D0706573

Anti-Semitism in Germany

Anti-Semitism in Germany

The Post-Nazi Epoch Since 1945

Werner Bergmann and Rainer Erb

Translated by Belinda Cooper and Allison Brown

Transaction Publishers

New Brunswick (U.S.A.) and London (U.K.)

Library of Congress Catalog Number: 96-36347
ISBN: 1-56000-270-0
Printed in the United States of America

Library of Congress Cataloging-in-Publication Data

Bergmann, Werner, 1950–
    [Antisemitismus in der Bundesrepublik Deutschland. English]
    Anti-semitism in Germany : the post-Nazi epoch since 1945 / Werner Bergmann and Rainer Erb ; translated by Belinda Cooper and Allison Brown.
        p. cm.
    Includes bibliographical references and index.
    ISBN 1-56000-270-0 (cloth ; alk. paper)
    1. Antisemitism—Germany (West). 2. Germany (West)—Ethnic relations. I. Erb, Rainer, 1945–   . II. Title.
DS146.G4B4713   1996
943'.004924—dc20
                                                                            96-36347
                                                                                  CIP

Contents

Preface

The collapse of the socialist regime in East Germany gave social scientists from the West their first opportunity to study attitudes of East German citizens toward Jews, Nazism, and the State of Israel empirically. The wave of xenophobic violence following unification, including anti-Semitic incidents, gave rise to fears that chauvinist, racist, and anti-Semitic tendencies would gain ground in a united Germany. This crisis-laden period of change led to an intensive phase of scientific observation of public opinion.

The Hamburg news magazine *Der Spiegel* planned a representative anti-Semitism study in late 1991 in eastern and western Germany. We served as advisors to this project. The evaluation of this survey gave us the chance to verify and update the findings and hypotheses of our basic anti-Semitism study of 1987. It was a scientific challenge to take advantage of the historically unique opportunity to compare the attitudes of two population groups that shared a common history up to 1945 and then lived under differing political conditions. West Germans lived in a liberal democratic, cosmopolitan, Western-oriented society that was economically prosperous and free of any major political crises, either domestic or foreign. East Germans lived in a communist state that was never certain of the loyalty of its citizens, controlling public life, the media, education, and science in an authoritarian manner. The East German leadership used the ideology of antifascism as a means of stabilizing the state and as a weapon with which to criticize the "imperialist" Federal Republic and the United States. This did not prevent it—together with other East-bloc countries—from following a strict anti-Zionist policy toward Israel. How would these different preconditions impact the attitudes of the citizens of unified Germany toward Jews, Israel, and the Nazi past? In addition to the two thematically broad-based anti-Semitism studies of 1987 and 1991, we included in our analysis all smaller studies and multiple-topic surveys conducted on our subject; this study thus offers a comprehensive picture of German anti-Semitism since the end of World War II.

Completion of such a project required the assistance and support of many individuals and institutions. In 1986, Abraham H. Foxman and Theodore Freedman, directors of the Anti-Defamation League in New York, approached Professor Herbert A. Strauss, then director of the Zentrum für Antisemitismusforschung der Technischen Universität Berlin, requesting a scholarly concept for a representative survey of present-day anti-Semitism in the Federal Republic of Germany. We would like to express our sincerest thanks to the Anti-Defamation League for this initiative and for its financial support of the study. The project was carried out in 1987, in cooperation with the Institut für Demoskopie in Allensbach, Germany. Dr. Renate Köcher, an expert on the subject as she had already conducted a survey on the same subject, led the group in Allensbach. We would also like to thank Professor Horst Skarabis of the Freie Universität Berlin for his assistance with statistical methodology in the planning phase and for referring to us one of his most competent staff members, sociologist Annemarie Lüchauer, who advised and assisted us in evaluating both studies. Werner Harenberg, who heads the public survey department at *Der Spiegel* with true journalistic professionalism, receives our appreciation for the fruitful exchange of ideas in the planning phase and for providing us with access to the data of the 1991 EMNID study.

We would like to thank the Deutsche Forschungsgemeinschaft for financial assistance in our evaluation of both studies. It is impossible to quantify the inspirational influence of the working environment at the Zentrum für Antisemitismusforschung. The critical advice and cooperation of Professor Strauss in particular was invaluable to our efforts. Our appreciation also goes to him for paving the way for an American edition of our book. We would also like to thank Inter Nationes, Bonn, and our publisher in Germany, Edmund Budrich of Leske und Budrich Verlag, for making this possible. Both contributed generously to the translation costs for an updated edition. Professor Wolfgang Benz, current director of the Zentrum für Antisemitismusforschung, deserves our thanks for additional financial assistance. We also appreciate the speedy and professional translation of the book provided by Allison Brown, Berlin, and Belinda Cooper, Berlin and New York, and our good working relationship with them.

We have attempted to incorporate all the helpful advice from our American reviewers. It provided us with direction in eliminating Euro-centricity in favor of a broader perspective. And we owe our thanks to Transaction Publishers for the patience they showed until the necessary revisions and updating could be completed.

Berlin, April 1995

1

Anti-Semitism in Germany (1945–1995)

Public Opinion

Anti-Semitism research in western Germany began right after the war, as the social scientific observations by the military authorities (OMGUS) of the popular mood in the American zone of occupation included questions of the persistence of anti-Semitic and racist attitudes, attitudes toward Nazism, the questions of collective guilt and on the process of "coming to terms with the past" (cf. Merritt and Merritt 1970, OMGUS Reports Nos. 49, 51, 68, 122, and 175 in the period 1946–1949). In the British zone, similar surveys were carried out; however, they have not yet been analyzed (PORO reports). Let us start with the studies on anti-Semitism conducted in the U.S. zone of occupation and in the early days of the Federal Republic. In the OMGUS studies, conducted in 1946, the following results were obtained: 20 percent showed only a slight tendency toward prejudice, 19 percent were nationalists, 22 percent racists, 21 percent anti-Semites, and 18 percent "hardcore" anti-Semites (Report 49, December, 1946). A repetition of the studies in April, 1948 showed a slight decrease in the proportion of anti-Semites to 19 percent and of "hardcore" anti-Semites to 14 percent (Report 122). This means we could expect that approximately 30 percent to 40 percent of the interviewees demonstrated clearly anti-Semitic attitudes in the early postwar years.[1] The interviews were certainly seen within the context of the policies of occupation and reorientation, to which some segments of the population objected. For this reason, the reliability of these early surveys should be judged with caution.[2] Nevertheless, the data provide evidence of a massive persistence of anti-Semitism after 1945, which was apparently rekindled as a result of specific postwar conflicts, such as the black market, displaced persons, and controversial restitution of Jewish property.

This was confirmed by the first survey under West German auspices. Shortly before the founding of the Federal Republic of Germany, the Institute for Public Opinion Research in Allensbach (*Institut für Demoskopie,* IfD) conducted a countrywide representative survey on anti-Semitism that was subtitled "a diagnostic contribution to domestic policy." Its purpose was to give "German officials an overview of popular opinion on the issue of anti-Semitism" (ibid., in the instructions to the interviewer). This offers us the earliest material on anti-Semitism after 1945, completely preserved and most thoroughly broken down according to socio-demographic characteristics (see table 1.1).

Self-appraisal was revealed to be the most certain indicator of anti-Semitism in our 1987 survey. In 1949 and 1952, 23 percent and even 34 percent, respectively, described themselves as openly anti-Semitic, whereas the group showing no prejudice comprised 30 percent to 47 percent. Since it can be assumed that a portion of the "reserved" and "no opinion" groups also harbor anti-Jewish sentiments, the proportion of anti-Semites in the postwar years can be estimated as between 30 percent and 40 percent. This result corresponds to the findings of a group experiment conducted in the winter of 1950–51 (Pollock 1955, table 9). This study was the first task taken on by the Institute of Social Research after it was reestablished in 1950, and followed in the footsteps of the famous *Studies in Prejudice,* that is, it took a psychoanalytical approach using a different methodology. In this experiments, discussion groups were formed to talk about specific issues, after the chairman had introduced certain "stimuli."[3] Of those speakers who made any statement at all on the subject of Jews in the group sessions (only 23 percent), 37 percent were assessed as anti-Semitic, 35 percent as ambivalent (somewhat anti-Semitic and/or pro-Jewish statements, some of which were

TABLE 1.1
"What is your general attitude toward Jews?"

	Openly anti-Semitic %	Emotional rejection %	Reserved %	Tolerant %	Openly friendly %	No opinion %
1949:	10	13	15	41	6	5
1952:	34		18	23	7	18

Source: IfD vol. I, 1957.

considered latent anti-Semitism), and 28 percent as non-anti-Semitic. The results provided impressive evidence that attitudes toward Jews after 1945 had indeed been affected by the Holocaust. Issues of guilt, guilt projection, attempts to rationalize, and silence were characteristic ways of coping with this complex; that is, anti-Semites found themselves on the defensive. For the participants in the discussions, anti-Semitism and Nazism were closely related. However, the results also indicated that Nazi education and propaganda had had a particularly strong impact on younger people and the better educated. Higher educational levels and youth do not have a moderating effect per se; more important is the prevailing political culture, and therefore also membership in a particular *political generation* (cf. Fogt 1982; Schuman and Scott 1989; Lang et al. 1993).

Combining the results of these four surveys in the postwar period, the following total picture emerges: at least one-third of the population must be categorized as openly anti-Semitic, almost one-third as somewhat anti-Semitic to ambivalent, and at least one-third as non-anti-Semitic.

The results of the 1954 survey commissioned by the *Bundeszentrale für Heimatdienst* (later renamed in *Bundeszentrale für politische Bildung*) and conducted by the EMNID Institute were comparable in magnitude. In answer to the free-association question "What comes to mind when you hear the word 'Jew'?," a third of those questioned indicated more or less positive attitudes, whereas a "more or less strong emotional rejection" was shown by approximately one-fourth (EMNID 1954, III). One-sixth of the interviewees were rated as harboring clearly negative feelings.[4] The remainder were either disinterested (13 percent—the authors of the study suspected that some of these also had negative attitudes in this respect) or made mixed or unemotional associations.

The wave of anti-Semitic incidents that broke out in the winter of 1959 through 1960 began in West Germany, but spread throughout the world. It served to motivate increased empirical research.[5] The large international comparative study "Intergroup Attitudes of Youth and Adults in England, France, and Germany" conducted by Melvin Tumin in 1961 and 1962 most likely also represented a reaction to the worldwide wave of anti-Semitism (Tumin 1962). Anti-Semitism played an important role in this study on racism and ethnocentrism. Using an anti-Semitism index, the study found that approximately equal numbers in each of the three countries (between 46 percent and 61 percent) exhibited anti-Jewish attitudes. This study, with its painstaking methodology, was never published in its entirety. Partial results were first published in 1980 by Badi Panahi, in conjunction with his own survey on this subject.

Once again, it was the Frankfurt Institute for Social Research that responded, this time to the trial of Adolf Eichmann, with two waves of representative surveys conducted in 1961, at the beginning and end of the trial (Schmidt and Becker 1967). This survey included a series of questions that could be used in anti-Semitism research. The same data, supplemented with a series of smaller surveys, formed the basis for a 1971 book by Michaela von Freyhold on "Authoritarianism and Political Apathy." It was significant for the approach we took in our study that von Freyhold found a clear correlation between anti-Semitism and Nazi sympathies. In her opinion, anti-Semitism in West Germany was "more (one) element of the rationalization of Nazism than a separate hostility"; she suspected "that authoritarians are infuriated not so much by some fixed stereotype of Jews, but by the silent accusation of the victims, which injures their collective narcissism" (1971, 97). Our study therefore employs this concept of "secondary anti-Semitism," rather than taking the completely ahistorical approach of Silbermann and Sallen, who proceeded as though modern anti-Semitism continued unchanged in Germany after 1945 (cf. the criticism in Fritzsche 1987).

Despite the Auschwitz trials and the 1965 and 1969 "statute of limitations debates" in the German *Bundestag,* all of which gained great public attention, there were no larger surveys on anti-Semitism until the 1970s, apart from a few questions occasionally included in surveys by the IfD (cf. *Jahrbuch der öffentlichen Meinung,* vols. III–V, 1958–1973). The subject was taken up again in the 1970s by academic sociologists such as Alphons Silbermann and Herbert A. Sallen, in their 1972–1975 German Research Society (DFG) project (main EMNID survey in 1974, publication of results in 1976, Sallen 1977, and Silbermann 1982), and Badi Panahi, in a representative 1977–1978 survey on "racism, anti-Semitism, and nationalism in West Germany today" (published 1980), in which he included Tumin's aforementioned results from 1961 through 1962. The Silbermann study received particular attention in public and political debates because of its findings.[6] Based on the degree of acceptance of twenty anti-Semitic items on an "anti-Semitism scale," the following results were obtained (table 1.2).

TABLE 1.2
"Intensity of anti-Semitic prejudice" 1974

Rejection	23,6 %
Mild acceptance	46,4 %
Medium acceptance	25,6 %
Strong acceptance	4,5 %
Total	**100.0 %**

Source: Silbermann 1982, 34.

Explaining that extreme values are often avoided in Likert scales even if these do in fact correspond to the opinions held by those questioned, Silbermann and Sallen combined the figures from strong and medium acceptance to form a group of 30.1 percent with strong acceptance of the anti-Semitic statements. Only 23.6 percent were rated "not anti-Semitic," and almost half (46.4 percent) of the West German population agreed somewhat with anti-Semitic statements. When these percentages were combined with two additional instruments (a social distance parameter and a behavioral orientation question), Silbermann and Sallen ended up with a slightly more favorable result. In addition to a tolerant group of approximately 30 percent and a strongly anti-Semitic group of approximately 20 percent, the authors concluded that half of the West German population displayed "at least latent remnants of anti-Semitic attitudes" (Silbermann 1982, 63).

Renewed interest in anti-Semitism at the end of the 1970s resulted once again from particular public events. The television series "Holocaust," which had a completely unexpected impact on the public and led to intensive discussion of the persecution of Jews, was accompanied by surveys asking about anti-Semitic attitudes, attitudes toward German guilt and Nazism and the like (Ernst 1979; Prokop 1981; Ahren et al. 1982; Gast 1982). The state political education authorities had primary responsibility for these studies; they hoped the findings would support their educational efforts. The results showed that the television series led to a short-term change in attitudes. However, because there were no follow-up studies (panels) at greater intervals and the material has not been published, it is not possible to estimate the stability of these changes in attitudes.

Some questions on anti-Semitism also appeared in the extremism studies commissioned by political authorities (the Ministry of the Interior and the Chancellor Helmut Schmidt's Office) in the late 1970s to measure the potential for right- and left-wing extremism in West Germany. This famous SINUS study (published in 1981) found that 13 percent of the electorate had a firm right-wing extremist worldview, which included anti-Semitism. However, a further "authoritarian-prone" share of the electorate (37 percent) was "immune to militarism, the *Führer* cult, and anti-Semitism" (93). In evaluating Nazism, and particularly anti-Semitism and racism, the IfD study on the "Potential for Extremism among Young People in the Federal Republic of Germany, 1984" made a similar distinction between right-wing extremists and "right-wing democrats" (Noelle-Neumann and Ring 1984, 77). Of active right-wing extremists, 17.9 percent answered "yes" to the statement, "The influence of the Freemasons and Jews in our country is still great today," but only 1.4 percent of right-wing democrats answered in the same way (ibid. R-Scale, table 5). These results indicate that active, hardcore anti-Semitism rarely appears as an integral element of a worldview. However, this does not mean that less absolute anti-Semitic attitudes are not found in the German population. Thus an anti-Semitism study must be designed to detect such less-pronounced, more diffuse anti-Semitism; otherwise it would have to be designed as a study of right-wing extremism. In 1985 and 1986, a series of major and minor "anti-Semitic incidents," particularly the dispute over the performance of the play *Der Müll, die Stadt und der Tod* ("Garbage, the City, and Death") by R. W. Fassbinder, once again led to a spate of anti-Semitism surveys, in which anti-Semitism was placed in the context of "coming to terms with the past." In February, 1986, the IfD was commissioned by *Stern* magazine to do a representative survey on "Germans and Jews forty years later." It was partially conceived as an international comparison, and included Austria—which had come under scrutiny due to the Waldheim affair—France, and the United States.[7] Renate Köcher prepared the following distribution for the 1986 IfD study, using a cluster analysis of a scale of nineteen items (table 1.3).

The results of the four most recent studies (IfD 1987, and EMNID 1989, 1992, Wittenberg et al. 1991) coincide to a large degree, despite the fact that they used different questions, rating methods, and boundaries between categories. They identify approximately 15 percent of the population as clearly anti-Semitic and between 50 percent and 60 percent as free of prejudice.

TABLE 1.3
"Extent of anti-Jewish sentiment" 1986

Pronounced positive attitudes	42,1 %
Mildly positive attitudes	13,1 %
Mildly negative attitudes	29,5 %
Strongly anti-Semitic attitudes (of those: hard core: 6 percent)	15,3 %
Total	**100.0 %**

Source: IfD 1986, Appendix: Cluster analysis.

For our 1987 study, Köcher also determined a group of 15 percent with clearly anti-Jewish sentiments [8 percent of which were categorized as vehemently anti-Jewish (IfD 1987, 51; for our own results cf. chap. 2)]. In response to the ultra right-wing *Republikaner* party's successful showing at the polls, as well as growing ethnocentricity, *Spiegel* magazine commissioned the EMNID Institute in the spring of 1989 to conduct a survey on "contemporary history," which included questions on attitudes toward Jews, Nazism, reparations, and the like. Using a twenty-seven-point scale, comparable values were obtained in 1989 (see table 1.4), although the criteria for distribution into the respective groups were not provided.

As far as the extent of residual anti-Semitic attitudes is concerned, the EMNID study obtained a somewhat less favorable distribution than the 1986 IfD study. It is understandable that the categories do not correspond entirely, since this involves making distinctions among very diffuse attitudes. In the end it is impossible to decide where to draw the line. If the criterion for the "not anti-Semitic" category were that none of the responses

TABLE 1.4
"Attitudes toward Jews" 1989

20–27 points: extremely anti-Semitic	4 %
14–19 points: quite anti-Semitic	10 %
6–13 points: somewhat anti-Semitic	40 %
0–5 points: not anti-Semitic	46 %
Total	**100 %**

Source: EMNID 1989, vol. 5.

to the scale statements demonstrate anti-Jewish sentiment, then little more than 25 percent would have been assigned to that group [in the 1987 IfD study, only 12 percent did not satisfy any of the negative conditions (51)]. This type of differentiation hovers in a nebulous gray zone, in which differences in attitudes are very difficult to determine with any precision.

In 1990, following German unification, it became possible for the first time to carry out public opinion surveys in eastern Germany without the supervision of the ruling SED party. In autumn of 1990, two representative anti-Semitism studies were carried out in eastern Germany, one of which also included the western German population for purposes of comparison (Wittenberg, Prosch, and Abraham 1991; Jodice 1991 for the American Jewish Committee). Both studies came to the conclusion, surprising to many, that anti-Semitism was far less widespread in eastern Germany than had been feared; at 4 percent to 6 percent, the percentage of the population that is anti-Semitic was lower than the western German figure of 12 percent to 16 percent anti-Semites.[8] Public and scholarly attention was focussed on eastern German young people by the reorientation crisis and the wave of violence against foreigners, primarily by young people, that became acute during the debate on the constitutional right to asylum triggered by the large number of asylum seekers in Germany. Starting in 1990, a series of regional studies on xenophobia and political orientation among young people appeared, each of which included some questions on attitudes toward Jews (Lederer et al. 1991; Förster et al. 1993; Melzer 1992; Sturzbecher, Dietrich, and Kohlstruck 1994; on a non-representative student survey cf. Brusten and Winkelmann 1994, Brusten 1995). These studies showed that the attitudes of fourteen- to twenty-year-old East Germans were more xenophobic and anti-Semitic than those of adults, and that both the attitudes and the political orientations of adolescents had radicalized still further between 1990 and 1994. There is no comparable amount of empirical material available on western German young people (except for one regional study by Infas in 1992). Not until the end of 1991 did the EMNID Institute carry out a survey, commissioned by the news magazine *Der Spiegel* and representative for the population over eighteen years old, on "Anti-Semitism in Germany" (EMNID Institute 1992). This study confirmed the results of the first ones in 1990.[9]

The electoral success of right-wing extremist parties after 1989, along with the continuing series of violent xenophobic and anti-Semitic incidents in Germany, has led researchers to include a number of questions on anti-Semitism and right-wing extremism within the context of other public opinion surveys (*Institut für Demoskopie* 1991, 1992, 1994; Noelle-Neumann 1993). Thus, we have a relatively large amount of data, permitting us to draw a differentiated picture of changes in public opinion.

In January, 1994, the American Jewish Committee repeated its 1990 study, adding a series of questions on the Holocaust (Golub 1994). The results indicated that the mood in Germany is characterized by concern over the increase in anti-Semitism, but that no negative trend in attitudes toward Jews had developed since 1990. Aggressive agitation by anti-Semites and a large number of attacks on Jewish sites apparently found no positive echo in the population. On the contrary, right-wing extremists have become the most unpopular group in Germany. A Forsa survey, "The Germans and National Socialism: Knowledge, Appraisals, Opinions" (1994), which included some issues central to present-day anti-Semitism (ending discussion of the past, the truth of the Holocaust), confirmed the impression that attitudes toward Jews and Nazism over the last few years had remained stable, while at the same time showing no apparent positive development.

Given the negative trend in attitudes among young people, it is possible to make only a limited prognosis on further developments. Whether the long-term decline in prejudice has been disturbed only temporarily by the specific crisis situation surrounding the process of German unity, or whether there has been an actual reversal of the trend, could not be determined by the end of 1995; additional empirical research will be necessary over the coming years.

Preliminary comprehensive evaluations of existing empirical data have been available since the 1980s (Weil 1980, 1987, 1990; Bergmann 1990; Bergmann and Erb 1991, 1995). All observed a continual decline in anti-Semitism in the Federal Republic of Germany since the early 1950s, along with a growing rejection of Nazism. West Germany's political culture has become largely comparable to that of other Western countries (cf. Conradt 1980; Baker et al. 1981; Berg-Schlosser and Schissler 1987). Comparisons of survey data for various Western countries reveal a general declining trend in anti-Semitism, while showing that anti-Semitism today is no stronger in Germany than, for example, in France, Austria, or the United States (cf. Weil 1987, 174f.; Bergmann 1996).

Anti-Semitism in the Political Arena

The Western Allies considered racial hatred and anti-Semitism to be the most terrible products of Nazi ideology. They attempted to open Germans' eyes to the consequences of this ideology through newspapers, photographs, and films (like the concentration camp film "Death Mills"; cf. Chamberlin 1981) as well as by directly confronting the public with the camps. The importance they attached to this issue was shown by the OMGUS surveys starting in 1946, which repeatedly posed questions pertaining to anti-Semitism, racism, and restitution for Jewish victims of persecution. Combatting anti-Semitism was an element of their reeducation policies (see Kellermann 1981, 90ff.) This included bans on Nazi films, removal of undesirable books, and expurgation of racial and anti-Semitic elements from curricula and textbooks. Teachers were often required to take part in "reeducation seminars," and those with tainted backgrounds were fired (Bungenstab 1970, 78). A classic study on prejudice by Gordon Allport (1948) was translated for use in political education by the "America House" cultural centers in 1951, indicating the importance that was attached to combatting anti-Semitism, especially by the Americans. Allied and German authorities cooperated on the local level on school policy, the organization of restitution for victims of Nazism, and return of stolen property.

The lively debate on German guilt that took place in numerous newly created political and cultural publications barely touched upon the aspect of anti-Semitism. The earliest statements by the churches in postwar Germany (the Stuttgart confession of guilt of 1945; cf. Boyens 1971) also made only implicit mention of guilt in regard to the Jews. As the churches saw themselves primarily in the role of victims of persecution by the Nazi dictatorship, they saw little reason to view their behavior towards Jews in the Third Reich self-critically. Thus, even these not particularly far-reaching statements met with widespread opposition from local congregations.

In the founding statements of the various parties in June of 1945, demands for the "liquidation" of National Socialism were accompanied by more or less clear acceptance of guilt or shared responsibility for the crimes of the Hitler regime and the duty to pay reparations. The murder of the Jews was not mentioned directly, but reflected in phrases such as "racial arrogance" or "incitement of racial hatred." All political platforms in this early period made reference to the elimination of any sort of "racial cult." But as the end of the war receded into the past, the willingness of all parties to address these issues lessened, though there was a significant difference between Left and Right (Billerbeck 1971, 56ff., for a recent analysis of postwar party politics concerning anti-Semitism and National Socialism see Bergmann, Erb, and Lichtblau 1995). After 1945, it was primarily the Social Democratic party (SPD), in particular its chairman, Kurt Schumacher, that condemned the persecution of the Jews and publicly raised the demand for reparations. At its party conferences in Nuremberg in 1947 and Düsseldorf in 1948, Schumacher declared it the SPD's task to push for compensation for the Jews, ban all anti-Semitic propaganda, and punish all those who had participated in the persecution (Shafir 1989, 192f.). It was also Schumacher who, as leader of the opposition, criticized Chancellor Konrad Adenauer's first government declaration because he found it "too lame and weak" in regard to the Jewish tragedy.

It would take from the founding of the Federal Republic until September, 1951 for then-Chancellor Adenauer to make a public government statement on "the Federal Republic's attitude towards the Jews" (Bundestag 1951). In this speech to the Bundestag, the Chancellor referred to the Basic Law in rejecting any form of discrimination, and assigned the educational system and the churches the task of raising the entire nation in the spirit of humane and religious tolerance. He announced that those who continued with anti-Semitic agitation would be punished severely. He said that the federal government and the great majority of the nation were aware of the immeasurable suffering inflicted on the Jews during the Nazi period, adding that the overwhelming majority of the German people had detested the crimes committed against the Jews and had not participated in them. Spokesmen for the parties represented in the Bundestag (SPD, FDP, German party, Bavarian party, and Center) then made similar statements; only the extreme right-wing parties and the KPD (Communist party) did not participate in the debate and refused to show any approval.

It was no accident that Adenauer's statement came at just this time. The backdrop was formed by demands for reparations by Israel, which had demanded such a declaration as a prerequisite to further talks (von Jena 1986, 462). It may also have been encouraged by the "Peace with Israel" initiative, called into being in summer 1951 by Hamburg's commissioner for culture, Erich Lüth; the initiative collected signatures to underscore its demand for the assumption of government contacts with Israel.

Adenauer's declaration formulated the basic outline of a policy against anti-Semitism that would continue to be a determinant of German government policies for decades. The great amount of latent, and to some degree manifest, anti-Semitism in the population, which politicians must have known about, was largely treated as nonexistent. The public was declared free of both moral responsibility for the Holocaust and anti-Semitic prejudice. Anti-Semitism was defined as the problem of small, extremist groups, made punishable, and otherwise turned into a public taboo. Schools and churches were given the task of raising young people in the spirit of religious, political, and ethnic tolerance. This view of the problem met with objections, mainly from the left wing of the political spectrum, which assumed that anti-Semitism persisted to a very great degree and recommended a different strategy to combat it—public discussion of its roots and its connection with the Nazi period. In this view, broad socio-political reforms were necessary to combat anti-Semitism, as it was related to the structure of capitalism and the authoritarianism of German society (Adorno et al. 1950).

In the first decade following the war, anti-Semitism and public discussion of it were closely connected with de-Nazification, restitution, and reparations. A representative case that gained great public attention in 1947 through 1949 was the Hamburg de-Nazification case of prominent film director Veit Harlan, who had, among other things, made the anti-Semitic film "Jud Süss" in 1940 (see Zielinski 1981). Public protest ensued in response to press reports that Harlan was to be classified as "free of guilt" (unbelastet). The investigation was never completed, as the expert commission on Harlan's denazification resigned. The Association of Victims of the Nazi Regime and the "Emergency Organization of People Affected by the Nuremberg Laws" then instituted legal proceedings against him. The trial, which took place with great public participation, mainly by people sharing Harlan's views, and the appeal ended in 1949 to 1950 with his acquittal. While the court judged the film to be anti-Semitic propaganda and acknowledged Harlan's participation, it said the responsibility for the film's production was divided; Harlan was declared responsible only for the artistic aspects, and thus not guilty in a political sense, while the film's anti-Semitic tendencies were attributed to Propaganda Minister Goebbels. During the trial, anti-Semitic attacks occurred against witnesses for the prosecution, some of whom were Jewish, and the acquittal was met with applause. The democratic public saw the acquittal as a "strike against democracy," and Hamburg's commissioner for culture, Erich Lüth, called on film distributors and the public to boycott the latest Harlan films, whereupon Harlan took him to court. The solidarity campaign that developed for Lüth led to a sharp polarization of the public. This debate reached its pinnacle in the winter of 1951 to 1952 in calls for boycotts and demonstrations by students against the showing of the newest Harlan film, during which the passers-by hurled insults such as "Jewish mercenaries" at the protesters. These incidents reveal the virulence of the anti-Semitism, the openness with which it was expressed, and the tensions it created, which were sometimes vented in physical attacks. The demonstrations and counter-demonstrations, as well as press reports for and against Harlan, made it clear that no anti-Semitic consensus existed as yet among the public.

Another focus for the crystallization of anti-Semitism was formed by the long-drawn-out debate over restitution of Jewish property (Erb 1990; Goschler 1992). Allied legislation obligated German property owners to return Jewish property acquired after 1933 to its Jewish owners or their heirs. There were especially bitter fights over the return of smaller properties (houses, summer homes, small businesses) that were important to the livelihoods of their new owners. The local press often criticized such restitution procedures and portrayed them as unjust. The founding of the Federal Republic allowed for the forming of organizations, and people affected by restitution were thus able to build up an organizational base with numerous publications. In these publications, they described isolated facts from the complicated restitution procedures in order to activate negative stereotypes of Jews on the basis of carefully selected cases, thus creating a impression of rumors, corruption, and personal enrichment. They warned against strict application of the laws, saying this would lend new impetus to hostility toward Jews. These denunciations and warnings were intended to encourage the federal government to revise the Allied laws.

While the debate over restitution kept alive negative cliches about Jews on a local level, reparations to Israel became a national issue. Surveys from 1952 show the public's overwhelmingly negative attitude, and the minutes of cabinet meetings and Bundestag debates give evidence of the political resistance to reparations, or to the size of the payments demanded. Chancellor Adenauer was only able to obtain ratification of the 1953 Luxembourg reparations treaty with the help of the opposition SPD, against the resistance of some of his own party in the Bundestag (Shafir 1989, 201f.). This specifically financial aspect of Bewältigung—"overcoming"—the Nazi past, which strongly influenced the relationship between Germans and Jews in the early post-war period, continues to this day to be a crucial factor in the German image of the Jews. As late as 1989, 46 percent of all West Germans considered reparations payments to be too high, and 29 percent saw them as a cause of anti-Semitism (Emnid 1989).

The restorative period of calm generally seen to have existed between 1953 and 1958 also applied to public interest in anti-Semitism. Isolated incidents such as graffiti and cemetery desecrations received only local attention and did not become significant national issues. Nor was there any widespread discussion within the churches of Christian anti-Judaism until the end of the 1950s. Missionary societies targeting Jews continued to carry out their missionary tasks after 1945. Only after the intervention of individual theologians did theology and the churches begin a process of critical self-reflection. Religious customs in which anti-Judaism persisted, such as the Oberammergau Passion Play and the pilgrimage to the "Deggendorfer Gnad" (having its origin in a host desecration legend from 1338), were performed in the traditional manner, but after "Auschwitz" they provoked criticism throughout the world. The rethinking process this set in motion had led by the early 1960s to a revision of the script of the Oberammergau play and a rededication of the pilgrimage. Paintings and relics that portrayed medieval "sins of the Jews" were removed from church buildings. The resolutions of the Second Vatican Council of October, 1965 were of considerable importance in restructuring the Catholic Church's relationship to Judaism. However, it took until well into the 1980s before Rome's decisions on the removal of anti-Jewish elements from religious custom had been completely carried out by local congregations.

The phase of latent anti-Semitism ended in the late 1950s as anti-Semitic scandals mounted. The case of the concentration camp doctor Hans Eisele, the teacher Ludwig Zind, who told a Jew that they had forgotten to gas him and his family, and the businessman Friedrich Nieland, who sent an anti-Semitic brochure as an open letter to all federal ministers and parliamentarians, gained national and international attention, particularly because of the actions of administrative and judicial officials. Dr. Eisele and Zind were able to escape to Egypt after being warned of their impending arrest by members of the judiciary; Nieland was acquitted at trial of libel and endangering the state. A motion for appeal by the Hamburg prosecutor's office was rejected by the state appeals court. Investigation of the Nazi past of the judge involved revealed that he himself had written anti-Semitic articles in the Third Reich. These anti-Semitic incidents ended in judicial scandals, as they made clear the continuity of personnel and ideology within the judiciary.

The oppositional SPD took up these scandals, and in January, 1959 it directed a parliamentary question on judicial policy at the federal government. The SPD criticized the fact that judges with Nazi backgrounds were allowed to make decisions on events in the Nazi period, and demanded a rethinking within the judicial branch. There were calls in the Bundestag for legal improvements in the prosecution of incitement to racial hatred, and a bill to that effect was introduced. While this bill was undergoing a second reading at the beginning of December, 1959, and various groups were articulating their dissatisfaction with having a "special law" to protect Jews, the 1959 Christmas holidays brought an outbreak of graffiti on the walls of the newly dedicated Cologne synagogue, followed by a wave of similar incidents inside and outside of the country. In West Germany alone, a federal government "White Book" counted 685 cases by the end of January, 1960. The fact that both the offenders in Cologne were members of the radical right-wing German Reich party (DRP), which immediately expelled them and distanced itself from them, turned the attention of the public and the Office for the Protection of the Constitution toward right-wing extremist organizations. Searches of the homes of functionaries led to the discovery of incriminating material. A countrywide ban on the DRP was suggested, but only actually instituted in Berlin and Rhineland-Palatinate. The public debate broadened to include, for example, former Nazis with posts in the Adenauer government and high positions in the judiciary and administrative agencies. Hans Globke, who had helped write the legal commentaries on the Nuremberg Laws, was an undersecretary in the Chancellor's Office; the minister responsible for German refugees from Eastern Europe, Heinrich Oberländer, was accused of participating in war crimes in Lemberg. This international criticism of the participation of former Nazis in a democratic state, leveled above all by the former occupying powers, Jewish organizations, and the East German government, led the judiciary to punish those responsible for the graffiti quite severely when they were caught. Politicians and journalists found the failure of schools and parents deplorable and demanded improvements in political education, which was actually achieved to some extent in the aftermath. The federal government countered Communist countries' accusations of fascism with countercharges that the "people pulling the strings" of the anti-Semitic graffiti writers could be found in East Berlin (Bergmann 1990, Mertens 1994, Wolffsohn 1995).

The extraordinary public response to these incidents, expressed in protests and outrage by almost all social groups, heralded a change in the treatment of anti-Semitism and the Nazi period. Within the framework of political education, in research, the churches, the press and broadcasting industries, intensive interest to study and combat prejudice and anti-Semitism emerged.

The process of dealing with the Nazi past, especially the Holocaust, continued in the 1960s with a series of major trials, the debate on the statute of limitations for violent Nazi crimes, and the emergence of the ultra-right NPD. The spectacular kidnapping of Adolf Eichmann and his trial in Jerusalem received great attention in the German media and society. The same was true of the two-year Auschwitz trial in Frankfurt, which lasted from 1963 to 1965 and involved eighteen camp guards and medical personnel. The extreme significance of these two trials lay in the fact that they exposed the entire complex of the "Final Solution," not only punishing individual perpetrators, but also illuminating the entire factual background of the Holocaust.

Writers took up these themes in popular theater pieces, in which the material was presented in a partly documentary and partly literary manner. Rolf Hochhuth's 1963 historical drama *The Deputy* (*Der Stellvertreter*), the theme of which was the Pope's moral responsibility for the Holocaust, triggered passionate arguments for and against the play (Grimm et al. 1963). While Hochhuth was interested in a historical reconstruction of the events and in personalizing guilt, other authors, such as Peter Weiss in his Auschwitz oratorium *The Investigation* (*Die Ermittlung*, premiere 1965) or Martin Walser in his play *The Black Swan* (1961), exposed the continued existence of the structures and people responsible for Auschwitz (Geiger 1973). The Federal Republic was once again confronted with the fact that the past was not really past when the statute of limitations for Nazi crimes was to come into force. In the restorative phase of the 1950s, the government and parliament had in 1955 allowed the deadline for crimes with a maximum sentence of ten years' imprisonment to pass without any discussion. On the statute of limitations for manslaughter in connection with Nazi crimes, too, there was only a short Bundestag debate in May, 1960, initiated by the SPD, in which an extension of the deadline was rejected with the argument that there should be no special laws for Nazi crimes. Not until 1965, when the statute of limitations for Nazi murders was scheduled to go into effect, was there an intense debate on the issue. The major trials and historical studies had created broader public awareness of the systematic character of the persecution of the Jews, which could no longer be played down as a crime "of the sort that can happen in wartime." Nevertheless, in 1965 neither the federal government nor the minister of justice took any action. The initiative was taken up by a single CDU member of parliament, Ernst Benda, and the SPD parliamentary group. No legal consequences were drawn from the singularity of the Holocaust. The Bundestag contented itself with shifting the beginning of the limitations period to 1949, as a proper system of law in German hands had existed only as of that point in time. Thus, the problem was back on the agenda in 1969, to be resolved temporarily with a general extension of the statute of limitations for murder to thirty years. It was hoped that all necessary investigations would be completed by 1979. However, this hope was disappointed, so that in the next debate on the statute of limitations in 1979 the Bundestag decided, under great domestic and foreign pressure, to lift the statute of limitations for murder. So as not to create special laws for Nazi perpetrators, the Bundestag refused to lift the statute of limitations for genocide alone. (In 1995 there were still more than 5,500 investigations on Nazi crimes pending.) While the Bundestag was able, after heated debates, to extend the statute of limitations repeatedly, the lifting of this statute and punishment of Nazi criminals were all but popular with the public. In 1962, only 14 percent of respondents thought it would have been better not to hold the Eichmann trial; for the Auschwitz trial the figure had gone up to 39 percent. In surveys in 1965 and 1966, 52 percent of all West Germans opposed further prosecution of Nazi crimes, sometimes making legal arguments, sometimes rejecting guilt through counter-charges, and sometimes using nationalistic arguments.

A comparison of the figures at the beginning and at the end of the Auschwitz trial shows only a minor educational effect; the number of those who wanted to see Nazi crimes punished, even twenty years after the war, rose only 4 percent, from 34 percent in 1963 to 38 percent in 1965 (IfD 1967, 165).

This tendency to demand a *Schlußstrich,* an end to discussion of the past, which has continued to increase up to the present day, reveals the growing gap between public opinion on the one hand, and the media and politics in and outside the country on the other. While German politicians since 1969 have increasingly emphasized historical responsibility for the deeds of the Third Reich, and are supported in this by the mainstream media, a growing feeling can be observed in the population that can be summarized as "enough, too much, too long." With regard to the Jews, in particular, the feeling is widespread that Germany has made enough reparations and has a right to a "normal" relationship with Jews and Israel. The impossibility of normalcy is seen as a refusal on the part of Jews (cf. the new image of the "unforgiving, irreconcilable" Jew), and leads to "secondary anti-Semitism" that remains private, since public opportunities to express it have been virtually nonexistent up to now. We thus speak of "communicatively latent" anti-Semitism (Bergmann and Erb 1986).

The anti-Semitic scandals of recent years involving statements of politicians and the planned performance of Rainer Fassbinder's play *The City, Garbage, and Death,* which presented the cliche of a "rich Jew" in a very negative role, were based in a partly populist, partly provocative break in this latency. The massive public response forced politicians either to apologize or resign, and the theater to cancel the performance of the Fassbinder play. In these cases, in part through protests by members of the Jewish community, anti-Semitism could be denied a public stage; however, it is possible that the price that was paid was the increase of anti-Semitism at the personal resentment level. This mechanism could be studied in the course of the Bitburg affair. The criticism by many organizations of this gesture of reconciliation between Chancellor Helmut Kohl and President Ronald Reagan at an inappropriate location was blamed on the "influence of certain East Coast circles." Thus, a classic anti-Semitic stereotype was used as an explanation—Jews have too much influence in the world (Funke 1986). In this case, too, protests forced the politicians to change the intended program, a fact which some took as the very confirmation of the anti-Semitic stereotype of "Jewish power." As in 1960, the increase in such *faux pas* led to intensified political and scholarly interest in anti-Semitism. Several surveys carried out in 1986 and 1987 permitted a more precise assessment of the structure and extent of modern-day anti-Semitism. Political science and journalistic analyses attempted to categorize the events in post-war West German history (Kiderlen 1986; Hartmann 1986; Levkov 1987). The Waldheim affair in Austria, which led to greater interest in anti-Semitism in that country, also had an impact on the West German debate.

At the request of forty-five members of parliament from the Green party, the SPD and the FDP, the Bundestag held a debate on 27 February 1986 on the subject of "the responsibility of all democratic parties in regard to emerging anti-Semitic tendencies." Chancellor Kohl, in particular, offered in his speech a strategy that could already be found in Adenauer's 1951 government declaration; anti-Semitic incidents were played down as isolated events, "the huge majority of our fellow citizens in the Federal Republic, especially the younger generation, is immune to anti-Semitism." According to this argument, anti-Semitism is localized at most as a minor sediment on the extreme right wing, and is thus isolated. While left-wing liberal speakers saw alarming trends, denial, and a lack of discussion of the Nazi past, representatives of the CDU/CSU party group spoke of the German's successful historical learning process. They relied on Jewish sources in support of their view. The Greens, in particular, accused the other parties of having avoided thorough discussion of anti-Semitism since 1945.

The Greens' involvement in this issue was an expression of a learning process by the "Left" that had just begun. While the KPD, until it was outlawed in 1956, followed the Soviet Communist party's anti-Zionist party line, the SPD followed a continuous policy of reparations and support for Israel. Left-wing party youth organizations supported this policy until the mid-1960s, and were committed to the Israeli kibbutz model. In the course of the student protest movement, the attitude of the "New Left" changed, becoming more critical of Israel and anti-Zionist. In domestic politics, this turning against Israel was expressed mainly in criticism of the philo-Semitism of the "Establishment," motivated primarily by its negative symbol Axel Springer and his press empire. The criticism was in part a reaction to support of Israel and admiration of its military achievements, which were compared with Wehrmacht campaigns, thus removing these campaigns from the context of Nazi warmongering. Many Germans' identification with the Israelis (headlines in the mass press read like this: "Moshe Dayan is Israel's Rommel;" "Our boys at Sinai") was interpreted by the Left as an attempt to exonerate themselves, and rejected accordingly. The conservative press and tabloids identified the Left with totalitarianism, according to the formula "Reds = Brown (shirts)," and accused it of anti-Semitism. In the eyes of the Left, this accusation confirmed the link between pro-Israel sentiment and "reactionary and anticommunist ideas." The theory of imperialism and the Vietnam War, which stamped the U.S. as a representative of aggressive imperialism, defined Israel as its proxy in the Middle East because of its close ties to the U.S. Support for liberation movements in the Third World also included the PLO. German terrorist groups were in contact with PLO commandos, from which they received military training and logistical support and with which they carried out joint operations, including those aimed at Jews and Jewish targets.

These positions were limited to isolated splinter groups that formed after the collapse of the student movement and whose publications lacked any broad impact. But the issue entered the Bundestag along with the Green party, making political waves mainly because of the first trip to the Middle East by a Green delegation. Some delegation members criticized Israel at a press conference and expressed their support for the "victims of the victims of fascism"—that is, the Palestinians whom they said had been "deprived of their rights"—as the veritable duty of an antifascist German party (see *Die Tageszeitung,* 2 January 1985). This insensitive behavior was sharply criticized in Israel and by the German public; it also triggered a discussion within the party that resulted in a more differentiated view of the Middle East conflict and a greater awareness of historical responsibility (Kloke 1990a). But the statements by various members of the party on the Gulf crisis in the winter of 1990 through 1991 showed that "cathartic acid tests" (1990b) continue to this day to characterize the Green party's debate on Israel.

While West Germany's political left seemed mainly to have an "Israel problem," which involved Israel's treatment of the Palestinians and did not turn into general anti-Semitism, anti-Semitic views on the far right appeared to strengthen. Anti-Semitism had always been an element of right-wing extremists' ideology, although they avoided openly propagating the issue, most likely out of fear of prosecution. To justify their own political position, they had to strive to deny or relativize the criminal character of Nazism. An international "literature of revisionism" (Broszat 1977) emerged; its central aim was and is to dispute the existence of extermination camps and "expose" the figure of millions of Holocaust victims as an exaggeration by Allied propagandists. Denial of the Holocaust is closely linked with anti-Semitism, as it is right-wingers who see Jews as the ones keeping alive memory of the past and trying to profit from it.

The SPD, and later the federal government, attempted to counter this insult to the victims with a "special law" against the "Auschwitz lie" (Cobler 1985). The proposed law was criticized from many directions as legally inappropriate and politically problematic, leading the government to withdraw its bill. Finally, in April, 1985 the Bundestag resolved to revise the libel and slander laws, over the opposition of the SPD and the Greens.

"Revisionist" theories, otherwise spread only through right-wing extremist literature and lacking any scholarly reputation, were widely discussed during the "Historian's Debate" (*Historikerstreit*) because of the publications of Ernst Nolte, whom critics accused of making revisionist ideas socially acceptable. The scholars involved found these ideas untenable and rejected them (*Historikerstreit* 1987).

The *Historikerstreit* made it apparent that two conflicting tendencies existed in the Federal Republic in regard to dealings with the past. On the one hand, scholarly and journalistic discussions had increased in intensity on the occasion of a series of commemorative anniversaries between 1983 and 1988, from the "Nazi seizure of power" to the "Kristallnacht." These discussions revealed the central significance of anti-Semitism and persecution of the Jews for Nazi ideology and politics. In particular, President Richard von Weizsäcker's speech on the fortieth anniversary of the end of the war once again brought the issues of Germany's historical guilt and responsibility back to the public consciousness. Interest in the Nazi period and the persecution of the Jews has become widespread, in regional and local historical research as well as in the creation and maintenance of memorials and research centers. Former Bundestag president Philipp Jenninger discovered how quickly the suspicion of anti-Semitism could arise in this newly sensitized climate after his unfortunate 1988 speech commemorating the "Kristallnacht" pogroms. He had to resign some days after his speech (Laschet and Malangré 1989).

On the other hand, there is also a widespread tendency to respond to this intensification with the slogan "enough of the past." This climate of opinion has been worsened by populist politicians who have enhanced the status of German history and national symbols. In their efforts to identify with an unbroken line of German history, Jews appear as annoying reminders. This complex is an important ideological element of the platform of the *"Republikaner"* party. Using "yes-but" rhetoric, the party calls itself non anti-Semitic, while rejecting "any interference" by Jewish representatives. The *Republikaner* party gained influence as a right-wing extremist party, purposedly breaking the taboo of anti-Semitism in certain cases and, thus, making it apparent that some of the public still responds to anti-Jewish hostility.

With the process of German unification in 1989 and 1990, the political Right was first reduced to the level of a splinter party. However, in eastern Germany violent attacks on foreigners and anti-Semitic and xenophobic graffiti indicated a revival of manifest right-wing extremism. The heavy influx of asylum seekers in the years 1991 through 1992 (cf. the entry "Germany" in Anti-Semitism World Report 1992, 1993) and the fierce debate on limitation of the right of asylum in the Basic Law for the first time served to place an issue on the public agenda that for years had been a central issue of right-wing extremist's xenophobic agitation. Thus, they were able to achieve considerable electoral success at the state level in the 1992 elections. Not until the democratic parties had shown their ability to take political action by changing the law on asylum was the drama removed from the issues of "asylum" and "immigration." The ban on neo-Nazi organizations instituted at the end of 1992 intensified investigation and prosecution of right-wing criminals by the police and the courts, and public protests against right-wing violence and xenophobia in form of candlelight vigils and mass demonstrations ushered in a change of climate; right-wing parties were unable to repeat their successes in the 1994 election year, remaining well below the 5 percent hurdle in all elections. Nevertheless, it can be said that along with xenophobic agitation and violence, anti-Semitic agitation and attacks on Jewish targets have increased (see Bergmann 1994a and 1994b). In Lübeck in 1994, a synagogue was the target of a firebombing for the first time since the war. The young perpetrators came from the same subcultural milieu that produces the majority of those have attacked businesses belonging to foreigners and hostels for asylum seekers. Politicians, the media, and the justice system have been firm in combatting anti-Semitism, which they have been forced to do again and again because of the frequency of such incidents; thus, the issue of anti-Semitism is more of a public and political issue now than it was before the fall of the Berlin Wall.

Notes

1. Taking into consideration objections that can no longer be verified with respect to the wording of the questions, corrected values lower than these were used by the authors to estimate that approximately 20 percent of the population were clearly anti-Semitic, 30 percent were indifferent, and 50 percent were non-anti-Semitic (ibid). It is thus not clear whether we can assume a figure of 20 percent or 40 percent anti-Semites for the early postwar period. The fact that the people would hardly have consistently expressed their true feelings to these delicate political questions for fear of possible repercussions and the findings of German studies on anti-Semitism in 1949 and 1952 support using the higher figure.

2. From the interview instructions for the 1949 IfD study: "We would first like to inform the interviewees that this survey is primarily intended to provide *German* authorities with an overview of public opinion on the question of anti-Semitism. The names of the interviewees will not be recorded" (italics in original). Cf. the corresponding observations for Austria in the early postwar years, in Hiller 1974, 162.

3. The authors considered this experiment a methodologically oriented pilot study and a case study for research in public opinion (Pollock 1955, 3ff.). Although many questions of methodology could not be resolved, and the study results were not representative, it nevertheless produced deeper psychological insight into the connection between repression of guilt feelings, projection, communicative latency, attitudes toward Nazism, and anti-Semitism.

4. If the statements collected into twenty-four associative complexes are examined, however, and the percentages of the negative complexes are added together, then in our opinion the proportion of negative associations is indeed higher (i.e., approximately 30 percent. Cf. EMNID 1954, 2–4).

5. Based on a nonrepresentative survey (N = 232), Schönbach (1961) recorded the reactions to this campaign. He identified a group of 16 percent showing "sympathy with anti-Semitic attitudes" and 24 percent free of any "recognizable reactions for or against anti-Semitic attitudes" (14). This was not a measurement of anti-Semitic sentiment per se, however, but only of feelings about anti-Jewish incidents, that is, the behavioral orientation and discrimination dimension, in which the figures are consistently less than in the stereotyping and emotional rejection dimensions. The 16 percent were certainly less than the total number with anti-Jewish attitudes in West Germany in 1960. The Federal Office of Political Education commissioned an EMNID study on "Expressions of Anti-Semitism in Assessments by the West German Public" (January 1960). As the ad hoc survey by Schönbach (1961) this study, along with several questions included in IfD surveys, was also not a broad-based anti-Semitism study; rather, it focussed on attitudes to the anti-Jewish incidents, of which a majority disapproved (IfD vol. III; EMNID 1960).

6. In our opinion, the Silbermann and Sallen study, like Panahi's, was too limited to an analysis of anti-Jewish stereotypes, without taking sufficient account of the changing historical context. There are limits to the extent to which anti-Semitism can be compared with "national prejudice" against other peoples or minorities.

7. In March, 1986, the *Westdeutsche Rundfunk* broadcasting company commissioned the EMNID Institute to do a representative study on "anti-Semitism." This one, however, had only five questions. The results are significant in that they clearly indicate the connection between anti-Semitism and the wish to end discussion of the past, as well as the phenomenon of "pluralistic ignorance" (cf. Bergmann 1988b). *Wiener* magazine (May 1988) commissioned the Wickert Institute to carry out 1,910 interviews; they found a surprisingly high level of agreement to the statements, although the wording was sensational, sometimes using Nazi terminology. The responses to some questions deviated considerably from the findings of other studies conducted at the same time. Despite requests on our part, we were not able to obtain any more specific information than the few tables published in *Wiener* (ibid., 3–6); it was thus impossible to determine the causes of these differences.

8. The first anti-Semitism study in the former East Germany in autumn 1990 by Wittenberg et al. (1991) used a scale created out of twenty-four anti-Jewish items; it included a series of stereotypes, as well as items on social distance and emotional rejection. The Erlangen sociologists identified three groups, without explaining their criteria more precisely. Those who agreed to a maximum of three items were described as largely free of prejudice (80 percent); those who agreed with nine to twenty-four items were counted as hard-core anti-Semites (6 percent); and an intermediate group (agreement to four to eight items) could be described as "somewhat anti-Semitic," as in the EMNID surveys (1989, 1992).

9. In constructing its scale, EMNID utilized sixteen separate questions dealing with anti-Jewish stereotypes and emotional rejection or presenting anti-Jewish statements. Without any clear methodological justification, all respondents giving six or more answers critical of Jews were categorized as anti-Semitic (13 percent of all Germans, 16 percent of those from the west and 4 percent of those from the east); those who gave zero or one "yes" response(s) were considered free of anti-Semitism (48 percent of all Germans). The group falling between the extremes (two to five "yes" responses—39 percent) were not placed in a precise category by EMNID; this group corresponded to the (West German) group classed by EMNID as "somewhat anti-Semitic" (40 percent) in 1989 (see above). Despite all the problems of comparison, the distribution for West Germans is very similar to those of the 1987 IfD Allensbach and 1989 EMNID surveys.

2

The Berlin Study on Anti-Semitism

Scientific examination of anti-Semitism has progressed quite irregularly in West German sociology and social psychology, generally intensifying only when the situation demanded. The Frankfurt Institute for Social Research (*Institut für Sozialforschung*) was exceptional in this development; after the return of Max Horkheimer, Theodor W. Adorno, and Friedrich Pollock from exile in the United States to West Germany, the famous *Studies in Prejudice* were continued until the late 1960s in numerous theoretical and empirical studies (Pollock 1955; Adorno 1959; Schönbach 1961; Schmidt and Becker 1967; von Freyhold 1971).

Conceptual Considerations

The most influential topic of discussion following the reestablishment of the Frankfurt Institute for Social Research was the authoritarianism theory, combining psychoanalysis with neo-Marxist social theory. Prejudice and aggression toward minorities were seen as an expression of a personality structure characterized by a weak ego and dependence on authority. According to this theory, this is caused by damaging childhood experiences due to an authoritarian upbringing. A weak ego leads to a low tolerance for frustration and a constant sense of external threat, resulting in the need for security in the in-group, projection of negative feelings onto out-groups, authoritarian fixation on strong authority, and rejection of weakness. People with weak egos do not direct the aggressions resulting from a repressive upbringing onto the loved yet feared authority figure; instead they shift them to other objects, primarily weak social groups. From this perspective, anti-Semitism—as well as prejudice toward other minorities—is relatively independent of the real object, functioning more as a form of social orientation by providing a clear, strongly polarized worldview. Anti-Semitism is seen here as one form of racism and ethnocentrism. This assumption was confirmed by Nazi racial politics, as well as by empirical findings from the United States that prejudiced people (those scoring high on the fascism and ethnocentrism scales) were not only anti-Semitic, but openly expressed hatred of and a desire to exterminate blacks, Japanese, and other ethnic minorities. This means that the object of this study is not specific types of prejudice, but the deep-rooted, comprehensive ideological and character structure (syndrome) responsible for rejection of *all minorities.* This theory is linked, via the notion of upbringing, to a critical theory of bourgeois-capitalistic society. Accordingly, anti-Semitism since 1945 has been closely linked to fascism and efforts to deal with it. Anti-Semitism remained an important subject in this theoretical tradition (and in the empirical research its followers initiated, cf. Pollock 1955; Freyhold 1971) until the mid-1960s. At the Fourth Congress of the "German Society for Psychotherapy and Psychoanalysis" in May, 1962—possibly in reaction to the wave of anti-Semitic incidents in 1959 and 1960—"the psychological and social prerequisites for anti-Semitism" were examined on the basis of the "psychodynamics of prejudice," which was the subtitle of the congress. Alexander Mitscherlich referred to anti-Semitism as a "disease of prejudice" (*Vorurteilskrankheit*), an "endemic, pathological occurrence in our culture, with epidemic waves spreading and aggravating the disease" (1962, 241). By far the most cogent book on efforts to come to terms with the past, *The Inability to Mourn,* by Alexander and Margarete Mitscherlich (1967, 1976), is written from this psychoanalytical perspective, which applies individual psychodynamics to the society as a whole. They describe insufficient confrontation with the Nazi past and the absence of education and reflection as repression and inner callousness, which are results of a narcissistic affront, a disappointed love of the *Fuehrer.* Repressed issues can be resolved by honest reevaluation—as in individual psychoanalysis. This form of social criticism was taken up by the student movement in its confrontation with the older generation.[1] In the movement's critique of capitalism and fascism, however, anti-Semitism was no longer a significant topic. Not until the 1980s did research on anti-Semitism revert to this Critical Theory tradition, and attempts were made to link psychoanalytical and Marxist approaches (Postone 1981; Claussen 1987). These studies offer little insight into post-Holocaust anti-Semitism, however, since they generally only analyzed modern anti-Semitism up to the Nazi period. At the same time, the consistently rejected charge that left-wing anti-Zionism could be a form of anti-Semitism was discussed self-critically in left-wing circles. It has become clear that in Europe, anti-Zionism cannot exist without anti-Semitism (cf. Wetzel 1983; Brumlik 1986; Broder 1986). This represents a new aspect of the theoretical discussion of anti-Semitism that must be taken into consideration in empirical surveys.

In recent years, self-critical questioning by the Left and the search for identity by younger German Jews (often occurring simultaneously) have evolved into a discussion dealing specifically with the unique forms of post-Auschwitz anti-Semitism and focussing on the connection between anti-Semitism and the German relationship to the Nazi past (Diner 1986; see also Bergmann 1988c, 228ff.). This discussion is essentially theoretical and abstract, making no attempt at empirical substantiation. We have taken these considerations into account in constructing our hypotheses.

An Anglo-American approach to research on anti-Semitism, as part of research on racism and minorities, was introduced after 1945, though it was not well received in Germany. The OMGUS studies of the late 1940s were based on this approach, in order to gain insight into the extent to which black American soldiers were rejected on account of skin color. It was mainly the projects sponsored by the United Nations (Leiris 1951 and Tumin 1962) that dealt with anti-Semitism in the context of racism and intergroup attitudes. This approach to research on racism and prejudice continued in West Germany in the 1950s within the scope of a larger research project on "national prejudices" (Sodhi and Bergius 1953; Sodhi, Bergius, and Holzkamp 1956). A methodological link was also made to early research by Daniel Katz and Kenneth W. Braly (1933, 1935); although these studies did investigate stereotypical images of Jews, this was not expanded into a theory of anti-Semitism. Research on minorities and prejudice then ceased to play any significant role in West Germany. German research on anti-Semitism after 1945 was conducted almost entirely within the context of Nazism, whereas research on minorities and prejudice was unable to develop at all, in view of the small, relatively invisible Jewish community in Germany and the absence of other minorities. New perspectives did not evolve until the 1970s, rather hesitantly, with the start of research on "guest workers" and foreign nationals.

This objective difference explains why intensive American research on anti-Semitism is difficult to apply to Germany (Bergmann 1996).

Attitudes toward the relatively large Jewish community in the United States are analyzed within the context of intergroup attitudes, and can be compared with attitudes toward blacks, Puerto Ricans, Italian-Americans, and so on (cf. Selznick and Steinberg 1969, chap. 9: "Anti-Semitism and Anti-Negro Prejudice"). This research deals with anti-Jewish attitudes within the scope of actual intergroup relations (Jews as neighbors, as presidential candidates, Jews in the business world, etc.) and current foreign policy issues (charges of "divided loyalties" to the United States and Israel). Christian anti-Judaism has also received considerable attention in this context. In a special study, Charles Y. Glock and Rodney Stark found a connection between religious dogmatism and anti-Semitism (1966). Because of the totally different situation in Germany, studies there can use neither the same questions and hypotheses nor the same theoretical approach (contact hypothesis, real conflict theory), although some phenomena are the same; for example, the influence of education and age on degree of prejudice can be observed in both countries.

Only Silbermann and Sallen analyzed anti-Semitism within the context of intergroup relations, which are basically determined by group rivalries and the sociocultural situation. They therefore maintained that modern anti-Semitism persists, and they distinguished among its various forms (economic, political, cultural, religious, and racist anti-Semitism), which at least in Germany no longer prevail in their previous form. Unlike typical intergroup conflicts, post-Auschwitz anti-Semitism does not seem to appear or intensify in times of social crisis; instead, it emerges from conflicts involving Nazi history and efforts to come to terms with the past, that is, in the final analysis, questions of German self-definition.

For this reason, our theoretical considerations did not take the same approach as American research on anti-Semitism. Instead, we based our research on hypotheses (and empirical procedures) developed since the 1970s by a small research group in Austria (Marin, Bunzl, Weiss). The various articles by Bernd Marin, in which he described a transformation of anti-Semitism in Austria, could also be particularly well adapted to West Germany. Anti-Semitism has largely lost its function as a political ideology, while continuing to exist as a personal prejudice. Not only is it "anti-Semitism without Jews," but also "anti-Semitism without anti-Semites." Personal hostilities can be exploited politically only in indirect ways via insinuations (1979, 1981). These considerations, as well as political incidents such as "Bitburg" and the Fassbinder and Waldheim affairs, have convinced us that present-day anti-Semitism in the Federal Republic of Germany is essentially tied to memories of Nazism, feelings of guilt, and the desire to end discussion of the past and return to normalcy. That means that rather than assuming an eternally unchanging structure of prejudice, we particularly wanted to measure the transformation and changes in the content of anti-Semitic prejudice, as well as the special, communicative latency of anti-Semitism today and the difference between private prejudices and public opposition to anti-Semitism. This perspective does not rule out the integration of theories of ethnocentrism, authoritarianism, and frustration-aggression models. All of these must be viewed from the proper angle, however, since current relations between Germans and Jews exist in the shadow of the Holocaust, and do not possess the structure common to competing ethnic groups. In their linguistic study of the major topics of prejudice in anti-Semitic discourse in Austria, Ruth Wodak et al. (1990, 279ff.) determined that these differ from those found by Teun van Dijk with respect to relations to "guest workers" and Moluccas in the Netherlands. The main concepts were "difference, deviance and threat"; that is, the emphasis was placed on the deviant behavior of the out-group, criminality, and the socioeconomic threat (cf. van Dijk 1984, 1987). These topics did not appear at all in anti-Semitic discourse; instead, the major topics there were "threat through political and financial power," "arrogance," and "dishonesty"; that is, mainly topics that are partly traditional and partly modified and adapted to current conflicts over the Nazi past.

The Outline of the Berlin Study of 1987

We started by evaluating both German and international research and compiling a list of hypotheses taking into account both individual dimensions of anti-Semitism and controversial political issues in the current relationship between Germans and Jews. In assessing foreign surveys on anti-Semitism, it became apparent that the historical and political prerequisites necessary for a comparison of "German anti-Semitism" with anti-Semitism in other Western countries (U.S., France, England) existed only to a limited degree. In addition to the different cultural traditions, the size of the Jewish community in each country was also a significant factor. In Germany, the issue of guilt, in particular, is closely tied to attitudes toward Jews; with the exception of Austria, there was no analogy to this in the other countries involved in the comparison.

In order to verify our knowledge of current aspects of and topics relating to present-day anti-Semitism, a series of exploratory interviews was conducted. Specially trained interviewers from the Institute for Public Opinion Research (IfD) in Allensbach carried out extensive depth interviews with twenty people, some of whom were clearly anti-Semitic, in late 1986. A manual of questions was used in conducting the interviews, in which the interviewees expressed their opinions in an unstructured manner. These interviews were intended to help us familiarize ourselves with views and opinions on issues important to the interviewee at the time. We also wanted to learn the actual wording used in expressing anti-Semitic prejudices and justification, as an aid in forming our hypotheses (for details of the results, see below).

Based on the exploratory interviews and general theoretical considerations (cf. Bergmann and Erb 1986), a comprehensive list of questions was compiled. It included historical and theoretical concepts and dimensions of anti-Semitism as well as everyday attitudes toward Jews.

A pretest was conducted in March, 1987 using the complete list of questions. The ninety questions (with numerous sub-questions) were answered by 344 people. This pretest was prepared in the form of a contrast group analysis,[2] that is, approximately 100 interviews were conducted with each of the following groups: a representative cross-section of the population (N = 121), people with clearly anti-Jewish attitudes (N = 95), and people showing markedly pro-Jewish sentiment (N = 128).[3] The interviewers were given the task of questioning people whom they knew or thought to hold anti-Jewish or pro-Jewish opinions. This procedure is of course in itself somewhat problematic, since the selection of extreme groups was made according to an undefined and individual concept of anti- or philo-Semitism, which varied from interviewer to interviewer. Possible interviewer subjectivity was difficult to ascertain and could not be eliminated even by briefing the interviewers. This fundamental criticism was taken into consideration in evaluating the interviews.

The contrast group comparison enabled us to verify whether the questions were capable of making relevant distinctions. Since we were interested in testing a large number of new hypotheses, in addition to using questions already included in other surveys, this comparison was of utmost importance. It allowed us to identify "dead-ends" and unproductive lines of questioning early enough to eliminate those questions from the main survey.

The list of questions in the pretest was revised and reduced to twenty-four questions (with additional sub-questions) for the main survey (survey period: 24 September through 5 October 1987; cf. appendix 2).

Due to methodological (and financial) considerations, we integrated the list of questions into the framework of a multiple-topic survey. We suspected that a survey dealing specifically with anti-Semitism would have been more strongly influenced in the direction of "socially acceptable" responses. An attempt was made to minimize this possibly unavoidable effect by changing subjects within the course of the interview.[4]

Exploratory Interviews

The IfD in Allensbach carried out a series of twenty open interviews lasting from one to two hours, throughout West Germany. These structured interviews had a common theme covering six subject areas with ten to fifteen supplementary questions each. The main purpose of these interviews was to determine whether certain attitudes even exist, and how coherent a structure they have. Especially since the questions dealt with a complex of attitudes that has been considered taboo for forty years and was not on the public and political agenda, it was important to determine the degree to which anti-Semitism still exists in the minds of West Germans, and the motives and issues at the root of present-day anti-Jewish sentiment. In order to ascertain the extent to which honest answers to questions on this taboo subject could be expected, we asked the interviewers following each session whether they had the impression the interviewees answered in an open, evasive, or restrained manner. According to the impression of the interviewers, the questions were answered openly in more than half of the interviews conducted. With respect to the remainder, it was generally the case that a few questions were answered either evasively or with restraint, though this never pertained to the interview as a whole. In reading the transcripts of the interviews, we generally felt that those questioned did indeed express their true opinions, and that public pressure did not result in any interviewee either expressing no opinion at all or indicating agreement with public opinion where this was not truly the case. Rather, the expression of extremely negative opinions was more often relativized or toned down. However, basic views could always be discerned behind more reserved answers. An interview situation is apparently felt to be private enough, and at the same time sufficiently anonymous, to allow the expression of true feelings, even if the subject is a "delicate" one. Most of those questioned would welcome an open conversation with Jews and did not wish to avoid the subject of Nazism and the persecution of the Jews. There was a desire for "normalcy." Only a few felt uneasy talking about the subject, though when such a situation was unavoidable, they preferred to express their sympathies.

Israel

The image of Israel was shaped by two subjects: the Middle East conflict and the country's special relationship to Germany, focussing on reparations. Sympathies were divided on the Middle East conflict. In some cases, interviewees took a neutral, descriptive position in which Israel was called a trouble spot, yet no judgment was made on the guilt or innocence of the involved parties. To some extent, interviewees accepted Israel's self-defense and settlement policies. In other cases, clear criticism of Israeli politics was expressed. In such cases, Israel was seen as responsible for taking land away from the Arabs and starting wars. This criticism was generally free of any clear anti-Zionist ideology, though there were also cases of anti-Zionist attitudes. This criticism was often event-related rather than ideologically motivated, as can be seen by the fact that such criticism and a positive picture of Israel ("I could live there") definitely could exist side by side. In our context, it is significant that what was seen as Israel's aggressive, hostile stance was considered by some of the interviewees to be a general characteristic of Jews—that they cannot coexist with others and always feel placed on the defensive, although they themselves are the aggressors. Old stereotypes of the "Chosen People" and their accursedness as "Christ killers" played an important role here, as Israeli policy was presented as part of a broad "historical" perspective. Other critical remarks were also made in the interviews, such as claims of too much emphasis on Israel in the media and complaints that criticism of Israel is not allowed, supported by old anti-Jewish cliches about the power of "international Jewry"—primarily with respect to U.S. support of Israel. Here, Israeli politics and their resonance throughout the world were still interpreted within patterns of modern anti-Semitism.

German-Israel relations, definitely seen as special, were seen entirely from the point of view of reparations, which most of those questioned did not support. Although some felt the political relationship between Israel and Germany was good, especially because of German reparations, most rejected further demands and accusations, calling them "impudent" and demanding the introduction of normal relations and an end to discussion of the past. The two opinions may indeed be related. The contradiction between Israeli and German perspective was definitely perceived: whereas Germans are interested not in forgetting the past, but in returning to normalcy, the interviewees felt that "Israelis think about the past too much and want to settle old scores." It was assumed that Israelis/Jews hate Germans and want to keep the German feeling of guilt alive. This is why some also felt that West Germany's good relations to Israel are "not genuine".

Jews throughout the World

When asked what connected Jews throughout the world, the most common responses were a common religion and a shared history of persecution. In only one case was Judaism defined not as a religion, but as a people: "A Jew is a Jew; first a Jew and then a German." Almost all of those questioned spoke of a strong sense of solidarity among Jews and their tendency to preserve their autonomy. In addition to neutral or positive connections, almost all of the interviewees also mentioned strong international business connections, which some interpreted as conspiratorial in nature. The insinuated position of economic and political power held by Jews had a generally negative effect on non-Jews, according to those questioned: "They want to oppress other peoples, because they have money." This influence, which some specified as a media influence, was usually simply suspected everywhere (big companies; "Jews have their fingers in everything"), rather than precisely stated. Only in one case was economic power in casinos and banks attributed to Jews in West Germany. It was typical for the vagueness of these responses that most of those questioned did not know about Jewish organizations. Some spoke of the Zionist Movement or a "Zionist Society" as an international combat force.

Opinions were divided on Jewish responses to particular current political events, such as the Waldheim affair. Whereas some of those questioned saw here an instance of great Jewish influence on the media, and viewed the actions of the World Jewish Congress as interference in Austria's internal affairs, others expressed understanding for criticism of Waldheim.

Stereotypes of Jews

When asked to describe Jewish physical traits, the traditional image of the "hooked nose," "dark hair," and "caftan" was addressed. Some expressed this without firm conviction, as if they were not stereotyping, but simply repeating what was common knowledge. Some had no feelings whatsoever regarding "Jewish appearance" or knew nothing about it. In the two cases in which interviewees had had contact with Jews, they claimed to be able to "sense" or "recognize with 90 percent certainty" if someone were Jewish. Especially in the second case, it was clear that contact with a few individual Jews at the workplace contributed to forming a general stereotype: Jews "wear a skullcap, have beards and hooked noses, are polite, have good manners, and wear a lot of jewelry." The ability to recognize Jews was not linked to any negative value judgment; it remained at the level of generalized individual experiences.

Some of those questioned knew relatively little about Jews. When asked about their opinions and interests, and about knowledge of Jewish subgroups, many were not able to give a response. Jews were seen as fully integrated people, like everyone else. In response to the question on positive views of Jews, however, the same interviewees said that they had never heard anything positive about Jews: "If anyone has a positive judgment of Jews, it can only be out of pity." This indicates that, with the exception of official statements, the subject "Jews" is usually mentioned only in a negative context.

The image of Jews is still dominated by stereotypes and economic-related prejudice. Sometimes the particular "aptitude" of Jews in business was emphasized in a more neutral fashion. Trade, banking, and the stock exchange, as well as media, film, law, and—in connection with Israel—agriculture, were mentioned as typical occupations. To some extent, these stereotypes revealed aspects of both old and new economic anti-Semitism: Leading positions in industry and research were viewed as successful infiltrations of these fields; business acumen eliminates the need to do physical labor; and business-mindedness was linked with arrogance and dishonesty. The economic stereotype was ambivalent: on the one hand, Jews were assessed as disciplined and business-minded, "like us;" on the other hand, Jews were rejected as the opposite of Germans (different from "Nordic peoples").

In some of the interviews, embitterment as a result of "not having come to terms with the past" was apparent. Reparations payments were rejected and Jews were criticized for continually confronting Germans with Nazism and "finding us guilty." A comparison of Israeli policy toward the Palestinians with the Nazi persecution of the Jews was mentioned reproachfully in this context.

All in all, the image of Jews appeared to be reduced to a few stereotypical characteristics, sometimes stated as facts and only rarely clearly expressed as an opinion. Very few interviewees had personal experience with Jews; nevertheless, they attempted to integrate new information (media impact in the U.S., agriculture in Israel, reports on diamond trading, etc.) into the traditional image.

National Socialism, the Third Reich, and the Jews

Very few interviewees had detailed knowledge of the persecution of the Jews in the "Third Reich." Ideas were often muddled and diffuse, with Jews sharing the blame for their fate. According to interviewees, the persecution of the Jews was not discussed in school; some of them had heard about the period from parents or grandparents.

Approximately half of those interviewed expressed abhorrence, or at least clear condemnation, of the Holocaust, though surprisingly enough, some of them would have had nothing against the deportation of the Jews ("like with the people seeking asylum"). One man questioned referred to his father, who had said, "it had to be done." Awareness of the magnitude of the crimes and the consequences appeared limited. Many were of the opinion that the Jews could have emigrated, and that "wealthy" Jews, in particular, all returned after the war. The interviewees gave the impression they thought only of German Jews as being among the persecuted, while Jewish victims from other European countries were apparently outside their frame of reference.

In addition to vague ideas in general, doubt about the existence of concentration and death camps was also clearly articulated ("who knows whom to believe"), going as far as implications that public opinion was manipulated by Jews and Americans. The truth was supposedly "prescribed by law."

In answer to the question on reasons for the persecution of the Jews, a majority of those interviewed assumed that Jews shared the blame. In addition to power and economic preeminence, other responses included the Jews' unwillingness to conform, too many foreigners (*Überfremdung*) and revisionist theses of Jews declaring war and agitating against Germany in the press. Even the accusation of murdering Christ and the tradition of persecution, illustrated with historical examples, were offered to explain such hatred ("There has been anti-Semitism here for over 5000 years!").

Disgust at the "Jewish problem" in general was perceptible in some of the interviews, in which those questioned did not want to hear anything more about it. They were opposed to "extolling Jews today," and the heavy focus on the subject in the media ("so much fuss"). Some suspected that those interested in keeping the subject alive had ulterior motives such as reparations and financial compensation. In general, the interviews gave the impression that knowledge, insight, and discernment, but most of all human sympathy for the victims of the Holocaust, were severely lacking. Rejection and projection of guilt were found instead.

Present-Day Relationships to Jews and Future Developments

"Jews" as an issue did not play a very significant role in the subjects' daily lives; "you don't hear anything about it," they said, although there were also complaints about media influence and attempts to keep memories of the past alive. Opinions diverged on the relationship between Jews and Germans. Many said the relationship today between the two peoples was good, whether because Jews have their own country and have acknowledged German reparations payments, or because German animosity has abated. Others saw a contrast between the official good relationship and unofficial tension and rejection of Jews. Some voiced fears that the good climate would last only as long as "the Jews get their money." Here, Jews were seen as the cause of possible tension. A third group believed the relationship between Germans and Jews was still strained, although they considered Jews in the Federal Republic of Germany to be well integrated. This group believed the cause of tensions lay in a subliminal anti-Semitism that has always been present among Germans.

Therefore, they refused to put an end to remembrance of history, insisting it was absolutely necessary to continue the discussion of Nazism. Overall, however, the demand prevailed that the debate be ended and financial reparations stopped. It was argued that historical obligations have been fulfilled. Although on occasion understanding was shown for the victims' point of view, including their refusal or inability to end the discussion, and a special obligation was recognized, the accusation prevailed that Jews want to "make money" by keeping the subject alive. Openly anti-Semitic interviewees rejected any further obligation to the Jews and accused them of fomenting hatred. They said reconciliation was impossible "because the Jews want to keep collecting" and "they keep on about National Socialism." Among these interviewees, there was also a clear tendency to project their own hatred of Jews onto the population at large [to the "false consensus effect" in the case of anti-Semites (cf. Bergmann and Erb 1991), claiming people were sick and tired of the issue and that there was a new anti-Semitic trend among Germans. Consistently enough, they demanded an end to the discussion as a prerequisite for understanding; that is, if the Jews gave up their claims, understanding would be possible. It is not surprising that they not only lacked any sense of German guilt or responsibility, but felt such guilt had been forced upon them through forty years of "reeducation." In their opinion, Germans suffer more immediately from the past, which "keeps being forced on us as a sense of guilt."

Thus, anti-Semitism is explained as resulting from the fact that "people just won't leave the Germans alone." A young man stated that young people, himself included, had nothing against the Jews, but simply did not want to be called "sinners" (adding the subtle threat that an ultrarightist party might otherwise emerge). In this context, suspicion was also voiced that Jews falsify history in order to maintain the accusation of guilt, which could in turn lead to hatred of Jews.[5] Thus, a tendency existed to make Jews themselves responsible for anti-Semitism. They were accused of artificially keeping alive and blowing out of proportion an issue that had in fact been forgotten.

Other interviewees suggested envy of Jews as a main cause of anti-Semitism, which they often believed was confined to specific groups such as the lower social classes, the elderly, or neo-Nazis. Opinions on the significance and extent of anti-Semitism differed. Some assumed that foes of the Jews, especially among the younger generation, had decreased sharply in number and that anti-Semitism was no longer a major issue. Some believed it was limited to neo-Nazis alone. However, others voiced the opinion that anti-Semitism had increased in recent years (evidenced by attacks on Jewish facilities). From an anti-Jewish perspective, this increase could be traced back to Jewish behavior, such as "playing up the Second World War." From a socially critical viewpoint, it could be seen in connection with xenophobia. Those holding the latter opinion were particularly critical of the younger generation for failing to work at coming to terms with Nazism and wanting to "rid itself of the idea of restitution." There were apparently two diverging motives for assuming a growth of anti-Semitism: an anti-Semitic desire that this be the case, and a skeptical attitude toward the public's ability to learn from the past.

Not all interviewees appeared to understand the concept of anti-Semitism. Some confused it with apartheid; others classed it with xenophobia, while still others had no clear idea at all of its meaning. Nearly all those interviewed rejected the idea of punishing anti-Semitic statements. When reasons were given, they included an emphasis on tolerance and rejection of special treatment for minorities. However, this rejection was also justified pragmatically, for example with the argument that punishment is not a suitable means of changing people's point of view. In contrast to the United States, for example, legal protection of minorities against discrimination seems to find little public acceptance in Germany.

Contact with Jews

The interviewees rarely had personal contact with Jews; where they did, they reported good experiences. This low level of contact comes as no surprise given the very small Jewish minority in Germany. Overall, knowledge and awareness of Jews in public life was also low and quite selective. Those with anti-Jewish views were more likely to identify Jews in public positions. One interviewee, for example, distinguished "unpleasant Jews," among which he included the famous "Nazi-hunter" Simon Wiesenthal and Heinz Galinski, at that time head of the Jewish community in Berlin, from positively viewed Jews such as the writer Ephraim Kishon. Another clearly anti-Semitic interviewee complained that Hans Rosenthal, a famous quizmaster, and Inge Meysel, a famous German actress in TV, were allowed publicly to voice their opinions on television. Knowledge of Jews in the arts and sciences was generally limited, and seemed to be closely linked to educational level.

A summary of impressions from the interviews furnishes the following picture: There are practically no current contacts or conflicts with Jews in West Germany today. Jews living in Germany are generally seen as well-integrated "people like you and me." However, marriage to a Jew generally meets with disapproval, with reference to religious differences. The subject "Jews and anti-Semitism" is generally of little contemporary significance. When it is discussed, the historical aspect prevails. Many of those interviewed had the impression that Jews used the past in order to make the Germans look guilty, and thus gain material advantage. They saw this as a cause of present-day anti-Semitism. Because of this tension, reconciliation was judged skeptically, even though many agreed that the relationship between Germans and Jews/Israelis was good, especially at the political level.

In addition to these resentments arising from the Nazi past, one encounters remnants of traditional stereotyping, such as the Jewish link to money and banking and their international influence, as well as physical stereotypes such as the nose and the caftan. However, these statements often had the character of learned responses; that is, people passed on "what you hear around," rather than deeply rooted personal attitudes. A statement on Jews' supposed international influence is not anti-Semitic per se, but must be interpreted within the context of the interview as a whole. To this extent, in both the preliminary and the main studies, agreement with specific anti-Jewish stereotypes should not be taken in itself as an expression of anti-Semitism.

While many of the interviewees made isolated "anti-Semitic slips of the tongue," these did not together form an "overall picture" of an anti-Semite. However, there were also obvious "Jew haters" who disliked Jews and felt no historical responsibility; at the same time, they were highly nationalistic, projecting the causes of anti-Semitism on the Jews while not shying away from threatening undertones. In these cases, it became clear to what extent the causes of current anti-Semitism were related to a constant sense of confrontation with moral accusations of guilt, which were then parried with counter-accusations and attempts to relativize the past. Our thesis of "secondary anti-Semitism" is strongly supported by these interviews.

Results of the Pretest

The comparison of contrast groups enables us to assess whether certain hypotheses and questions can be used to measure anti-Semitic attitudes; it allows a comparison of answers from people with anti-Jewish, average, and pro-Jewish views. In the following we briefly present results not included in the evaluation of the main survey.

In our study, we did not start with a concept of personality theory along the lines of the "authoritarian personality," but in the pretest we did attempt to gain a picture of the "anti-Semitic personality" using questions on self-description, family socialization, and existential views. Those with anti-Jewish attitudes described themselves as assertive leadership types with a tendency toward order and punctuality, but also as outsiders and loners. As far as friends and social contacts were concerned, however, they seemed to be socially integrated persons, though somewhat less trusting and more pessimistic than the average. Thus, we included several questions on subjective mood in the main questionnaire (cf. chap. 9). Questions on upbringing showed no deviation from the average; however, with respect to Jews, it was conspicuous that anti-Semites less often reported that their families had had Jewish friends and acquaintances, while reporting more frequently that their families were anti-Jewish (27 percent, compared with 3 percent in the overall population). Among anti-Semites of the older generation, family upbringing was more significant as a source of learned attitudes. In comparison, the influence of the media seemed to be slight. People with anti-Jewish attitudes were less likely to read clearly liberal publications (*Die Zeit, Der Spiegel*), but this may be more the influence of education, as they read fewer newspapers overall than the average. None of them reported reading the right-wing extremist newspaper *Deutsche Nationalzeitung*.

Subjects with anti-Jewish attitudes described themselves as interested in politics (68 percent, compared with 60 percent among the total population), with political positions ranging from right to right-wing extremist and anti-liberal. Thus, 32 percent of them would support a new right-wing extremist party, or would welcome its creation (10 percent of the total population). But this third was offset by a majority of people with anti-Semitic views (48 percent) who would oppose a right-wing extremist party; that is, anti-Semitic attitudes were by no means overwhelmingly linked to an active right-wing extremist orientation, although the anti-Semites did exhibit a somewhat greater proclivity toward violence. They tended to hold particularly well-defined nationalist or chauvinist views (57 percent believed Germans were superior to other peoples), another side of which included strong xenophobia in addition to anti-Semitism. Here, too, socialization proved influential: anti-Semites were more likely to report that their parents were always cautious in regard to foreigners (43 percent, compared with 18 percent among those with pro-Jewish attitudes).

People with anti-Jewish attitudes, like the population in general, had little contact with Jews (such contacts were more likely among those with pro-Jewish opinions), but they were far more likely to reject any form of contact or cooperation with Jews or Israel. This disinterest included an element of mistrust regarding direct contact with Jews; the anti-Semites were far more likely to ask if someone was Jewish (57 percent, compared with 12 percent in the general population).

This social distance accompanied a decisive rejection of any special obligation involving help or reparations for Israel (88 percent) and Jews (42 percent saw no obligation, as compared with 18 percent of the total population). Shared guilt or responsibility was widely rejected. Although those with anti-Semitic views seldom saw the Holocaust as a unique event (14 percent), and few of them assumed that it could never be atoned for (17 percent), they were, on the other hand, overwhelmingly skeptical about the possibility of reconciliation between Jews and Germans. Only 5 percent thought it possible in the foreseeable future, while 69 percent did not believe in a "real reconciliation" (46 percent of the total population also believed this). Those with anti-Jewish outlooks thus did not see the Holocaust as a crime for which amends could never be made, instead blaming the absence of reconciliation on the "Jewish character." There is a tension between this skepticism and the anti-Semites' strong wish to put an end to the discussion of the past [*Schlußstrich ziehen* (94 percent)].

With regard to level of awareness of the Nazi past and the persecution of the Jews, there were few differences between the two groups of interviewees. The level of knowledge seemed quite high; anti-Semites also believed they knew enough about the issues and did not want to hear any more about them. This attitude concealed tendencies toward denial and defensiveness, as is revealed by the attitude, shared by 45 percent of the anti-Semites, that "a lot of what is said about the concentration camps is exaggerated" (7 percent of the total population said the same). They also remembered much less about the concentration camps than about the war. Concerning their overall attitude toward National Socialism, anti-Semites tended to perceive the crimes of the Third Reich as the acts of a few Nazi leaders (83 percent), while exonerating the majority of the people. They believed the Jews, and especially "international Jewry," shared responsibility for the persecution of the Jews. Twenty-three percent of those with anti-Semitic views described the Third Reich in positive terms (4 percent of the total population). This attitude may be encouraged by certain ways of passing down information. Thus, by their own account, their own families were less often opposed to the Nazis, and the anti-Semites spoke more frequently with parents and grandparents about this period. Where they had personally experienced the Nazi period, the anti-Semites did not differ from the other two groups of interviewees.

The anti-Semites were divided with regard to our questions on how they dealt with the subject of "Jews." On the one hand, they were less likely than other interviewees to call the subject uninteresting; on the other, however, they avoided it as far as possible, and were less likely than the average to say that it was possible to have an interesting conversation on the issue (14 percent to 26 percent). This suggests that anti-Semites prefer to avoid the subject when talking to people who do not share their views. Talking to an Israeli, they would feel forced to apologize and would expect to be ostracized. But some of the anti-Semites claimed they would take the offensive in such a situation; they would "tell them a thing or two." They would be happy to talk to opponents of the Jews, however; 67 percent of them said they had many anti-Jewish friends (17 percent of the total population). Over half of those with anti-Jewish attitudes believed anti-Semitism to be widespread; a third even believed it was on the increase.

Tolerance of anti-Semitic remarks in private circles was, as could be expected, widespread among the anti-Semites (59 percent, compared with 25 percent of the total population). In other areas, too, they exhibited greater tolerance for anti-Jewish activities. Only half of them advocated equal treatment for Jews in Germany. The potential for discrimination in this extremist group proved surprisingly high; that is, it can be assumed that the interviewers, in choosing their interview partners, did indeed find particularly anti-Jewish persons.

For the main survey, which could only include a fourth of the pretest questions, we chose primarily those questions that clearly discriminated between the anti-Semites and the two other groups of interviewees. Such a procedure is imperative, especially if one assumes that anti-Semitic attitudes today are quite diffuse and no longer comprise a firm world view. But the many questions and aspects that were not included in the main survey also gave us a reservoir of background knowledge that was invaluable in evaluating the survey.

Construction of the Anti-Semitism Indices

We followed the approaches used in former studies by Charles Y. Glock and Rodney Stark, and Herbert Sallen and Alphons Silbermann in constructing our indices, by creating a partial index for each dimension of anti-Semitic prejudice (for a detailed discussion of these earlier attempts to develop an instrument for measuring anti-Semitism and for problems in the construction of scales see appendix 1). Unlike the authors mentioned, we determined the group of anti-Semites on the basis of all three dimensions of prejudice.

Anti-Jewish Stereotypes

We chose from the overall list of stereotypes those negative anti-Jewish stereotypes that loaded onto one factor in a factor analysis. First, we added all other negative cognitive judgments of Jews from our questionnaire, and subjected the items to a correlation analysis. For the final construction of the index, we eliminated those items whose correlation fell beneath $(r) = .40$. Seventeen individual questions remained (cf. appendix 4), which were used to form the "anti-Jewish stereotypes" index (AS-Stereotype; see table 2.1).

Combining all seventeen negative stereotypes into an aggregate measure showed, on the one hand, that anti-Jewish cliches were widespread (on the average, each interviewee gave 3.3 negative responses), but that, on the other hand, a *consistent* anti-Jewish image was found only among a minority. Approximately one in four people gave no anti-Jewish response to any of the seventeen questions. At what point can one begin to speak of clearly anti-Jewish image? In defining the interface, it must be taken into account, first of all, that negative views of Jews among the interviewees were clustered around particular complexes of stereotypes; that is, even those with clearly negative views of Jews would make choices, and would disagree with certain aspects of the cliche (such as religious or economic aspects). Second of all, the method of questioning (presenting a list of

TABLE 2.1
Index: AS-Stereotype

yes answers	N	%	% cumulative
0	509	24,2	24,2
1	374	17,8	42,1
2	275	13,1	55,2
3	184	8,8	63,9
4	158	7,5	71,5
5	127	6,0	77,5
6	105	5,0	82,5
7	82	3,9	86,4
8	80	3,8	90,2
9	46	2,2	92,4
10	38	1,8	94,2
11	41	2,0	96,2
12	22	1,0	97,2
13	23	1,1	98,3
14	10	0,5	98,8
15	13	0,6	99,4
16	9	0,4	99,9
17	3	0,1	100,0
missings	3	0,1	
Total	**2102**	**100,0**	

Guttman Split-half: .82   Mean x = 3.3
Spearmen-Brown: .85
Reliability alpha: .86

characteristics) is structured such that non-agreement with a characteristic does not mean explicit rejection. That is, an interviewee need not agree with all or a majority of the characteristics provided in order consistently to express his or her individual anti-Jewish cliche. We believe that agreement with more than a third of the characteristics should warrant being ascribed a consistent anti-Jewish attitude. That would draw the line between five and six "yes" responses, which would mean 22.5 percent of the interviewees had a consistently negative view of Jews (see table 2.1).[6] However, this group of people could not be lumped together as "Jew haters," as only some of them showed any emotional involvement.

FIGURE 2.1
Stereotyping and Social Distance

Number of 'yes 'responses to stereotypes

Index: Soc. Distance

- ■ Zero 'yes' responses
- ▨ 1 'yes'response
- ▨ 2 'yes'responses
- ▨ 3 'yes'responses

About half the population assessed Jews in an inconsistent manner (43.3 percent = one to three "yes" responses). Within this group, a further distinction can be made. If we use the mean of all "yes" responses as the basis (3.3), we can define another interface between three and four responses, thus separating out a group of approximately 40 percent. This formal argument is supported by the fact that, of those who agreed with one to three anti-Jewish characteristics, very few attached anti-Jewish feelings to this stereotyping.

After these observations, we can distinguish three groups:

No or limited anti-Jewish stereotyping (zero to three "yes" responses)	64.0 %
Inconsistent anti-Jewish stereotyping (four to five "yes" responses)	13.5 %
Consistent anti-Jewish stereotyping (six to seventeen "yes" responses)	22.5 %

This group definition is somewhat arbitrary, and can only be justified theoretically. We must assume that today anti-Jewish stereotypes are transferred fragmentarily, and that these traditional views can be neither reinforced nor called into question through primary experience. The open interviews that we conducted in preparing the survey showed that fragments of the anti-Semitic world view still exist, but in only a few cases actually merge to form a coherent overall picture. Anti-Jewish stereotypes are part of the collective store of knowledge, but for most people they have no current, personal significance. Neither are they anchored in primary experience, which could justify corresponding emotions. The interviewees constantly pointed out the lack of contact to Jews, and often expressed their ignorance and lack of preoccupation with the issue.[7] The intermediate group we identified has been shown to be open to influence by negative or subtly anti-Jewish reporting in the media.[8]

In comparison with the two following indices of emotional rejection and inclination to discriminate, the AS-Stereotype index—in accordance with the theory of prejudice—is a softer indicator with a broader range. While agreement to even one or two questions in the other two indices must be recognized as obvious anti-Semitism, agreement with a range of negative stereotypes of Jews need not be seen as a definite sign of anti-Semitic views. This is also shown by the fact that only 24 percent of the interviewees agreed with none of the stereotypes, while in the other indices (which, however, also consisted of fewer items, see below), 65 percent to 80 percent did the same. To achieve a corresponding degree of selectivity for the stereotypes, this index must contain a larger number of items than is necessary for the other indices. Studies of national stereotypes regularly indicate that foreign peoples are ascribed a number of positive as well as negative characteristics. A few negative stereotypes thus do not justify being regarded as hostile cliches. Caution is also necessary because the index only included hostile characteristics, without taking account of the balancing positive characteristics that are even more often ascribed to Jews by the population than the negative ones. These reasons serve to justify our refusal to judge agreement with one to three negative statements on Jews as an expression in itself of an anti-Semitic outlook.

Emotional Rejection and Social Distance

In preparing this index, we used three items that clearly express antipathy toward and dissociation from Jews: "It's better not to have

TABLE 2.2
Index: AS-Social Distance

yes answers	N	%	% cumulative
0	1703	81.0	81.0
1	263	12.5	93.5
2	76	3.6	97.1
3	60	2.9	100.0
Total	**2102**	**100.0**	

(Mean x=.28, Reliability: alpha .65)

too much to do with Jews" (question 1a); "People who don't like Jews" (question 7); "It would be best for us Germans if all the Jews would go to Israel" (question 10). The correlations among the three items lie between r = .62 and .77, assuring a statistically acceptable connection among them.

Of those questioned, 81 percent answered "no" to all three of these "social distance" questions. This is partly due to the fact that an index consisting of only three items, especially very harsh and highly correlated ones as is the case here, makes the group of those who showed approval smaller and more selective than the AS-Stereotype index, which has a broader distribution. On the other hand, this result also signifies that emotional rejection and social distance are less widespread in the population than anti-Jewish stereotypes. It can be concluded that many of those questioned did not attach any great emotional significance to some of the anti-Jewish stereotypes they support, nor was their social relationship to Jews exclusively determined by these stereotypes. As expected, there is a significant positive correlation between the AS-Stereotype and AS—Social Distance indices (r = 0.55). Nevertheless, it is clear that the two indices measure different dimensions of anti-Semitic prejudice. On the basis of these considerations, we generated the following groups:

No rejection or distance (zero "yes" answers)	81 %
Pronounced rejection or distance (1–3 "yes" answers)	19 %

Inclination to Discriminate

In preparing this index, all items were included which call for discriminatory behavior toward Jews. "One shouldn't go to Jewish doctors" (question 16/10); "Jews should be prohibited from either immigrating or returning to Germany" (question 16/13); "Jews shouldn't be allowed to hold high public offices here" (question 16/2); "Letters to the editor should be written strongly criticizing reparations payments to Israel" (question 16/16); "We should discontinue reparations payments to Israel" (question 16/8).[9] The correlation analysis shows that the statistical correlations between the items are acceptable (between r = .48 and .78).

TABLE 2.3
Index: AS-Discrimination

yes answers	N	%	% cumulative
0	1366	65,0	65.0
1	454	21,6	86,6
2	180	8,6	95,1
3	54	2,6	97,7
4	34	1,6	99,3
5	14	0,7	100.0
Total	**2102**	**100.0**	

(Mean x=0.56, Reliability: alpha .62)

The percentage of those supporting at least one form of discrimination against Jews is very high (35 percent). This finding would contradict the prejudice theory, which assumes that a higher degree of prejudice is required for active behavior than for passive, emotional rejection. The breakdown of the number of "yes" answers per item shows that a large proportion of those who affirmed only one item were opposed to further reparations payments to Israel, that is, the least discriminatory demand included in this list (292 of 454 questioned). Half of all those who supported this demand did not support any other anti-Jewish demands. For this reason, it made sense to put those who answered "yes" to only one item in a separate intermediate group.

On the basis of these considerations, the following groups were formed:

No inclination to discriminate   65.0 %
  (zero "yes" answers)

Intermediate inclination to discriminate   21.6 %
  (1 "yes" answer)

Pronounced inclination to discriminate   13.4 %
  (2–5 "yes" answers)

Determination of Anti-Semitic Potential

These three partial indices each measure a particular dimension of anti-Semitic prejudice. The correlation coefficients between the respective indices, which can also be assumed to be a validity test of the results, are relatively high: .57 (AS-Discrimination/AS-Social Distance); .55 (AS-Social Distance/AS-Stereotype); and .61 (AS-Discrimination/AS-Stereotype). Since the indices are intended to measure different aspects of anti-Semitic prejudice, a greater correlation cannot be expected theoretically.

Combining the three partial indices into one comprehensive index is not advisable, primarily because the relative weight of the individual dimensions cannot be determined theoretically. A "yes" response to a stereotype on the AS-Stereotype index must be evaluated differently than a "yes" response to one of the statements expressing discriminatory behavior or strong emotional rejection on the AS-Discrimination or AS-Social Distance indices, respectively. The problem cannot be resolved by combining three indices of equal length in a 1:1:1 ratio; nor does it help to give the shorter indices correspondingly greater weight. As regards content, weighting of any kind is problematic. For this reason we refrained from compiling a comprehensive index and instead combined the categorization (see above) made with respect to each of the partial indices in identifying a person as anti-Semitic. In this way, it was possible to integrate the three dimensions of prejudice.

To distinguish between anti-Semitic and non-anti-Semitic persons, standards of varying intensity can be formulated.

1. We applied very strict criteria in identifying the group of hardcore, vehement anti-Semites. In this category we included all those who demonstrated pronounced anti-Semitic attitudes as we defined them for each of the three partial indices, that is, *vehement anti-Semitism (VAS)* = six or

more "yes" answers in the AS-Stereotype index; one or more in the AS-Social Distance index; *and* two or more in the AS-Discrimination index.

Using this procedure, we established a group of 6.9 percent (N = 146) hardcore anti-Semites.

2. Persons responding with an above-average (relative to the mean value of all affirmative answers) number of "yes" responses in all three dimensions of prejudice can also be regarded as anti-Semitic.

According to this criterion, 11.6 percent (N = 244) of those questioned were categorized as *strongly anti-Semitic (SAS)*. Since the mean value in a sample varies with the extent of anti-Semitism and its distribution in the population, the proportion of people categorized as anti-Semites using this procedure need not necessarily increase, even if anti-Semitism in society in general grows. That means that this method is only appropriate for measuring anti-Semitism at a particular point in time, and cannot be compared with later results unless the original mean value is used as a standard in later calculations.

3. When the three partial indices (AS-Stereotype, AS-Social Distance, and AS-Discrimination) are compared, it can be seen that some interviewees received a high rating in one partial index, but a low rating in the other two. This was particularly the case regarding people with a strong, often emotionally grounded negative view of Jews, who often, however, displayed no inclination to discriminate. There were also cases which satisfied the strict criteria we defined (VAS) in only one or two prejudice dimensions. Despite the lack of coherence, these people cannot be considered free of prejudice. We therefore created an additional category of anti-Semites which includes all those satisfying the following conditions in at least one of the partial indices: six or more "yes" answers in the AS-Stereotype index; *or* one or more "yes" answers in the AS-Social Distance index; *or* two or more "yes" answers in the AS-Discrimination index. According to this procedure, we established a group of 33.2 percent (N = 697), which we classify in a broader sense as being *potentially anti-Semitic (PAS)*.

We have tested a variety of categorization criteria and compared the results. If all partial measurements are taken into consideration, 33 percent of the population may be said to have anti-Semitic attitudes (PAS). Twelve percent of the population is strongly anti-Semitic (SAS), and 7 percent are hardcore, vehement anti-Semites (VAS).

Notes

1. Hermann Lübbe received considerable public feedback as the primary critic of the Mitscherlich thesis of repression (and of course its instrumentalization). In Lübbe's view, it was necessary, in the interest of reconstruction, for former Nazis and victims of the Nazi regime to come to some form of consensus after the war by becoming "mute" with respect to the past (1983).
2. For information on the contrast group analysis procedure developed by Erp Ring, cf. Noelle-Neumann and Ring 1985, 23–26.
3. In the cross-sectional group, the sample was representative on the basis of gender, age, level of education, and residence; in the group with anti-Jewish leanings, there was a disproportionate number of men (65 percent of this group) and members of the older generation (64 percent of this group was over fifty years of age); in the more pro-Jewish group, there was a greater percentage of people with higher education; only 35 percent of this group was over fifty years old.
4. The persons questioned were all at least sixteen years of age and living in the Federal Republic of Germany (West Germany) or West Berlin. The survey sample was comprised according to a representative ratio corresponding to official statistics. The sample was distributed among the states and districts; within each of these regional units, further divisions were made among large, medium-sized, and small cities and rural communities; between men and women; and by age, profession, and occupation. The percentages are representative for each of the categories. There were no quotas for religious affiliation or marital status.
5. This suggests that conflicting reports on the number of victims, the existence of gas chambers, and so on are registered attentively and seen as proof of the manipulation of historical writings on the Holocaust.
6. If Selznick's and Steinberg's criteria for distinguishing among categories are taken as a basis (see appendix 1), then the cumulative number of yes responses for each item starting with point 5 on the AS scale reaches the value of the total count for each individual item. In that case, 28.5 percent of the interviewees would have to be classified as having a clearly negative view of Jews. This formal distinguishing criterion leads the line to be drawn in a similar way to our idea of choosing the theoretical argument of consistency of the anti-Jewish image as the criterion.
7. In the pretest, we asked a question on how often the "persecution of Jews" came up in conversation with family and friends. Fifty-two percent of those questioned said they had "almost never" spoken about this subject in the last three to four years, 41 percent said they had spoken about it "now and then," and 4 percent claimed to have spoken of it often. Because those with "pro-Jewish leanings" more often claimed to have spoken about this subject (17 percent "often" and 48 percent "now and then"), one can assume there is a correlation between discussion of the subject and attitude (one's own and that of family and friends) toward Jews.
8. The panel study on the activation of anti-Semitism through the Waldheim affair in Austria showed that the greatest change of opinion in an anti-Semitic direction came for those who had previously held slightly anti-Semitic views. Cf. Költringer and Gehmacher 1989, 559.

9. The only question we did not use was the following: "Would you support some-one in a conversation who says something against Jews?" (Question 16/14). The evaluation showed that many of those interviewed misunderstood the question, thinking it supported standing up for someone against anti-Semitism.

3

The Distribution of Anti-Semitic Attitudes in West Germany

By constructing an anti-Semitism scale, we were able to estimate the extent of anti-Semitic attitudes in the population as a whole. This scale also makes it possible to isolate differences in attitude according to the socio-demographic categories of age, gender, education, occupation, religion, size of residential community, and political orientation. We will analyze our findings within the context of West German and international surveys, linking them with specific issues, attitudes toward Nazism, the extent of anti-Jewish stereotypes, inclination to discriminate, attitudes toward Israel, latency, and xenophobia.

The Distribution of Anti-Semitic Attitudes by Age

There is a connection between anti-Semitic prejudice and the age of the interviewee, though anti-Semitism does not increase consistently with age. Rather, particular political generations can be distinguished. Four separate groups can be identified.

1. The eighteen through forty-four age group (born 1943 to 1969; N = 1085; 51.6 percent). A trend showing a decrease in anti-Semitic attitudes could no longer be identified within this age range.[1]
2. The forty-five through fifty-four age group (born 1933 to 1942; N = 351; 16.7 percent).
3. The fifty-five through sixty-four age group (born 1923 to 1932; N = 268; 12.8 percent): this group includes the Hitler Youth generation.
4. The over-sixty-five age group (born prior to 1923; N = 398; 18.9 percent).

The categories we created in identifying groups of people with anti-Semitic attitudes (PAS, SAS, VAS) yield the following figure (3.1) for the four age groups mentioned.

FIGURE 3.1
Anti-Semitism by Age Group

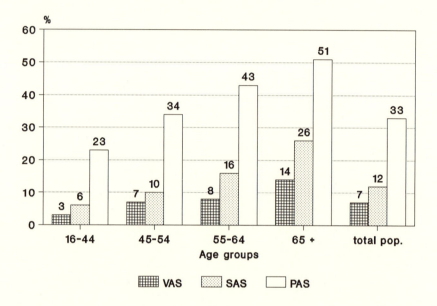

The generational structure and the distinct gaps between some age groups suggest that the findings represent a series of political generations, rather than an life-cycle effect (i.e., a trend toward increasingly conservative attitudes with advancing age). Attitudes toward Jews seem to depend on whether or not major parts of a person's life and/or socialization took place in the period before 1945.[2] It must be remembered that an anti-Semitic political climate and anti-Semitic socialization in schools and the family existed even prior to 1933, toward the end of the German Empire and during the Weimar Republic, and that this became more radical when the Nazis came to power. The age distribution for anti-Jewish attitudes in the 1949 IfD survey (table 3.1) confirms this assumption.

With the exception of the oldest cohort (born prior to 1885), whose anti-Jewish attitudes were less pronounced than expected under the life-cycle hypothesis, all other age groups showed a similarly high level of anti-Semitism. The youngest age group (under thirty years of age) dem-

TABLE 3.1
"What is your general attitude toward Jews?"

Age	Openly anti-Semitic %	Emotional rejection %	Reserved %	Tolerant %	Openly friendly %	Indifferent %
under 30	11	15	16	38	2	18
30–50 years	11	12	16	43	7	11
50–65 years	10	15	13	40	8	14
65 and older	7	10	10	46	10	18

Source: IfD 1949, 39.

onstrated above-average rejection of Jews and an especially low percentage of "philo-Semites." The impact of anti-Semitic Nazi propaganda on this age group (born between 1919 and probably 1931 through 1933), which had undergone most of its socialization during the Nazi period, was especially strong. According to their own statements, a disproportionate share of this age group based their attitudes on Nazi racial theory and political conviction, and on the writings and reports of others (IfD 1949, 41ff). Approximately 30 percent answered that they "believed anti-Jewish propaganda" (only 13 percent to 19 percent of the other groups gave this response). Only 17 percent of this age group considered the propaganda abhorrent (as opposed to 28 percent to 37 percent of the older groups, ibid., 7). This group's resistance to Nazi anti-Semitism was also relatively low.[3] A survey of 685 German prisoners of war conducted in July, 1944 confirms that 57 percent of the younger soldiers (under twenty-one years old) accepted Nazism and continued to believe in it. This figure was far higher than for the over-forty age group [25 percent (cf. Zinnecker 1985, 329)].[4] Zinnecker summed up a 1953 EMNID survey, saying that at the time "a considerable percentage of the young continued to be faithful to the nationalist, militarist legacy of the past" (1985, 330) and at the same time felt humiliated at having lost the war.[5]

The current distribution of anti-Semitism clearly shows, however, that while a disproportionately high ratio of this Hitler Youth generation does still have anti-Semitic attitudes, it is far lower than among the over-sixty-five-year-olds, who were in the over-thirty group in 1949. A larger proportion of the Hitler Youth generation changed their attitudes toward

TABLE 3.2
Attitude toward Jews by Age of Participant
(percentages refer to speakers in the individual age groups)

Age	up to 20 %	20–35 %	35–50 %	50 and older %
Not anti-Semitic	29	31	25	30
Pro-Jewish	10	4	13	15
Somewhat anti-Semitic	18	21	32	23
Anti-Semitic	43	44	30	32

Source: Pollock 1955, table 32.

Jews than of those who were already middle-aged when the war ended. This probably followed a "phase of defiance and reorientation," during which they first responded to politics with apathy and abstinence ("no more politics, no more political parties"; cf. Holtmann 1989, 149ff.).[6] From a psychological point of view, this change may have been easier for the younger generation, since they were exonerated—politically and legally—as a "generation led astray"; accordingly, they felt less responsible for Nazism and its consequences.

In all West German surveys, the age-specific distribution of attitudes toward Jews proves to break down into a series of political generations.[7] The "group experiment" of 1950 through 1951, which was nonrepresentative and took a different methodological approach, obtained the same age distribution as the 1949 IfD survey (see table 3.2).

Compared to the IfD survey, the above table paints a more negative picture of the virulence of anti-Semitism in the early postwar years. Between 55 percent and 65 percent of all participants in the group discussion exhibited some anti-Jewish attitudes, the younger age groups proving to be more extreme: 44 percent of them—the largest percentage of any group—proved to be strongly anti-Semitic, and only 4 percent—the smallest of all groups—exhibited pro-Jewish attitudes. This can most probably be traced back to the radically anti-Semitic climate in which they grew up and attended school. This is not a sufficient explanation, however, as a study on the outbreak of anti-Semitic incidents in 1959 through 1960 showed that the youngest cohort (eighteen to thirty years of age, i.e., born 1930 to 1942) had the highest percentage (23 percent) of sympathizers with anti-Semitic attitudes [average: 16 percent (Schönbach

1961, 54)], although many of these young people experienced only a short period of anti-Semitic education in the "Third Reich." Schönbach assumes that anti-Semitic tendencies were in fact more prevalent among older interviewees than younger ones, but "older people tended to conceal their anti-Semitism out of reluctance stemming from their memories, whereas younger people expressed their feelings openly" (1961, 57). This might indeed be the case, but it does not change the fact that 23 percent of the eighteen to thirty-year-olds had to be classified as anti-Semitic and another 26 percent as indifferent. It seems that Nazi anti-Semitism continued to have an impact in families until the 1950s, while the authoritarian climate of the time did not support liberal, democratic political leanings in public or in the schools. Only 19 percent of adolescents clearly and definitively dissociated themselves from anti-Semitic attitudes or actions (ibid., 54).[8] It appears that the anti-Semitic outbreaks and subsequent political and educational reorientation led to a perceptible shift in attitudes toward Jews and Judaism.

The 1974 survey by Silbermann and Sallen shows both the stability of the attitudes acquired by the older generation and the decrease in anti-Semitism among generations socialized after the war. Sallen recognized a change starting with the forty-year-olds (born 1934). An increase in the percentage of anti-Semites could be observed for those born before 1935 (Sallen 1977, 311).[9] Another jump could be observed at the interface to the fifty-four-year-old age group (born 1919 and earlier).

Recent surveys show a similar distribution pattern according to age, confirming the findings of social psychologists that attitudes acquired during the impressionable socialization phase remain stable, changing only minimally despite changes in the political culture.[10] However, it seems that the radical political changes after 1945 experienced by members of the Hitler Youth generation, who identified strongly with Nazism, did lead to a change in attitude after a certain period of time. This suggests that fundamental changes in attitude are obviously tied to personal or collective situations involving change and crisis that permit or force political and moral reorientation.[11]

With respect to changes in opinion among the older generations, as well as the age groups that attended school after the war (1929 through 1939), it is unfortunate that the main sources of information regarding knowledge and opinions of Nazism were either personal experience (especially for the age group born 1929 through 1933) or oral documentation passed down by contemporary witnesses (this was the primary source for the age group born 1937 through 1939). Only a very small percentage gave "school" as a source of information [only 26 percent of those born 1929 through 1939 (cf. Zinnecker 1985, 338f.)]. As is known from personal accounts, the history of the Nazi period was taboo in the *Gymnasium* (college preparatory high school) in the 1950s. Today, adolescents experience a totally different situation (Dudek 1982, 109ff). In 1984, 93 percent of the fifteen to twenty-four-year-old adolescents questioned said school was a source of information on the Nazi period for them. This figure is considerably higher than for conversations with older people (44 percent), media (38 percent), and books (36 percent) (Zinnecker 1985, 338).[12] In this age group, 74 percent considered it "important" or "very important" to deal with the issue of Nazism, and only 7 percent considered it "not at all important." In contrast to these figures, adults between forty-five and fifty-four years old (born 1930 through 1939) were split on this question [54 percent important, 47 percent less important, 23 percent of those "not at all important" (cf. ibid. 341)]. Today, schools and the political climate in general support a critical examination of Nazism and anti-Semitism, instilling opposition to anti-Semitic attitudes. Our survey also clearly shows that socialization within the family no longer has much influence on the formation of anti-Semitic prejudice. Only 4.5 percent of the sixteen through twenty-nine-year-olds said that their "family used to have very negative feelings toward Jews," whereas 17 percent of the over-sixty-year-olds still gave this answer (total population: 9.7 percent).

There is a significant correlation between past anti-Semitic attitudes of the family and the interviewees' current feelings: 42 percent of the vehemently anti-Semitic (VAS) and 34 percent of the strongly anti-Semitic (SAS) have the same opinions as those expounded in their respective families (PAS 18 percent).[13] Of the 203 persons who confirmed anti-Semitic attitudes in their families, roughly two-thirds (PAS = 63 percent) had to be classified as anti-Semitic to some extent themselves. It appears that dominant family attitudes toward Jews led a majority of the individuals to take on that prejudice. With respect to the older interviewees, this phenomenon might have been strengthened by the general political climate during their formative years. Today the family no longer plays a very significant role in passing on anti-Jewish attitudes.

The distribution calculated for the different age groups today (see above) applies for all three dimensions of anti-Jewish prejudice—stereotypes, social distance, and inclination to discriminate. It also applies with respect to attitudes toward other minorities and toward Nazism and "coming to terms with the past." It does not apply to the same extent to attitudes toward Israel. Attitudes of the different generations are not as polarized with respect to Israel; in fact, the answers to many Israel-related questions did not reveal any age distinctions (cf. chap. 7).[14] Except for approval of extremely negative statements on Israeli policy, in which the basic anti-Semitism of the oldest age group was particularly visible, age distribution on this topic appeared to deviate from the general pattern. The generation of forty-five to fifty-nine-year-olds supported Israeli policy to a great extent, while the younger generations were more critical. This also reflects the particular experiences of the respective generations. Older generations are still greatly influenced by anti-Semitism; the critical attitudes of the younger generations are more influenced by a stronger orientation toward the "Third World" and perceptions of current politics. Since 1973, Israel has been seen increasingly not as the threatened David, but as the Middle East's mighty Goliath, with superior military strength. These younger age groups never experienced Israel in a threatened position. The fact that Israel has lost a tremendous amount of support since 1973 shows that the perception of Israel as vulnerable is generally fading, and that the country is being judged by current political standards. From the Yom Kippur War in 1973 until February, 1983, the percentage of those supporting Israel in the Arab-Israeli conflict decreased from 60 percent to roughly 20 percent in all age categories, and support for the Arab side grew from approximately 7 percent to 15 percent (Wolffsohn 1988, table 4).

The Influence of Education

In addition to age, education (measured according to level of formal education completed) plays a significant role in accounting for anti-Semitism. Our results concurred with West German and international studies in which anti-Jewish sentiment decreased with level of education. The following figures (see table 3.3) were obtained using the Anti-Semitism index.

The table essentially shows a linear correlation: the higher the educational level, the lower the level of anti-Semitism (i.e., a lower value on the AS index). There are two exceptions to this pattern. First, not finishing school appears to create a situation that fosters feelings of resent-

TABLE 3.3
Highest Level of Education Completed
(mean value of the standardized AS-index)

Some secondary school	.95
Hauptschule (junior high school completed)	.31
Some *Realschule* (basic high school)	-.25
High School Diploma	-.42
Some *Gymnasium* (college preparatory high school)	.29
Abitur (university entrance qualification examination)	-.64
Some college	-1.37
College graduate	-.78

(Mean value for the total population -.03)

ment. This was particularly true in cases where high social expectations were connected with completion of the *Abitur*. Disappointment seems to feed the tendency toward prejudice. Second, not completing a college degree did not necessarily denote career failure and the corresponding frustration.[15] This group showed the lowest level of anti-Semitism at all stages of the evaluation. Even if they had not completed college, it is possible that they achieved a successful career outside of normal channels, leading to social contentment. In the "some college" category, the younger age groups (students) represented a combination of positive factors with respect to both education and age, therefore demonstrating the lowest level of anti-Semitism.

The correlation determined in the mean value comparison can also be seen among the groups formed according to the PAS/SAS/VAS criteria for measuring degrees of anti-Semitism. There is one interesting deviation: of the college graduates questioned, the proportion of strongly and vehemently anti-Semitic persons (SAS and VAS) rose to the same level as among *Realschule* (basic high school) graduates. If this figure is examined taking age into account, it becomes clear that college graduates born between 1908 and 1916 represent the majority of hardcore anti-Semites with this education level (of five VAS with a college degree in our sample, three were over seventy years of age and the remaining two were between forty-five and fifty-four years old). Despite the small number of cases, this confirms the surveys of the early 1950s (cf. Pollock

FIGURE 3.2
Anti-Semitism and Level of Education

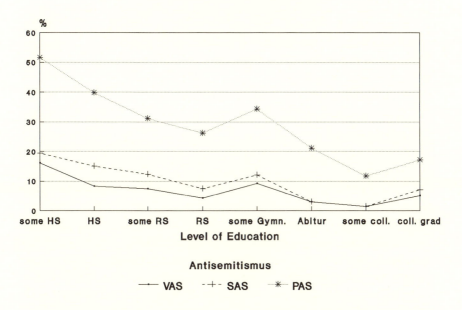

1955), which found that college graduates in particular strongly identified with Nazi anti-Semitic ideology. Thus, prejudice is by no means
eliminated by education per se.

Measuring educational level against each of the individual dimensions
of anti-Semitism yields the same results. The same pattern as for the
aggregate level of the Anti-Semitism index described above results for
the extent of negative stereotyping, emotional rejection of Jews and inclination to discriminate. Some deviations can be observed, however, for
individual indicators. The above-mentioned influence of education applies with respect to most of the anti-Jewish stereotypes, though the "overly
sensitive, unforgiving/irreconcilable and arrogant" stereotype represented
an exception to this, in that no difference with respect to education was
observed for the youngest age group (sixteen through twenty-nine). On
the one hand, this suggests that traditional anti-Jewish cliches are diminished by better formal education, the impact of the mass media, and
family upbringing; on the other hand, cliches that grew out of German-

TABLE 3.4
"Please rate your feelings about Jews living in Germany/Israel."

	Total Pop.	Elementary School without / with apprenticeship or training		Junior HS / Abitur High School	College
German Jews	0.7	0.4	0.5	0.8	1.3
Israeli Jews	0.4	0.2	0.3	0.7	0.7

Source: Emnid 1989, table 61.

Jewish postwar experiences were apparently not combatted in the same (self-)critical manner by socializing institutions. Our thesis of "secondary anti-Semitism" seems to confirm that these cliches are not dependent on education. By conveying correct, factual information, the media and political education authorities are more likely to eliminate historical prejudice, whereas their impact on attitudes toward current political issues is contradictory or not as great. It is politically concerned individuals in particular who react to events and public opinion trends, thus making them more prone to new prejudices (cf. Költringer and Gehmacher 1989 on anti-Semitism in Austria). One of the findings of the 1989 EMNID study confirms these observations, that is, the measurement of feelings about Jews living in Germany (on a scale of +5 to -5) shows the expected effects of education.

Positive attitudes increase with the level of formal education. As regards sympathies for Jews living in Israel, not only are feelings generally less positive than for German Jews, but the effect of higher education is also weaker. This suggests that feelings for Jews living in Germany are more closely connected to Nazi persecution, while perceptions of Israelis are also affected by current Israeli politics.

Although all surveys conducted in Western countries currently show a positive influence of education, and for Martire and Clark, education is even "clearly the most powerful demographic correlate of anti-Semitic beliefs" (1982, 38), education per se by no means ensures immunity from prejudice. Education encourages acceptance of socially prescribed norms; under a totalitarian system that made anti-Semitism a fundamental component of its ideology, it was particularly the educated and the elite who adopted Nazi racial ideology and anti-Semitism.[16] These findings concur with those obtained from 1948 though 1952, which show that higher education in West Germany correlated positively with racism and anti-Semitism. In the 1949 IfD survey, 34 percent of those questioned who had completed elementary school rated themselves "anti-Semitic" to "reserved," and 50 percent as "tolerant" and "friendly," compared with 48 percent and 40 percent, respectively, for those who had completed the university entrance qualification examination (39). College graduates' identification with Nazi anti-Semitism was indirectly apparent in the noticeable restraint they displayed when making statements on this subject in the discussions conducted within the scope of the "group experiment." Nevertheless, their comments were so consistently anti-Semitic that 92 percent were classified as anti-Semitic or somewhat anti-Semitic. Of those who had completed *Volksschule* (elementary school), 55 percent were classified in this way, though 45 percent were classified as not anti-Semitic or pro-Jewish (Pollock 1955, 169). Since there are no statistics for the 1950s and 1960s, it is not possible to determine precisely whether, and if so, when, college graduates changed their opinions or when subsequent college classes displayed a new distribution of attitudes. By 1974, this trend started to reverse, and a positive correlation between higher education and lack of prejudice continues to appear (Sallen 1977, 310).

For each of the age groups in our study, the impact of education was investigated separately. It became clear that at all ages up to seventy (born 1917 and earlier), anti-Semitism decreases with higher formal education (with the exception of higher level secondary school students who did not complete the *Abitur* examination). However, the distribution established in 1950 and 1951 by Pollock could be observed in the over-seventy group; that is, anti-Semitism among this age group increased with higher formal education.[17] Attitudes of individuals with higher education are apparently not easily influenced, even by a totally changing political culture.

Prejudice can be reduced by improved education only if this occurs within a liberal, democratic society whose values are conveyed by the education process, and if politics and public opinion are prepared to continually reaffirm the norms of group coexistence.

The Influence of Occupation and Income

The answers given by particular occupational groups in the studies conducted shortly after the war reveal the traditional middle-class base of anti-Semitism. At that time, education, now a major factor, was less significant. According to the findings of the 1949 IfD survey and the 1950 to 1951 "group experiment," those "self-employed in trade and industry" and farmers, followed by freelance workers, college students, and salaried workers, were particularly anti-Semitic at that time. Since the time of the German Empire, most of the support for modern anti-Semitism had come from these occupational fields, due to worldview, competition or fear of social decline (Kampe 1988; Puhle 1975; Volkov 1978; Hamel 1967; Lichtblau 1994). In 1949, besides civil servants, it was above all laborers and housewives who were less often classified as anti-Jewish or made fewer anti-Jewish statements in the group discussions (cf. IfD 1949, 39; Pollock 1955, 170). Aspects of social-democratic tradition, which consistently rejected anti-Semitism on political grounds,[18] might have survived among the working class. Housewives were probably less anti-Jewish, or made the most "non-anti-Semitic" statements, as a result of their general lack of involvement in politics and their counter-ideological experiences with Jewish businesspeople.

A comparison of different occupational groups over time is difficult, as every social historian knows, since occupational categories continue to exist, but the composition and character of different occupations often change dramatically over time. The following historical comparison is limited by the uncertainties resulting from this problem.

The data collected by Schönbach (1961, 68) already showed the beginnings of change. The higher level occupational fields (civil servants, independent professionals, management and mid-level salaried employees, wholesalers) were the least anti-Semitic and authoritarian, though this was also the case for skilled and unskilled workers. On the other hand, the greatest proportion of anti-Semites was still found among those self-employed in trade and industry and among lower level civil servants and salaried employees (farmers were not included in this sample, which was limited to the area around Frankfurt/Main).

In the 1974 survey by Silbermann and Sallen, the trend observed by Schönbach continued and education started to have an increasingly greater impact in diminishing anti-Semitism. On the one hand, among farmers[19] and the self-employed, former job-specific anti-Jewish leanings continued to have an effect. Strong feelings of anti-Semitism were displayed by 42 percent of farmers and 32.5 percent of the self-employed (Sallen 1977, 251).[20] Civil servants as a group continued to demonstrate relatively weak

FIGURE 3.3
Anti-Semitism and Occupation

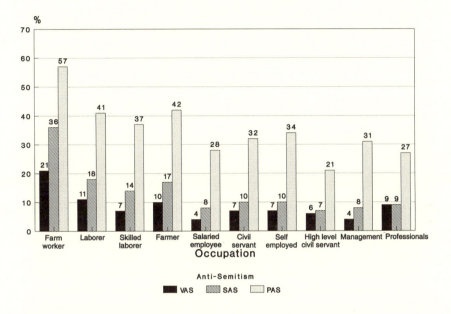

anti-Semitic tendencies (22 percent). The attitudes of laborers and salaried employees—both rather global job classifications encompassing many different fields—showed great change as compared to 1949. A disproportionately high level of laborers were "strongly anti-Semitic" (30 percent), while salaried employees (20.5 percent) were farthest below the average of 27.2 percent (ibid). The fact that their traditional environment was beginning to dissolve, as well as their relatively low level of education, might be responsible for the change in attitudes among laborers. Figures for salaried employees were most likely due to long-term participation in the economic success of West Germany and the general impact of the rise in education.

If the correlation between occupational category and the Anti-Semitism index is examined, it is once again farmers and farm workers, as well as unskilled laborers, who were most strongly anti-Jewish, while higher-level civil servants, salaried employees, and, initially, independent professionals were most clearly below the average mean value for the total population.[21] Persons in occupations that required a higher level of school and university education expressed, on the average, the lowest level of anti-Jewish sentiment.

This suggests that no particular social class now forms a support base for anti-Semitic attitudes, since Jewish influence does not in any way determine the social position of any occupational group. Rather, we are dealing with a complex of ideological issues which is passed down, and decreases in strength with increasing formal education. All in all, this reflects the close correlation between level of education and occupational group.

There is a definitive correlation between anti-Semitism and occupation via level of formal education. Within each individual occupational category, those who achieved a higher level of education are the ones who are less anti-Semitic. For example, the ratio between skilled laborers who did not complete *Hauptschule* (junior high school) and those with a *Realschule* (basic high school) diploma is very large (mean value = 1.86 to -.56).

The correlation between level of education and anti-Semitism showed that a disproportionate number of persons who interrupted their education, that is, did not complete either high school or college, were anti-Semitic. If the relationship of education and future career to anti-Semitism is examined, it becomes clear that resentment is most likely to be experienced by those whose later job positions lie beneath the qualification level of the educational level they failed to achieve. High school students who did not receive a diploma, and then became laborers or unskilled laborers, displayed an above-average level of anti-Semitism for this job category. The same phenomenon emerged for *Gymnasium* (college preparatory high school) students who do not complete the *Abitur* examination and ended up working as laborers, salaried employees, or lower- and mid-level civil servants.

This finding appears to confirm the theory of social deprivation and, in a broader historical context, theories of crisis, which assume that individuals whose social expectations are disappointed have a greater tendency toward xenophobia and anti-Semitism (for details, cf. chap. 9).

Income level does not have any specific impact on anti-Semitic attitudes; rather, it is an expression of education and training, the resulting occupation, and age. The level of anti-Semitism is statistically higher among members of lower income groups (earning up to 1750 DM per month). This is based on the fact that this income category includes a very high number of retired persons; it is not an expression of social deprivation.

In 1949, when anti-Semitism was not concentrated in the older age groups, but was found primarily in the middle and younger groups and among the better-earning college educated, a different correlation emerged between monthly income and attitudes toward Jews. Besides those with the lowest incomes (up to 50 DM monthly; 42 percent "reserved" to "anti-Semitic" and 41 percent "tolerant"), 51 percent of the highest income group (500 DM and above) was "reserved" to "strongly rejecting" in its attitudes toward Jews; only 37 percent (the lowest ratio) of this group was "tolerant." The intermediate income groups showed less rejection (34 percent to 42 percent) and more tolerance [38 percent to 49 percent (IfD 1949, 39). This finding supports the claim that income is not an independent factor in measuring tendencies toward prejudice.

Gender-Specific Differences

Due to gender-specific differences that continue to exist in political and family socialization, it can be assumed that men and women will also differ in their attitudes toward Jews, the state of Israel, and the Nazi past. In Renate Köcher's evaluation of a partially comparative international study in 1986, she already commented that West Germany evidenced a greater gender disparity with respect to responses to some questions than the other countries included in the comparison [U.S., France, and Austria (IfD 1986, 31); Martire and Clark found no gender-specific differences in the extent of anti-Semitic prejudice in the United States (1982, 36)].

A comparison of mean values using the Anti-Semitism index yields the following gender-specific difference: men were on the average more anti-Semitic than women, though the difference at this aggregate level is minimal. The difference exists in all age groups (with the sole exception of the thirty-five to thirty-nine age group).

If anti-Semites are isolated from the remainder of the population according to the PAS/SAS/VAS criteria, slight differences can be observed, though the correlations between gender and anti-Semitism are not significant. A significant gender-specific difference can only be identified

TABLE 3.5
Anti-Semitism by Gender

Anti-Semitism	Total Population %	Male %	Female %
PAS	33.2	35.7	30.9
SAS	11.6	13.2	10.2
VAS	6.9	8.6	5.5

in the group of hardcore, vehement anti-Semites (VAS 6.9 percent of the population). Approximately 60 percent of this group are men.[22]

The relatively weak expression of anti-Semitic attitudes among women in general can be explained above all by their less definite political judgments.[23] All anti-Semitism surveys have found that women tend to respond "don't know/undecided" more often than the men, and that they avoid extreme answers, particularly negative ones.[24] Differences between men and women are most evident in their positions on issues of a more political nature ("power of Jews, influence of Israel, charges of political radicalism"), in emotional attitudes toward the Nazi past ("ashamed of Nazi crimes against the Jews"), and in the obligation to pay reparations; in these situations, women often exhibit more positive attitudes than men. Men apparently more strongly identify with their country and its history and politics [32 percent of the men and 26 percent of the women considered Germans to be superior to other peoples (question 6)]. Women agree with negative stereotypes of Jews less often than men, though no difference can be observed for positive stereotypes. Here as well, the gender-related difference is greater with respect to politics and power-related stereotypes, and smaller for economic stereotypes.

The questions on social distance, which deal with more personal relationships, present a different picture. It is men who more often "want to have more to do with Jews," who accept Jews in their circle of friends, and would more often accept the idea of marrying a Jew. The greater distance shown by women is not motivated primarily by anti-Semitism, but stems from greater insecurity and reservations toward strangers in general. The responses to two survey questions confirm this interpretation. First, 14 percent of the women (and 11.6 percent of the men) prefer not to have too much to do with "Jews," but only 7 percent with "German Jews" [9 percent of the men (question 1/6)]. When the Jews were identified as German, that is, not foreigners, the social distance indicated by the women diminished. Second, the gender-specific difference disappeared or reversed in favor of the women when dealing with relationships of a less intimate nature, that is, with neighbors or co-workers (IfD 1986; IfD vol. 6, 26).

Köcher's observation, quoted earlier, that attitudes toward Jews diverge more in Germany than in the other countries included in the comparison seems to apply only to the above-mentioned issues of reparations, political influence, and shame. In general, it can be assumed that judgments by men and women are becoming more similar. The 1989 EMNID survey (tables 61, 66, 68, and 75) shows no gender-related differences whatsoever with respect to like and dislike of Jews, or in questions pertaining to dealing with the past and Nazism.

In the early postwar period, these differences were more pronounced. In the "group experiment," women made fewer "anti-Semitic" or "somewhat anti-Semitic" statements than men (52 percent of the women versus 68 percent of the men) and were more often "pro-Jewish" or "not anti-Semitic" [48 percent of the women versus 32 percent of the men (Pollock 1955, 168)]. In addition, women were more willing to carry on a discussion on this subject. (Could this be because women have less cause to feel guilt?) The women probably considered this subject less of a taboo because they felt they drew their opinions of Jews more often from experiences in the family, everyday situations, and religion, which were not as heavily discredited as Nazi ideology and political anti-Semitism. They were less likely to respond that they had been influenced by anti-Semitic propaganda, and their memories of Jews were 10 percent more "positive" than those of the men [42 percent to 32 percent (IfD 1949, 31)]. When asked about their attitudes toward Jews, the major difference between men and women—similar to today—lay in the lesser degree of open, aggressive rejection displayed by the women [15 percent to 6 percent; there was no significant difference in "emotional rejection": 13 percent to 14 percent (ibid., 39)]. The 1949 IfD survey could not verify a greater degree of tolerance and pro-Jewish attitudes among women.

The generally greater social distance shown by women with respect to marriage with a Jewish partner, treatment by a Jewish doctor, and shopping in a Jewish store, are rooted in the role prescribed for women in the 1940s and 1950s, as well as in the impact of the segregationist Nazi

racial laws and ideology, which comprised the basis for individual behavior at the time. The stronger reservations expressed by women in
consulting a Jewish doctor continued to exist until the 1960s, though
they gradually diminished and can no longer be distinguished from those
of men. [In 1961, 18 percent of the women and 10 percent of the men
expressed such reservations; in 1965, it was 15 percent of the women
and 12 percent of the men (IfD vol. 3, 218 and vol. 4, 96).] An evaluation by age shows here, too, that the decrease was due not so much to a
change in attitude among older women as to the emancipation of women
and the attitudes of the next generation, which was not influenced by
Nazi ideology. Today, reservations with respect to visiting a Jewish doctor have all but disappeared [total population 2 percent (question 16/10)]
and appear only in the over-sixty age group (5 percent).

Anti-Semitism studies conducted since the 1960s (Tumin 1962, 67;
Sallen 1977, 247; Panahi 1980, 70; EMNID 1989) have found no gender-specific influence on attitudes toward Jews. As we have shown, differences only emerged in specific areas and with regard to radical
anti-Semitism. American and Austrian studies conducted beginning in
the mid-1960s had the same findings (Selznick and Steinberg 1969, 101f;
Martire and Clark 1982, 36; Weiss 1984, 55; Kienzl and Gehmacher
1987).[25]

Political Orientation and Anti-Semitism

In our study, we ascertained the correlation between political orientation and anti-Semitism in two ways: in the pretest we asked those with
anti-Jewish and pro-Jewish tendencies and the "average" group how they
would classify themselves politically on a 100 point scale (from 0 =
extreme left-wing to 100 = extreme right-wing). In the main survey, we
did not use this scale, but instead ascertained political orientation according to party preference.

Among those with anti-Jewish attitudes (N = 95), the predominant
self-appraisal was center-right (cf. figure 3.4). Only 11 percent of those
with anti-Jewish views classified themselves as left of center, while 43
percent described themselves as right to extreme right-wing. Among those
with pro-Jewish views, the pattern was reversed: over 55 percent classified themselves as left of center, and only 9 percent as extremely right-
oriented (7–10 points). Although the 344 people questioned in the pretest

FIGURE 3.4
Anti-Semitism and Political Self-Appraisal 1987

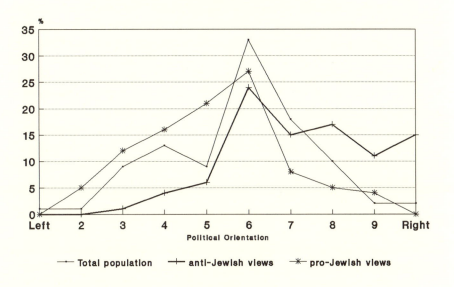

FIGURE 3.5
Anti-Semitism and Political Self-Appraisal 1989

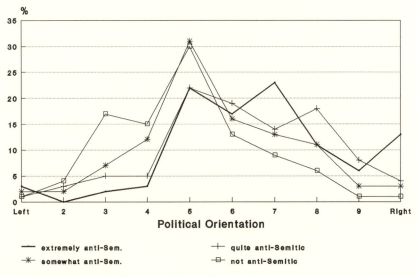

(Source: Emnid 1989, tab. 12)

were not a representative sample, there was a definite correlation between anti-Semitism and right-wing political views.[26] This was confirmed by the 1989 EMNID survey, in which the interviewees were also asked to position themselves on a political scale [1 = ultraleft, 10 =ultraright (cf. figure 3.5). The same pattern can be discerned here; approximately a third of those with extremely or quite anti-Semitic views referred to themselves as "far right" (scale values 8–10), while another third stood right of center (6–7). It is extremely rare for anti-Semitism to go hand-in-hand with an extreme left-wing orientation (scale values 1–3). On the other hand, "mild" anti-Semitism was not linked with an extreme right-wing position, but rather with a center position (scale values 4–7; 72 percent of those with "somewhat" anti-Semitic views). The political views of those who are not anti-Semitic tended more toward the left (two-thirds were left of center—scale values 1–5). An ultraright-wing orientation is extremely rare among non-anti-Semites (only 8 percent indicated scale values of 8–10).

As could be expected, the same right-left pattern is found when the correlation between political orientation and anti-Semitism is measured by party preference, though it is more difficult to recognize in that case. The respective parties' voters can vary greatly according to age and education, so that political orientation may be concealed by generational and educational effects. In addition, at the time of the survey, neither an ultraright-wing nor an ultraleft-wing party of any significance yet existed. In 1987, the ultraright-wing *Republikaner* was only a tiny splinter party, and the German Communist Party [DKP, *Deutsche Kommunistische Partei* (N = 2)] and the right-wing German National Party [NPD, *Nationaldemokratische Partei Deutschlands* (N = 7)] were hardly represented in the sample, in accordance with their proportion of votes in the 1986 parliamentary elections. Thus, no statistical generalization can be made here.[27]

To avoid any misunderstanding, it must be pointed out in advance that the following involves an analysis of party preferences of the interviewees, which must be distinguished from both the views and the actual policies of the parties themselves. If we measure the views of the voters of the various parties, we obtain the following mean values (table 3.6).

In addition to the generally applicable right-left pattern, there seems to be a difference between the main parties and smaller ones with specific issue-related platforms that contradicts the schematic right-left di-

TABLE 3.6
Anti-Semitism and Party Preference

Party	Mean	N
Not entitled to vote	-.80	41
CDU/CSU	.56	645
SPD	-.29	689
FDP	-.67	139
Greens	-1.18	114
DKP	1.50	2
NPD	8.43	7
Others	1.75	4
Don't know	.06	196
Don't vote	.16	117
No answer	-.42	145

Mean total pop. -.03   N=2102

vision. A heterogeneous electorate backs the two main parties (*Volksparteien*). In our opinion, the conservative profile and decades-long integration of right-wing electoral groups in the Christian Democratic Union (CDU) explain why this party deviates from the mean in the Anti-Semitism index, in the direction of greater anti-Semitism. The mean for SPD (Social Democratic) voters most closely corresponds to the population average. The clear difference between the two main parties cannot be attributed solely to a deviation in the age structure of the respective electorates. Although it is true that the CDU/CSU's share of older voters is somewhat greater, the differences remain even when comparisons are made within particular age groups. There are no educational differences within the electorates of the main parties [cf. the breakdown of groups in the electorate by education for 1986 (Jaide and Veen 1989, 136)]. Therefore, one can assume that different political orientations and values among voters are responsible for the differences in attitude toward Jews.

Among FDP (liberal) voters, in 1987 anti-Semitic views were far below average in all age groups. This indicates a greater homogeneity in the electorate, which is faithful to liberal values on this issue. The high level of education among its voters was also a contributing factor. FDP voters were more likely than the average to have had higher education;

the two lowest types of school diploma were rarely encountered.[28] Bourgeois liberalism was free of anti-Jewish prejudice. The general right-left pattern is broken here (this has changed since then, cf. chap. 12).

Among the Greens, three reasons can be found in 1987 for the low incidence of anti-Semitic prejudice: first, a basic political position that opposes racism and discrimination against minorities; second, the age structure, which is completely different from that of the other parties; third, the higher average educational level (cf. also Jaide and Veen 1989, 136). Ninety percent of the Green voters questioned in our survey were under forty years of age; that is, the more anti-Semitic older generation is virtually unrepresented among Green voters.

The attitudes of nonvoters and those who gave no party preference did not differ from the average. The suspicion that these groups—which fail to vote or cannot choose a party because of political disillusionment, disinterest, or extreme political views—might represent a latent anti-Semitic potential could not be confirmed for the groups as a whole. Motives for not participating in elections are apparently heterogeneous, and revealed no predominance of extreme anti-Semitic attitudes. However, a definite share of dedicated anti-Semites can be found among nonvoters. A disproportionately high number of those who refused to give a party preference indicated no anti-Semitic sentiment whatsoever.

Measuring the correlation between party preference and anti-Semitism yielded the same results. Because of its vividness, the following figure (3.6) is used to illustrate the ratio of those classified as strongly anti-Semitic according to party preference.

The figure shows that double the percentage of CDU/CSU voters can be classed as anti-Semitic in comparison to the percentage of anti-Semitic SPD voters. Among FDP and Green voters, it is as little as a fourth of the CDU/CSU voter share. In the group "vehement anti-Semites" (VAS), our sample found no Green voters at all; this is primarily due to the aforementioned different age structure, as the hard core consists largely of older people. The few NPD voters included in the sample (N = 7) proved to be clearly anti-Semitic (except for one). Because of the small number of cases, no conclusions can be drawn about the DKP and those voting for other splinter parties.

In the EMNID study of March, 1989, there was a trend toward the same correlation between party preference and attitude toward Jews. Measuring emotional attitude toward Jews living in Germany on a sympa-

FIGURE 3.6
Anti-Semitism by Party Preference

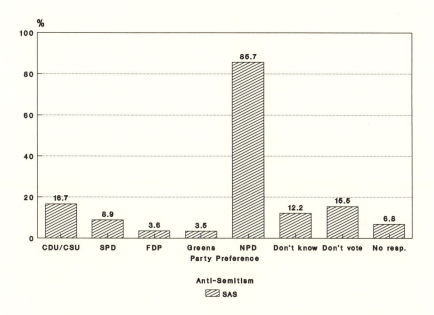

thy-antipathy scale (from +5 to -5) produced the highest sympathy value among Green voters (1.3). SPD and FDP voters were almost equal (1.0 and 0.9, respectively), and CDU/CSU voters achieved a figure of 0.6. On the average, voters for the parties represented in parliament had a neutral to slightly positive attitude toward Jews living in Germany. Only voters for ultraright-wing parties—for the first time, this EMNID study was able to question *Republikaner* voters in a statistically significant quantity (N = 104)—disliked Jews (*Republikaner* voters: -1.1; NPD voters: -1.2). An interesting result emerged from EMNID's attempt to distinguish between core and marginal *Republikaner* voters: while dedicated voters strongly disliked Jews (-4.6), rejection was plainly lower among marginal voters (-0.8), though still within the negative range. In other questions on nationalism and anti-Semitism (reparations, truth of the Holocaust, etc.), *Republikaner* and NPD voters took extremely anti-Semitic positions. The consistent difference between core and marginal

TABLE 3.7
Republikaner Voters and Anti-Semitism

Image of Jew	Total pop.	"Republikaner" regular core	Voters margin
	%	%	%
The dangerous Jew	19	52	38
The Jew with ties to a cohesive community	60	58	62
The good Jew	21	15	23
The ugly Jew	5	22	9
The greedy Jew	32	61	54
The unforgiving Jew	35	65	51

Source: Noelle-Neumann 1993, table A7.

Republikaner voters gives rise to the conjecture that there may be serious differences in degree between the radical party platform and the convictions of its more involved members and voters on the one hand, and the mass of its voters on the other, despite their similar basic orientation.[29] The *Republikaner* party enjoyed continued success in the years following its first major election victory in early 1989 in Berlin, including the 1990 European Parliament elections and several state and local elections. Consequently, several voter profiles of the party (cf. for a summary Falter 1994) were conducted. Elisabeth Noelle-Neumann (1993) analyzed the anti-Semitic potential of *Republikaner* voters on the basis of IfD surveys from the years 1992 to 1993. Her study confirms the difference between staunch supporters and marginal voters; the former hold extremist right-wing views, and thus are almost all anti-Semitic as well; the marginal or protest voters are less often anti-Semitic than the core voters, but they display anti-Jewish attitudes much more often than the popular average. The following table expresses the list of stereotypes (cf. appendix 3: Factor Analysis of Stereotypical Images of Jews) in individual cliches.

Table 3.7 shows the extent to which *Republikaner* voters hold stereotypical views of Jews, whether positive or negative. There was also a considerable negative deviation among the core voters, as compared to less hardcore and marginal voters, in other dimensions, such as attitudes toward Israel, willingness to be reminded of the Nazi past, and assess-

FIGURE 3.7
Party Preference and Affinity for Jews (like-dislike)

December 1991

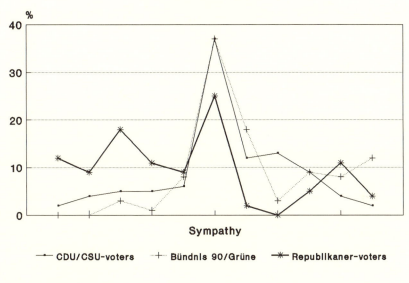

Source: Emnid 1992, tab.20

ment of the Nazi regime.[30] In late 1991, *Republikaner* voters were most likely to reject Jews on an emotional level,[31] measured on an eleven-point like-dislike scale (-5 = strong dislike; 0 = neutral; +5 = strong liking).

The statement "I do not like Jews" is a very good indicator of anti-Semitism. Figure 3.7 confirms our assumption that *Republikaner* voters, in particular, often reject Jews emotionally. If the "dislike" figures from -2 to -5 are combined,[32] then 46 percent of *Republikaner* voters can be classified as anti-Semitic, 16 percent of CDU/CSU voters, and 4 percent of *Bündnis 90*/Green voters[33] (total population: 14 percent). Attitudes of voters for the two ultraright-wing parties that have also been fairly successful in the last few years, the DVU (*Deutsche Volksunion—* German People's Union) and the NPD, showed the same pattern as that for the *Republikaner.*

A difference in attitude was also found among Green voters, in which core voters held a more positive view of Jews (2.0; marginal voters 1.1).

This positive view was probably based on their common background and participation in social movements fighting for integration of minorities and equality of the sexes and ethnic groups. Thus, core voters make up a particularly active group with a high degree of ideological unity in these areas, which need not hold true to the same extent for marginal voters.

The party spectrum in united Germany has been expanded by the post-communist "Party of Democratic Socialism" (PDS). The PDS is the successor to the official East German communist party, the SED, and claims to be dealing with the Stalinist past in a self-critical manner. It views itself as a party of the democratic Left. The overwhelming majority of its members were formerly members of the SED, and most of the party's voters are in the new federal states in eastern Germany.[34] Anti-Semitism researchers are concerned primarily with two questions regarding the PDS: (1) Since it can be assumed that PDS members and voters had a particularly close relationship to the East German state, the question arises how the explicitly anti-fascist and anti-racist self-image of this group is reflected in its attitudes toward Jews; (2) An additional question emerging from this special closeness to GDR ideology is the extent to which East Germany's anti-Zionist politics had an impact on the attitudes of this group toward Israel (cf., on this point, chap. 7, "Attitudes toward Israel"). A profile of PDS voters shows deviations as compared to the other parties (EMNID 1992). The high proportion of neutral (51 percent) and not unfriendly self-assessments (34 percent chose +1 or +2 on the like-dislike affinity scale) is striking. Significantly fewer PDS voters expressed an outspoken liking for Jews living in Germany. Only 7 percent chose values of +3 to +5, and in comparison with voters for all (!) other parties, PDS voters were least likely to express philo-Semitic attitudes (CDU/CSU: 15 percent; SPD: 15 percent; FDP: 19 percent; Bündnis 90/Greens: 30 percent). Nine-tenths of PDS supporters could be classified non-anti-Semitic, but 9 percent expressed emotional rejection (-2 to -5 on the like-dislike affinity scale). Compared to the share of anti-Semites among voters for the pre-existing West German parties (CDU/CSU: 16 percent; SPD: 12 percent; FDP: 13 percent), PDS voters scored somewhat more favorably. Despite the state-propagated anti-fascist self-image of the GDR, the educational, propagandistic, and repressive methods at its disposal, and the state control of mass media, the SED/PDS was not able to pull anti-Semitism "up by the roots"—not

TABLE 3.8
Political Orientation/Anti-Semitism 1949
"What is your general attitude toward Jews?"

	Openly anti-Semitic	Emotional rejection		Reserved	Toler-ant	Openly friendly	Indif-ferent
	I	II	I+II				
	%	%	%	%	%	%	%
CDU/CSU	5	13	18	12	49	7	14
SPD	7	7	14	16	46	9	15
FDP	10	17	27	16	36	5	16
KPD	13	3	16	3	54	10	17
Sonstige	12	14	26	15	39	6	14

Source: IfD 1949, 40.

even among its own voters. The "prescribed anti-fascism" of the GDR was by no means more successful than the open and conflict-laden process of dealing with anti-Semitism in the pluralist society of the Federal Republic, especially not among supporters of the former state party. In this case, they could have been expected to adopt the progressive elements of their ideology. PDS voters come off less favorably than the Greens, the left-wing party in the western part of Germany (4 percent anti-Semitic voters).

The parties and the potential voters they address have changed considerably since the founding of the Federal Republic of Germany. In regard to anti-Semitism, the right-left pattern was already discernible in 1949, but the parties that still exist today occupied different positions within this pattern (see table 3.8).

The left-wing parties had the lowest ratio of anti-Semites, at 14 percent and 16 percent, and the largest percentages of tolerant persons and philo-Semites (55 percent and 64 percent, respectively). Christian Democratic voters occupied the middle ground, which corresponded to their political standpoint at the time. They had not yet integrated the voters from right-wing extremist and right-wing conservative parties, who at the time voted for the FDP and the other right-wing parties (Deutsche Reichspartei, Deutsche Partei, WAV).[35] The right-wing, nationalist-conservative position of the FDP in 1949 was reflected in the data: 27 percent of its voters classified themselves as pronounced anti-Semites, a ratio that was 1 percent higher even than the electorate of the remaining parties, which were largely catch-alls for anti-democratic and former Nazi voters.

If we take the KPD (*Kommunistische Partei Deutschlands*) and the FDP as the poles on the left-right continuum, an extreme divergence which is no longer found among voters for parties represented in the *Bundestag* was apparent in views regarding anti-Semitism. The divergence was particularly striking on questions involving the political and legal consequences of the Nazi persecution of the Jews. Restitution claims, that is, claims for return of property that Jews were forced to sell to non-Jews after 1933, were acknowledged in 1949 by 68 percent of KPD voters, but only 34 percent of FDP voters (CDU/CSU: 40 percent, SPD: 42 percent, Others: 37 percent). An obligation to pay reparations was accepted by 48 percent of FDP voters, as opposed to 57 percent of KPD voters. Punishment of people who had committed anti-Semitic acts was approved of by 44 percent of KPD voters and only 13 percent of FDP voters. Punishment was opposed by 53 percent of the latter [KPD: 26 percent (IfD 1949, 20ff.)].

This basic pattern remained intact until the early 1960s. Only then did the ban on right and left-wing extremist parties [SRP (*Sozialistische Reichspartei*) banned in 1952 and the KPD banned in 1956], and the integration of voters from parties that fell below the 5 percent minimum during the 1950s, begin to change the party landscape to the one that would determine the course of politics in West Germany until the early 1980s.

Voters for the FDP/DVP continued to be most attached to the Nazi past. They had a much more positive attitude toward Hitler and a new, hypothetical "National Socialist Party" than did CDU/CSU and SPD voters.[36] They also clung most tightly to anti-Semitic views. In 1960, 55 percent of FDP/DVP voters were opposed to a Jew becoming Chancellor; in the SPD, the figure was only 47 percent, and in the CDU/CSU, 42 percent (IfD vol. 3, 1964, 218). These figures alone show that at the time, it was still CDU/CSU rather than SPD voters who were most critical of the Nazi period, and who expressed the least reserve with regard to Jews. In their assessment of the "20th of July" resistance and Adenauer's policy of reconciliation with Israel, the CDU/CSU voters also expressed the most positive views (IfD vol. 3, 1964, 235 and vol. 4, 1967, 191). However, voters' opinions differed from their parties' policies. The process of de-Nazification and prosecution of Nazi criminals was supported primarily by the KPD and the SPD. And the SPD supported reparations payments to Israel quite early on, providing a parliamentary majority in 1953 for Konrad Adenauer's policies, which were opposed by segments of his own party and the FDP.[37]

The 1960s were a time of great transformation in Germany's historical and political consciousness. The FDP developed from a conservative nationalist to a liberal, middle-class party, while the SPD, with the Godesberg Program, changed from a workers' to a peoples party and succeeded in attracting new social groups and intellectuals with its reformist policies since the 1966 Great Coalition. Responses to the question whether "Hitler would have been one of Germany's greatest statesmen if it hadn't been for the war," taken up again in 1972, illustrated the changing composition of the electorate. Now, agreement was lowest among FDP supporters, at 23 percent, while supporters of the CDU/CSU made up the right wing of the opinion spectrum with 40 percent [SPD: 32 percent (IfD, vol. 5, 1973, 204)]. Here a basic pattern was set that still holds today.[38] This did not rule out the possibility that deviations from this pattern might exist for certain subjects in our survey (attitude toward the Nazi past, to Jews, to the Middle East conflict, etc.).

We would like to sketch this specific opinion profile of the electorate in light of two issues: their attitude toward the Middle East conflict and toward attempts to deal with the past. In the *Middle East conflict,* the sympathies of CDU/CSU, SPD, and FDP voters were clearly on Israel's side from 1967 until the beginning of the 1980s. FDP voters had slowly abandoned their pro-Arab attitude of the 1950s.[39] Nevertheless, to this day they have a greater attachment to Arab countries than do CDU/CSU and SPD voters. In 1967, only NPD voters expressed a pro-Arab position that was almost certainly motivated by anti-Semitism.[40] With the 1982 Lebanon war, voters of all parties underwent a radical change of opinion in favor of the Arabs. This change was very pronounced among SPD voters, and especially among the Greens. However, the sympathy felt by SPD and Green voters for the Arab side in the Middle East conflict should not be interpreted as a rejection of Israel; on the contrary, voters from these parties were highly conscious of Germany's special historical responsibility toward Israel, and even preferred good relations with Israel to economic advantages from trade with the Arab countries (IfD vol. 8, 648).

As an indicator of attitudes toward the past, we can include support for demands for an end to the discussion of the past.

TABLE 3.9

"Are you personally in favor of continuing to prosecute Nazi crimes, or are you personally in favor of putting an end to this?"* (Schlußstrich ziehen)

Party	1969		1974		1987		1989		1994+	
	yes / no		yes / no		yes / no		yes / no		yes / no	
	%	%	%	%	%	%	%	%	%	%
CDU/CSU	73	21	68	19	78	12	75	24	58	35
SPD	61	30	56	30	61	27	65	35	46	47
FDP	71	22	56	25	60	25	70	30	49	46
Grüne	—	—	—	—	41	44	39	61	27	70
NPD/REP.	96	—	—	—	—	—	92	8**	89	7
PDS	—	—	—	—	—	—	—	—	32	63

* Question as formulated in 1969; wording changed in subsequent surveys; + East and West Germans (Forsa 1994, 17).
Sources: IfD vol. 5, 1973, 232; *Informationen* 1/2, 1974, table 4;
IfD 1987, table 16;** EMNID 1989, table 75.

For voters from the major parties, the table shows a constant high rate of affirmative responses to the question whether discussion of the Nazi past should come to an end. Events that greatly influenced public opinion, such as the major Nazi trials and the broadcast of the TV film "Holocaust" (1979) regularly interrupted this tendency, though it always resumed after a period of time. In questions of national history, FDP voters took up an intermediate position between the CDU/CSU and the SPD, whereas their attitudes toward minorities and groups suffering social discrimination were more liberal, more closely resembling those of Green voters.

Anti-Semitism and Religious Affiliation

Scholars consider Christian anti-Judaism to be one of the roots of modern anti-Semitism. After the Holocaust, isolated Church officials and theologians began—after some delay—to acknowledge their shared responsibility and blame, and to redefine their relationship to Judaism (cf. Rendtorff and Hendrix 1988). This rethinking was manifested in numerous Church declarations and theological and liturgical reforms; it gradually trickled down from the Church theological elite to local congregations

TABLE 3.10
"One sometimes hears that the Jews have so many problems because
God is punishing them for crucifying Jesus Christ."

	1974		1987
Strong agreement:	8.3 %	Agreement:	8.0 %
Mild agreement:	19.6 %		
Mild disagreement:	24.2 %	Disagreement:	75.7 %
Strong disagreement:	45.3 %		
Don't know:	2.6 %	Undecided:	16.3 %

Source: Sallen 1977, 278; our survey: question 23.

and religious instruction, though critical analyses of religious textbooks still reveal subtle forms of anti-Judaism in traditional negative judgments of Jews.[41] It can be assumed that this learning process in the Church had a positive effect on the attitudes of congregation members to Jews and Judaism, but it is almost impossible to measure its direct influence. First of all, Germany lacks empirical findings on this issue; second of all, the specific effect of the Christian enlightenment is difficult to distinguish from the effects of the process of secularization in Western societies and the general decline in anti-Semitism.

In face of this lack of data, we repeated a question on anti-Judaism already asked by Silbermann and Sallen in 1974 (See Table 3.10). The difference in possible responses makes a comparison difficult. If we consider the disagreement quotient, the statement was rejected by three-quarters of the interviewees. This quota rose only negligibly between 1974 and 1987. However, the effect so often observed is once again apparent—anti-Jewish opinions do not transform into their positive converse, but lead to a position of indecision for both sides. It is likely that many of those who chose the category "mild agreement" in 1974 would have preferred the response "undecided." It is also possible that many lacked knowledge of these issues, so that an above-average proportion of those with a low level of education (and a surprisingly large number of young people) chose these responses.[42] Between 1974 and 1987, there was a decrease in agreement with this central Christian accusation against Jews.[43] The trend is even more perceptible if we consider the age distribution of our 1987 survey. Only 4.5 percent of the sixteen to forty-four age group agreed with this statement, rising to 9 percent among forty-five to sixty-four-year-olds and 12 percent of the sixty-five to seventy age group; agreement peaked among those over seventy at more than 16 percent.

Is there any difference between members of the two largest Christian denominations in their responses to the "Christ killer" accusation? A significant difference can be found between Catholics and Protestants: 11 percent of Catholics and 6 percent of Protestants agreed with the causal connection "murder of Christ and persecution" [question 23 (this reflected the influence of different theologies: the Protestant Church abandoned the Christ-killer thesis in its theology long before the Catholic Church did)]. The lowest figure was achieved by those with no religious affiliation (4 percent). This difference can largely be explained by the religious upbringing of older people; for those over sixty-five, there was 21 percent agreement among Catholics and 13 percent among Protestants. There are no differences between younger Protestants and Catholics in their responses to this question (4 percent agreement for each).

Church membership in itself reveals nothing about attachment to the Church or intensity of faith. In public opinion research, the degree of religiosity is generally measured by frequency of church attendance. This frequency strongly correlates with agreement with the "Christ killer" question. People who attended services every Sunday or almost every Sunday showed a significantly higher level of agreement—19 percent and 16 percent, respectively—than those who attended services occasionally, rarely, or never (under 6 percent). An interesting generational effect indicating the success of the Church's educational work among church-affiliated young people is the fact that, of those under twenty-five who attended church every or almost every Sunday, not a single one answered "yes" to the question, and only a few declined to answer.

The age and educational influences on anti-Judaism are basically the same as for anti-Semitism.[44] In general, we gave relatively little weight in our study to the religious aspect of anti-Semitism. Glock and Stark (1966), who devoted an entire study to this issue, were able to question the specific subpopulations involved (members of various churches and Protestant pastors) in detail. In contrast, we had to emphasize different aspects, as our survey involved the population as a whole. In addition, our pretest, like other studies of anti-Semitism (cf. Weiss 1984), had indicated that anti-Judaism does not play a major role today in the complex of causes of hostility toward Jews (interviewees' calls for discrimination rarely arose from Christian reservations about Jews and Judaism), and that religion and church affiliation had little influence in molding anti-Semitic attitudes.[45] The 1989 EMNID survey confirmed this assumption. In answer to a question about causes of "critical views" toward Jews, the item "Jewish religion" on the list provided was chosen least often (8 percent). Based on the total count, neither Catholics nor Protestants showed a correlation between responses and frequency of churchgoing (EMNID 1989, table 83).[46] Because not all of those 8 percent who believed the Jewish religion could be a cause of anti-Semitism necessarily shared this religious anti-Semitism themselves, the number of those for whom the Jewish religion comprised the central aspect of their anti-Semitism must have been below 8 percent. In the same survey, no correlation was found between frequency of churchgoing and a liking for Jews living in Germany. For nonchurchgoers and those with no religious affiliation, this was, at +0.5, somewhat lower than for Catholic (+0.7) and Protestant churchgoers (+0.9; total population, +0.7).

In contrast to these empirical findings, Godwin Lämmermann continued to ascribe central importance to the religious component in his sociological and educational observations on religious anti-Semitism. In his opinion, explicit religious anti-Semitism has abated; nevertheless, he saw traces of unconscious religious motivation in secular anti-Semitism, in which only the form had been altered (1984, 69ff.). In his opinion, 80 percent of the anti-Semites in West Germany continued to be influenced in part by religious motives, when one considers both conscious and unconscious or subconscious justifications (ibid., 68). His views are supported by the continued frequent characterization of Judaism using the Christian church's traditional anti-Jewish interpretations, such as "vengeful, obstinate, full of Talmudic rhetorical cunning." Thus, those with anti-Jewish views still believe the fundamental principle of Jewish or Israeli legal thought could be found in the biblical passage "an eye for an eye, a tooth for a tooth." In more modern, Christian-influenced literature, the pseudo-exegetically justified assertion that a special ethical code exists within the Jewish community can still be found. However, this occasional anti-Judaism can no more form the basis for an estimate of anti-Semitic public opinion than Lämmermann's barely discernable underground motivations. In our survey, religious anti-Judaism proved to be a relatively insignificant form of hostility toward Jews, and the one that correlated least with other forms of anti-Semitism. A special study aimed more specifically at the various Christian denominations (Lutheran and Fundamentalist), and which better distinguishes the degree of Christian faith is still lacking for Germany and Austria.[47]

Apart from the question whether religious anti-Semitism is an important dimension of general anti-Jewish prejudice today, we were interested in whether religion and degree of religiosity have an identifiable influence on anti-Semitic attitudes.

Religious affiliation had no significant influence on degree of anti-Semitism. A comparison of the mean against the Anti-Semitism index showed Catholics having a slightly, though not significantly, higher tendency toward anti-Semitic views (8.1 percent of Catholics and 6.1 percent of Protestants were "hardcore" anti-Semites). This tendency was not pronounced throughout all age groups; it first appeared—very strongly—in the above-sixty-five age group. Of those with no religious affiliation, 7.4 percent could be classified as "hardcore." This relatively high figure was largely a result of the small number of older, strongly anti-Semitic people found in this group. Affiliation with one of the two Christian denominations was not significant for emotional distance, stereotyping, or inclination to discriminate.

A more clearly differentiated picture results if the assessment is based not on religious faith, but on ties to the church and frequency of churchgoing. People who go to church every or nearly every Sunday scored significantly higher on the Anti-Semitism index than people who seldom or never go to church. This had to do with the different age composition of the various groups. While 80 percent and 72 percent of weekly and almost weekly churchgoers, respectively, were over forty-five years old, the ratio was reversed among those who seldom (40 percent) or never (32 percent) go to church.

There was, however, no linear correlation between frequency of churchgoing and anti-Semitic attitudes. The evaluation revealed the following pattern: The highest degree of anti-Semitism was exhibited, irrespective of denomination or age, not by those who went to church "every Sunday," but by those who did so "nearly every Sunday." Among those who said they went "now and then" or "seldom," the anti-Semitism rate fell, only to rise slightly among those who never went to church—although here the share of older people was the smallest (only 32 percent were over forty-four years old).

TABLE 3.11
Frequency of Churchgoing/PAS[48]

Every Sunday	34.6 %
Nearly every Sunday	41.6 %
Now and then	36.4 %
Seldom	28.0 %
Never	31.3 %
Average in the population as a whole	33.2 %

p<.001, chi^2 21.3

The difference between the first two categories can be explained by the fact that far less than the average number of those under sixty who attend church every Sunday held anti-Semitic views, while this was not as pronounced among those in the same age group who go to church "nearly every Sunday." There was no difference between the two categories among older churchgoers. Presumably, members of the younger generation with close church ties were positively influenced by the church's learning process. The higher scores in the group that go to church almost every Sunday can be explained by the fact that these people did not completely experience the church reforms. Younger generations in this group were no different from those with more distance from the church. The fact that those who go to church "now and then" and "seldom" nevertheless revealed a lesser degree of anti-Semitism was due to the difference in attitudes of the older generation. Particularly among those who attend seldom, the scores of older people were clearly lower than in groups attending church more frequently. As mentioned above, among those with no religious affiliation and those who said they never go to church, an above-average proportion of those over sixty-five were anti-Semitic.

In summary, we can say that religious tolerance and a changing religious and theological view of Jews and Judaism in the church is shared by younger Christians. Among older Christians, religious traditionalism and conservativism seem to have hindered this learning process. Here, older generations with fewer church ties proved more tolerant. Theological preachings directed against Judaism that have burdened Christian-Jewish relations for centuries find almost no acceptance today among younger churchgoers. They reject polemics about "Christ killing," the influence of "religious fanatics" in Israel, and the "Jewish claim to be the Chosen People" much more emphatically than do their less frequently churchgoing peers. For older generations, the reverse is true; here, those questioned who had closer ties to the church accepted these polemics more readily than older people with more distance from the church. That is, in order to determine the influence of religious faith upon attitudes toward Jews and Judaism, the generations must be studied separately. Otherwise, the contradictory attitudes cancel each other out, making it seem that no influence exists.

The Influence of Region and Size of Residential Community

An urban community—which is associated with modernity, cosmopolitan attitudes, better education, and occupational opportunities—as well as its location in a particular region could exercise an influence upon the anti-Semitic attitudes of residents, especially if the regional focusses of anti-Semitism in recent German history are taken into account.

The influence of community size on anti-Semitism is not significant. A disproportionate number of those we classified as anti-Semitic live in communities with populations of under ten thousand. The lowest figures were found in medium-sized cities with populations of 50,000 to 500,000, while a slightly higher tendency emerged in major cities. This pattern was observed in the 1989 EMNID survey (table 61) in the ratings of how well Jews living in Germany are liked or disliked, and other questions relevant to our subject. In their survey, Silbermann and Sallen discovered a pronounced, reciprocal correlation between size of residential community and extent of anti-Semitism. In towns with populations of up to 5,000, they recorded 39.2 percent with strongly anti-Semitic tendencies; in cities with 50,000 to 500,000 residents, the figure was approximately 29 percent, and in large cities, 18.6 percent (Silbermann 1982, 67). Silbermann explained this distribution with reference to the lesser mobility of opinion in smaller communities, where residents tend to hold more firmly onto traditional views (cf. above, Roof's explanation of anti-Jewish prejudice as resulting from a "localistic world view"), and their different informational behavior. In smaller towns, sources of information on Jews are most likely to be the family and neighbors; in larger cities, the mass media are preferred (ibid.).[49]

Our data also showed that negative stereotypes of Jews have persisted longer in villages than in cities. A greater sense of traditional and a more narrow definition of group membership are reflected in the fact that anti-Jewish demands, such as "Jews should not be able to become civil servants," a ban on immigration, and boycotts of Jewish doctors were supported more strongly in villages (21 percent in villages and 15 percent in large cities; for a prohibition on immigration, the figures were 11 percent and 4 percent, for a boycott of Jewish doctors, 3.2 percent and 1.3 percent). The truth of the Holocaust was also more frequently denied in villages, discussion of the Nazi past rejected, and the demand that no reparations be paid to Israel more frequently made (34 percent rejection in villages and 26 percent in large cities).[50] On the other hand, no difference could be discerned in emotional attitude or social distance to Jews.

Whether the observed urban-rural dichotomy can be traced to the difference in milieu, or whether it results from age and educational effects, remains to be studied. A difference in age distribution among residents of various larger communities can be ruled out as an explanation, as age groups are equally distributed. However, there is a pronounced educational gap between city and country. Overall, villages lack residents with higher education, especially college students; that is, the milieu effect can be partly traced to an educational effect. The fact that the difference between large and smaller cities with respect to anti-Semitism had blurred almost entirely in our study, and had been reduced even for villages in comparison with Sallen's and Silbermann's results, could also be interpreted as a tendency for different worlds to come together, especially in larger urban areas. If education is held constant, an independent effect of residential community size on attitude toward Jews is observable only as a weak tendency.

As in the case of religious influence, however, a representative survey is not sufficiently sensitive to measure all urban-rural differences. The qualitative methods of more recent studies of local history and folklore are better suited to record the village milieu and more precisely describe the contradictions of a village's means of dealing with the Nazi past and history (cf. Jeggle et al. 1988). Such qualitative comparative studies on attitudes toward Jews in towns and cities of different sizes might reveal residential influences (particularly in cases of local conflict) that cannot be registered by our less precise method of measurement.

The latter is also true of the analysis of regional differences. Social and religious distinctions in different regions of Germany have lessened as a result of the immigration of refugees and exiles after 1945, the emergence of new industrial centers, and resulting mobility. Therefore, differences in attitude can be recorded only by analyzing smaller areas. The requirements of a representative survey do not permit regional differentiation below the state level. Some state and regional borders bisect areas historically settled by Jews and traditional centers of anti-Semitism, or bury their unique features within large regional units (cf., for example, the fact that Main-Franconia has been divided up, with parts belonging to the states of Bavaria, Baden-Württemberg, and Hesse).

In our evaluation, we found no correlation, or only a very weak one, between the variable "state" and anti-Semitism. Overall, a North-South dichotomy existed, reflected in the electoral showings of right-wing extremist parties such as the NPD and the *Republikaner* (cf. Roth 1989, 14f.).[51] Agreement with anti-Jewish statements was less frequent in northern German states than in the south. In the city-states of Hamburg and West Berlin it was far below average, while Bremen represented an exception, sometimes coming out above the level of the southern states.[52] Negative Jewish stereotypes, in particular, seem to have persisted more stubbornly in the south than in the north. Certain differences also existed in attitudes toward the Nazi past and acceptance of the consequences of that past. In comparing North Rhine-Westphalia in the north to Bavaria in the south, for example, one may assume that these differences result not only from differences in social structure, but also from the policies of the respective SPD and CSU governments; they have dealt with these issues very differently in public statements and educational and cultural policies. Tracing regional differences in political ways of handling these subjects is a task for historians and political education departments in the respective states.

Notes

1. While general age distributions in all recent surveys on anti-Semitism concur, our survey and the 1989 EMNID findings differ consistently with respect to the figures for younger generations. The sixteen to twenty-nine age group did not differ significantly from the thirty to forty-four age group in our survey; in some cases, in fact, the latter group appeared less prejudiced. The EMNID survey, on the other hand, showed a clearly discernible trend toward less prejudice on the part of the younger generation for all questions dealing with anti-Semitism. There is a difference not only between the thirty to forty-four-year-olds and the younger generation, but even between the eighteen to twenty-four and twenty-five to twenty-nine age groups (on questions involving their appraisal of Nazism, the amount of reparations payments, etc.). We can simply point out this discrepancy, although we are not in a position to explain it. Our data tend to indicate a low

plateau had been reached for the under-forty-four age groups; the EMNID data, however, show a continuing progressive decrease in anti-Semitism.

2. On the stability of attitudes acquired by a particular generation, cf. the results of the panel study by Marwell, Aiken, and Demerath (1987), which found that the political values of the 1960s generation in the United States differed decisively from preceding and subsequent generations, even after twenty years.

3. These results correspond with general sociological findings regarding adolescents in the 1940s and 1950s, summarized by Zinnecker as follows: "Adolescents in the 1950s were authoritarian as compared to the same age group in the 1980s. They supported authoritarian state views in many ways—strong state, one-party system—while some, at least the oldest among them, even continued to flirt with National Socialism after 1945" (1985, 323). In contrast to today, in which rigid authoritarianism and neo-Nazism are characteristic of marginal groups, open or latent leanings toward Nazi ideology in the 1940s and 1950s were considered one of many possible "political-cultural alternatives" (ibid, 325).

4. When interpreting these figures, the year (1944) and the particular situation of prisoners of war must be taken into account. Schörken (1990, 114ff.) described the prisoner of war camps as places with an isolated Nazi atmosphere.

5. Schörken's qualitative study using interviews and diaries depicts a different image of the adolescent generation. Nazism appeared as a "weak ideology" which, after the war, had obviously lost its function as an orientation and worldview. In his opinion, this included biological racist ideology (1990, 145ff.). The representative data of postwar surveys show, on the other hand, that anti-Semitic convictions, including elements of racism, were clearly retained, especially by adolescents.

6. On this reeducation phase, cf., for example, Holtmann's observations of former Hitler Youth leaders and the shift in their attitudes toward those of the Social Democratic Party (SPD) in the city of Kamen (1989, 240ff.).

7. The succession of political generations in Austria was also closely linked to Nazism. As in postwar Germany, surveys conducted by U.S. authorities in the American zone of Austria revealed that the generation of eighteen to twenty-nine-year-olds (born 1919 to 1929) continued to support Nazism and its ideology ("National Socialism a good idea"). In a 1973 survey, this same generation supported the most intensely anti-Semitic views [e.g., 47 percent of this age group was opposed to marrying a Jew, compared to an average of 35 percent in the population as a whole (cf. Hiller 1974, 159, 165)]. Attitudes toward Jews in general held by later political generations in Austria have not been investigated in detail, however. Recent surveys seem to suggest that generational developments in Austria did not coincide with those in West Germany.

8. It is, however, conceivable that the group of eighteen to thirty-year-olds actually represents *two* political generations: one strongly anti-Semitic group raised during the Nazi period (born up to 1934) and a younger, less anti-Semitic group. On the basis of available data this cannot be reconsidered. Cf. in the following, the stable dividing line separating the generations born in the early and late 1930s.

9. This interface corresponds exactly to the one Zinnecker discovered for inclination to deal with issues pertaining to the Nazi period. In 1979, half of the interviewees up to the age of forty-four (born 1935) thought it made sense to confront issues of Nazism, whereas the figure for this question in the forty-five and older group dropped to between one-fourth and one-third (1985, 341).

10. Surveys in the United States also found a low level of individual changes in attitude, and a greater degree of social, generational changes. The average level of anti-Semitism (measured using the same scale) did not change between 1964 and 1981 for the same age groups (eighteen to fifty-five years old in 1964 and thirty-five or older in 1981), though individual anti-Jewish prejudices did. The drop in anti-Semitism from 1964 to 1981 can be attributed to the more tolerant subsequent generations (Martire and Clark 1981, 23f.).

11. In terms of political education, this finding means that formation of prejudice and negative attitudes toward minorities must be nipped in the bud, that is, stopped at the time the attitudes emerge in adolescents. Prevention of prejudice at a later age will not change basic attitudes. At most, the attitudes will be repressed into communicative latency.

12. A nonrepresentative survey of 4000 schoolchildren and adolescents in 1984 in the Stuttgart/Esslingen area yielded similar results. School and television were mentioned as the main source of information on the history of the Jews and their persecution during the "Third Reich" (67 percent). Parents were listed in third place, with 38 percent. The fact that "friends and acquaintances" were seldom mentioned (11 percent) implies that the adolescents considered Jews merely a historical subject discussed in class or by their parents. With respect to information on current events about Israel, "school" and "parents" decreased in importance in comparison to "media" as a source of information (Roth 1986, 60). In a 1994 Forsa survey, school and parents were mentioned as the main source of information about the Nazi crimes (65 percent and 38 percent). Television, books and grand parents seem to play only a minor role (1994, 9).

13. A series of questions in the pretest dealing with attitudes in the family on issues pertaining to the "Third Reich" and persecution of the Jews suggests that those with pro-Jewish attitudes acquired them through conflict with their parents. They responded that they often asked questions, initiating discussion on these issues in the family and with friends. They rarely show any understanding for the fact that people in the "Third Reich" did not stand up to the political system.

14. In answer to the question on personal opinion regarding diplomatic relations with Israel, even in 1965 there were no discernable age distinctions [though a definite effect of education could be observed (IfD vol. 4, 470)].

15. The category "some college" included students who had yet to achieve a particular career position. The positive appraisal of this group pertains not only to these younger age groups, however; it can be observed for all age groups in this category.

16. In a psycho-social study of the attitudes of laborers and salaried workers conducted from 1929 to 1931 under the direction of Erich Fromm, however, interviewees who had adopted Nazi propaganda slogans often stated that the Jews were the cause of all problems, as was common in Nazi ideology (Fromm 1980, 111).

17. An analysis of the education factor as pertains to voters for the ultraright-wing German *Republikaner* party shows the same correlation. In the younger and intermediate age groups, the highly educated represent the lowest percentage of *Republikaner* voters; in the over-sixty age group, the percentage is higher for those with intermediate and higher formal education than for elementary school graduates (cf. Roth 1989, 13, table 6).

18. Cf. Hans-Helmuth Knütter, *Die Linksparteien,* in Mosse 1965, 323ff. Arnold Paucker cites a December, 1929 election analysis by the organization of German Jews, the *Central-Verein deutscher Staatsbürger jüdischen Glaubens,* which stated

that the Nazis were unlikely to have much effect upon the firmly entrenched organizations of the Social Democratic party (SPD) and even the German Communist party (KPD), in contrast to the middle-class parties (Paucker 1969, 166f.).

19. In their criticism of Silbermann, Wolfgang Erler and Ursula Schlude assumed that the unfavorable values for "premodern societal zones" could be relativized by means of a context analysis of the village environment. They said that "rural residents, farmers, and provincials" wandered into the language traps of the prejudice researchers (1985, 159 with note 6).

20. Survey data for 1965 confirm this perpetuation of career-specific prejudice among lawyers and doctors; 18 percent and 16 percent, respectively, attributed too much influence on political life to the "Central Association of Jews in Germany" (Zentralvereinigung der Juden in Deutschland). In comparison, 3 percent of Catholic and 6 percent of Protestant clergy said the same thing (IfD vol. 4, 337).

21. The very rough classification according to occupational categories in the 1989 EMNID study basically confirmed these observations. The lowest popularity values for Jews living in Germany (0.2) were found among laborers, the highest among civil servants (1.1), though salaried employees and self-employed/ independent professionals were only marginally below this level [0.9 and 0.8, respectively (cf. table 61)]. The percentage of Republikaner voters in various occupational groups yielded the same results: Farmers, unskilled and skilled workers made up the largest voter contingent; and management-level civil servants and salaried employees, as well as housewives, the smallest (Roth 1989, 13, table 7).

22. If age is then taken into consideration, thirty-seven of the sixty-one anti-Semitic women and only forty-one of eighty-five anti-Semitic men are over sixty years old. The percentage of radical anti-Semites is, however, much lower for women over 60 (11.5 percent VAS) than it is for men in that age group (20.5 percent VAS).

23. In his 1959–60 study on the wave of anti-Semitic incidents, Schönbach found that women more often preferred to take the middle ground and were less willing to give a more definite opinion "for" or "against" the Jews. He explained this on the basis of his finding that women show less interest in politics in general (1961, 52f.). In an 1987 ipos survey 60 percent of the men and 38 percent of the women were classified as interested in politics. (For a summary see Roth 1989, 11–12). These differences could not be explained on the basis of age and education differences.

24. In our questionnaire, we chose almost exclusively dichotomous response options; thus we could prevent attempts to avoid giving a clear answer. On the other hand, women who were truly undecided may have been forced to give a definite response, thus concealing their true neutral to undecided attitudes and creating a total picture more positive than it really was. Selznick and Steinberg also found a gender-specific difference in response patterns for the United States, but they found gender did not influence the extent of anti-Semitism: "Men are slightly more apt to score as anti-Semitic (42 percent versus 33 percent), but women are less likely to have opinions. The net result is that the proportion of men and women who score as convinced non-anti-Semites is precisely the same— 49 percent" (1969, 101ff.).

25. Regarding Austria, Weiss's findings from the years 1976 and 1980, and the 1987 findings of a joint survey by several public opinion research institutes, contradict a representative survey conducted in January, 1989 in which women clearly

made up a smaller proportion of "hardcore" and "latent" anti-Semites (hardcore anti-Semites: men 14.8 percent, women 7 percent: latent anti-Semites: 35 percent versus 21 percent). At the same time, this study found no effect based on age or education (Haerpfer 1989, 38ff). These dramatic changes were interpreted by the author as impacts of the conflict, starting in 1986, surrounding the presidential candidacy of Kurt Waldheim. The influence of political education that had been observed since the 1970s and the country's liberal political culture had largely been lost, according to the author; in dealings with ethnic and religious minorities in Austria, the situation has returned to the *status quo ante* (ibid., 45). The question remains why men and women responded differently to these political conflicts. The most plausible explanation is that men responded in a more strongly anti-Jewish manner because of their greater interest in politics. However, this contradicts the findings of the panel study by Költringer and Gehmacher (1989, 559), which observed a negative change in attitudes among women in particular.

This finding challenges future empirical researchers on anti-Semitism to pay attention to gender-specific reactions to public events, and clarify the specific causes of these differences through detailed investigations.

26. However, for most anti-Semites this right-wing orientation was purely cognitive; except for a small minority, it did not mean a right-wing behavioral orientation. Thus, only 13 percent of those with anti-Jewish leanings in the pretest would welcome and support an attempt by a right-wing extremist party to come to power. An additional 19 percent would welcome it, but do nothing actively to assist it. Forty-eight percent would be opposed, of which 21 percent would even do whatever they could to prevent a right-wing extremist party from coming to power. However, rejection of a left-wing party's attempt to take power was much stronger among anti-Semites, at 84 percent, of which 45 percent would even work actively against it. Anti-communism and rejection of leftist positions is thus a basic component of the ideological equipment of almost all those with anti-Jewish views.

27. However, because the responses of NPD voters corresponded to all previous information on this party, general statements can be made about the group.

28. A breakdown of voter groups by education level showed a large percentage of voters with the *Abitur* (college entrance qualification) and college education among FDP supporters in 1986 (25 percent, as opposed to 18 percent in the total population). Only 10 percent of FDP voters had only basic education and no apprenticeship; one third each had basic education with an apprenticeship (34 percent) or had completed the first level of secondary school *(Mittlere Reife)* (31 percent—total population, 19 percent and 41 percent, respectively). Cf. the figures in Jaide and Veen 1989, 137.

29. Based on its voters, Lepszy classified the *Republikaner* as a "heterogeneous protest party." A populist, ultraright-wing program exists relatively independent of its electorate; that is, an analysis of the program does not allow any generalization on the motives of the voters. Regarding the *Republikaner,* there is an especially significant difference between the party of the program and the members, on the one hand, and the party of the voters, on the other. (Lepszy 1989, 4).

30. The Forsa survey on Germans and National Socialism (1994) shows that the historical consciousness of *Republikaner* voters consistently deviates from that of the population at large: 30 percent of them blame other countries for World War II (total population, 3 percent), 63 percent would want to live in Germany if

Hitler and the Nazi regime had won the war (total population 14 percent), 76 percent find Nazi ideology to be "not that bad at all" (in comparison: 30 percent of CDU/CSU voters gave this response, 24 percent of SPD voters, 15 percent of Green party voters, and 12 percent of PDS voters).

31. *Republikaner* voters were the only group that clearly disliked Jews (-1.2). Among voters for other parties, Jews were either liked or assessed neutrally. The like-dislike figures fit into the right-left political spectrum as follows: CDU/CSU: 0.3; FDP: 0.6; SPD: 0.6; Greens: 1.2; only PDS voters (0.5) do not fit into this pattern formed by the western German parties [total population 0.5 (EMNID 1992, table 20)].

32. We do not consider an expression of slight dislike (-1) as indicative of anti-Semitic feelings, since an anti-Semite can be expected to express more definitive negative feelings toward Jews.

33. The civil rights movement *Bündnis 90* (Alliance 90) was founded in the GDR in the year 1990. In 1993 it merged with the West German Green party to form the *"Bündnis 90*/Green party."

34. The PDS has had seats in the *Bundestag* since 1990, when it received over 5 percent of votes in the new eastern German states. In the 1994 *Bundestag* elections, it did not attain the necessary 5 percent of the total German vote to be represented, but since it received four direct mandates (in the eastern part of Berlin), it nevertheless received 30 seats (4.4 percent of the vote) in the *Bundestag*. The PDS is also represented in all state parliaments in the eastern German states and in all local governments.

35. On the development of right-wing and right-wing extremist parties after 1945, cf. Dudek and Jaschke 1984, vol. 1, 59ff.; Stöss 1989.

36. In 1956, the question "Would you say Hitler would have been one of Germany's greatest statesmen if it hadn't been for the war?" was answered "yes" by 56 percent of FDP/DVP supporters, 36 percent of CDU/CSU voters, and 43 percent of SPD voters (IfD vol. II, 278 f.).

37. On reparations policies, cf. Herbst and Goschler (eds.), 1989; Goschler 1992; on SPD policies, Shafir 1989, 191 ff.

38. From the 1950s through the 1970s, the publications of public opinion research institutes contain occasional questions on issues of interest to us, but these were often not broken down by political orientation of those questioned. That is, our data base for the correlation between political orientation and anti-Semitism is small for this period. Incomprehensibly, Silbermann and Sallen asked nothing at all about party preference in their representative survey on anti-Semitism in 1974.

39. During the Six-Day War of 1967, the party itself was less pro-Israeli, emphasizing Germany's "strict neutrality" and voting against supplying gas masks to Israel's civilian population (Deligdisch 1974, 134).

40. Thus, the *National- und Soldatenzeitung* (National and Soldiers' Newspaper) reported on alleged murders and atrocities by Israelis; in these reports, interestingly enough, they compared the Israelis with the Nazis, and Zionism with Nazism (Deligdisch 1974, 138). Apparently, the paper could not resist the general consensus and linguistic usage under which particularly abhorrent atrocities always invite comparison with Nazi crimes. Similarly, during the Lebanon war, the Sabra and Shatila massacres were also called a "Holocaust."

41. Cf., for example, Kastning-Olmesdahl on Protestant religious textbooks (1981) and Fiedler on Catholic religious instruction (1980). See also the critical evalu-

ation in Lämmermann 1984, 58ff. See the latest analyses of (Catholic) religious textbooks by Reck-Hog 1990, 1994, painting a more positive picture of new developments in religious instruction.

42. The educational gap is particularly striking in the "Christ-killer" question:

Highest level of education completed	Yes %	No %	Undecided %
some secondary school	14.5	48.5	37.0
Hauptschule (junior high school completed)	10.6	72.3	16.8
some *Realschule* (basic high school)	4.7	74.5	18.9
High School Diploma	4.7	78.5	16.8
some *Gymnasium* (college preparatory high school)	8.6	78.6	12.9
Abitur (university entrance qualification examination)	4.5	84.2	11.3
some college	—	92.6	7.4
college graduate	2.0	90.9	7.1

$p < .001$, chi^2 91.2.

43. In secularized societies Christian anti-Judaism loses its impact on anti-Semitism. This can be exemplified by results of the 1991 Emnid-survey (1992, table 12). Fifty-eight percent of the East Germans, raised in an atheistical society, felt unable give an answer to the question "if the Jews were to be blamed for the death of Christ," because they never reflected upon it (West Germans: 30 percent).

44. However, there is one remarkable deviation. Independent of religion, age, or education, women were more likely to agree with this religious form of anti-Semitism than were men. But this gender difference appeared only among those in their mid-forties or older. We can offer no explanation for this phenomenon on the basis of our data.

45. In 1974, Sallen and Silbermann (Sallen 1977, 245) found a correlation of gamma = .37 between religious hostility and general anti-Semitism. Less than half of the strongly anti-Semitic shared the religious prejudices; among the mildly anti-Semitic, it was less than a third, and religious hostility without general anti-Semitism appeared in about 5 percent of all those questioned. In our study, an analysis of the correlation between various dimensions of anti-Jewish prejudice (emotional and aggressive rejection, anti-Zionism, etc.) indicated that religious prejudice had the least correlation with the other dimensions [gamma value between .27 and .40 (cf. IfD 1987; Köcher 50)].

46. As early as the 1949 IfD study, the Jewish religion was seen as a cause of anti-Semitism by only 12 percent (without any significant age difference). There was no difference among Catholics, Protestants, and the non-affiliated or members of other religions (45f.).

47. The study by Glock and Stark in the early 1960s, which was conceived in this way and established a close correlation between orthodox and particularist Christian faith and anti-Semitism, did not go unchallenged. Critics claimed the positive relationship between Christian faith and anti-Semitism resulted not from

religious dogma, but from factors such as education, age, and ethnic group (Martire and Clark 1982, 73–75), a thesis that has been confirmed by our data. Another explanation was provided by Roof (1974, 643ff.), who blamed the self-imposed social isolation of fundamentalist groups and their resulting "localistic world view" for this correlation. A further possibility was offered by Middleton (1973), who suggested, in addition to a range of socioeconomic factors, socio-psychological characteristics such as anomia, authoritarianism, and conservativism.

48. A significant correlation existed only between potential anti-Semitism (PAS) and frequency of churchgoing. For the strongly anti-Semitic group (SAS), the correlation was lower, and for the vehement anti-Semites (VAS) it was no longer significant.

49. In 1989, the question on "sources of information on the Hitler period" showed that in towns with up to 4,000 residents, reports by older people were still the most frequent source (52 percent, with multiple responses possible), while in larger cities they were mentioned by between 37 percent and 43 percent (EMNID 1989, table 73).

50. Assessments of Hitler also varied depending on size of town. In 1989, in towns of up to 4,000 residents, 47 percent of those questioned considered Hitler one of Germany's greatest statesmen if it had not been for the war and the persecution of Jews; in major cities, the figure was 32 percent (EMNID 1989, table 70).

51. In addition to this traditional gap, already observed in the NPD's electoral results in the 1960s (the NPD did well in Baden-Württemberg, Hesse and Bavaria), there are also old "nests" in the north, such as Bremen and Lower Saxony; Hamburg, Schleswig-Holstein and North Rhine-Westphalia, however, had the lowest number of NPD, DVU and *Republikaner* voters, both then and in 1989 (on the election results, cf. Roth 1989, table 12).

52. The small size of the sample from Bremen (N = 28) must, however, be taken into account; with such a small number of cases, slight distortions can occur. However, ultraright-wing parties have traditionally done well in Bremen; in 1967, the NPD garnered 8.8 percent, its second-best state parliamentary showing, and in the 1989 European Parliament elections, the *Republikaner* and the DVU reached a combined total of 7.6 percent, the highest showing outside southern Germany (cf. Roth 1989, table 12).

4

Anti-Semitism as a Social Prejudice

The Concept of Prejudice

There is no consensus in the scholarly debate on the extent to which prejudice can be distinguished from other judgments other than through normative decisions (cf. Bergmann 1994, 575). In this context it is irrelevant whether prejudices differ in terms of their over-generalization, their rigidity, or their distortion of reality, as we are not examining the question of the psychological formation of attitudes. We apply a sociology of knowledge; attitudes and prejudices will be viewed as an integral aspect of the value system and the collective knowledge of a group, learned in the course of socialization. These attitudes then form a schema, which determines the social perception of the members of the group (on the schema concept, cf. Ruhrmann 1989, 43ff.). These attitudes are both elastic and permanent (Sodhi and Bergius 1953, 15), that is, they continue to exist even in a changed situation and can integrate contradictory experiences. We characterize a prejudice as negative when it is socially undesirable, that is, when it violates rational norms and standards of humanity and justice (equality) (on this normative concept of prejudice, cf. Harding et al. 1969; Estel 1983).

The multidimensionality of prejudice is significant in analyzing anti-Semitism. Social psychologists distinguish among three dimensions: cognitive (stereotypes), affective (emotions), and conative (the inclination to act on the basis of these attitudes). Anti-Semitism surveys have often focussed too strongly on the cognitive dimension, solely measuring agreement with anti-Jewish stereotypes. This does not suffice, however, to estimate the extent and intensity of anti-Semitic attitudes in the population. Emotional attitudes, social distance, and inclination to discriminate must also be ascertained, since this is the only way of accurately judging

99

the significance of agreement with anti-Jewish stereotypes. All three dimensions should therefore be taken into consideration in creating an index to measure anti-Semitism.

Stereotypical Images of Jews

There are only approximately 70,000 members of the Jewish communities living in the Federal Republic of Germany today.[1] The chances of having Jews in one's circle of acquaintances are thus slight. Surprisingly enough, however, 12 percent of all those interviewed claimed to know Jews. That would mean that each and every German Jew would have about 180 non-Jewish acquaintances.[2] This statistic seems to express a wish and sign of approval rather than accurately reflecting the actual situation.[3] Although this exaggeration can be taken to suggest an outspoken interest in Jews and Judaism,[4] the fact is, half the population said they had neither Jewish acquaintances, nor did they know of people in the media or in the area where they lived who were Jewish. This lack of knowledge is more an expression of disinterest than of outspoken anti-Jewish sentiment. Psychological studies have shown that anti-Semites have considerable interest, albeit negative, in identifying Jews in private and public spheres. They are more likely to claim to "recognize Jews" (cf. the research summary in Bergmann 1988a, 288ff.).[5] This is confirmed in many of the pretest results. Of the anti-Semites, 57 percent expressed interest in identifying someone in their circle of friends as a Jew, whereas only 12 percent of the contrast group expressed such an interest.[6] Persons with anti-Semitic views also claimed far more often than others that they were able to identify a Jew from his or her appearance (41 percent to 13 percent), or claimed to know if public personalities were Jewish (50 percent to 44 percent).[7]

Despite the fact that most of the population lacked any personal experience with Jews, they had a relatively detailed idea of what a "typical" Jew was like. Sodhi and Bergius, in their study on "National Prejudices," determined that the German picture of Jews was very clearly differentiated, widespread, different from stereotypes of other nationalities, and ambivalent (1953, 80).[8]

It must be assumed that cultural traditions have been passed down through the family, media, the schools, and the churches. Such images are not rooted firmly in the personal experiences of the individual because they have never been "confirmed" by first-hand experience. This means that in interpreting stereotypes of Jews, it must be taken into account that these are cognitive value judgments, which do not necessarily say anything about their emotional significance for the individual.

The list of characteristics for the questionnaire used in the main survey was compiled according to a two-fold procedure. First, features mentioned in the open interviews were collected and categorized; second, typical characteristics were selected from the historical image of Jews and from previous surveys, in order to determine a possible evolution in the stereotypical picture of Jews.[9] All dimensions of anti-Semitism were taken into consideration: political and economic rejection, a negative physical image, ambivalently judged "special abilities" of Jews, their religion, and their group consciousness. Positive qualities were also included, as well as the image of Israel and qualities most often mentioned by Germans in describing themselves.[10] In order to be able to compare the results with those of previous surveys, items from these surveys were also taken into consideration in forming the list of characteristics.

The method we used in presenting the interviewees with the list of characteristics was first used in research on prejudice in 1933 by Daniel Katz and Kenneth W. Braly. This method has been sharply criticized, as it predetermines the results to a certain extent (Sodhi and Bergius 1953, 20ff.; Brigham 1972; for a summary, cf. Bergmann 1988a, 457ff.). The interviewees could agree with characteristics they might never have mentioned if the question were left open, and some qualities missing from the list could remain unconsidered. This method is favored in representative studies for reasons of practicality and facility in evaluating responses. In addition, in comprising a character list, anti-Semitism researchers can draw upon an empirically substantiated picture of Jews with clear historical contours. Interviewees were asked to provide a current description of characteristics in order to recognize any shift in the image of Jews in the population, and as a control for our own primary experience. Some of the qualities included in the list of characteristics in the pretest were deleted, since agreement was significant neither by anti-Jewish nor pro-Jewish interviewees. Decisions regarding the final list of qualities used in the main survey were thus part of a complex selection procedure.

We then subjected the resulting list of thirty-two qualities (see questionnaire, question 20) to an exploratory factor analysis to provide the structure of the image of Jews. The low explained variance (49 percent) can be explained by the fact that stereotypes are diffuse and somewhat contradictory by nature.

The factor analysis yielded six factors (see appendix 3). Factor 1 can be interpreted as the *classical anti-Semitic image of Jews*. It includes the following negative characteristics:

- the power-hungry Jew (power-hungry, politically radical/ruthless);
- the dangerous Jew (sinister, unpredictable, false/conniving, destructive/subversive, conspiratorial);
- the unforgiving Jew (unforgiving/unreconcilable, arrogant);
- the greedy Jew (avaricious/greedy).

Aside from the religious component of anti-Judaism and the negative physical picture of Jews (factor 5), all other anti-Semitic stereotypes loaded onto this factor. Statements relating to an economic threat (point 4) loaded only weakly onto this factor and form an independent factor with negative economic-related characteristics.

The stereotype of the unforgiving, unreconcilable Jew is linked with classical stereotypes. It has a long religious tradition,[11] though it has certainly gained in relevance since the Holocaust. Jews are "annoying reminders" who are "arrogant" in morally condemning the Germans. This stereotype also appears as an individual factor (6), which means that to some degree it also exists independent of traditional anti-Judaism.

Agreement with individual items of factor 1 is between 4 percent and 28 percent (mean value 16 percent). The stereotype of the power-hungry Jew was agreed with most often. If this is combined with the responses to the question about Jewish influence ("Jews have too much influence in the world"), the picture becomes even more clearly defined: 33 percent of those questioned thought Jews have too much influence. In contrast, the traditionally rooted complex of the sinister Jew who secretly exercises his subversive influence—the anti-Semitic image of the parasitic Jew—did not find as much approval. The image of a covert, not totally comprehensible influence of Jews in Germany was shared by only 13 percent of those questioned (IfD 1986), whereas the influence of Jews internationally, where not as much is known about the distribution of power, was assessed by the interviewees to be considerably higher. Today, German resentment of Jewish influence is primarily triggered by the image of Jews active around the world whose influence in other countries is greater than in the German context (IfD 1987, 24). Since this image is most prevalent among the elderly and less educated, we presume it has to do with a traditional picture of Jews which these groups have not revised; it has much less relevance among younger generations and those with higher education. This traditional aspect is demonstrated by the fact that with respect to the "power-hungry" stereotype, an unexpectedly high proportion of those questioned answered that their own families had anti-Jewish attitudes. The stereotypes of "power-hungry," "greedy," and "unforgiving" Jews have been retained, whereas anti-Judaism and a racist, negative physical picture of Jews have not. This is partly because these cliches received "environmental support" following World War II. In order to verify this connection, we correlated the "power-hungry" stereotype with accusations against Israel that pertained to power, war, annexation, and the like. The comparison showed a significant correlation. Of those who were classified as anti-Zionist according to the Anti-Zionism index (cf. chap. 7), that is, those who saw Israeli policy as ruthless and jingoistic, 42 percent considered Jews in general to be "power-hungry," while only 11 percent of those not classified as anti-Zionists felt that way.[12]

The "power-hungry" prejudice has been nourished not only in terms of Israel, however. A large percentage of those sharing this prejudice also felt that the World Jewish Congress interfered unduly in Austria's domestic affairs during the Waldheim Affair (42 percent; 27 percent considered the interference necessary; 16 percent were undecided). Corresponding to stereotypical perceptions, the stereotype need not be "confirmed" through particular events and can remain relatively diffuse. Thus, 67 percent of those who find Jews to be "power-hungry" assign Jews, entirely unspecifically, "too much influence in the world" (19 percent do not see too much influence, 14 percent undecided).

At first glance, factor 2 appears to include positive stereotypes depicting Jews as a *"religious, traditionally motivated group showing a high degree of unity."*[13] More than two-thirds of all those questioned felt this was true. The same proportion saw Jews as successful businesspeople. Although positive virtues such as a sense of tradition, religiosity, industriousness, and bravery predominate in this assessment, however, some stereotypes that also appear in the generally negative factor 4 (intelligence, ambition, and business acumen) also have negative overtones. Indeed, one-third of the interviewees who regard Jews as "religious" or assume they stick together also feel that Jews consider themselves the "chosen people" and therefore look down upon others. Aside from the fact that every in-group normally overestimates the unity of out-groups, interviewees attributed such a cohesiveness to Jews in particular.[14] Deviations from this pattern are seen as isolated examples of individual dissidence and do not lead to a revision of the general assessment (only 21 percent of those interviewed said that Germans stick together, while 70 percent assumed this of Jews). The monolithic character assigned to Judaism forms the basis for the image of a connection among Jews throughout the world, and thus also for the negative complex of Jewish power and conspiracy.[15] Almost half of all those questioned who assumed that Jews "stick together" insinuated that Israel has "much covert influence" (45.5 percent), and somewhat more than one-third attributed to Jews in general "too much influence in the world" (35.7 percent agreement; 41.6 percent disagreement; 22.6 percent undecided). The proportion of interviewees who perceived this solidarity as very negative and threatening is, however, smaller; only 13 percent see Jews as "conspiratorial."

The views of different age groups and educational levels largely coincided, particularly with respect to agreement with the generally positive characteristics. Unlike factor 3, which is entirely philo-Semitic, factor 2 also includes a series of ambivalent character descriptions. Religiosity and cohesiveness can be seen as a sign of "arrogance and being the Chosen People;" cohesiveness can also be perceived in connection with the covert influence of Jews worldwide, leading even to the stereotype of the "conspiratorial Jew." Today's view of Judaism is obviously determined to a large degree by the traditional image of the religion and of Jewish economic activities. This image does not integrate real developments within Judaism (secularization and the statistically inconspicuous career structure).

Factor 3 shows a clearly *philo-Semitic image of Jews* with mostly positive, middle-class character traits that apply more to individual Jews than to Jews as a group. This picture of Jews is largely marked by (secondary) virtues that also dominate Germans' self-image, such as honesty, loyalty, sense of duty, orderliness and cleanliness, bravery, modesty, industriousness, and so on (agreement ranges from 11 percent to 46 percent, mean value of all items = 23 percent). Qualities such as "intelligence" and "ambition" also took on a positive connotation in this context. In contrast to the negative factors (1, 4, 5, 6), the positive images of Jews (factors 2 and 3) showed no generational or educational effect. This suggests that a reduction in prejudice is more likely due to neutralizing effects than to the construction of a philo-Semitic counter-stereotype among younger generations, who are definitely less anti-Semitic than the older generations, but no more philo-Semitic. In seeking reasons for these pro-Jewish stereotypes, actual facts often seem very relevant. There are significant correlations to the corresponding characteristic descriptions of Israel. Of those who consider Israelis to be an "industrious people," 71 percent said the same of Jews in general; and of those who regard Israel's agriculture as exemplary, 60 percent hold Jews to be "industrious." Significant correlations also exist between the stereotype "brave" and the image of Israelis as an "industrious people" (0.25), as good soldiers (0.18), and as the "Germans of the Middle East" (0.13).[16]

The proportion of those questioned who strongly identified the German self-image with the image of Israel ["They are like us. The Germans of the Middle East" (10 percent agreement)] attributed "German" virtues to Jews to a very large extent. The highest value (70 percent) was achieved with respect to the trait "industrious;" 51 percent for "brave" and only 36 percent for "orderly." This group scored up to double the values of the population at large for the positive character traits. Identification between Germans and Israelis exists primarily in two areas. Cultivation of the land, achievements in building the country, and military victories are aspects of the complex Israeli social situation with which Germans can identify. Other aspects of the German self-image such as orderliness, loyalty, and honesty, on the other hand, are mentioned less often by the group identifying strongly with the Israelis, though in any case more than by the rest of those questioned.

As expected, almost all of those in the pretest tending to have anti-Jewish attitudes denied Jews these virtues. The only exceptions were "industrious" and "brave," which were certainly influenced by the perception of Israel (cf. table 4.1 below).

Factor 4 includes the *economic-related negative characteristics* often ascribed to Jews (cunning/shrewd, avaricious/greedy, miserly, intelligent, successful in business). This complex of negative aspects received the most widespread agreement (20 percent to 75 percent; mean value of all items = 42 percent).[17] For persons with anti-Jewish attitudes, this represents the most dominant image of all, with over 75 percent expressing agreement.

The traditional association of Jews with trade and money has been maintained as a negative complex in the general image of Jews. Attribut-

TABLE 4.1
Agreement with Selected Stereotypes

	Total pop. %	Those showing anti-Jewish tendencies
Industrious	55	33
Brave	42	31
Sense of duty	36	10
Orderly/clean	21	11
Modest	16	4
Honest	15	0
Loyal	15	5
	N= 121	N=95

Source: Pretest.

ing intelligence and business acumen to Jews involves an element of acknowledgment of business capabilities, though it harbors a negative connotation of Jewish business acumen, as illustrated by the strong association with negative traits such as "cunning," "greedy," and "stingy." In this context, talent and industriousness are seen in the end to serve personal profit and economic exploitation, thus giving qualities like "intelligent" and "successful" an ambivalent to negative connotation. Intelligence and business acumen are apparently traits consistently attributed to Jews. Philo-Semites and anti-Semites agree in this characterization. Of course, the different contexts in which these traits are seen result in their taking on contrasting meanings (cf. factors 2, 3, and 4).

The traditional stereotype of the Jewish businessman is even stronger and more clearly negative among the older generation. This commonly held view, "Jew = Business," is still a living memory, accentuated in a negative manner by the economic anti-Semitism practiced until 1945. Surveys from the early 1950s show the predominance of this image. Of expressions used exclusively to characterize Jews, Sodhi and Bergius (1953, 41), in their 1951 study, found primarily economics-related terms such as "usurer" (74 percent agreement), "crafty" (66 percent), "greedy" (60 percent), and "exploiter" (43 percent). In addition, "nation of traders" (81 percent), "avoid physical labor" (68 percent), and "money-maker" (47 percent) were mentioned.[18] In answer to the free association question "What do you think of when you hear the word 'Jew'?" the 1954 EMNID study found that the second most common answer referred to the activities of Jews as businesspeople. The younger generation has no corresponding everyday experiences, and their perceptions are no longer formed by officially propagated anti-Jewish cliches. Of course, the stereotype did not immediately disappear, though it is indeed starting to fade. In general, anti-Jewish prejudice is also weaker in the younger generations and in persons with higher education. The effect of formal education can be seen with respect to clearly negative stereotypes; a difference of six to twelve percentage points was found between persons having completed *Hauptschule* (junior high school) and those with higher degrees.

Today the complex of motives for economic anti-Semitism is determined much more by reparations obligations to Israel and the Jews than by ideologizing a real experience of competition. From the very start of the reparations debate until the present day (cf. chap. 10), these obligations meet with strong disapproval and are seen by many of those questioned in surveys as a fundamental reason for the perpetuation of anti-Semitism. Our survey confirmed this correlation of negative stereotypes and disapproval of reparations. Almost half (49 percent) of the opponents of reparations payments regarded Jews as "greedy/avaricious" and 63 percent as "cunning/shrewd," whereas only 19 percent and 34 percent, respectively, of those not opposed to the payment of reparations agreed with these attributes. The correlation is even more obvious if the stereotypes "greedy" and "cunning" are compared in relation to the statement: "Many Jews today attempt to gain advantage from the 'Third Reich' at Germans' expense" (question 21). This confirms the close relationship between the stereotype of extreme economic ability and reparations.

The stigmatization of minorities by means of a *negative physical image* (weak, cowardly, ugly) is found again and again in research on prejudice. This characterization, including the distorted picture created by anti-Semitic caricatures and comics of the weak and unathletic Jew who shirks or is unfit for military service, can be found in factor 5. Physical weakness is associated in this stereotype with negative character traits such as cowardice and falseness. "Manifest characteristics" are thus used to draw conclusions about related yet invisible traits. According to this stereotype, a weakling is not strong enough to fight, and therefore must lie and use underhanded, conniving tactics (the qualities "conspiratorial" and "sinister" also loaded weakly onto factor 5). The image of the "Jew as parasite" was still apparent here in the background. The low level of agreement with this prejudice in the sample as a whole (4 percent agreement) suggests that this old image of Jews is no longer plausible in modern society. The perception of the modern Israeli as a victorious soldier also reveals this cliche to be totally unfounded.[19]

In view of the very low level of agreement with this complex, the effect of age and higher education is correspondingly weak. The slight generational effect is surprising to the extent that the image of Jews as ugly and unsoldierlike still existed in the early 1950s. In 1954, 20 percent of those interviewed still considered the external appearance of Jews to be a cause of anti-Semitism (EMNID 1954, 37) and in 1951, "hooked nose" (88 percent agreement) and "unsoldierlike" (58 percent) were given as typical Jewish characteristics (Sodhi and Bergius 1953, 41).[20] Historical experience with Israel has apparently triggered a far-reaching change in attitudes.

The characteristics of the *overly sensitive, unforgiving Jew* (oversensitive, unforgiving/unreconcilable, arrogant) comprise factor 6. There is relatively high agreement with this compendium of traits (from 15 percent to 32 percent, mean value of all items = 24 percent). We believe this factor reflects the German-Jewish relationship since 1945. The traditional stereotype of the vengeful Jew from the Old Testament is not the decisive image in this factor, as one might initially assume, although that image certainly provides a strengthening or authenticating effect. Rather, this complex is based on the feeling that Jews refuse to exonerate Germans of their guilt and their obligations resulting from the Nazi past. Persons who recognize this obligation and want to keep alive memories of the crimes that were committed very rarely judge Jews as unforgiving. This pattern can be seen with respect to all questions concerned with coming to terms with the past.

Thirty-two percent of the interviewees regarded Jews as "oversensitive," 26 percent as "unforgiving/unreconcilable," and 15 percent as "arrogant." Oversensitivity was judged ambivalently, though unreconcilability and arrogance had a definite negative connotation. The small difference between age groups in assessing Jews as "oversensitive" supports this assumption, while "unforgiving" and "arrogant" met with increasing approval as the age of the interviewees increased. Oversensitivity was apparently perceived by some of those interviewed as "sensitive"; assignment of this characteristic within a historical context indicated the problematic nature of the German-Jewish relationship. All in all, there was a significant correlation between the "oversensitive" and "unforgiving" assessments. The third stereotype belonging to this complex, "arrogant," must be interpreted within the framework of coming to terms with the past, that is, as an expression of a Jewish moral superiority, forcing the Germans to live "in sackcloth and ashes." Of those who judge Jews to be "arrogant" (15 percent), 50 percent also accuse the World Jewish Congress of having interfered unduly in the Waldheim Affair (question 24b). Factor 6 seems to be more an expression of "secondary anti-Semitism," emerging from problems in dealing with the past.

In summary, the German image of Jews can be divided into three partial images: a consistently positive one, a positive one with ambivalent characteristics, and a severely anti-Jewish one. Factor 1 loaded the highest, encompassing the traditional anti-Semitic picture of Jews with all its facets except for physical stigmatization. As demonstrated in factors 4, 5, and 6, the negative image is then subdivided into clearly defined partial images: the racist, physical picture; the economic component passed down by traditional anti-Semitism; and a new image reflecting the problems of the German-Jewish past.

These partial images differ by generation. We conducted a factor analysis to determine the image of Jews for the sixteen to twenty-nine, thirty to fifty-nine, and sixty-and-over age groups. The positive images for the respective generations generally concur.[21] In all age groups, the dominant image was that of the "dangerous Jew." The negative images of Jews differed among age groups with respect to the extent of differentiation. While the oldest cohort merged all negative qualities into one picture, apparently integrating new experiences into an already existing framework, the younger interviewees held various coexisting negative images. The youngest group separated out negative physical appearance and divided the economics-related stereotypes into two partial images: that of the successful, intelligent, and industrious businessperson, and that of the greedy, conspiratorial Jew.

The intermediate age group differentiated the most in various aspects of the negative image. In addition to the dominant picture of a conspiratorial and power-hungry Jew, they distinguished between the partial images of the "greedy" and the "unforgiving" Jew, as well as stereotypical physical appearance. The middle generation had the strongest negative stereotype of the greedy and cunning Jew, in which intelligence and success in business took on an obviously negative connotation.

The oldest generation appeared to have a relatively unified cognitive schema in which all negative attributes are linked together. In the youngest cohort, this unity was not an expression of a highly organized schema, but the result of a relatively low level of knowledge and interest, so that the few personal experiences and remnants of an anti-Jewish tradition were lumped together into a sweeping judgment. The middle generation had the most differentiated negative cliche since, as contemporaries, they probably reacted most strongly to the historical and political events of the last few decades. In contrast to the oldest group, this age group could not fall back on a rigid schema to integrate these experiences into their negative picture.

Gender-specific differences with respect to the image of Jews were not very widespread.[22] There was a separate factor for the men concerning the "unforgiving Jew" (oversensitive, arrogant, unforgiving), while women integrated these traits into the classical anti-Semitic picture of Jews. This might suggest greater attention on the part of the men to the current German-Jewish relationship. There was a separate factor for the women comprising the image of the "sinister Jew" (sinister, conspiratorial), whereas the men integrated these traits into factor 1 (the "dangerous Jew") and, in connection with negative physical appearance, into factor 5 as well. In general, a greater tendency to separate aspects into individual partial images could be observed among the women.

The German image of Jews has thus proved not at all uniform, feeding on different traditions and present-day perceptions. This has consequences for both a scientific analysis and for attempts to deal with anti-Semitism publicly and politically. The partial images each have their own "logic" and direction of development; they are distributed differently among age and educational groups and can be influenced to different extents. Domestic and foreign events can either affect individual partial images or strengthen ambivalence and negative images in general.

Changes in the Image of Jews

There are very few samples in survey research (IfD 1960, 1961, 1965, 1986; Noelle-Neumann 1993) that allow a comparison of the images that Germans have of Jews. Those that do exist include only a few stereotypes that correspond to the stereotypes on our list of characteristics. Generally, there have been no changes in either the negative or the posi-

TABLE 4.2
Agreement on "Jewish Characteristics"

	1960/61 %	1965 %	1986/87 %	1992
Artistically talented	39	—	39	38
Intelligent/gifted	52	—	49	52
Greedy	23	20	20	
Cowardly	19	15	4	—
Arrogant	11	14	15	—
False/hypocritical	13	—	9	16
Calculating	30	30	31	
Exploiter*	34	25	14	—

Source: IfD vols. 3, 4, 9 1986, 1987, 1993.
* Sodhi and Bergius determined the nonrepresentative figure of 43 percent agreement in 1951; 1953, 41.

tive characteristics, with two exceptions. The appraisal of Jews as "cowardly" decreased continuously, from 19 percent in 1960 to 15 percent in 1965, and finally to only 4 percent in 1987. Israel's military victories can be cited as the source of this shift. There is also very little agreement with the "exploitation thesis," which has to do both with the shift in political semantics toward discreditation of a class struggle vocabulary and with the disappearance of the supervisory/subordinate German-Jewish employment relationship.

These few comparative data suggest stability, as predicted by the prejudice theory, particularly with respect to the negative aspects of the image of Jews; this contrasts to some degree with the shift in attitudes among the younger generations. Positive developments, however, were not as strong as would be expected in light of this shift. It appears that up to the present day, negative characteristics are still discussed more often than positive ones in communication about Jews. In response to the following pretest question: "When there is discussion about *the* Jews today, is it usually about their good or their bad characteristics?" 43 percent said "more likely about the bad ones" and only 8 percent said "about the good ones." With respect to those with anti-Semitic attitudes, the ratio was even higher, at 62 percent to 4 percent. Even among the philo-Semites, only 11 percent said that the good qualities are usually talked about. The subject of Jews is assessed as not very important, though when the subject does come up, it is usually in a negative context.

An International Comparison of Anti-Jewish Stereotypes

Up to now, the 1986 IfD study was the only international comparison of people's images of Jews that used lists of character traits to make the comparison. Some comparative data thus exist for Austria, France, and the United States. Sweeping negative judgments found more support in these three countries than in the Federal Republic of Germany, while the values for some of the positive characteristics (brave, culturally significant) were higher in France and the United States. (Brave: West Germany = 45 percent; Austria = 40 percent; France = 66 percent; U.S. = 63 percent. Cultural life would be impoverished without Jews: West Germany = 38 percent; Austria = 29 percent; France = 33 percent; U.S. = 65 percent). There are several explanations for these national differences. The low level of agreement with positive and negative stereotypes in the Federal Republic of Germany might imply that the picture of a people or a minority fades when there is no longer any direct, everyday experience of dealing with them. In such a case, both positive and negative biases lack any "environmental support." The data for the United States would support this interpretation, as they reflect both positive experiences ("Jews are competent businesspeople" and "Cultural life would be impoverished without Jews") and conflicts ("Jews have too much influence in politics" and "Jews are often arrogant") between the majority and minority populations. The figures for Austria do not support this interpretation, since negative attributes scored particularly high there, although, as for Germany, actual group relations no longer have any significance. Germany's and Austria's particular past must be taken into account in interpreting this data. In the Federal Republic, a standard of opposing anti-Semitism and attempting to deal with the Nazi past—no matter how insufficient this process might be—represented a learning process, on the one hand, and forced anti-Semitism into communicative latency, on the other (cf. chap. 11). In Austria, however, this process was far less extensive [see the public reaction to the Waldheim Affair (cf. Gottschlich and Obermair 1988; Gehmacher and Költringer 1989; Mitten 1992)], enabling anti-Semitism to continue relatively unchecked. Thus, the low figures in West Germany resulted in part from fading stereotypes, which have lost all meaning in Germans' everyday lives, and in part from the special way of dealing with anti-Semitism resulting from the legacy of Nazism. In France and the United States, where this burden of guilt does not exist, judgments are much more openly negative. The degree to which the low figures in Germany are distorted due to latency will be examined later (chap. 11).

In their 1951 study, Sodhi and Bergius found a relatively broad consensus between the image of Jews described by U.S. college students (corpus of Katz and Braly 1933) and the image described by their German sample (also primarily college students); the Germans did, however, elaborate more on Jewish talent and the Americans more often checked off "obstinate" and "aggressive" (1953, 49). The findings of the international, comparative survey conducted by the IfD in 1986 had shown that the stereotypes in France and the United States, both of which have large Jewish minorities, were different from those in West Germany (and Austria). This can clearly be seen in the different assessments of the "power of Jews." The wording of the question in the U.S. and France always pertained to the power of Jews in the respective country. One-fifth of those questioned, both in the United States [20 percent in 1981 as opposed to 11 percent in 1964 (Rosenfield 1982, 436) and in France (21 percent in 1988, 17 percent in May 1990)[23] believed that Jews in their country had too much power. In the Federal Republic of Germany, the question more generally concerned the influence of Jews throughout the world, which was estimated to be relatively strong ("Jews have too much influence in the world;" 33 percent agreement in 1987, in 1990 12 percent agreed strongly and 32 percent agreed somewhat). However, there has been a constant decrease in "yes" responses to the question—asked repeatedly in EMNID studies since 1959—on whether the influence of Jews *in Germany* is too great.

When the question was posed more concretely, concerning the influence of certain Jewish organizations in Germany, even fewer West Germans felt that Jews exerted excessive influence; in 1971, only 6 percent felt the *"Zentralverband der Juden in Deutschland"* (Central Association of Jews in Germany) had too much political influence (IfD vol. 5, 217); in 1966, the value was 13 percent (IfD vol. 5, 174). We also asked about Jewish influence in the pretest, though the wording of the question alluded more strongly to the anti-Semitic context of a "covert Jewish conspiracy." Of those questioned who believed it was not the sovereign powers of state in Germany, but "others who pull the strings," over 40

TABLE 4.3
"Do you think that the groups listed below[24] have more influence,
less influence, or just as much influence in West Germany as they should?"
(in percent).

Jews	1959	1961	1964	1967	1975	1981	1984	1986	1994
More influence	23	19	18	19	14	20	16	11	24
Less influence	26	16	20	16	18	34	34	—	9
As much as they should	39	23	26	25	36	43	46	—	32
No response	12	43	36	40	32	3	4	—	36

Source: EMNID-Informationen 7, 1965, 11/12 1984, EMNID 1986, table 1; AJC 1994, table 4b—the figures for the East Germans in 1994 are 8 percent, 12 percent, 24 percent, and 56 percent, respectively.

percent mentioned the world's superpowers or multinational corporations, while only 4 percent thought it was the Jews who were pulling the strings.

In contrast to the United States, where Jewish influence is considered to be concentrated in certain areas [journalism, film, international banking (cf. Martire and Clark 1982, 19)], West Germans assessed the influence of Jews in their country as relatively weak, believing their influence to be greater internationally.[25]

Even the negative stereotypes of the tricky, unreliable businessman and the aggressive, arrogant, dominating Jew, as well as the positive stereotype of Jews as sustainers of culture, are expressed more concretely, and find relatively strong acceptance, in U.S. surveys. In the Federal Republic of Germany, these stereotypical traits are still recognizable to some extent, though they are starting to become increasingly abstract, lacking any content or experiential context. The fading of stereotypes and the process of dealing with prejudice against Jews at a societal level, both of which have taken place in West Germany, have led to a generally decreasing tendency to stereotype Jews, particularly among the younger generations.

The positive impact of social efforts to break down prejudice in the Federal Republic of Germany is becoming visible, in comparison to

Austria and the countries of Eastern Europe, which have only small Jewish minorities. The image of Jews in Poland, Hungary, Romania, and to a lesser extent Czechoslovakia, was still characterized in 1973 through 1974 by images of aggression and the desire to dominate [30 percent to 40 percent agreement (cf. Radio Free Europe 1980, 6; see for data from the early 1990s Cohen and Golub 1991)].[26] The IfD international comparison showed that anti-Jewish stereotypes were retained more strongly in Austria than in West Germany [IfD 1986, table 25 (on developments with respect to the process of coming to terms with the past in Austria, cf. Pelinka and Weinzierl 1987)].

German Autostereotype and Jewish Heterostereotype

One method of assessing the significance of the image a particular group has of others is by comparing it with the group's image of itself. A careful analysis of national prejudice conducted in 1951 by Sodhi and Bergius find similarities with the German auto-stereotype in the characterization of Jews as good scientists and doctors (whereby the picture of "German Jews" might have predominated in this case over that of "Eastern European Jews") and in the description of intelligence, talent for languages, industriousness, and family ties. The great difference between the German self-image and their image of Jews became apparent in particular with respect to characteristics assigned exclusively to one of the two groups.

While Germans have a picture of themselves as an industrious, reliable, emotional, and highly civilized people, they characterize Jews primarily through their negatively valued business activities. Some traits emerge as direct opposites. The German characterization of Jews falls into the categories of negatively viewed ethical behavior, economics, talent, and attitude toward their own group or homeland. In describing themselves, Germans prefer the categories of positively viewed ethical behavior, desire and achievement, level of culture, artistic endeavor and talent (cf. Sodhi and Bergius 1953, 57–59).

We chose a different method in order to determine the differences between the German self-image and their image of others. For each of the given characteristics, we measured the difference in agreement by Germans regarding each of the two groups. Three different complexes emerged: (1) character traits which were often attributed to one's own

TABLE 4.4
Characteristics Attributed Exclusively either to Jews or Germans

Jews	Germans
Hooked nose	Sense of duty
Usurer	Thorough
Crafty	Reliable
Greedy	Brave
Feeling of solidarity	Animal lovers
Shrewd	Poets and Philosophers
Unsoldierlike*	Militaristic
Without a homeland	Lovers of their homeland*
Exploiter	Respectable
Materialistic	Idealists
Racially conscious*	Overrate everything foreign
	Sustainer of culture
	Bureaucratic
	Involvement in clubs, groups
	Show endurance
	Comradely
	Pleasant, easy-going
	sentimental

Source: Sodhi and Bergius 1953, 37 and 41.
* Each of these characteristics is nonexclusive.

group, but rarely to the foreign group; (2) an area of overlap, in which the same characteristics were applied to the same extent to both groups; and (3) traits which were more often attributed to the foreign group than to one's own group.

Germans and Jews were assessed as similar with respect to business acumen and the ability to push through their ideas at all costs, even to the point of ruthlessness. With respect to the dominant characteristics of the German self-image—that is, order, industriousness, honesty, and national pride—a major difference can be observed in their use to characterize Jews.[27] These traits are attributed to Jews to a much lesser degree. The characteristics that supposedly distinguish Jews from Germans the most are those describing Jews as a shrewd, oversensitive group that sticks together. The comparison shows characteristic differences, whereby some

TABLE 4.5
Autostereotype versus Heterostereotype

1st Group:	Orderly/clean	+67
	Sense of duty	+47
	Arrogant	+39
	Industrious	+33
	Ambitious	+33
	Loyal	+29
	Honest	+23
	Power-hungry	+12
2nd Group:	Brave	+7
	Ruthless	+5
	Successful in business	-4
	Modest	-4
	Conspiratorial	-8
	Greedy	-9
3rd Group:	Sense of tradition	-13
	Unforgiving	-16
	Artistically talented	-16
	Intelligent	-19
	Oversensitive	-21
	Cunning, shrewd	-39
	Stick together	-65

Source: Pretest—characteristics with less than 10 percent agreement were not taken into consideration.

of the characteristics included in group 3 are part of the anti-Semitic stereotype (cf. Hortzitz 1988). This can be confirmed by evaluating the responses of those tending to express anti-Jewish attitudes (AS), as this group attributes positive traits to Jews less often, and mentions negative ones more often. Tables 4.6 and 4.7 contain the figures for this partial group in comparison to the overall population.

As expected, a very different picture emerges if, instead of describing a stereotypical image of the "Jew," the characteristics are attributed to a Jew whom the interviewee knows personally.

First of all, willingness to make a stereotypical judgment drops dramatically if the person described is known to the interviewee; that is, not

TABLE 4.6
Attribution of Positive and Negative Stereotypes

	Total pop. %	A S %
Sense of tradition	74	55
Unforgiving	35	71
Oversensitive	47	48
Intelligent	66	57
Cunning, shrewd	55	84
Stick together	86	83

Source: Pretest, multiple entries.

only do negative attributes decrease, as could be expected, but even positive ones are mentioned less frequently. "Typically Jewish" group traits (solidarity, sense of tradition, business acumen) lose from fifty to seventy percentage points, while the other individual characteristics "intelligent," "artistically talented," and "industrious," which also score rather highly, are the most important ones in assessing Jews personally known to the interviewee. Typically "German virtues" (honesty, loyalty, orderliness, modesty) maintain their level of agreement. Aside from the two ambivalent stereotypes "ambitious" and "(over)sensitive," which are attributed to Jews to approximately the same degree by the average population and by people tending to have either anti-Jewish or pro-Jewish attitudes, no clearly negative characteristics find more than 2 percent acceptance (exception: cunning/ shrewd = 8 percent). The assessments of those tending to have anti-Jewish attitudes deviates much less from that of the overall population if they know a Jew personally. The greatest difference can be seen in the clearly lower assignment of "German virtues" and in the higher agreement to economics-related negative stereotypes. Even the attributes rejuvenated by the Nazis, that is, "arrogant" and "unforgiving," have values of 17 percent and 10 percent, respectively, which is considerably above the average for the overall population. It can be shown for the population as a whole that the negative picture of Jews was not derived from descriptions of Jews the interviewees knew from personal experience; rather, the general Jewish stereotype was formed independently, evolving out of the anti-Semitic tradition. Anti-Semites are somewhat more favorable in their judgment of Jews they

TABLE 4.7
Autostereotype/Heterostereotype by Group

Characteristics	Self-image			Image of Jews					
	tot. pop.	AS*	PJ*	tot. pop. +		AS*		PJ*	
	%	%	%	%	%	%	%	%	%
orderly, clean	88	97	91	20	(28)	11	(22)	38	(32)
industrious	88	94	86	46	(31)	33	(28)	73	(42)
sense of duty	83	93	86	29	(25)	10	(18)	47	(31)
successful in business	74	76	77	75	(25)	86	(37)	83	(29)
sense of tradition	61	56	51	65	(16)	55	(16)	84	(23)
brave	49	85	43	34	(11)	31	(6)	60	(15)
intelligent, smart	47	75	39	49	(39)	57	(33)	75	(49)
loyal	44	59	35	11	(15)	5	(7)	23	(23)
honest	38	60	26	11	(27)	—	(7)	23	(37)
artistically talented	30	46	31	39	(30)	34	(17)	70	(38)
stick together	21	26	13	70	(14)	83	(15)	83	(20)
ambitious	87	90	88	49	(28)	53	(34)	64	(28)
arrogant	56	25	68	15	(2)	37	(17)	10	(2)
power-hungry	28	12	32	19	(—)	56	(7)	9	(2)
oversensitive	26	20	26	32	(12)	48	(19)	47	(24)
greedy and avaricious	24	11	31	28	(2)	78	(17)	17	(—)
ruthless	21	13	30	15	(2)	50	(7)	13	(2)
stingy	19	5	26	20	(2)	48	(7)	16	(2)
unforgiving	19	11	29	26	(1)	71	(10)	14	(2)
crafty, shrewd	16	10	11	42	(8)	84	(24)	38	(8)
cowardly	9	2	7	4	(—)	13	(4)	2	(—)
false, conniving	7	1	5	9	(—)	41	(6)	2	(—)
destructive, subverive	4	5	8	4	(—)	25	(2)	2	(—)
conspiratorial	3	1	1	11	(—)	39	(7)	6	(—)

* AS = those tending toward anti-Jewish attitudes   * PJ = those tending toward pro-Jewish attitudes
( ) = those with Jews in their circle of acquaintances—pretest   + = main survey
Source: pretest and main survey

know, but the anti-Jewish stereotype influences their personal experiences to a very great degree. This means that central complexes of prejudice come into play even with respect to individual Jews known to the person, whereas the population as a whole does not usually make this projection.

Notes

1. It is estimated that an additional 25,000 who are not registered members of any Jewish community live in Germany. In response to our question (no. 22) on the number of Jews living in the Federal Republic of Germany, only 6 percent of the population were within range of the correct answer. Another 70 percent could not offer any answer at all. The assumption that anti-Semites systematically overestimate the number of Jews, which would correspond to their worldview, was not supported by our data.

2. In the study by Glock and Stark, 75 percent of those interviewed claimed to have invited Jews into their homes. This figure seemed improbable to the authors: "If 75 percent of our sample have had Jews in their home, one suspects that Jews in the San Francisco Bay Area would have few opportunities for a quiet evening at home" (1966, 156).

3. Cf. Frank Stern on the postwar situation, in which many Germans rediscovered their Jewish "friends and acquaintances" (1992, chap. 6). Even in the 1954 EMNID study, the authors were struck by the large share of people who claimed to know one or more Jews well (30 percent of the interviewees). As an explanation of this figure, they suggested that many people answered yes to the question, even if they were only very indirectly acquainted with Jews. The fact that these acquaintances were almost entirely judged positively (two-thirds, as compared to 5 percent who considered the personal relationship to be a bad one), confirms Frank Stern's statement. Personal contact to Jews was considered by many to be a way of certifying their anti-Nazi, nonprejudiced attitudes (EMNID 1954, 49ff.).

4. In response to the question in the pretest "Are there any Jews in your circle of acquaintances?" 34 percent of those considered to have pro-Jewish attitudes answered affirmatively; only 10 percent of those with anti-Jewish attitudes answered in this way.

5. Galtung empirically studied this correlation between anti-Jewish attitudes and the desire to recognize a Jew as such. He concluded that "for the negatives (i.e., those with anti-Jewish attitudes), 'no way' of identifying the group which one endows with so many undesirable characteristics means to increase the danger; 'they may be sneaking in on you without any way of telling before it is too late.' The belief in clear and visible characteristics can reduce at least this fear" (1960, 62).

6. In her Austrian survey, Hilde Weiss also found this negative interest among anti-Semites in identifying a Jew as such. Of all Austrians questioned, 19.8 percent agreed with the following statement: "Children should be raised to be able to identify a Jew; it could prove very useful in life" (1984, 47ff.). In a factor analysis, this very emotionally charged statement loaded onto the "general anti-Semitism" factor (51).

7. People with anti-Jewish attitudes generally orient themselves more according to a person's appearance in judging his or her national identity. Of those with anti-

Jewish attitudes who were questioned, 20 percent claimed to be able to identify a Frenchman by appearance, while only 10 percent of the overall population made this claim (pretest).

8. In terms of both intensity of prejudice (measured by means of the degree of concurrence in the assessments made by the interviewees), in which Jews were second to Germans, and the number of characteristics appearing in the list and their contrast to judgments about other national groups, Jews always ranked very high [3.5 among the national groups (cf. Sodhi and Bergius 1953, 64ff.)].

9. The extent to which the Nazi persecution of the Jews shaped the "image of Jews" after the war can be seen in the nexus with the word "Jew" measured in the 1954 EMNID survey. Most imaginations had to do with aspects of persecution and the Nazi period, pity, understanding, and guilt. Aside from the relatively common connections to trade and business, the racist stereotype of Jews and the religion were mentioned by only a very few (EMNID 1954, 2ff., and 56). The image of the persecuted Jew, which obviously represents an important dimension of how Jews are perceived by their environment since the Holocaust, has to our knowledge not been included in any list of stereotypical prejudice toward Jews. This is primarily due to the fact that lists of characteristics too strongly retained traditional, negative typologies.

10. In the pretest, interviewees were asked to mark the qualities common to Germans. The most common (over 50 percent) responses were orderly/clean, industrious, ambitious, possessing a sense of duty, home-loving, successful in business, possessing a sense of tradition, arrogant, and brave.

11. Christianity disparaged Judaism as a religion of revenge. Certain Biblical passages were referred to as "proof," such as "an eye for an eye" and "Vengeance is mine, sayeth the Lord." This interpretation continues to be espoused by Christian bible scholars, who see the decisive difference between the "Old" and "New" Testaments as the supposed principle of restitution in kind, and distinguish the Jewish religion of "renewed vengeance" from the Christian faith, which is characterized by brotherly love and the renunciation of vengeance (Vetter 1989, 13).

12. The correlations between the "power-hungry" stereotype and anti-Israel statements such as "a state that stops at nothing" (question 14/8), "A country that simply does not want peace" (question 14/18) and "They start wars" (question 14/19) are significant, though not excessively high, with values of .25, .23, and .30, respectively. This means Israel's politics represent only one source of this anti-Jewish stereotype.

13. This image is also widespread in the United States. It combines positive traits ["Jews have a strong faith in God) 71 percent agreement)] and negative accusations ["Jews stick together too much" (40 percent agreement); "Jews don't care what happens to anyone but their own kind" (16 percent agreement; cf. Martire and Clark 1982, 17)]. The assumption that Jews are clannish becomes more concrete with respect to the labor market in the following opinion: "Jewish employers go out of their way to hire Jews" (37 percent agreement).

14. In the 1951 study by Sodhi and Bergius, from a list of fourteen nations, "feelings of solidarity" were attributed exclusively to Jews by 65 percent of those questioned. A "sense of family" was also seen as a striking quality of Jews, though this was shared with other peoples—the Chinese, the Germans, and the British (1953, 41).

15. In the pretest, 51 percent of the interviewees felt there was such a thing as "World Jewry," 18 percent did not believe there was such a thing, and 31 percent answered "don't know."

16. On the other hand, those who considered Jews "cowardly" did not judge the achievements of the Israeli army positively, and tended to accuse Israel of ruthless politics.

17. In 1988, the Wickert Institute even found 88 percent agreement with the following statement: "Jews are clever businesspeople." They found no differences according to age (*Wiener* 1988).

18. The latter qualities were typically attributed to Americans and the British, in addition to Jews. With respect to their sense of business, they were identified with capitalism and plutocracy.

19. The Six-Day War of 1967 marked a turning point here. Germans suddenly discovered that Israelis were courageous, brave, industrious, and reliable; these characteristics were sometimes compared with highly valued German character traits. A preliminary examination of daily newspapers from the time (*Die Welt, FAZ, Bild,* and the Berlin *Tagesspiegel*) supports this impression. This fundamental shift in attitudes can apparently also be identified in letters to Ben-Natan, then Israeli ambassador in Bonn (cf. Deligdisch 1974, 138f.).

20. To this day, a "hooked nose" is the main characteristic mentioned for a "typically Jewish" appearance. At 46 percent, this trait was far ahead of the skullcap [yarmulke (15 percent)] and the traditional side curls [peyes (14 percent)]. The "Jewish hooked nose" today appears to be considered common knowledge, without necessarily having a racist, discriminatory connotation (pretest). Of those questioned, 24 percent could name no traits and 9 percent stated that there were no typically Jewish characteristics.

21. The image held by the oldest age group deviates from the others insofar as they distinguish between a middle-class picture of Jews and one of Israelis, in which the qualities of soldiers and settlers are of foremost importance (brave, dutiful, industrious, radical).

22. In their 1951 study, Sodhi, Bergius, and Holzkamp found no interpretable differences between men and women, except for the fact that men agreed more in their assessment of Jews than women did. The authors interpreted this as a sign that men were psychologically "closer" to Jews than women, for whom Jews were of more peripheral interest (1956, 288). In his nonrepresentative 1960 study, Schönbach also found that men and women expressed similar attitudes toward Jews (cited in Galtung 1960, 4).

23. According to a telephone survey commissioned by the "France Inter" broadcasting station, cited in *Frankfurter Allgemeine Zeitung,* 18 May 1990. The figure for May, 1990 must be seen in light of the nationwide outrage (96 percent of those questioned were shocked) at the desecration of a body buried in the Jewish cemetery in Carpentras, which occurred several days prior to the survey.

24. In addition to Jews, the following groups were listed: Protestant and Catholic clergy, bankers and major industrialists, farmers' organizations, unions, the Freemasons, and exiles' organizations.

25. In the comparative 1986 survey, the following picture was obtained:

"Jews have a great deal of influence on politics in this country."

	U.S.	France	Austria	Germany
Agreement	55 %	37 %	32 %	26 %

Source: IfD 1986, table 25.

26. The 1973–74 survey of visitors from these countries was by no means representative. This is a methodological shortcoming that could not be entirely compen-
sated for, even by weighting over- and underrepresented groups. Today we have
more reliable data from the surveys done by the American Jewish Committee in
these countries in the early 1990s (Cohen and Golub 1991; Gudkov and Levinson
1992).

27. Cf. the study by Panahi (1980, 118) on the self-image of Germans in 1978,
which obtained similarly high figures and a similar order of comparable character traits (hard working, intelligent, conceited, domineering, brave). EMNID
obtained the following striking character traits in the German self-image in 1961:
industriousness, conscientiousness, reliability, and assiduity (up to 47 percent
agreement), followed after a considerable gap by punctuality, thrift, loyalty, and
intelligence. The major negative character traits in the German self-image were
stubbornness, conceit, selfishness, thoughtlessness, and militarism (*EMNID-
Information*, No. 32, 1961).

5

Emotional Rejection of and Social Distance from Jews

Agreement with anti-Jewish stereotypes says little about the extent to which these judgments are emotionally significant to the person involved. The analysis must therefore be expanded, with the stereotypical image of the Jew seen in relationship to emotional and social attitudes toward Jews.

Emotional Rejection

We asked about emotional attitudes in two ways. First, we used a word preference test that measured the subjects' emotional response to key notions in the survey field (question 5). In evaluating the results, we found that the scale could be interpreted in isolation, but that its results could not always easily be related to other indicators of anti-Semitism and social distance toward Jews. Apparently, dislike of a notion (such as race or Talmud) provides only limited evidence of dislike of those referred to by the notion, especially when the meaning of the word is unclear to many of those questioned (such as Talmud).[1] An additional indicator was targeted at subjective assessments of the subject's own emotional attitude toward Jews. The question whether the subject counted him or herself as someone "who does not like Jews" was intended to allow subjects to categorize themselves as consciously hostile to Jews (see table 5.1). Of those questioned, 5.8 percent classed themselves as exhibiting emotional rejection of Jews. This self-categorization proved to be the best single indicator of anti-Semitism.[2] Those who classed themselves in this way were disproportionately over sixty years old, male rather than female (6.6 percent versus 5 percent), less educated, and (also related to education) working at unskilled jobs.

125

TABLE 5.1
"I consider myself a person who does not like Jews."

		Age groups							
Total pop.		16–29		30–44		45–59		60 and older	
%	N	%	N	%	N	%	N	%	N
5.8	122	3.0	18	3.2	17	5.2	26	11.8	61

N = 2102

In historical comparison, there has been a sharp drop in the number of Germans who describe themselves as anti-Jewish, as well as a major change in their age distribution. The 1949 IfD survey included a direct question on emotional attitude toward Jews (see table 5.2).

Over the years, there has been a gradual decline in emotional rejection of Jews in Germany, a trend that stagnated mainly in the early post-war years.[3] In its 1954 study, EMNID used an associative question ("What do you think of when you hear the word 'Jew'?") to ascertain "spontaneous and unreflected" attitudes, emotions and opinions on "the" Jews. One in four of those questioned was found to feel "a more or less strongly negative emotional aversion," which seemed to have been heavily influenced by Nazi propaganda (EMNID 1954, III and 1ff).[4] The study contained no evaluation by age for this question. In a simultaneous "special survey" of schoolchildren and adolescents, university students, and teachers, age distribution can be roughly established. College students clearly expressed a stronger dislike than teachers and school-age youths (EMNID 1954, 56). Among the younger group, the smaller degree of antipathy probably resulted from changed socialization in a political culture in

TABLE 5.2
"What is your general attitude toward Jews?"

		Age groups			
	Total pop.	Under 30	30–50	50–65	65+
Openly anti-Semitic	10	11	11	10	7
Emotional Rejection	13	15	12	15	10
Reserved	15	16	16	13	10

Source: IfD 1949, 39.

FIGURE 5.1
Word Preference Test: Like-Dislike of Foreign Groups

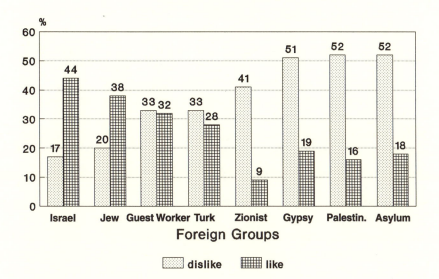

which anti-Semitic propaganda had been discredited as immoral and undemocratic.

The results of these early surveys were confirmed by studies by youth sociologists indicating that young people had been most influenced by Nazi ideology and were most likely to acquire and keep anti-democratic, authoritarian, and anti-Semitic views (cf. Zinnecker 1985, 322ff.). Those who were twenty to thirty years old then are now over sixty. The relatively minor decline in emotional rejection in this age group indicates how difficult it is to change attitudes acquired and emotionally anchored in the course of a lifetime.[5] This generation experienced Nazism while in a formative, impressionable phase. Given the contrasting fact that of today's younger generation, only 3 percent reject Jews emotionally, it can be established as an intermediate finding that liberal, democratic models and education that encourages tolerance and rational conflict-solving have largely succeeded in preventing the emergence of anti-Jewish feelings. On the other hand, forty years lived in a democratic state have had only a partial educational effect on the older generation. Approximately half of the members of this generation who were anti-Semites in 1949 had discarded their anti-Jewish feelings.[6]

The infrequency of self-classification as "emotional anti-Semite" contrasts with "objective" measurements using other indicators. In a word preference test,[7] 20 percent disliked the word "Jew" (see figure 5.1). This figure can best be understood in comparison with the like-dislike figures for other groups and ideologies. Thus, the words "Jew" and "Israel" were classed as clearly more likeable and less unpleasant than the words for other foreign groups.

This trend held across all age groups, although the word "Jew" was disliked twice as frequently by those over sixty (30 percent) than by the sixteen to forty-four age group (15 percent). The generation gap was narrower for "Israel," at 24 percent and 14 percent, respectively. As already observed for subjective emotional rejection of Jews, antipathy toward Jews has decreased only slightly in the older generation since 1961. Then, 32 percent of those questioned answered "true" to the statement, "In my opinion, the word 'Jew' still sounds bad" [47 percent responded with "false" (IfD vol. 3, 228)].

The absolute figures and the age structure of the word preference test with respect to the word "Jew" were largely confirmed by the 1989 EMNID survey. Those questioned were asked for like-dislike ratings for particular groups. Eighteen percent disliked "Jews living in Germany" [47 percent liked them, and 33 percent were neutral (EMNID 1989, table 61)]—15 percent of the eighteen through forty-four-year-olds, and 24 percent of the over-sixty-year-olds. There has been a social learning process in regard to Jews living in Germany, as shown by the clearly more positive view of them compared with all other ethnic minorities in Germany, as well as by the fact that "German Jews" were liked more than "Jews living in Israel," who were judged approximately 6 percent more negatively by all age groups. The image of Israelis was particularly distinct from that of Jews among younger age groups. More empathy was felt with "German Jews," perhaps because they were seen as victims of the Nazi regime, than with Israeli Jews, who were seen more negatively as a result of Israeli policies in the occupied territories. This differential with respect to feelings toward "German Jews" and Israelis in 1989 was probably the result of Israel's loss of support after the beginning of the Intifada in December, 1987; in our October, 1987 word preference test, "Israel" continued to be liked more than "Jews."

Historically, attitudes toward Jews in the Federal Republic have been closely tied to views of Nazism. That is, one can make indirect statements on emotional attitudes toward Jews by measuring like or dislike of "persecutors of Jews." Key phrases such as "Third Reich," "anti-Semite," and "fanatic" were disliked the most (60 percent to 84 percent) and liked the least (around 5 percent) of all items on the list. Of course, the far-reaching discreditation of Nazism, which included anti-Semitism as one of its central ideological elements, does not imply a transformation into "philo-Semitism." It does, however, form a cognitive and emotional barrier against acceptance of anti-Semitic views, greatly impeding attempts to follow in the footsteps of Nazi anti-Semitism or other forms of hostility toward Jews. In contrast, "secondary anti-Semitism" not directly connected with the Third Reich, but rather with the problem of "dealing with it," meets with greater emotional acceptance. For key phrases in this complex, such as "reparations" and "coming to terms with the past," the public is divided into two main camps: 36 percent and 42 percent, respectively, dislike these words, while 38 percent and 28 percent, respectively, like them. Similarly, we find an emotional debate between these two camps throughout the history of the Federal Republic of Germany, culminating in the "historians' debate" (*Historikerstreit*). If we correlate dislike of Jews with dislike of "reparations" and "coming to terms with the past," we find that rejection correlates twice as highly with rejection of Jews as for those who feel no antipathy toward these words. Emotional rejection of attempts to deal with the Nazi past ("end the debate" mentality) thus seems to act as a good basis for anti-Semitism.[8] In comparison, groups that liked or disliked the "Third Reich" did not differ as much in their rejection of Jews (on the relationship between attitudes toward coming to terms with the past and anti-Semitism, cf. chap. 10).

Social Distance

To measure social distance, the distance scale developed in 1925 by Emory Bogardus is usually used.[9] We did not use this scale because the intervals between the distances are not equal, and it is multidimensional (cf. criticism by Sallen 1977, 137f.). Instead, we developed our own social distance questions, enabling us to compare distance toward Jews with distance toward other groups. In this way, it was possible to investigate whether hostility to Jews is an aspect of general xenophobia, or whether it is motivated by other forces.[10]

TABLE 5.3

"Suppose there was a football game between Germany and Israel, and the spectators included German Jews. Whom do you think they would cross their fingers for, who would they root for?"

	Total pop.	Anti-Jewish attitudes	Pro-Jewish
Germany	47	13	24
Israel	40	66	35
Undecided	13	21	41
Total N=344	100 %	100 %	100 %
	(N=121)	(N=95)	(N=128)

We expanded this complex of issues by adding a question on Jews' national loyalties. Since the eighteenth century, the assumption of strong Jewish loyalties (cf. the high level of agreement to the stereotype "Jews stick together") has led to accusations that Jews form a "nation within a nation" or "state within a state" (cf. Katz 1982, 124ff.). Today, a new variant of this distrust is observable, involving the state of Israel and the strong sense of attachment to this state among Jews living outside Israel. In U.S. studies, the question of the "divided loyalties" of American Jews to the United States and Israel has proved to be a point of conflict in which Jews are suspected of lacking sufficient attachment to the U.S.[11] We included a question in the pretest (see table 5.3) that created a hypothetical situation requiring a decision.

All three groups assumed relatively little identification with the German team. Those with anti-Jewish tendencies, themselves feeling greater social and emotional distance from Jews, suspected Jews of feeling a similar distance toward the German team.[12] Like the very high agreement to the stereotype "Jews stick together" in the main survey (70 percent), these results indicate the persistence of a traditional anti-Jewish accusation, namely, that Jews' loyalty to other Jews is stronger than their identification with the country in which they live.[13] The question then arises whether this suspicion leads people to refuse to recognize German Jews as Germans, to deny them nationality (see table 5.4).

Although only a small percentage of those questioned believed that German Jews would identify with the German team in an international sports competition, two thirds did not deny them their German nationality. The fact that 20 percent saw them more as Jews or Israelis than as

TABLE 5.4
"What do you think about the following: Would you consider a Jew born and raised in Germany more a German or more a Jew?"

| | Total pop. | Age groups | | | |
| | | 16–29 | 30–44 | 45–59 | 60+ |
	%	%	%	%	%
More a German	65	72	69	66	52
More a Jew	20	13	16	20	33
Undecided	15	16	15	14	15
Total	**100**	**100**	**100**	**100**	**100**

N = 2102

Germans in the national sense, while 15 percent were undecided, shows that it cannot be taken for granted today that Jews born in Germany will be acknowledged as Germans. But this need not result per se from anti-Semitic sentiment; it could also signify sympathy with the difficulties Jews experience in feeling German since the Third Reich. However, when we examine the extent to which denial of nationality is connected with anti-Semitism, anti-Jewish motives prove to be the main basis for this judgment.

Of those classified as not anti-Semitic (according to SAS), only a few viewed a Jew living in Germany as first and foremost a Jew, while two-thirds of the anti-Semites felt this way.[14] The strong generational influence (cf. table 5.4) supports this interpretation; only half of those over sixty considered a Jew born in Germany to be a German, while over two-thirds of the sixteen to fifty-nine-year-olds did the same. Of the latter, only 13 percent would categorize a German Jew as a Jew rather than a German, while a third of the older generation would do so.[15]

TABLE 5.5
Anti-Semitism (SAS): Is a German Jew more a German or more a Jew?

	More a German	More a Jew	Undecided
Not anti-Semitic	70.3 %	14.4 %	15.5 %
Anti-Semitic	24.4 %	64.3 %	12.3 %
Total	**64.8 %**	**20.2 %**	**15.0 %**

FIGURE 5.2
Identification and Desire for Jewish Emigration

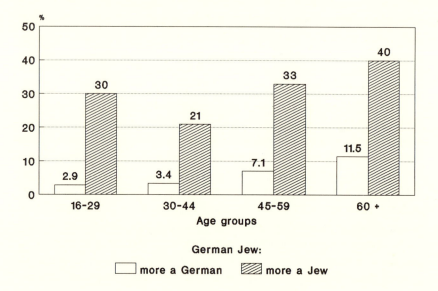

German Jew:
☐ more a German   ▨ more a Jew

Those who deny German citizenship to Jews do not necessarily reject the idea of living with them. There was very little support for this strong form of creating social distance, for example in a preference for emigration or prohibition on immigration or return by Jews. The statement "For us Germans it would be best if all Jews would go to Israel" (question 10) was answered "yes" with by 13 percent, 67 percent said "no," and 20 percent were undecided. This distance also increased markedly with increasing age (7 percent of those sixteen to twenty-nine, but 24 percent of those over sixty agreed). Agreement with an explicit prohibition on immigration or return to Germany for Jews was even lower, at 6 percent (question 16). This difference between desire for emigration and prohibition on immigration is partly the result of the fact that the first question was formulated to suggest voluntary emigration to Israel and represented an abstract opinion, while the second involved a concrete political demand. Only a small group agreed to such demands (cf. chap. 6). Only one-third of those who expressed a desire for Jewish emigration also supported a prohibition on immigration or return to Germany.

The fact that 20 percent of the main survey (see table 5.4 for the age distribution) considered a Jew born and raised in Germany to be more a Jew than a German does not imply any doubts about his or her German citizenship and national reliability.[16] The questions on "desire for emigration" (question 10) and "immigration prohibition" (question 16) allow examination of whether identification as a Jew is coupled with such discrimination.

The evaluation shows that a wish for Jews to go to Israel is significantly linked with identification as a Jew. When this identification was made, agreement to Jewish emigration was much higher than when they were considered Germans. The fact that identification as Jews need not coincide fully with an inclination to discriminate was shown by the responses of the thirty to forty-four-year-olds. They identified German Jews as Jews more frequently than did the sixteen to twenty-nine-year-olds, but were still less likely to want them to emigrate to Israel. Among the thirty to forty-four-year-olds, identification as Jews coincided in only 21 percent of all cases with a desire to discriminate (average: 35 percent). Among those over forty-five, desire for Jewish emigration and identification as Jews rose simultaneously with age. Among those seventy-one to seventy-nine years of age, 30 percent called for emigration, and 36 percent saw a German Jew as more Jewish than German. Among the oldest interviewees, identification of German Jews as Jews was seen as a negative characteristic; 40 percent of those who made this identification also wanted all Jews to emigrate to Israel. Their social distance from Jews was so strong that even among those who considered German Jews to be Germans, 11.5 percent still wanted them to emigrate.

Whereas among younger people, identification of German Jews as Jews tended not to have consequences, and seemed less important to the group in general (high rate of nonresponse—over 20 percent), intermediate age groups showed a slightly philo-Semitic tendency. Those over sixty had definite opinions (lowest rate of nonresponse—under 10 percent), linked with negative views.

In a second step of the evaluation, we linked support of a prohibition on *immigration* for Jews with identification of German Jews as Jews. The trend here was similar. Identification of German Jews as German very rarely coincided with support for a prohibition on immigration; for identification as a Jew, this was much more frequent. The age groups up to forty-four years old had a disproportionately low rate of agreement; from forty-five years of age upward, agreement rose discontinuously, reaching a maximum of approximately 14 percent among sixty-five-year-olds.

In general, it can be said that identification of a Jew born and raised in Germany as a German provides him or her more protection from discrimination. Identification of this person as a Jew is strongly connected with discrimination in the minds of older people (up to 50 percent).

Measuring social distance from a minority that is hardly perceptible due to its small size and level of integration in German society has a strongly hypothetical quality. This greatly distinguishes Germany and Austria from France and the United States,[17] where everyday contact is a normal experience.[18] While earlier surveys on social distance in Germany could still take advantage of memories of relatively close social contact (memories of personal acquaintances, the presence of Jewish businesses, etc.), these questions disappear as historical distance increases—they have become implausible for younger generations. Thus, very little data is available with which to analyze the development of social distance; in addition, variations in the wording of the questions makes it difficult to compare them.

An international comparison, for which some data is available, faces the aforementioned problem that Jews are a large, visible minority in places such as France and the United States, so that the problem of social distance affects daily life in a very different fashion than in Germany or Austria.

There has been a definite decrease in emotional rejection and social distance from Jews, as shown by surveys on various dimensions of distance in the last four decades. This development occurred in Germany simultaneously with similar trends in other Western countries.[19]

In the following, we will discuss the survey data for various dimensions of distance—from rejection of significant social contacts, usually measured through marriage, to geographic isolation from an entire group.

Reservations about the most intimate contact, marriage to a Jewish spouse, have decreased most sharply. Although the questions were formulated differently (in 1949, 1961, and 1969, a question was asked about the conceivability of one's own marriage; in 1954, 1968, 1986, and 1987, the question involved reservations about marriage between a Jewish and a non-Jewish partner; and in 1988, it concerned objections to such a

TABLE 5.6
Marriage to a Jewish Partner

	1949	1954	1961	1968	1969	1986	1987	1988
Yes	8	72	14	53		79*		
No	70	25	54	29	29	11	9	26
Undecided	22		3	32	18			12
	100	100	100	100		100		

Source: IfD 1949, 1986, 1987. EMNID 1954, EMNID-Info 6, 1968; Weil 1987; Wickert 1988.
* Pretest, not representative

marriage by one's own child), the trend appears unmistakable.[20] The unusually positive figures in the 1954 survey resulted, first of all, from the romantic formulation of the question ("Two young people are in love; one is Jewish. Do you believe they can have a happy marriage?"). Secondly, unlike the 1949 and 1961 surveys, the question did not ask about one's own willingness to enter such a marriage (see table 5.6).

Two reasons can be identified for a disapproval of mixed marriage. Those who did not believe in 1954 that a happy marriage was possible between a Jew and a non-Jew justified their response on both religious and racist grounds. In the special survey of teachers, school-age youngsters, and college students, the same generational effect was apparent as was found in other surveys. While teachers more frequently gave religious reasons, school-age youngsters, and especially college students, more often had racist reservations (EMNID 1954, 14 and 60).[21] In 1961, 73 percent of all those questioned still considered Jews "a different race" (IfD vol. 3, 214), and in 1974, Silbermann still found 31 percent racially anti-Semitic (cf. 1982, 45; Sallen 1977, 280); nevertheless, both religious and racist reservations against marriage to Jews have decreased over the years.[22]

To better assess social distance in regard to marriage to Jews, we used surveys that simultaneously asked about rejection of marriage to members of other peoples, races, or religions. In 1968, 18 percent expressed disapproval of marriage between members of the two major Christian denominations, 29 percent of marriage between Jews and non-Jews, and 47 percent of marriage between "whites and non-whites" (EMNID-Info 6 and 11/12 1968). Figures for 1986 showed that marriage to a Jew met with significantly lower disapproval (11 percent) than marriage to an

TABLE 5.7
Rejection of a Jewish Neighbor/Co-Worker (in percent)

1975	1981	1986	1987	1992	1994
16	14	22	11	7	22

Source: IfD 1976, 1983, 1986, 1987 Pretest; Wickert 1988; IfD 1992; Gollup 1994.

Arab (62 percent disapproval), a black person (46 percent), a Turk (42 percent), or a British person [15 percent (IfD 1986, table 23)]. With the disappearance of racially grounded reservations, Jews have come to be considered part of secularized Western European-American culture, accepted with few problems as marriage partners. In contrast to Islam (cf. the strong disapproval of Arabs and Turks), the Jewish religion no longer seems to be grounds for strong reservations.

The position of women in the Islamic religion was most likely responsible for the fact that those questioned so often expected marriage to a Muslim to fail. Ethnic and racial differences were the grounds for the strong disapproval of marriage to a black partner.

Let us now compare West German developments with those in Austria, France, and the United States. In Austria, the "marriage question" was posed only four times, starting in 1968. The trend here seems similar to that in Germany, though to a greater extent: in 1968, 40 percent opposed marriage to a Jew, in 1969, 36 percent had reservations, in 1973 the figure was 35 percent, and in 1980, 23 percent would try to prevent their child from marrying a Jew (EMNID-Info 6/1968; Marin 1976, table 1; Weiss 1984, table 10/2). In France, disapproval had already begun to decrease by the late 1960s, from 37 percent to 16 percent, and remained at this level until the end of the 1970s (EMNID-Info 6/1968; Weil 1987, 177). No clear trend can be established for the United States (Weil, ibid.). Overall, disapproval was above the level of the European countries surveyed [1981: 43 percent (Martire and Clark 1982, 28)].[23]

At first glance, it may seem surprising that in 1986, 89 percent of all Germans would have had no objections to a Jewish spouse, but in 1987 only 49 percent would "like to have Jews in (their) own circle of friends." The difference can be explained by the contrasting purposes of the two questions. The first looked at whether the person questioned actually discriminated, while the second asked whether he or she actively desired Jewish friends. The 89 percent who did not disapprove of marriage to

FIGURE 5.3
Rejection of Ethnic Minorities

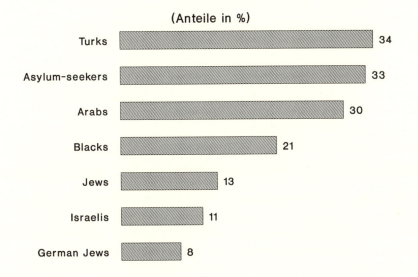

(Anteile in %)

Turks	34
Asylum-seekers	33
Arabs	30
Blacks	21
Jews	13
Israelis	11
German Jews	8

Jews did not express a desire for a Jewish spouse, but merely general, nonbinding acceptance. The question that has often been posed since 1974 on acceptance of Jews in one's circle of friends showed a gradual rise in acceptance of social contact up to 1987: from 32 percent to 41 percent between 1975 and 1981, reaching 49 percent in 1987 (Weil 1987, 177; IfD vol. 6, vol. 8, 1987). We lack comparable data on this question from international studies.

An intermediate social distance from a group is often measured through group members' acceptance as neighbors and co-workers. For this area our data only extended back to 1975, and indicated a relatively stable, low level of disapproval (cf. table 5.7).

Rejection of closer contact ("I would not like to have too much to do with Jews/Israelis"), in a question which did not more closely define the type of contact, brought a similar rate of agreement.

Social distance was reduced by the addition of the adjective "German," rejection fell to 8 percent.[24] Rejection of closer contacts could be

TABLE 5.8
Could imagine Jews as neighbors.

	West Germany %	Austria %	France %	U.S. %
Yes	52	37	85	91
No	22	30	10	7
Undecided	26	33	5	2
	100	100	100	100

Source: IfD 1986, table 16.

based on anticipation of problems, and did not necessarily result from anti-Jewish prejudice. Such national identification reduced the social distance from "German" Jews, eliminating any feared language difficulties.

In comparison with all other ethnic groups (cf. figure 5.3), contact to Jews was most rarely rejected (for a more detailed discussion, cf. chap. 8). In drawing an international comparison, these figures indicate ways of dealing with minorities specific to a given country.

A comparative survey of four countries by the IfD in 1986 asked how the population felt about neighborly relations to Jews, Arabs, blacks, and Chinese people (see table 5.8).

In countries with a long liberal tradition of ethnic coexistence, in which Jews form a relatively large segment of the population, neighborly contact was accepted almost across the board. (However, this was also true for the other three groups mentioned.) While marriage partners from one's own group were preferred, professional and social contacts outside ethnic and religious boundaries were considered normal. In Germany, and even more markedly in Austria, ethnic plurality was still felt to be unusual, and close social contact met with disapproval and precariousness.[25] The high percentage of "undecideds," in comparison with the nearly unanimous views of the Americans and French, showed that the situation was still too new for many to have been able to, or want to, take a definite position.

Renate Köcher (IfD 1986, 29) called attention to the fact that the distanced attitude of Germans and Austrians also reflected a lack of direct personal experience. While only 12 percent of the German population and 15 percent of the Austrian population said they "knew Jews personally," the percentage was 35 percent in France and 65 percent in

TABLE 5.9
"Would you say it would be better for Germany if there were no Jews in the country?" (%)

	1952	1956**	1958	1963	1965	1983	1987*	1992
Better	37	26 (29)	22	18	19	9	13	18
No	19	24 (35)	38	40	34	43	67	54
Wouldn't make a difference/ Don't know	44	50 (36)	40	42	47	48	20	28
	100	100	100	100	100	100	100	100

Source: IfD 1986, 23, *1987 slightly altered question: "It would be best for us Germans if all Jews would go to Israel" (**cf. note 26); IfD 1993, IX, 1001.

the United States. An additional evaluation provides confirmation of the contact hypothesis (cf. Bergmann 1988a, 294ff.), that is, the positive correlation between social tolerance and actual, positively perceived social contacts: 11 percent of Germans who knew Jews personally rejected them as neighbors, while 71 percent accepted them in their circle of friends (averages in the total population 22 percent and 52 percent, respectively).

Since Bogardus's study, the question of a group remaining in one's own country has been used as an indicator of great social distance. Since 1952, the IfD has regularly repeated the same question in reference to Jews, so that anti-Semitism researchers have the most dense time series for this dimension of social distance.

The data series clearly shows "anti-Semites" fading away, and growing acceptance of Jews in Germany.[27] First of all, it can be established that a large percentage was undecided or had no opinion. One might suspect that this group possesses an anti-Jewish potential but avoided openly taking a position, resorting instead to this neutral category. A comparison of the two results from 1956 contradicts this assumption. When the possible answer "wouldn't make a difference" was omitted, the percentage of "anti-Semites" increased only slightly (from 26 percent to 29 percent), while the percentage of "philo-Semites" grew from 24 percent to 35 percent. This indicates that, among supporters of Jewish life in Germany, some were less committed or dedicated. Overall, one can expect that the group of those either with no opinion or indifferent is very large.

TABLE 5.10
"Someone recently said that it would be best if all Jews would go to Israel, since that's their country" (in percent).

	West Germany	Austria	France	U.S.
Agree	20	24	17	9
Disagree	56	40	65	87
Undecided	24	36	18	4
Total	**100**	**100**	**100**	**100**

Source: IfD 1986, table 20.

A relatively extreme shift in opinion took place in the 1950s, but did not continue into the early 1960s. Unfortunately, there is no survey data available for the period of political change in the late 1960s and early 1970s, a time that also saw the definitive change in generations, so that we do not know whether the process was continuous or whether the changed climate of opinion led to an abrupt change in attitudes toward Jews. The higher figure of 13 percent measured in 1987 for those who thought the absence of Jews would be better for Germany need not indicate a new trend; it could have resulted from the slight change in the wording of the question. In contrast, the rollback in those with no opinion in favor of the "philo-Semitic position" indicated a continuation of the trend.

A 1986 question that focussed on the Jews' interest in emigration to Israel (see below) received 20 percent agreement (disagreement 56 percent, undecided 24 percent). Apparently, the change of perspective in the formulation of the question caused the higher rate of agreement. It seems one can support settling all Jews in a state of their own without this necessarily being tied to German self-interest or a wish to discriminate against Jews.[28]

Nevertheless, this agreement can be interpreted as doubt with respect to the possibility of smooth neighborly relations between Jews and non-Jews. An international comparison shows that Americans have no sympathy with attempts to resolve the difficulties of group coexistence by sending all Jews to their own country.

In West Germany, and even more so in Austria, this idea met with approval, whereas in France, it was overwhelmingly rejected, and in the United States almost unanimously rejected. As in the question on neighbors, European societies apparently continue to believe in the ideal of a homogeneous nation-state; while for the United States, historically a land of immigrants, a multi-ethnic society is a given. This ideal of homogeneity may explain the following remarkable result: According to the Bogardus scale, keeping alien groups out of one's own country would signal the highest level of social distance, encompassing all other forms of distance. But this theoretically predictable result was not confirmed by our survey. 12,7 percent (N = 266) agreed with the item "It would be better for us Germans if all Jews would go to Israel" (question 10). Of these, a third rejected personal contacts with Jews, thus acting in a "consistent" manner; but two-thirds did not reject such contacts, although they represent a lesser degree of social distance. Rejection of Jews as a group with its own interests and specific domestic and international demands appears to follow from the ideal of a homogeneous nation-state; but this does not entirely determine personal contacts to individual Jews. Conversely, rejection of such personal contacts (N = 214) correlated more closely with the demand for total social distancing (N = 100, or 47 percent). Among people with strongly anti-Jewish attitudes, this distance pattern was even more pronounced: sixty of seventy-four people questioned in this category (that is, 81 percent) agreed with both social distance statements. How can it be that many of those classified as not anti-Semitic felt it would be better not to have Jews in the country, yet did not reject personal contact? Apparently, collective and personal considerations are categorized separately. Coexistence in a collective is judged on the basis of cultural patterns and issues of status, which have a different emotional significance than direct personal contacts. In terms of national distance, the collective image of the Jew is that of the "dangerous, powerful Jew." Traditional anti-Semitism itself was characterized by a difference between the hated collective ("The Jew") and the actual Jewish neighbor, who, as the "exception to the rule," was omitted from the collective assessment, and with whom one could very well have personal contact.

Demographic Distribution of Emotional and Social Distance

Individual questions on emotional and social distance met with different levels of agreement. To make an overall assessment of the extent and distribution of rejection of Jews at this level of prejudice, we created the AS-Social Distance index. It includes three central variables from this complex of issues: question 7, "People who don't like Jews"; question

TABLE 5.11
Index: AS-Social Distance

Yes-answers	N	%	% cumulative
0	1703	81.0	81.0
1	263	12.5	93.5
2	76	3.6	97.1
3	60	2.9	100.0
Total	**2102**	**100.0**	

1a, "Don't want to have too much to do with Jews"; and question 10, "All Jews to Israel" (cf. chap. 2 on the introduction of this index).

The selected variables formulated a pronounced rejection of Jews, so that those who answered "yes" to even one question could be described as emotionally anti-Jewish. However, an evaluation of the AS-Social Distance index in conjunction with the AS-Stereotype and AS-Discrimination indices showed that only a small portion (one-fifth to one-third) of those who agreed once, strongly stereotyped and discriminated.[29] The group of those with emotionally anti-Jewish attitudes thus included all those who agreed twice or three times, and some of those who agreed only once. That is, we estimate that approximately 11 percent of those questioned had emotionally anti-Jewish attitudes.

There was no gender difference in emotional rejection. The major characteristics contributing to the formation of this group were age and education.

Four different generations can be distinguished. People up to forty-four years of age showed the least amount of emotional rejection (between 2 percent and 3.5 percent); the figure was slightly higher (5 percent) for those between forty-five and fifty-four years of age. The next oldest age group, fifty-five to sixty-four years of age, agreed twice as frequently (7.5 percent) as the youngest cohort. However, there was a clear generation gap between this group and those over sixty-five years of age, who expressed the strongest emotional rejection of Jews (17 percent). Aside from a degree of conservativism born of age, the ideological influence of the Third Reich on this generation appears to have left lasting emotional traces.

Education, and the sounder judgment it teaches, diminish emotional responsiveness to hostility. Groups with less education expressed the

FIGURE 5.4
AS-Social Distance by Age Group

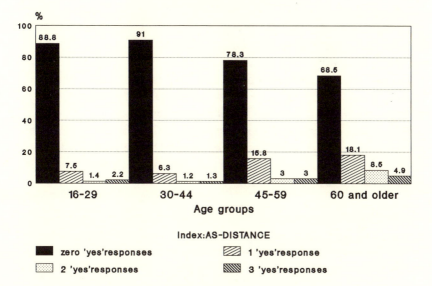

FIGURE 5.5
AS-Social Distance by Educational Level

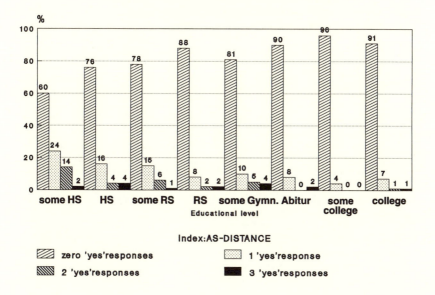

greatest emotional distance toward Jews. Interrupted education appears to favor the development of hostility; people who had begun at a *Gymnasium* (college preparatory high school) but failed to complete the *Abitur* (college entrance qualification exam) were more likely to harbor hostilities than those who had successfully completed high school. When age and higher education coincided, as in the case of young college students, hostility disappeared almost entirely. Of sixty-eight students questioned, only three answered "yes" once on the AS-Social Distance index (4 percent); not a single one answered "yes" two or three times.

The overall increase in higher education in Germany, as well as the emergence of younger generations unburdened by the past, allows us to assume that emotional rejection of and social distance from Jews will continue to diminish in the future.

Notes

1. Ignorance about the Talmud is the first indication that the tradition of anti-Semitic polemic against the Talmud no longer exists.
2. This direct question on self-classification was not often posed. Therefore, there is little international data to compare with German data. In 1966 in France, 10 percent of those questioned said they disliked Jews (4 percent expressed a liking for Jews, 80 percent neither/nor), while 9 percent called themselves anti-Semites (Bensimon and Verdes-Leroux 1970, 60).
3. In their study on national prejudice, Sodhi and Bergius (1953, 75ff.) attempted to determine affective attitudes toward various groups. They asked their subjects to classify the ascribed characteristics used in the study on a scale of values. The evaluation yielded the highest positive emotional value for the Germans' stereotype of themselves; Jews ranked ninth among fourteen nationalities in the range of emotional values. With a point value of +0.03, Jews were close to the "neutral point." The authors interpreted this as an expression of an ambivalent emotional state, in which positively valued talents were offset by negative characteristics. However, this method of cancelling out fails to take into account that characteristics (such as intelligence, business acumen, national solidarity, etc.) can take on a negative connotation in the context of negative feelings; Jewish talents could be perceived as a threat by anti-Semites.
4. One in four also indicated emotionally indifferent associations combining positive and negative elements. Fifteen percent gave no response, and one-third expressed a positive attitude that was strongly intertwined with feelings of guilt (EMNID 1954, IIf.).
5. The difficulty of changing individual attitudes is shown by the distribution of responses to questions in the study by Weiss (1984, 66ff.) that pertained to subjective changes in opinion. For the question "When you think about the past, did you have a different opinion of Jews than you do today?" 16.8 percent said they had "had a lower opinion in the past," while 76.9 percent claimed not to have changed their opinion (3.6 percent had a higher opinion in the past, 2.5 percent gave no answer). Those born in the years 1926 to 1930 experienced the greatest

change of opinion. This generation had been indoctrinated in school and youth groups, but was not as heavily influenced or involved as older groups, and could thus more easily overcome learned anti-Semitism (ibid., 67).

6. For combating social anti-Semitism, a dual strategy is thus indicated: Among younger people, the emergence of prejudice can and should be nipped in the bud by liberal schools and public opinion; older people must be prevented from publicly expressing their anti-Jewish views, as it is very difficult to change the opinions of this age group radically.

7. Spontaneous expressions of like or dislike for certain notions is more a "soft" indicator of emotional attitudes. One should not consider like-dislike values in terms of their absolute value in isolation; more significant are the intervals between the notions involved. They provide information on the approximate position of the notion on a like-dislike scale.

8. The strong correlation (.43) between the AS-Social Distance index, which measures the emotional component of anti-Semitic prejudice, and the Past index, which measures attitudes toward the past, confirms this relationship. Cf. chap. 2 and the end of this chapter on the introduction of these indices.

9. It allows selection of one of seven categories of distance, ranging from intimacy (marriage) to relations with neighbors and co-workers, to strong rejection [deportation or prohibition on immigration (Bogardus 1925 and 1933)].

10. In his survey of American high school students, Galtung came to the conclusion that the views of those with anti-Semitic attitudes "to a large extent form parts of a general syndrome of attitudes toward minorities." These people also rejected blacks, Catholics, and Germans with above-average frequency, but were especially opposed to Jews: "but they specialize in Jews" (Galtung 1960, 64).

11. Cf. the summary of results from 1964 to 1982 in Rosenfield 1982, 433ff. Approximately 30 percent of those questioned in this period agreed to the statement: "Most American Jews are more loyal to Israel than to the United States." Cf. also Weil 1987, 176.

12. In 1960, Galtung provided empirical evidence that those with anti-Semitic attitudes assumed that Jews felt corresponding emotions of hatred, contempt, and superiority. He interpreted this as a typical conflict phenomenon: those who consider themselves in conflict with another group require a reciprocity of these negative feelings, and thus must assume that the other group feels the same negative emotions that they themselves perceive (Galtung 1960, 64). For the anti-Semites, this projection has the function of avoiding inconsistency and dissonance.

13. In 1974, a projection question asked for estimates of the national orientation of Jews: "Jews feel tied mainly to Israel. They are only marginally interested in the affairs of the country in which they live." Fifty-five percent of Germans questioned expressed strong or mild agreement, 30 percent strong or mild disagreement, and 15 percent no opinion (cf. Sallen 1977, 281). This agreement may reflect a knowledge of the great significance that the state of Israel has for Jews throughout the world; however, it may also reflect reservations on the loyalty of native Jews, as the second part of the question has polemic undertones.

14. On the other hand, it is still true that categorizing a Jew living in Germany as a Jew and not a German cannot lead to an assumption of anti-Semitically motivated ostracism. Of the 424 people questioned (20 percent) who saw German Jews as more Jewish, only 37 percent could be classed as clearly anti-Semitic.

15. In a 1949 survey conducted under the auspices of HICOG, it was still the youngest cohort of all those under thirty who denied German Jews their German na-

tionality. To the question "In your opinion, is a Jew whose parents and grandparents were born and raised in Germany a real German or not?" 38 percent of them answered "no," in contrast to 26 percent of the thirty to forty-nine-year-olds and 22 percent of those over fifty. The fact that in 1949, only 28 percent of all those questioned answered "no" indicates strong adaptation to what was socially desirable at the time. At the same time, this response pattern rejected the Nazi definition of Jews as a race (HICOG report no. 1, Dec. 1949, 13, data representative for the U.S. zone).

16. Doubts about the national reliability of Jews living in Germany seem minimal. In 1979, before the television series "Holocaust" was broadcast, only 2 percent of those questioned disagreed with the statement "Jews in Germany are just as good citizens as everyone else"; 80 percent agreed with it, and 19 percent were undecided (Ernst 1979, 239). Interesting insight into acceptance of Jews could be gained with a question that, for example, connected their legal status with the universal duty to serve in the military.

17. In 1986, 535,000 Jews lived in France (in 1994: 600,000), while the number in the United States was estimated at 5,814,000 (cf. American Jewish Yearbook 1987, 221 and 167; in 1994: 5,8 Mill., Antisemitism World Report 1994).

18. Twelve percent of those questioned in our survey said they had one or more Jews in their circle of friends.

19. For some of the Eastern European countries like Poland, Russia, and Slovakia, the data of studies from 1990 show the great social distance toward Jews in all these countries (cf. Gudkov and Levinson 1992 for Russia, Cohen and Golub 1991 for Poland, Hungary, and Czechoslovakia).

20. The number determined by the Wickert Institute in 1988 must be judged with skepticism outside the context of this survey; in our opinion, it does not signal a new trend.

21. The 1949 HICOG report on the "State of German Nationalism" indicated that racism continued to exist in the U.S. zone. From December, 1946 to October, 1949, between 42 percent and 54 percent of those questioned agreed with the statement, "Do you think that some human races are more fit to rule than others?" and between 34 percent and 43 percent believed in the inferiority of some "races" (Report no. 1, 1949, 10ff.).

22. In our pretest, 13 percent of those questioned still said they spoke of the Jews as a race. On religious-based rejection of Jews, cf. chap. 3.

23. EMNID provided a comparative international "snapshot" for 1968:

Question: *"Are you for or against marriage between:"* (in %)

State	Catholics/Protestants for / against		Jews/Non-Jews for / against		Whites/Non-Whites for / against	
West Germany	72	18	53	29	35	47
Austria	78	14	51	40	39	53
Netherlands	48	25	44	19	51	23
France	74	14	64	16	62	25
Great Britain	61	24	50	23	29	57
USA	63	22	59	21	20	72

Source: EMNID-Info 11/12, 1968.

24. Half the sample was given the question worded as not wanting to have too much to do with "Jews," and half with the wording "German Jews."

25. For 1988, Wickert found that 12 percent would reject a Jewish family as neighbors (among eighteen to twenty-nine-year-olds the figure was only 3 percent, among thirty to forty-nine-year-olds it was 10 percent, and for fifty to sixty-nine-year-olds, 17 percent). A Turkish family was rejected by 20 percent, with the age difference less pronounced. Seventeen percent of the youngest cohort, 15 percent of the intermediate cohort, and 27 percent of the oldest cohort would reject a Turkish family as neighbors (Wiener 1988, 4). On the other hand, right-wing extremists today experience a much greater social nonacceptance or social distance: in 1992, 77 percent of the West and 79 percent of the East Germans rejected them as neighbors. As was found in comparative research, in no other European country were they rejected as strongly as in Germany (Noelle-Neumann 1993).

26. Galtung called attention to the strong influence the possible responses have on the results. Thus in 1956, two versions of the question were posed: the one cited here, including the two response choices "don't know"—17 percent and "undecided"—33 percent, which are combined in the source to 50 percent; and another version without the "undecided" response category. In the latter, answers were distributed as follows: "better"—29 percent, "not better"—35 percent, and "don't know"—36 percent (Galtung 1960, 3). That is, those who evaded an answer by choosing "undecided" were only rarely hostile to Jews. This breakdown is of general significance to our subject because it refutes the thesis that many people hide their true anti-Jewish opinions behind indifference and ignorance.

27. Comparable figures for France in 1966 yielded similar results to those of the 1965 West German study. Approximately 20 percent of all French wanted as many Jews as possible to go to Israel; 63 percent were indifferent, and 3 percent wanted as many Jews as possible to remain in France (Bensimon and Verdes-Leroux 1970, 71).

28. This observation is supported by the results of public opinion research in Austria. There, the question "Would you say it would be better for Austria if no Jews were in the country?" was frequently posed (in %).

	1973	1986	1987	1988	1989
Yes	21	15	11	8	13
No	47	58	71	83	68
Other	32	26	18	10	19

Source: Haerpfer 1989, 37.

A comparison of 1986 response distributions for this question with responses to the wording "if all Jews would go to Israel" for the same year (see table 5.10, above) indicates that the wording of the question does, in fact, play a decisive role.

29. In general, we can clearly establish a correlation between the three dimensions of anti-Jewish prejudice. The correlation between AS-Social Distance and AS-Stereotype is .55; the correlation between AS-Social Distance and AS-Discrimination is .57 (significant on the 1 percent level).

6

Inclination to Discriminate and Intolerance

The way people act in a real situation cannot be measured by means of public opinion polls. Only verbal statements that can be used to ascertain their *inclination to act* can be gathered in this manner. In this sense, a measurement of inclination to discriminate is one attitudinal dimension. Opinions are divided among researchers of prejudice as to the extent to which attitudes influence actual behavior, since actions are carried out in a normatively determined context in which a variety of social factors function simultaneously (Benninghaus 1976; Frey 1972; McGuire 1985, 251ff.; Ajzen and Fishbein 1980). It can be assumed, however, that if a person agrees with demands for discriminatory behavior, this agreement represents a bridge to actual action and signifies the person's conscious and emotional involvement. Support for anti-Jewish demands is thus a far better indicator of pronounced anti-Semitism than agreement with cognitive stereotypes or social distance. This can be seen in the 1987 pretest, which showed a large deviation between the popular average and those with "anti-Semitic leanings," whose inclination to discriminate was four to five times higher.

This minority is inclined to discriminate, in contrast to the great majority of the population, which supports equal rights and equal treatment. Seventy percent of the respondents were of the opinion that "Jews and non-Jews should be treated the same, legally and generally." In the sixteen to fifty-nine age group, 73 percent supported this statement, as did 63 percent of those over sixty years of age. This legal principle is occasionally used as a formal basis for argumentation by lay people when applying principles of equality to unequal groups. The principle of equal treatment under the law is then used as a basis for rejecting historically based special treatment of Jews. Only 26 percent agreed with the statement "Jews should be helped in every way possible, since they have

149

suffered a lot." We examined the notion of equal treatment of unequals within the context of Jewish demands to practice their religion and education in a Christian environment. The finding of 69 percent agreement to the statement "Jewish children should go to the same schools as other children" is ambivalent. On the one hand, it expresses interest in integration, while on the other hand indicating a potential area of conflict with respect to acceptance of autonomous Jewish educational and cultural institutions.

In our survey, we considered three expressions of the inclination to discriminate:

- inclination to take personal action against Jews;
- demands for legal discrimination;
- inclination to tolerate anti-Jewish comments and actions by other persons or groups.

Personal Inclination to Discriminate

To start with, it is important to note that far fewer people are inclined to take personal anti-Jewish action than are willing to support anti-Jewish stereotypes or express social distance toward and rejection of Jews. Of those questioned, 2 percent to 7 percent could be regarded as inclined to discriminate. Two percent agreed with the statement "People shouldn't go to Jewish doctors" (question 16/10); 5 percent felt that letters to the editor should be written strongly criticizing reparations payments to Israel (question 16/16); and 7 percent expressed an inclination to "support people who say things against Jews in conversation" (question 16/14).[1] In general, such demands were more strongly supported by the older age groups. This was particularly blatant in regard to Jewish doctors. While 5 percent of those over sixty still disapproved of going to Jewish doctors, obviously reminded of and restating the Jewish boycott during the "Third Reich," the younger age groups showed absolutely no support for such a demand. Such discriminatory behavior, which in the 1950s and 1960s was still very much a part of the everyday consciousness of many Germans, has now become virtually meaningless, especially for the younger generations. In 1961 and 1965, 14 percent of those questioned still had reservations about being treated by a Jewish doctor. The sixteen to twenty-nine age group expressed below-average support for the statement in those years (10 percent and 8 percent, respectively). The distinction between Jew and non-Jew had by then apparently already become irrelevant for them. The women did express higher than average reservations (18 percent compared to 10 percent of the men, IfD 1964, 218). This reflects the residual effects of racist Nazi propaganda that condemned any close contact with Jews as "besmirching" and depicted Jewish men as sexually aggressive. The gender-specific differences in this regard gradually diminished with time (1965: 12 percent of men and 15 percent of women) and are no longer found today (2.2 percent to 1.9 percent in 1987). As in the question of visiting a Jewish doctor, the prolonged effects of the Nazi boycott policy can be observed in the early postwar years. In 1949, 25 percent of those questioned rejected the idea of shopping in Jewish stores, even if the prices there were lower (IfD 1949, 35). At that time, it was particularly the well-educated who would have turned down favorable prices, spurning all economic rationality [30 percent versus 22 percent of those having only completed *Volksschule* (elementary school equivalent)]. This group was greatly influenced by Nazi propaganda and initially stood by their convictions, as verified by the "group experiment" in the early 1950s (Pollock 1955).[2] We did not include any questions like this one in our 1987 survey, since it seemed to provide information about vestiges of anti-Jewish tradition that are irrelevant to the reality experienced by younger people, rather than about areas of conflict which are relevant in present German-Jewish relations. Today, more support is expressed for political demands directed towards Jewish representatives and Israel; that is, even among a majority of anti-Semites, the point is not to support an active boycott of Jews living in Germany, but to discontinue special aid and reject the special status they believe exists.[3]

Demands for State-Sanctioned Discrimination

In contrast to personal anti-Semitic activities, which were seldom encountered (see for the Jewish perception Silbermann and Sallen 1992), demands for state discrimination were much more common. Especially strong feelings were voiced against Jews in government or administration (see table 6.1).

This rejection expresses the assumption that Jews have divided or unclear loyalties, on the one hand, and the long-standing tradition of excluding Jews from government positions, on the other. This calls to

TABLE 6.1
"Jews should not become government ministers or high level
civil servants here" (in %).

| | Age groups | | | |
Total pop.	16–29	30–44	45–59	60 and older
16.1	9.1	11.8	17.2	27.0

mind, not only the "Third Reich," in which racial legislation "legalized" exclusion of Jews from public service, but also the concept of the Christian-Germanic state, which excluded non-Christians and non-Germans per se (Erb and Bergmann 1989). The strong generational difference points to the virulence of this ideology. Among younger people, raised with a democratic, egalitarian notion of the state, 11 percent supported the statement, whereas even today, 27 percent of those over sixty years of age agreed with it.[4]

Resistance to Jews in high political office has been examined several times in public opinion research in order to measure discrimination, each time with the question worded somewhat differently. The question was first asked in a study on sixteen to twenty-five-year-old adolescents conducted in 1956 by DIVO (see table 6.2); parts of it were repeated in 1961.[5]

The figures for 1956 show that young people expressed strong disapproval of Jews holding political office; the figure of 55 percent was almost as high as the one for disapproval of former Nazi leaders. As among the adults, both perpetrators (Nazis) and victims (Jews and emigrés) were rejected to a similar degree. The latter were acknowledged neither as victims of Nazi persecution nor as representatives of a "better Germany." It is therefore not surprising that two-thirds of all those responsible for the wave of anti-Semitic graffiti (*Schmierwelle*) in 1960 were between fourteen and thirty years old. Cold war anti-communist ideology, which can certainly be considered a functional equivalent of anti-Semitism and Nazi ideology (Galtung 1960, 5; Mitscherlich and Mitscherlich 1967, 42), led to virtually total rejection of communists among adolescents, although at that time anti-communism had not yet replaced the anti-Jewish attitudes of many Germans. Anti-Semitism and anti-communism existed side by side in the minds of many Germans in the 1950s. The 1961 figures denote a relatively strong decline in anti-Jewish reservations among the next generation of youths. Part of the sixteen to twenty-five age group

TABLE 6.2

"What is your opinion: Should people belonging to one of the following groups be allowed to hold high positions in the German government?"

| | Strong/Some Reservations | | No Reservations | | No Opinion | |
| | 1956 / 61 | | 1956 / 61 | | 1956 / 61 | | 1956 / 61 | |
	%	%	%	%	%	%	%	%
Leading industrialists	25	—	30	—	28	—	17	—
Communists	63	—	17	—	7	—	13	—
Nazis	33	39	27	23	17	13	23	25
Jews	29	19	26	19	24	35	21	27
Emigrés	—	14	—	23	—	35	—	28

Source: DIVO Pressedienst, July 1961, 7ff.

in 1956 (born 1931 to 1940) attended school during the "Third Reich" and was therefore subjected to racist biological indoctrination. In 1961, however, this age group was comprised of people born between 1936 and 1945; these young people experienced only fragments of this influence, to some extent within the context of anti-anti-Semitic attitudes. The more favorable 1961 figures might also be a consequence of the far-reaching social impact of the wave of anti-Semitic graffiti. It triggered heightened activity against anti-Semitism and education on the Nazi persecution of the Jews.[6] In the June, 1961 survey, adolescents and adults did not differ in the degree of reservations they felt against Jews holding high public office. Of those questioned, a total of 18 percent had strong reservations, 23 percent had some reservations, and 33 percent had none.[7] The second survey, at the time of the Adolf Eichmann trial in February, 1962 (DIVO, cited in Schmidt and Becker 1967, 132), came to the same conclusion as in June, 1961. Approximately 45 percent of those questioned had reservations against Jews "holding high federal positions in West Germany"; 20 percent had no opinion. In the 1990s, two surveys included the question if one would approve or disapprove a Jew as a candidate for president of Germany (Golub 1994, Spiegel-Special 1994). Both reveal a still very strong minority disapproving a Jewish candidate: 30 percent in former West Germany, 20 percent in former East Germany (AJC 1994, table 7).[8]

In the United States, a question on support for a Jewish presidential candidate has been asked repeatedly in surveys since the end of the 1930s. It serves as a good indicator of the degree of political and social discrimination against a group. Almost 50 percent of those questioned rejected the notion of a Jewish candidate until the mid-1950s. This figure is just as high as the one for West Germany in 1960. The figure for the United States had already dropped to 28 percent by 1958, and decreased steadily thereafter (1963: 17 percent; 1965: 15 percent) to 7.4 percent in 1969 (Smith 1991, table 10).[9] This very low level was measured at a time when the civil rights movement was at its peak; it has not been reached again. The rejection of Jewish candidates rose up to 12.5 percent in 1978. In the 1970s, with a slightly different wording of the question, the figures were even higher: in 1974, 32 percent thought a Jewish candidate would be "bad for the country," and 24 percent were unsure. In 1981, 21 percent thought it would be either "very" or "somewhat" disturbing to have a Jew nominated as a presidential candidate (cf. Rosenfield 1982, 442; Weil 1987, 176). The figures dropped to 7 percent in 1983 and 6 percent in 1987.

A similar trend, comparable in magnitude to the one in West Germany, could also be observed in France. In 1966, 50 percent of the French still disapproved of voting for a Jewish candidate; the figure had dropped to only 24 percent in 1978 (Weil 1987, 176). In 1990 it dropped even further, down to 9 percent. The same trend also applies to Austria, though with a definite shift in time frame. In 1976, 45 percent of the Viennese questioned were of the opinion that "we should make sure that no Jews take on influential positions in our country"; the figure dropped to 23 percent of all Austrians in 1987 and to 20 percent in 1991 (Weiss 1984, 46; *Journal für Sozialforschung* 1988, 84; Karmasin 1992, table 13, but in 1991 27 percent said "Don't Know" or did not answer the question).

Despite the fact that ethnic, religious, and historical conditions vary from country to country, a sharp decline in, if not the total disappearance of, political discrimination against Jews can be observed in western democracies. The trend toward individualization that accompanied modernization also loosened traditional religious and other group ties, so that a Jewish candidate is no longer considered primarily an exponent of that group. As compared to the United States, the western and middle European countries have experienced a certain "delay" in terms of the decline in political discrimination against Jews. In most of west-

TABLE 6.3
"Jews should no longer be permitted to immigrate or return to Germany."

	Age groups			
Total pop. (%)	16–29	30–44	45–59	60 and older
6.4	2.8	3.6	7.2	12.6

ern Europe the trend could not be observed until the 1970s, and in Austria it came even later.

For Germany and Austria, public attitudes about the return of emigrants or immigration of Jews must be viewed within the context of an inclination to discriminate. As demonstrated by conflicts surrounding displaced persons and the postwar discussion on the return of Jewish property, German attitudes toward Jewish returnees and refugees were extremely negative. In Austria, 46 percent of all respondents in 1946 felt that "the Jews should not return." There are no corresponding survey data for Germany, but attitudes on this issue in the western zones of Germany were probably similar to the finding for Austria. Contemporary sources, such as public opinion reports prepared by the Allied military administrations, mentioned virulent anti-Semitism and strong rejection of Jews in the country (Dinnerstein 1980). Attitudes toward laws prohibiting Jews from returning or immigrating were not examined again in surveys until 1987.

Today, only a recognizable hard core of anti-Semites supports such a prohibition. A larger segment of those over sixty years old favor it, while it plays a negligible role for younger generations. Thus, an old option in "solving the Jewish problem" (cf. Erb and Bergmann 1989), namely, territorial segregation by means of emigration and a prohibition of immigration, finds no support among younger Germans today. The disappearance of this form of discrimination demonstrates that German-Jewish relations are no longer viewed as a traditional majority/minority conflict that could be resolved by expelling the minority from the country.[10]

As in the case of personal inclination to discriminate, demands for state discrimination are voiced by only a small minority of the population. Aside from a traditional rejection of Jews, another cause of the greater disapproval of filling a representative government position with a Jew—observable to a similar degree in several western countries—lies

TABLE 6.4
"Should people who are involved in anti-Jewish activities in Germany today be prosecuted or not?"

	1949 %	1958 %	1960 %	1987 %	1992 %
Yes, definitely or yes, in serious cases	41	50	82	82	90
Not, not as a rule or No, it would be undemocratic	43	20	8	10	6
Undecided	16	30	10	8	4
	100	**100**	**100**	**100**	**100**

Source: IfD 1949, 1987, 1992.[11]

in the existence of a Jewish state, and the resulting suspicion of divided loyalties of Jews (see also chap. 5).

After analyzing personal inclination to discriminate and demands for state discrimination separately, the combined interaction of these dimensions will be presented. We formed an index based on five discriminatory demands (AS-Discrimination, cf. chap. 2 for details). Using this index, 13.4 percent were calculated as having a strong inclination to discriminate (agreement with two to five statements in the index). An extremely hostile group of 5 percent supported more than half of the discriminatory demands.

Tolerance of Intolerance

In determining attitudes toward minorities, we must take into account whether or not public opinion and the population as a whole tolerate discrimination. For this reason, the surveys always question attitudes toward anti-Jewish statements and actions.

One such question has been repeated in surveys since 1949, making it possible to trace developments over the last four decades (see table 6.4).

In 1949 the population was equally divided into two groups on this question, whereas today those believing anti-Jewish actions should be prosecuted have a clear majority. The social climate has changed completely in this respect. Criminal prosecution of vandalism, libel, and slander is supported by a broad base of the population and discrimination against Jews is generally disapproved of. However, the collective learning process progressed much more slowly than the table suggests. This impression is given by an anomaly in 1960, that seems to show an abrupt shift in opinion compared to 1958. The 1960 figures are deceptive, however, since that survey was conducted during a phase of public outrage over the wave of anti-Semitic incidents that occurred in the winter of 1959–60 (Schönbach 1960, Bergmann 1990). It must be assumed that this represented a temporary swing in public opinion rather than a stable trend,[12] since even the 1987 figures do not reach the 1960 level (the 1987 figure for "yes, definitely" was 39 percent, lower than the 1960 figure of 55 percent). This question was not repeated in surveys in the 1960s and 1970s, so that we cannot substantiate our suspicion with empirical data. According to the changes from 1949 to 1958, the shift in attitudes progressed quite slowly, though it continued throughout the 1960s, as demonstrated by answers to the question on Jewish emigration to Israel. We can thus assume that the impact of the reaction to anti-Semitic activities at the time was indeed temporary.[13]

Today's fairly unanimous condemnation of anti-Jewish actions does not, however, mean that the public or the press takes particular pains to register and criticize such incidents.[14] On the contrary, at a local, everyday level there is more of a tendency not to talk about the importance of graffiti and waves of "Jewish jokes," or to play them down. Thus, there appears to be a contradiction between the socially desired disapproval of anti-Jewish actions, and actual behavior in concrete cases. This phenomenon is universal, however, since concrete situations always include additional conditions leading people to deviate from their convictions. It is indeed possible to be opposed in principle to anti-Semitic discrimination yet still refrain from criticizing a specific situation, play down its significance, or even ignore it totally, due to outside influences. In the prevailing climate of public opinion which criticizes anti-Jewish actions, it is primarily people with anti-Semitic attitudes who resort to this strategy. In order to check these assumptions, we included a question in the pretest about the best way to respond to anti-Jewish actions. Of those interviewed, 69 percent advocated having the media publicize the incident. For those with pro-Jewish leanings, the figure was as high as 85 percent, while only 39 percent of those with anti-Jewish leanings supported such publicity. An above-average proportion of this group also preferred "not to talk about" such incidents (16 percent as opposed to 9 percent in the total population). These figures confirm our suspicion that it is above all anti-Semites who have a good nose for the public opinion climate they face, and therefore try to avoid public discussion of anti-Jewish actions.[15]

The coherence of the pro-Jewish climate of public opinion can also be measured according to the extent to which public disapproval is expressed, not only with respect to criminal actions, but also toward anti-Jewish comments made by public figures. Pertinent questions were not asked in surveys until 1986, when scandals surrounding remarks made by politicians became more frequent (cf. Schwinghammer 1986). Most of the survey responses opposed anti-Jewish comments by politicians. In 1986, 55 percent considered such comments "very bad," and another 28 percent "bad." Sixteen percent felt they were "not worth mentioning" (EMNID 1986, table 5). Trivialization of such comments came partly from those with anti-Semitic attitudes, though the major factor in evaluating such comments was the respondent's relationship to the Nazi past. Of those who advocated constant reminders of the Nazi past, only 3 percent considered such statements trivial, while 25 percent of those in favor of ending discussion of the past (*Schlußstrich ziehen*) felt this way. Those considering anti-Jewish remarks "not worth mentioning" tended much more strongly to deny the existence of any anti-Jewish sentiment in Germany at all (35 percent).[16]

In response to the debate on Kurt Waldheim's presidential candidacy in Austria, the IfD in Allensbach prepared its 1986 study on anti-Semitism to include an international comparison on this issue, and surveys were also conducted by Austrian public opinion research institutes, giving us access to some international data on the Waldheim affair. In the IfD survey of February through March 1986 (IfD 1986, table 32), interviewees in four countries were asked to respond to the question whether high-level politicians demanding that "Jews should not be allowed to hold important positions in this country" should step down and/or withdraw their statements. A clear majority (over 70 percent) of those questioned in West Germany, France, and the United States called for resignation or withdrawal of the statement. Austrians were less inclined to oppose such behavior (56 percent) and 40 percent in Austria felt that politicians "can feel free to say such things." In contrast to the three other countries, in Austria the population was divided into two almost equal groups, so it is not surprising that anti-Semitic hostilities have been exploited in political discussion (cf. Gottschlich and Obermair 1988; Mitten 1992). The debate on anti-Semitism in Austria, taken up by the international media with great intensity, as well as foreign criticism influenced the climate of public opinion in Austria. A February, 1987 survey showed a dramatic change in attitudes, with the distribution corresponding more to other western countries; 71 percent now considered it "very bad" or "quite bad" if an Austrian politician attempted to make political capital out of anti-Semitic remarks. Only 1 percent felt it was acceptable behavior, and 25 percent did not care (*Journal für Sozialforschung* 1988, 86). Discrimination or public slander or libel of Jews was also rejected by 74 percent of the Austrian population. A greater degree of understanding was granted the press, however, if it disparaged Jews. Only 38 percent found this behavior greatly offensive, another 35 percent somewhat offensive, and 24 percent were not offended at all. This difference in the leeway granted politicians and the press can most likely be explained by the particular nature of the "Waldheim debate." In response to foreign criticism, freedom of speech and press was used to justify media reporting, whereas it was felt that representatives of state needed to be more diplomatic. The changes in public opinion that emerged within a year more likely signify an opportunistic reaction to domestic and foreign criticism than a widespread shift in personal attitudes toward Jews. In fact, Richard Költringer and Ernst Gehmacher ascertained a reversal of the trend, moving toward greater anti-Semitism, since it was specifically those with vague anti-Semitic sentiments whose attitudes had changed (1989, 559ff.).

At the public opinion level, West Germans largely disapprove of anti-Semitic remarks and demand that such behavior be punished. For decades, policies aimed at prohibiting anti-Jewish discrimination in public and taking a clear moral stand on the issue. This led to a relatively broad-based anti-anti-Semitic consensus in West Germany. The question must be raised whether the creation of such a taboo also had an impact on individual communication. In 1986, surveys in four countries included a question on tolerance of anti-Semitic remarks made within one's circle of friends.

The answers for Germany and Austria reveal a different pattern than those for France and the United States. This can probably be explained by the connection to Nazism in the respective countries and the resulting relationships to Jews and anti-Semitism. In Germany and Austria, taboos obviously delve further into personal relationships, so that fewer

TABLE 6.5
"Suppose an acquaintance of yours says that all Jews should be expelled from our country. If the remark was really meant seriously, could you imagine staying friends with that person, or would that be unlikely?"

	Germany %	Austria %	France %	U.S. %
I could imagine that	40	40	54	68
Unlikely	26	18	23	26
Couldn't say	34	42	23	6
	100	100	100	100

Source: IfD 1986, table 31.

people were willing to tolerate anti-Semitic statements within their circle of friends.[17] The proportion of people who would break off a friendship in such a situation is not higher, however, in these two countries than in France and the United States. The large share of "undecideds" in Germany as well as Austria indicates uncertainty as to how to act in this situation. It seems difficult for many to apply the public anti-anti-Semitic norm to their private lives. On the one hand, they do not wish to tolerate anti-Semitism in the private sphere, but on the other hand, such an offense does not seem serious enough to require such harsh personal consequences. People with explicitly pro-Jewish attitudes reacted more harshly to the violation of the norm; two-thirds felt it was "unlikely" that the friendship could continue, and only 12 percent of whom would prefer to remain friends. Among the explicitly anti-Jewish interviewees, the ratio was just the opposite (Pretest 1987). There was considerable acceptance of the norm in response to this hypothetical question, though it remains questionable whether everyday behavior would indeed be affected. Of the respondents, 43 percent also said that the "bad" characteristics are the ones generally mentioned when the subject of Jews comes up in conversation [even 29 percent of those with pro-Jewish attitudes said this (Pretest)].

A majority of West Germans were opposed to discrimination against Jews. However, there were differences depending on the type of discrimination and the level of communication. Punitive action in response to anti-Jewish activities, for example, against religious institutions or persons, was demanded almost across the board. Anyone not agreeing with this must be considered a hardcore anti-Semite. Verbal *faux pas* by political representatives were not condemned as universally. There was also no general agreement as to what is considered a *faux pas* or deliberate defamation, so that problems of definition arise. The public responded more sensitively to anti-Semitic comments made publicly than to those made in private. However, the low tolerance for such remarks in Germany and Austria indicates that the effect of the social norm opposing anti-Semitism extends into the personal sphere in those countries. This norm becomes problematic in connection with assessing friendships, a conflict which many avoided by answering "undecided."

Notes

1. The 7 percent agreement with the last mentioned question should be seen somewhat skeptically, since a portion of those questioned obviously misunderstood the question in a pro-Jewish sense. The phrasing of the question might have been understood as referring to lending support to the Jew being attacked rather than to the attacker.
2. The strong inclination to discriminate led to violent incidents during the wave of anti-Semitic incidents in the winter of 1959–60. Unlike the situation in the United States, where this primarily involved adolescent vandalism by high school students (only 6 percent of those arrested were over twenty-three years of age), in West Germany a large proportion of the offenders were adults [44 percent were over twenty years old (cf. Galtung 1960, 8)]. The greater support among adults in Germany indicates a potential capable of activating an inclination to act.
3. The question remains whether a new norm has been established in opposition to the Nazi persecution of the Jews. In answer to the following question asked in the 1988 Wickert Institute survey: "Assuming that a new Hitler came to power and made an appeal to fight the worldwide Jewish conspiracy, would you hide a Jew in your home?" 93 percent answered "yes" (Wiener 1988, 6).
4. In the 1988 Wickert Institute study (we had no information on the methods and conception of the study) 30 percent of those questioned supposedly "did not wish to be governed by a Jewish chancellor." In the under-thirty age group the figure was 14 percent, and for older generations approximately 35 percent (Wiener 1988, 5).
5. Particular hope was placed in the youth for the democratic renewal of Germany after 1945, though great concern also existed. Special attention was given to these questions in numerous empirical research projects on adolescents (cf. Hübner-Funk 1990, 218ff.).
6. Public and political outrage over the wave of anti-Semitic incidents led to reactions in many social institutions. The causes of anti-Semitism were discussed at conferences and symposia, the Conference of Ministers of Culture resolved in 1960 to change school curricula and take educational measures, public opinions polls were conducted, and the incidents were one impetus for the "Germania Judaica" exhibition in Cologne in 1964 (cf. Bergmann 1990, 253ff.).

7. This finding corresponds to data collected in 1960 by the IfD. At that time, 45 percent of those questioned were opposed to "a Jew becoming German Chancellor," and 24 percent were undecided (IfD vol. 3, 218).

8. In the Spiegel-Study on German youth between fourteen and twenty-nine, even 41 percent gave a negative answer to the question "Could a German Jews become president of Germany (*Bundespräsident*)?" (Spiegel Special 1994, 68).

9. The general trend toward liberalization of U.S. society can be seen in the fact that between 1958 and 1965 the right of political participation was extended to other disadvantaged groups in society. The decline in reservations against women in political positions was minimal (1958: 43 percent disapproved of women in political positions; 1963: 41 percent), and even reservations against blacks remained at a high level [decline from 53 percent to 34 percent (*EMNID-Informationen* 46, 1963 and 35, 1965).

10. The high level of agreement with the statement (question 10): "It would be best for us Germans if all the Jews would go to Israel" (13 percent), combines two motives: the classical motive of deportation and a pro-Israeli, nationalistic one. The high level of approval thus cannot simply be interpreted as a new form of the former idea of expulsion.

11. A similar question was posed to East and West Germans in 1990: "Do you think that the German government should, after the unification of the two German states, ban anti-Semitic groups?" 80 percent of the West German population, and 78 percent of the East Germans answered "Yes", 12 percent and 15 percent said "No" (Jodice 1991, table 6a).

12. This is substantiated by the overwhelming condemnation of the wave of anti-Semitic incidents in 1959 and 1960, for which only 1 percent of the population expressed open approval (80 percent condemned the actions, 10 percent trivialized them). The strong pressure of public opinion in this situation contributed to the virtually unanimous disapproval. EMNID therefore estimated the proportion of those who were anti-Jewish and/or approved of the actions to be higher—approximately 4 percent [or a maximum of less than 10 percent (*EMNID-Informationen* 9, 1960)]. Although this magnitude might very well be accurate with respect to the extent of support for open anti-Semitism, it certainly underestimates the number of those with anti-Jewish sentiments.

13. Our assumption is indirectly confirmed by the Boynton and Loewenberg study (1974, 461), which in 1960 also found a strongly negative trend regarding support of the "Hitler regime" by West German citizens. In 1961 and 1962, this support rose once again, so that data from 1960 proved to be a temporary deviation. In the time frame from 1955 to 1967, the curve of support for Hitler decreased *consistently.*

14. When asked about the frequency of "actions against Jewish institutions," only 9 percent of those questioned said that such actions occur often. Of pro-Jewish observers, 17 percent gave this answer, along with 3 percent of those with anti-Jewish attitudes (Pretest 1987). The perception of anti-Semites is obviously influenced by their desire to avoid publicity for these actions, since they know that the public and the media respond to them negatively. Faced with taboos and repression of prejudice, they opt for social inconspicuousness.

15. Since there are no reliable statistics available on the type and number of anti-Semitic actions, the following table is intended to provide a general idea. It includes those suspected to be acts of Arab terrorism in Europe. These statistics were presented by Michael May (Institute of Jewish Affairs, London) to an in-

vestigative committee of the European Parliament. We have no information as to the extent to which the reports applied uniform criteria.

Anti-Semitic Incidents 1981–1983

	1981	1982	1983
Austria	28	32	23
Belgium	28	26	19
Britain	314	312	221
Cyprus	—	1	—
Denmark	2	11	9
Finland	7	5	2
France	100	116	93
Germany	88	120	88
Greece	20	34	17
Ireland	—	1	1
Italy	70	95	28
Netherlands	8	52	20
Norway	1	7	7
Portugal	—	3	1
Spain	16	10	10
Sweden	11	8	7
Switzerland	6	22	7
Total	**699**	**855**	**554**

Source: European Parliament 1985–86, Document A2-160/85, Appendix 120.

16. Tolerance of intolerance varied greatly with educational level. Interviewees who had completed high school or college were almost unanimously opposed to such statements ("very bad" 76 percent; "quite bad" 20 percent), whereas those with less education did not support the norms of liberal culture as strongly ("very bad" 49 percent: "quite bad" 31 percent of those having completed elementary school).

17. Another question on tolerance of extremist views in one's circle of friends, namely, with respect to "dedicated Nazis," was met with the highest degree of rejection. Of all those questioned at all ages and educational levels, 90 percent rejected having a "dedicated Nazi" among their friends (question 1b/8). Since anti-Semitism was a basic conviction of Nazi ideology, it can be assumed that this rejection of Nazi supporters also includes a rejection of extreme anti-Semitism.

7

Attitudes of Germans toward Israel

Germans' Image of Israel

With the founding of the state of Israel in 1948, for the first time in almost 2,000 years Jews once again had their own state. The significance of this event is far reaching, in part with respect to the history of hostilities toward Jews. It must be expected that this would have an impact on the perception of Jews and Judaism.[1] This has given researchers the task of examining the extent to which Israel is turned into a new object of anti-Semitism (anti-Zionism = anti-Semitism?) and to what extent the existence and accomplishments of Israel as an independent state have brought about a change in the image people have of Jews. The close relationship felt by many Jews in the Diaspora to Israel has also given new form to traditional suspicions of divided loyalties and the strong sense of group solidarity ("a state within a state"). Thus, Diaspora Jewry is collectively blamed for Israeli policy, while observers assume that Jews have greater loyalties to Israel than to their own respective countries. This could represent a new source of anti-Semitism.

In examining the effects that Israel has on people's image of Jews, the categorical difference between attitudes toward a country and those toward an ethnic group must be kept in mind. Opposition to the policies of a state is not the same as attitudes toward its population. Public opinion regarding state policy is much more closely related to specific events than are attitudes about peoples, which represent long-term historical developments and are more stable than individual events. The way Israel is perceived is dependent primarily on its role in international politics, within the context of foreign policy. In this regard, there is a high level of agreement in the perception and assessment of Israel by populations of various western European countries (Wolffsohn 1984).

The Holocaust has lent German-Israeli relations a very pronounced, distinctive historical dimension. On the one hand, it is characterized by great sensitivity and antagonism, and on the other hand, by a particular sense of German responsibility. In Deligdisch's analysis of attitudes in the Federal Republic of Germany to the state of Israel, he developed the thesis of a moral and political dual nature (1974). Because of this relationship, Germans and Israelis view themselves from a strongly moral perspective; conflicts thus appear virtually unavoidable, as it is known that morality has a "provocative" nature.[2]

In order to ascertain the different facets of relations to Israel and Israelis, we asked questions in our survey on feelings of like/dislike and social distance, not only toward Jews, but toward Israeli politics and reparations payments, and on Germans' expectations regarding attitudes of Jews/Israelis toward them. We performed a factor analysis on this cluster of questions and arrived at seven factors, three of which provided a positive image of Israel, three a negative image, and one neutral (see appendix 3).

The variables with the highest explained variance that loaded onto factor 1 were those viewing *Israel as the aggressor in the Middle East* ("They start wars and blame others," "Israeli politics are ruthless and narrow-minded," "A country that simply does not want peace," "A state that stops at nothing," etc.). This image was based entirely on Israel's role in the Middle East conflict, which was judged absolutely negatively. Israel was seen as aggressive, ruthless, warmongering, and expansionist. Israel's role was seen in isolation; support was expressed neither for Israel's adversaries, nor was the external threat taken into consideration as a political reason or justification. Israel's actions were in part explained vaguely as fated by a curse burdening the people, and partly by the influence of religious fanatics. Although this factor had the greatest explained variance, agreement to individual statements was not higher than 21 percent (average: 17 percent).

The variables for factor 1 generally did not show any significant effect of age or level of education, with the exception of variables including remnants of the traditional anti-Jewish stereotype. In the sixteen through twenty-nine age group, 11 percent agreed with the statement "The Israelis start wars and blame others," but in the over-sixty age group, the figure was 21 percent. Support for this statement decreased with increasing education. The same pattern was revealed in responses to the statement "There is a curse on that people." Both of these statements draw on old anti-Jewish allegations. The "curse" on the Jews stems from religious opposition to them, while Nazi propaganda put great stress on accusations that Jews stir up animosity among people, putting the blame on others. The oldest cohort and the less educated obviously transferred traditional anti-Jewish prejudices onto Israel with respect to these questions. This was not the case, however, regarding the "political" statements, in which hardly any generational difference could be distinguished.

Factor 2 represented the image of a *strong Israel,* a country subjected to an external threat, yet militarily and agriculturally strong. It was seen as having international allies and political influence. The noted dependence on the United States and "covert influence" add a slightly critical tone to what is otherwise a positive image. The questions loading onto this factor received the highest level of agreement, between 21 percent and 48 percent. Thus, a largely positive image of Israel existed among the West German population.

The age distribution here deviated from the usual "anti-Semitism distribution." The intermediate age groups, particularly the forty-five through fifty-nine category, showed the greatest agreement for the positive and ambivalent stereotypes. For the youngest age group, the lower level of agreement can be traced to the fact that on the whole, it was less prepared to assign people generalized characteristics, and secondly, this group felt less responsibility toward Israel, basing its opinions on the current political situation. The low level of agreement expressed by the oldest age group, which was more pro-Israel than the youngest, might be related to skepticism coming from the traditional image of Jews. The pro-Israel attitudes of the middle generations were probably due to the positive reception of Israel in its founding phase, Israel's successful cultivation of the desert, its idealism embodied in the Kibbutzim, and its military assertiveness. The consciousness of Germany's particular historical responsibility for Israel might also have contributed to this positive image. Statements relevant to the current political situation (good army, dependence on the United States, external threat) received more support from those with higher education, whereas no educational influence was found for the strong value judgments (industrious, Israel can truly be proud of itself).

A very distinct group saw *Israel as beneficiary of German guilt* (factor 3). This group saw German-Israeli relations entirely from the point of view of the Nazi past and the resulting financial burdens. Since these people felt Israel profits from the past and lives off German reparations payments, there was strong opposition to such payments. A small minority was even prepared to express this opinion publicly (writing letters to the editor: 5 percent). This image of Israel is rounded off by the assumption that it has covert influence throughout the world and a sense of national superiority. Age and education had the same effect on this factor as on the general anti-Semitism pattern: younger and more highly educated respondents tended to be more accepting of reparations payments stemming from the "Third Reich."

The most positive image of Israel is contained in factor 4, which includes all items depicting *Israel as a positive example*. Two aspects comprised this thoroughly positive image: (1) West Germany's obligation to support Israel politically; and (2) Recognition of Israel's accomplishments, tied to a demand to learn from them.

The effects of age and education were different for each of the two aspects. There was a similar low level of agreement in all age and education categories for political support of Israel (between 21 percent and 24 percent). The intermediate age groups, in particular, considered Israel a positive example, while the younger and older groups—as was the case for factor 2—were to some extent less enthusiastic and more skeptical.

Factor 5 included the desire for *personal contact with Israelis and support for Israel*. This generally unpolitical image focussed on efforts to acquire personal contact to Israelis. Many expressed a desire to have Israelis in their circle of friends, and wanted to see an intensification of contact through public support of tourism and political partnerships at a local level. All forms of contact were welcomed much more strongly among the younger age groups (sixteen through forty-four years of age). This might be a result of tourism and international awareness.

Unlike factor 1, not only was Israel charged with being an aggressor in factor 6, but active support for Israel's opponents/"victims" was sought as well. The demand for *support for the Palestinians* (16 percent agreement) dominated this factor. The interviewees obviously identified strongly with those seen as suffering the most in the Middle East conflict. That it loaded weakly (.20) onto the question about Israel's dependence on the United States can be assessed as an anti-imperialistic statement, since the conflict is interpreted as the result of political situations and not as its fate (rejection of the item "There is a curse on that people"). There was a very slight age and education effect on the variables of this factor. The

TABLE 7.1
Word Affinity: Likes/Dislikes (question 5)

	Total pop.	Age groups			
	%	16–29	30–44	45–59	60 and older
Like					
Israel	44.1	44.7	50.7	46.1	35.0
Palestinian	15.9	20.8	15.8	15.4	11.0
Zionist	8.9	7.5	11.5	10.6	6.2
Dislike					
Israel	14.9	14.4	13.0	16.3	23.9
Palestinian	51.7	44.0	51.3	55.2	57.2
Zionist	41.0	36.8	39.9	40.9	46.9

N = 2102

youngest and oldest age groups, as well as the more highly educated, tended to express more sympathy with the Palestinians.[3]

Factor 7 presented a *neutral image of Israel.* Political normalcy was stressed, even if this bore some resemblance to the positive self-image ("The Germans of the Middle East"), and any comparison of Israeli occupation policy with the persecution of the Jews during the "Third Reich" was rejected. The generations agreed on this factor, though the Israel-Germany comparison had no relevance for the youngest cohort. Persons with higher education tended to judge Israel's political normalcy more skeptically than others.

Emotional Rejection and Social Distance from Israel(is)

The view of Israel by the German population is primarily determined through its *position in the Middle East conflict.*

There was much more sympathy in Germany for Israel than for its Palestinian counterpart, whom half of those questioned "disliked." Only a small number disliked Israel, and even the term *Zionist,* which according to much of the German population represents Israeli expansionism, was rejected less than the term *Palestinian* (41 percent versus 51 percent). The distribution of sympathies according to age differed from the typical anti-Semitism distribution pattern. Israel was liked the most by the intermediate age groups, while its popularity dropped slightly for the youngest age group, and amounted to only 35 percent in the oldest age category. The sixteen through twenty-nine year olds, in particular, liked Palestinians; their popularity among the older respondents was lower.

The 1989 EMNID Institute data showed no change in trend among the younger generations. Although they were less likely to rate Palestinians with "dislike" on an eleven-point scale (from 5 to +5) (32 percent of the eighteen through twenty-nine year olds versus 41 percent of the over forty-five year olds, EMNID 1989, table 61), the Palestinians, with a slightly negative value of 0.1, did not reach the slightly positive + 0.5 value of the Israelis. What distinguished the generations from one another was not their attitudes toward Israelis, which varied relatively little over all age categories (or generally in a positive direction for the younger age groups), but the more positive assessment of the Palestinians by those under thirty years of age. This assessment expressed both a particular political attitude and a general tendency among younger generations to show a greater openness and liking toward other peoples. The fact that only Green party voters on the average made a slightly positive evaluation of Palestinians resulted from this combination of specific age categories and general political orientation. On the eleven-point scale mentioned, Israelis attained a weakly positive value of +0.4 among a cross-section of the population, which was between the value of +1.7 for Americans and 0.4 for Palestinians.

Between 1989 and late 1991 (the date of the latest EMNID survey) the Middle East experienced major turmoil, including the Intifada and the Gulf War. These were followed by intensive diplomatic activity and the beginnings of a peace process. Press and television followed these developments closely. Although a majority of the German public (79 percent) was very skeptical about the chances of a lasting peace between Israel and its neighbors, approval of both Israelis and Palestinians rose equally in all age groups in comparison with 1989 (Israelis: from +0.4 to +1.0; Palestinians: from -0.4 to 0.0, EMNID 1992, table 20). The gain in sympathy of Israelis probably had to do with the fact that Iraqi missile attacks during the Gulf War brought home the threat to Israel. Since the 1967 Six-Day War, it has been observable that approval of Israel rises among Germans in situations where it is threatened.[4]

Israel was also perceived as a *Jewish* state, and therefore placed in the context of German-Jewish relations strongly influenced by the Nazi past.

As a result of anti-Semitism, the word "Jew" (*Jude*) has taken on a negative connotation and was rated "liked" less and "disliked" more than the
word "Israel" (like: 38 percent to 44 percent; dislike: 20 percent to 17
percent). As could be expected, there was a rather high correlation (0.48)
in the evaluation of these terms. Almost two-thirds of those who disliked
the word "Israel" said the same for the word "Jew," whereas the other
way around, only half of those disliking the word "Jew" said the same
about the word "Israel." This means that rejection of Jews or greater
liking for Israel did not coincide entirely.[5]

In addition to the like-dislike dimension, we also asked about feelings
of social distance toward Israelis. Of those questioned, only 11 percent
reported that they would "not like to have too much to do with Israelis."
This figure shows that the distance from Israelis was far less than toward any other foreign or socially stigmatized group included in the list
given to each interviewee (question 1a). The acceptance of Israelis corresponded to that of Jews, with "German Jews" rejected somewhat less
than "Jews" (8 percent versus 13 percent). At .56, the correlation in the
distance toward Israelis and Jews was rather high. When asked whether
interviewees would accept certain groups within their circle of friends,
"Israelis" were rated somewhat worse (39 percent) than Jews/German
Jews (49 percent). The correlation in this case was also high (.62). This
difference can be explained by reservations against foreigners in general
(language problems, cultural differences, etc.). The younger age groups
once again demonstrated a greater desire for contact, as they also did for
other groups, such as Turks, asylum-seekers, Arabs, and so on (question
1b). Acceptance of Israelis in one's circle of friends was twice as high
among sixteen through twenty-nine year olds (49 percent) as it was for
the over-sixty age group (25 percent).[6]

Public Opinion toward German-Israeli Relations

Personal attitudes toward Israelis must be distinguished from attitudes
toward Israel. To Germany, concerned at the time with the physical and
political consequences of the war, the founding of the state of Israel in
1948 seemed largely a distant event in the Middle East.[7] Not until 1951, in
connection with demands for reparations, did Israel become a subject of
political and public discussion. Aside from this subject, which still plays
an important role in determining attitudes of many Germans to Israel (see

below), the Middle East conflict and the issue of West Germany's special
political relationship with Israel also shape public opinion.

The Middle East Conflict

Sympathy and antipathy toward Israel are largely influenced by its
role in the Middle East conflict. Generally, in wars in which Israel was
perceived as a "David" who had to defend himself against superior Arab

TABLE 7.2
Sympathies in the Arab-Israeli Conflict 1956–1991

	Sympathies		neither/nor	undecided
	Israel	**Arabs**		
	%	**%**	**%**	**%**
1956 Suez War*	10	56	6	28
1965	24	15	44	17
1967 June: Six-Day War	55	6	27	12
1967 July/August	59	6	27	8
1970	45	7	32	16
1971	43	8	29	20
1973 April	37	5	37	21
1973 October: Yom Kippur War	57	8	25	10
1973 October: after end of war	40	6	45	9
1978 Israel invades Lebanon	44	7	33	16
1981 Begin attacks Schmidt	21	24	43	12
1982 Beirut massacre	20	26	39	21
1983	19	15	51	15
1987	39	17	—	44+
1991 March	38	16	—	46+
1991 December	8	14	53	25

Source: IfD *Jahrbuch*; Allensbach Report No. 41/1973, *EMNID-Informationen* No. 11-12/1973;
EMNID 1992.
* The 1956 survey included questions about sympathies for Egypt, on the one hand, and France and
England, on the other. The 10 percent for France and England has been entered for Israel, as an ally
of the two Western powers (IfD, *Jahrbuch I,* 355).
+ IfD, *Jahrbuch IX,* 1993, 999—no category: neither/nor.

TABLE 7.3
"Do you think Israel's actions in Egypt were right or not right?"

	right %	not right %	no opinion %
Australia	31	43	26
Canada	25	43	32
Denmark	28	44	28
Finland	12	70	18
Germany (West)	9	60	31
Italy	20	55	25
Netherlands	42	24	34
Norway	11	89	—
USA	23	43	34

Source: EMNID-Informationen 45, 1956, 1f.

might, German sympathies were on the side of Israel. Michael Wolffsohn followed changes in sympathies in the Arab-Israeli conflict, preparing a series of graphic representations based on available survey data (cf. 1988, table 2). Since the Suez War in 1956, surveys on attitudes toward the conflicting parties have been conducted during and after major military conflicts or whenever German-Israeli-Arab topics were on the public agenda.

The data shows that particular events led to large fluctuations in the distribution of sympathies. Until the Six-Day War in 1967, only a small minority supported one side or the other, the majority showing special sympathy for neither of the two sides or remaining undecided. An international comparative survey evaluating the Suez War of 1956 showed that Israel enjoyed only slight support among West Germans as compared to the other countries. A spot survey by the Gallup Institute in nine Western capitals revealed that West Germany deviated considerably in terms of public opinion (similar only to the Scandinavian countries), generally due to fear of war and opposition to military aggression.

The high level of disapproval for Israel's actions should not be interpreted as fundamentally anti-Jewish or anti-Israeli. This can be seen in the even greater level of disapproval of military actions by France and England (right: 2 percent, not right: 74 percent), and in the considerable fear

TABLE 7.4
"Do you think it is right or wrong to show moral support for Israel?"

	right %	wrong %	no answer %
SPD	55	25	20
CDU/CSU	58	20	22
FDP	44	39	17
NPD	24	58	18
non-voters/voting preference not given	42	20	38

Source: EMNID-Informationen 8, 1967, 5ff.

that the Suez conflict could escalate into a larger-scale war (threat of war—yes, 46 percent: no, 33 percent). All in all, though, West Germans did not show any great sympathy with Israel in the 1950s.[8] Support for Israel was thus at the same level as the countries of the east bloc, which was low due to the cold war (*EMNID-Informationen 15,* 1957, 3).

The 1967 war polarized opinions in Israel's favor. The West German government followed a neutral policy of nonintervention, but the German public, the media, and certain organizations (such as the Federation of German Trade Unions) took Israel's side, expressed in donations and medical aid (cf. Deligdisch 1974, 137ff.). An EMNID survey in June through July 1967 confirmed that one in two West German citizens felt it was right to give moral support to the Israelis (24 percent considered it wrong). These figures were comparable to those for other western countries.[9] Willingness to show support varied according to level of education and political party preference.[10] Compared to people having completed only elementary school (49 percent of whom expressed support), 58 percent and 62 percent, respectively, of those with intermediate or higher education supported Israel.[11] Support for Israel decreased the further right the preferred party was on the political spectrum. It must be kept in mind that up until the mid-1960s, FDP voters represented a conservative, nationalistic political orientation. Emanuel de Kadt was correct in emphasizing that for Germany and Austria, an anti-Israel reaction still was related to a general world view that contained anti-Semitic elements (1967, 11).[12]

As is data on attitudes toward Jews, support for Israel also revealed no left-right distinctions with respect to voters for the two main parties. There was a broad-based consensus, particularly in terms of the foreign policy position toward Israel. Moral support for Israel was based on the assumption that not Israel, but the Arab countries—together with the Soviet Union—were to blame for the conflict (52 percent of West Germans held the Arab countries responsible, 22 percent the Soviet Union, and 8 percent Israel; in contrast, in France, 17 percent held Israel responsible for the conflict). The attitudes of NPD and FDP voters were clearly more anti-Israel. Thirty-one percent and 18 percent, respectively, blamed Israel. The moral judgment by West German citizens did not have any impact on their actions, however, with the exception of private donations. Of those questioned, 77 percent wanted to retain a strict policy of political neutrality in this conflict. Despite sympathies for Israel, there was a greater desire to remain in the position of observers than to intervene on Israel's behalf.

This abundance of support gradually decreased up until the Yom Kippur War in 1973, although support for the Arabs did not increase during this time. The war itself then served to quickly boost support for Israel once again.[13] Not until after the 1978 war in Lebanon was there a fundamental shift in public opinion with respect to the Middle East conflict. Support for Israel dropped to half of what it had been, while at the same time support for the Arab side increased to approximately the same level. The long-term nature of the conflict, which more and more people were starting to consider unresolvable, led the public to withdraw their support for either of the conflicting parties or to become undecided.[14] This distribution of sympathies was similar to that in other western countries; that is, it did not reflect the special German-Israeli relationship.[15] The observed shift in public opinion took place to the same extent throughout the entire population and cannot be traced to a particularly anti-Israeli or pro-Arab shift among the younger age groups. A survey conducted in May, 1978 on the occasion of the thirtieth anniversary of the founding of Israel—shortly after the start of the war in Lebanon—to assess Israeli policies in the Middle East revealed a difference in opinion. Of all respondents, 52 percent considered Israeli politics balanced and 41 percent considered them aggressive. This finding becomes even less favorable when we take into account that a majority of those interested in politics (the more highly educated and residents of major cities), that is, those setting the course of public opinion, considered Israel to have an aggressive foreign policy [elementary school: 35 percent, high school and college: 53 percent (*EMNID-Informationen 6,* 1978, 12)]. International response was especially negative after Israel's invasion of Lebanon and the massacres in Sabra and Shatila. Support in West Germany for the Arabs was initially greater than for Israel (see above). In other western countries as well, these events served to increase support for the Palestinians considerably (cf. de Boer 1983, 123ff.), whereas Israel was criticized more vehemently.

The fact that in 1989, 40 percent of respondents believed Israel's policies in the occupied territories were the reason why Jews were viewed critically supports the assumption that sympathy with Israel declined after the outbreak of the Intifada in December, 1987 (EMNID, table 83). Occupation policies were mentioned most frequently as a cause of anti-Semitism. A critical change in opinion, with views turning against Israel, could be observed in other western countries after the start of the unrest. Thus in the United States, approval of Israel reached its lowest point in fifteen years.[16] In western Germany, sympathy with Israel's position in the Middle East conflict fell to 8 percent, its lowest point ever (EMNID 1992, table 32).[17] This loss of support was not accompanied by increased support for the Arab side (which has remained constant since 1983); rather, the situation was seen as increasingly insoluble and hopeless, so that three-quarters of the respondents felt sympathy for neither side of the conflict.[18] A solution to the Israeli-Palestinian conflict was expected—though still considered "unlikely" in 1991—only if both sides were willing to compromise (two thirds of the respondents). Twenty-five percent of all Germans believed Israel would have to make greater concessions in the conflict, while few expected this of the Palestinians [7 percent (EMNID 1992, table 34)].

By the end of 1991, no difference was apparent between western and eastern Germany in how approval was distributed and responsibility ascribed. Nor could attitudes be distinguished according to age group or educational level. Thus, the attitude toward Israel is the only dimension of attitudes toward Jews in which eastern Germans did not differ *positively* from western Germans. In fall 1990, 33 percent of both eastern and western Germans agreed completely or partly with the claim that "Zionism is racism," as formulated in the UN Resolution No.3379 (Jodice 1991, 24ff.). The effect of anti-Israeli propaganda in the former East

Germany varied depending on closeness to the communist state. Voters who supported the CDU after 1989 had more pro-Israeli attitudes than the average in the German population, while supporters of the communist successor party PDS showed above average support for the Arab states (36 percent, in comparison with the average of 13 percent). PDS supporters accordingly demanded that Israel yield. This anti-Israeli, pro-Arab attitude, which clearly deviated from the average structure of opinion among eastern Germans, can be traced in part to ideologically established anti-Zionism among the PDS supporters. This hard core of PDS voters is surrounded by a majority of less strongly ideological PDS voters. Among the handful of western German PDS supporters (less than 1 percent of the electorate), a dogmatic left-wing profile is even more apparent. While 44 percent of the eastern German PDS voters demanded Israeli concessions in the Middle East conflict, 74 percent of their fellow western German party members did so (EMNID 1992, table 34). For some of the latter, ideologically motivated antipathy toward Israel carried over to the Israeli population, while eastern German PDS voters apparently strictly separated the two; they did not dislike Israelis as individuals (EMNID 1992, table 20).

Germany's Political and Moral Relationship with Israel

Attitudes toward Israel are heavily influenced by its special *bilateral relationship* with Germany. Aside from reparations, which we will consider below, survey questions on German-Israeli relations generally involve military and economic cooperation.

In the early 1950s, the public opposed close cooperation with Israel with relative clarity (37 percent; in comparison, 12 percent opposed close cooperation with France, and 60 percent with Poland). By 1959, the rate of opposition had decreased by half (IfD vol.III, 1964, 187). We have a relatively large amount of data on this issue.

The rise in the sympathy curve in Israel's favor during the 1967 and 1973 wars was reflected in the desire for close cooperation. While only 13 percent to 19 percent advocated such cooperation before the Six-Day War, by October, 1968 and the following years the figure was 24 percent, rising to 27 percent in 1974. However, not even half of those expressing support for Israel favored closer cooperation. Economic cooperation was sought considerably more often with Western European

TABLE 7.5
"Which of these countries should we work with as closely as possible?"

	1954 %	1959 %	1963 %	1968 %	1972 %	1974 %	1975 %	1980 %	1983 %
France	46	48	70	68	63	69	63	69	66
Israel	13	19	17	24	25	27	19	18	18
Russia	22	31	27	35	49	42	38	20	38
Egypt							16	14	

Source: IfD vol. V, 1974, 533; vol. VI, 1977, 291; vol. VIII, 1983, 596.

neighbors and international trading powers. But among economically comparable countries, the wish for close cooperation with Israel was relatively strong, reflecting Germany's special relationship with Israel.

In the public mind, a desire for close political and military cooperation with Israel involved balancing consideration for German interests in regard to the Arab countries against Germany's special obligation to Israel. The debate over diplomatic relations with Israel revealed this dual character. Until the mid-1950s, Israel refused any official contact with West Germany, as the legal successor to the Third Reich. When Israel changed its mind on this issue, the West German government delayed an exchange of ambassadors to preserve good relations with the Arab states, as well as in order to uphold its claim to be the only legitimate representative of Germany (the Hallstein Doctrine). Thus after 1955, West Germany's policies collided more and more with the principle of moral responsibility (Deligdisch 1974, 10). Domestically, after 1962 the German Federation of Trade Unions (*DGB*), *Aktion Sühnezeichen,* and other organizations pressured the German government to take up diplomatic relations with Israel. Not until the head of the East German Council of State, Walter Ulbricht, made an official visit to Egypt in 1965, making concern for the Hallstein Doctrine superfluous, was this step hurriedly taken.[19]

Deligdisch spoke of a radical change in Germany's Middle East policy during the Middle East crisis of 1964–65 (1974, 11). Public opinion was split: in 1963, 27 percent were against diplomatic relations with Israel (38 percent for, 35 percent undecided). During the public debate over the decision, which continued until February, 1965, the number of opponents increased by 10 percent.[20] Public opposition to diplomatic relations was not of a fundamental historical and political nature; it was

instead influenced by foreign policy interests (IfD 1967, 470). Advocates of immediately taking up diplomatic relations with Israel, on the
other hand, were less concerned with political reservations than with
history; of the advocates, 81 percent stood by their views even when
confronted with the disadvantages—that is, the likelihood of diplomatic
relations between East Germany and Egypt (*EMNID-Informationen 17,*
1965, 2f.).

In this phase, too, the public refused to accept any special responsibility for Israel despite the threat posed by the Arab states. Seventy-five
percent voted to remain neutral if Israel "were attacked and defeated by
Egypt or other Arab countries." Only 10 percent would have helped Israel in such a situation (IfD vol.IV, 1967, 471). In the same year, a two-
thirds majority supported halting weapons supplies to Israel (11 percent
supported weapons deliveries). Thus, the policies of the federal government, which were more strongly oriented toward Israel's interests, did
not enjoy the support of a majority of the population.

Pragmatic interests again carried the day between 1981 and 1983,
when the discussion on oil supplies to Western industrialized countries
again required a decision between pragmatic politics and historical responsibility toward Israel (Neustadt 1983). In 1983, fifty-two percent of
the respondents refused to prioritize good relations with Israel over Arab
oil. Only 18 percent advocated a particularly friendly relationship with
Israel because of Germany's historical guilt (IfD, vol. VIII, 1983, 648).

The controversy between Chancellor Helmut Schmidt, who in 1981
called for Palestinian self-determination, and Israeli Prime Minister
Menachem Begin, who refused to shake hands with Schmidt because he
had served as a German soldier in the Second World War, underlined the
sensitivity of German-Israeli relations and the continued explosiveness
of history (cf. Neustadt 1983, 475ff.). West Germans proceeded to characterize Begin as ruthless, aggressive, and unpredictable (*EMNID-
Informationen 5–6,* 1982, 17). While half of all Israelis identified with
Begin's refusal, a majority of Germans took Schmidt's side (57 percent);
only 18 percent thought he was partly responsible for the controversy.
An IfD survey showed how quickly, in the context of the sensitive German-Israeli relationship, political criticism and polemics could cause a
renewed outbreak of old hostilities. Forty-one percent of all West Germans believed that after Begin's attacks, "prejudice against Jews will
again increase here" (IfD vol. VIII, 651). The fact that this fear was

expressed most often by older people (sixteen through twenty-nine years old, 33 percent; forty-five years old and above, 47 percent), who were more likely to be anti-Semitic, suggests that it was not an unrealistic concern, but at least in part an actual upsurge in anti-Semitic sentiment.

German Attitudes toward Reparations to Israel

The issue of "reparations" was mentioned frequently during the exploratory interviews (chapter 2). In general, those interviewed were opposed to reparations. This issue appears very closely linked with the image of Israel, although reparations to Israel make up only a fraction of all reparations payments (as of 1 January 1994, they made up 3 billion DM out of 93.3 billion DM; on the financial dimension, Bundesministerium der Finanzen 1994, 42).[21]

A factor analysis of the image of Israel (see above) indicated a partially negative image accusing Israel of exploiting German guilt. When we added a new variable, composed of all five items in our survey involving reparations, only a third of those questioned made no negative comments on reparations. That is, two-thirds of the population opposed reparations in some form or other. No other dimension of our evaluation produced such a high negative rate of agreement (for the opinions of eastern and western Germans after unification see chapter 12).[22] This confirmed our hypothesis that the German relationship to Israel, and Jews in general, was heavily influenced by the past and the financial, political, and moral obligations arising from it. Israel and its representatives were seen as "annoying reminders," who insisted upon reminding the Germans of a past they preferred to forget; their claims and demands were no longer accepted as a consequence of Nazi injustice, but instead viewed as "items in the Israeli budget." Opposition to reparations was central to Germans' domestically motivated negative view of Israel. These reservations were not linked very strongly with anti-Zionist attitudes or support for adversaries of Israel. The relatively low correlation (maximum .36) between items on reparations and the anti-Zionism[1] index (see below) supports the view that strong rejection of Israeli policies in the Middle East and historically motivated criticism of its attitude toward Germany involve two distinct, only partially related attitudes.

The central significance rejection of Israeli demands for material and moral reparations had for anti-Semites was indicated by the significant

FIGURE 7.1
Israel Lives off Reparations/PAS, SAS, VAS

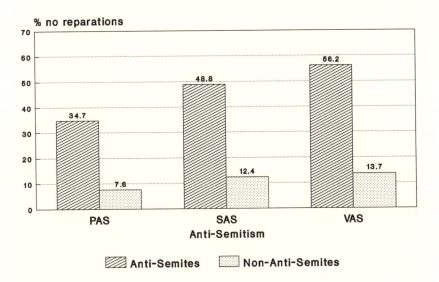

correlation between opposition to reparations and the three measures of anti-Semitism.

Ninety-three percent of those classified as "vehemently anti-Semitic" claimed Israel took advantage of the Nazi past (SAS 91 percent, PAS 79 percent). This finding confirmed our hypothesis that present-day German anti-Semitism is triggered by an "unmastered past" (*unbewältigte Vergangenheit*).

Reparations payments and their "abuse by individual Jews" were the main cause of critical views of Jews, according to anti-Semites (cf. chapter 10), while those classified as non-anti-Semitic ascribed significance to this complex much less frequently.

Attitudes toward reparations indicated the usual generation effect. Approximately one-quarter of sixteen through fifty-nine-year-olds were against any payment of reparations to Israel at all, while 37 percent of those over sixty were opposed to such payments. When we asked about the appropriateness of the amount of the payments, rather than for a justification of reparations, the number of those in all generations who considered the payments "too high" was perceptibly greater.[23]

Looking back at forty years of relations with Israel from the perspective of public opinion polls, the following pattern becomes apparent: In the Middle East conflict, German sympathies have tended more toward the Israeli than the Arab side, a trend that has increased during wars. However, as far as practical policies are concerned, people prefer a neutral attitude and would like to "see Israel as a state like any other." Very few Germans acknowledge a special historical obligation or recommend it as a guideline for German policy. In particular, a majority of the population oppose any further reparations. Overall perceptions and judgments of Israel are determined more by relations at any given time and by Israeli policies than are perceptions of Jews, in which historical relationships and anti-Jewish traditions play a greater role.

Anti-Zionism and Anti-Semitism

An oft-discussed issue in anti-Semitism research and in public political debate concerns the relationship between anti-Semitism and anti-Zionism. One theory maintains that anti-Zionism is no more than veiled anti-Semitism. Because the latter can no longer be expressed openly, hostility toward Jews takes the form of extreme criticism of Israel, which is more acceptable in public. Another, contrasting theory holds that criticism of Israeli policies has been discredited as anti-Zionism, and thus linked with anti-Semitism, in order to prevent such criticism.[24]

Zionism and anti-Zionism are political concepts that are very difficult to define precisely in a public opinion survey. Neither is it possible to fall back on operationalizations in older or foreign studies, as no anti-Zionism indicator has been developed so far.[25] In the literature on this subject (cf. Broder 1976 and 1986, Bauer 1983, Heinsohn 1988, Volkov 1990, Wistrich 1990), individual texts and statements are generally criticized for being anti-Zionist, though no explicit, generalizable criteria are provided. Statements denying Israel a right to exist and describing Zionism as an imperialist, racist ideology are clearly anti-Zionist.[26] Regarding other criticisms of Israel, an assessment as "anti-Zionist" depends on one's political standpoint. The criteria mentioned above most likely apply to extreme left-wing criticism of Israel, but cannot provide the basis for a general public opinion survey, as the public does not think in categories such as racism or left-wing imperialism theory. Rejection of Israel among the population at large is more likely to be linked with events presented by the mass media, which are evaluated in the context of existing anti-Jewish attitudes. Our view is supported by the fact that the 1975 UN Resolution No.3379, stating that "Zionism is a form of racism and racial discrimination," did not enjoy a great deal of support in a 1975 EMNID survey of West Germans. Seventeen percent considered the comparison accurate (in England, the figure was 27 percent, in France 28 percent, and in Switzerland 13 percent), 41 percent disagreed with it, 42 percent had no opinion (*EMNID-Informationen 12,* 1975, 4f.; in 1990, 33 percent of western and eastern Germans agreed strongly or somewhat, Jodice 1991, table 5a). The high percentage of "no opinions" suggests that the public did not view Zionism in the categories provided.

In our list of questions on views of Israel, we included very harsh, exaggerated criticisms of Israeli policies. We created an "Anti-Zionism Index" from the statements that loaded onto the factor "aggressive Israel" in the factor analysis of the view of Israel; they showed a high correlation with each other. The index included the variables "They take land away from their neighbors illegally" (question 14/16); "They start wars and blame others" (question 14/19); "A country that simply does not want peace" (question 14/18); and "The way the state of Israel treats the Palestinians is in principle no different from how the Nazis treated the Jews in the Third Reich" (question 15). The question on "support for the Palestinian struggle" (question 16/5), which is part of the anti-Zionism complex in substance, was not included in the index because it did not load onto the "aggressive Israel" factor and correlated only slightly with corresponding items. Rejection of Israel was apparently not strongly linked to support for its opponents; the only exception here was a group of younger, better educated interviewees (see above).

The decision on how many negative statements would be necessary to classify someone as "anti-Zionist" could not be made automatically from the data, but had to be justified with the help of additional information. We used the following criteria as an orientation: before someone was ascribed a complex of ideological views, agreement with anti-Israeli statements had to appear *repeatedly*. Thus, those who gave only one "yes" response were not immediately counted as "anti-Zionists." Further, the correlation of the anti-Zionism Index with other anti-Israeli statements indicated a clear pattern: those who answered "yes" once on the AZ index still fell within the

TABLE 7.6
Index: Anti-Zionism

"yes" responses	N	%	cumulative %
0	1216	57.8 %	57.8
1	431	20.5	78.4
2	238	11.3	89.7
3	101	4.8	94.5
4	80	3.8	98.3
5	36	1.7	100.0
Total	**2102**	**100.0**	

(Reliability - alpha = .67)

overall average in their agreement with such statements; agreement clearly increased only with a "yes" response to two or more statements in the index. For example, only obvious anti-Zionists supported the "Palestinian struggle" with above-average frequency (45 percent, compared with 16 percent in the total population), and they were also more likely to see no threat to Israel (approximately 65 percent compared with 52 percent). From this perspective, approximately 22 percent of the population would have to be classified as anti-Zionist.

Are anti-Zionists also anti-Semites? The correlation between the anti-Zionism index and the anti-Semitism index was quite obvious, at .56 (p < .001). The more radical the anti-Semitism, the greater the overlap between anti-Semitism and anti-Zionism.

Thus, the stronger the anti-Semitic convictions, the more likely it is that they will include anti-Zionist views. The same is true in reverse, with anti-Zionism as the starting point: when a hard-core (10.3 percent = 3–5 "yes" responses on the anti-Zionism index) of anti-Zionists was isolated, anti-Semitism rose with the intensity of anti-Zionist convictions. This partly confirms the identification of anti-Zionism with anti-Semitism that is repeatedly made in the literature.

On the other hand, we identified a large number of anti-Zionists who expressed no anti-Semitic convictions. Even under a very broad definition of anti-Semitism (through the PAS conditions), 36 percent of the anti-Zionists and 22 percent of the "extreme anti-Zionists" had to be classified as non-anti-Semitic.[27]

FIGURE 7.2
Anti-Semitism and Anti-Zionism

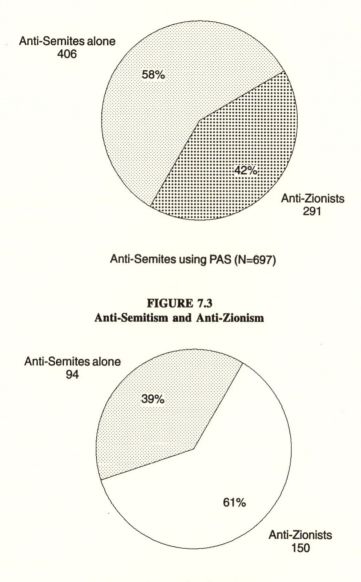

Anti-Semites using PAS (N=697)

FIGURE 7.3
Anti-Semitism and Anti-Zionism

Anti-Semites using SAS (N=244)

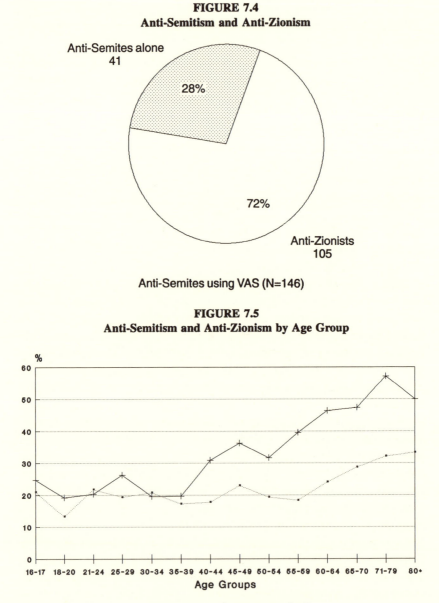

FIGURE 7.4
Anti-Semitism and Anti-Zionism

Anti-Semites alone
41

28%

72%

Anti-Zionists
105

Anti-Semites using VAS (N=146)

FIGURE 7.5
Anti-Semitism and Anti-Zionism by Age Group

····■···· Anti-Zionists   ──+── Anti-Semites (PAS)

FIGURE 7.6
Anti-Semitism by Party Preference

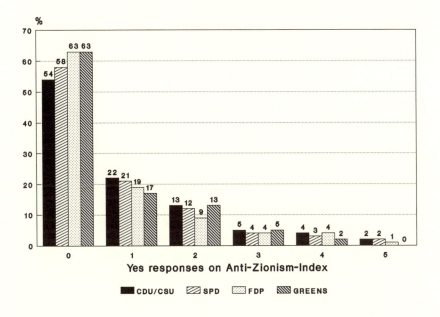

Thus, negative attitudes toward Israel can be explained only in part by anti-Semitism. They also partly comprise an independent complex of attitudes nourished by other motives. The distinction was indicated, first of all, by the fact that the age distribution on the anti-Zionism index differed from that on the anti-Semitism index: the age-related increase was less strongly marked on the Anti-Zionism index. The clear generation gaps found for anti-Semitism were lacking.

In contrast to the case of anti-Semitism, voters for the four parties in the *Bundestag* (in 1987) hardly differed in their strong rejection of Israel. For the first time, opinions among the Greens corresponded to those found in other parties.

The special sympathy for Israel felt by the "Left" until 1967 has since fallen consistently, approaching the popular average (Ludwig 1995). What was summarized by the index as anti-Zionism could have resulted from

TABLE 7.7
Support for the Palestinians / Anti-Zionism Index / Party Preference

"yes" responses	CDU/CSU %	N	SPD %	N	FDP %	N	Greens %	N
0	10.0	335	12.7	51	8.0	7	4.2	3
1	16.5	23	15.6	23	37.0	10	15.0	3
2	19.5	16	30.0	24	30.8	4	46.7	7
3	20.0	7	30.8	8	80.0	4	66.7	4
4	25.9	7	33.3	8	16.7	1	50.0	1
5	53.8	7	70.0	7	100.0	1	—	—
Total N		**95**		**121**		**27**		**18**

(In the sample, 16 percent of all respondents advocated the call to "support the Palestinian struggle for their homeland.")

various political motivations. Traditional anti-Semitism was probably responsible for rejection of Israel by the "Right" (also indicated by the fact that all seven NPD voters in the sample gave more than two "yes" responses); that is, Israel was identified as a "Jewish state" and viewed in a correspondingly negative light. Here anti-Semitism and anti-Zionism coincided. For liberal and left-wing voters, it was necessary to investigate the extent to which criticism of Israel grew out of a low assessment of the threat to Israel,[28] from its military and occupation policies, or from pacifist motives. Here we are dealing with a rejection of Israeli policies that contains hardly any anti-Semitic elements. Among these voters, total rejection (four or five "yes" responses on the anti-Semitism index) rarely appeared, totalling only 2 percent to 5 percent.

Our assumption that there were two different aggregates of motives used to justify anti-Israeli attitudes was confirmed when we broke down the relationship between anti-Zionism and "support for the Palestinian struggle for their homeland" (question 16/5) according to party preference.

Among CDU/CSU voters, willingness to support the Palestinians rose only slightly as anti-Zionism increased; it became very strong only in the group with five "yes" responses. That is, only among a very small number did a negative attitude toward Israel coincide with a pro-Palestinian position (a total of only one-quarter of anti-Zionists among CDU/CSU voters supported the Palestinian cause, compared with 33 percent among SPD, 40 percent among FDP, and 52 percent among Green voters). The situation was different among voters for other parties. There, the number of people with pro-Palestinian views was clearly higher among those giving more than two "yes" responses (our cutoff for classification as an anti-Zionist). However, because of the small sample from the two smaller parties, these statistics must be viewed with caution. Thus, it appears that CDU/CSU voters judged Israel and its policies negatively for reasons largely connected not with the Middle East conflict, but with a generally anti-Jewish attitude, while voters for the other parties—especially the Greens and the Free Democrats—based their objections more on a critical perception of Israeli policies toward the Palestinians and on support for the latter. However, this support by people we had been classified as anti-Zionist did not go so far as to approve more frequently of "selling weapons to the Arabs."[29]

Israel was judged more within the context of anti-Jewish prejudice by voters for the two larger parties than by supporters of the smaller parties in Parliament. This was indicated by the significantly higher level of agreement by anti-Zionist CDU/CSU and SPD voters with the statement "There is a curse on that people" (question 14/2). A third of them agreed with it, compared with a quarter of "FDP anti-Zionists," and only an eighth of Green voters (overall total: 21 percent).

No evaluation could be made for splinter parties because of the small number of cases. Of the seven NPD voters in the sample, all had to be classed as anti-Zionist, and all were opponents of Israel for historical and political reasons.[30] It is conspicuous that, in contrast to the mainstream right, the militant right strongly supported the Palestinian struggle.

Overall attitudes toward Israel were more heavily influenced by current events and political views than were attitudes toward Jews. Rejection of Israel increased among older generations, but distinctions between political generations were not as apparent. Among women, the total level of disapproval of Israel was lower, increasing more slowly with age. Men were slightly overrepresented in the group of anti-Zionists: 25 percent of all men and 19 percent of all women fell into this category. Further, there was only a slight gender difference in critical attitudes toward Israel resulting from the troubled German-Jewish past. While 72 percent of the men rejected reparations and reminders of German guilt, the figure for women was 64 percent (significant at the 5 percent level).[31]

We suspected that two different aggregates of motives were involved in political anti-Zionism and in rejection of Israel resulting from a wish to end discussion of the past. This was once again confirmed by the fact that education had a different effect on each of the two. The better educated had a more positive attitude toward Israel's claims to reparations and reminders of the past; higher education and assumption of political models helped them better understand the historical background that legitimized these claims. Here a significant link existed between educational level and attitudes toward Israel's demands. While some 70 percent of people with or without *Hauptschulabschluss* (junior high school equivalent) took a critical attitude, the figure was 62 percent for those with a high school education, and 55 percent among the college educated. However, opposition to Israel's claims was so strong that even among the college educated, more than half took a negative position.

Education had still other effects on opposition to Israeli policies. Among people with junior high school and basic high school educations, we saw the familiar pattern of a positive educational influence (34 percent rejection among junior high school students without a diploma, 25 percent among junior high school graduates, and 18 percent among basic high school graduates). Rejection did not decrease with completion of the *Abitur* (college qualification exam), as might have been expected; it remained at the same level as that of basic high school graduates, even rising among people who had completed college to the level of those with only junior high school diplomas (22 percent). The only exception here were university students, who evidenced the lowest degree of anti-Zionism, at 13 percent.[32]

We can suggest the following as reasons for the differing attitude expressed by the college educated toward Israel's claims arising from the German past and toward the Middle East conflict. In the first case, a high level of political awareness may lead to a learning process and objective political judgments. The liberal political consensus on this issue is perceived as an obligation and supported by the successful and better educated. In judging Israel's current policies, no such consensus exists; expressing anti-Israeli views is thus less of a taboo. Anti-Zionism thus *might* be a way of expressing latent anti-Semitic hostilities. But it cannot be ruled out that Israel is more closely observed by the better educated, and its policies judged by high political and moral standards.[33] The backdrop is formed by liberal values such as nonviolence, protection of minorities, self-determination, and the like, along with a critique of imperialism and support for "Third World" national liberation movements. Intensively scrutinizing Israel and applying particularly high standards to its behavior are probably a means of turning around Israel's own moral criticism of Germany, trying to judge Israel by its own stringent moral standards.[34] This negative assessment can be used for moral rationalization, to relativize Jewish or Israeli criticism of Germany, and to exonerate Germany, for example when Israeli policies toward the Palestinians are compared with Nazi persecution of the Jews (cf. question 15: agreement 17 percent, undecided 33 percent, disagreement 50 percent). Israel's behavior has been compared with that of Nazi Germany, as indicated by the extraordinarily harsh criticism of the massacres in the Sabra and Shatila refugee camps during the 1982 Lebanon war, which were condemned as a Holocaust of the Palestinians. It is often difficult for the German public to free its assessment of Israeli policies, whether pro or con, from historical and political interests.

Notes

1. Cf. the remarks in Strauss 1990.
2. Cf. Luhmann 1978, 43ff.
3. The negative image of Israel was most accentuated among the thirty through forty-four-year-olds (born 1943–1957). An anti-Zionist image of an aggressive Israel was combined with pro-Palestinian attitudes ("Support the struggle of the Palestinians") in two of the age groups (sixteen through forty-four and forty-five through fifty-nine). The oldest age group combined pro-Palestinian demands with a rejection of reparations payments. Generation-specific value judgments seem to be very significant here. The older interviewees took the side of the Palestinians, for whom they showed no particular affinity (11 percent "like Palestinians"), as a reflection of anti-Israel attitudes connected to the Nazi past. The younger age groups, on the other hand, had pro-Palestinian attitudes as an expression of a pacifist, international human rights orientation, as well as support for the struggles of the "Third World."
4. Criticism of the behavior of the German peace movement during the Gulf War does not often distinguish sufficiently between the situation before and after the Iraqi missile attacks on Israel. During the first phase of the conflict, the peace movement opposed military intervention and supported a boycott of Iraq; it changed its views after Israel was actually attacked.
5. Hilde Weiss's study on the attitudes of the Vienna population (1978, 13) confirmed that sympathy for Israel can exist independently of negative attitudes toward Jews. Eighty percent of those who attained a high value on an anti-Semitism scale had a positive image of Israel (versus 92 percent of all those questioned). Only 20 percent exhibited a congruency of attitudes between anti-Semitism and the rejection of Israel. When asked if their own image of Israel influenced their opinion of Jews, 47 percent of those considered to be anti-Semites said "no." Weiss interpreted this phenomenon as a defense mechanism used to prevent the cognitive insecurity of a threat to their attitudinal system. If a person's anti-Semitic prejudice was less strong, defensiveness

was clearly lower (31 percent of the "mid-range" anti-Semites), and the transmission effect of a positive image of Israel onto attitudes toward Jews was considerably greater (67 percent in comparison to 48 percent of the vehement anti-Semites).

6. Agreement with statements encouraging support of contact via tourism to Israel or through city partnerships was 26 percent and 37 percent, respectively. Though agreement appeared relatively high here, no conclusive evaluation of the data is possible since comparative data for other countries or from older surveys are not available. With respect to age distribution, the same pattern emerged for approval of publicly supported contact as for personal contact.

7. In the first opinion polls, questions about Israel were still asked entirely from a German perspective, that is, within the context of the "Jewish question." Two-thirds of those questioned considered "the formation of the state of Israel [to be] a solution to the Jewish question," with only 14 percent disagreeing (IfD 1949, 47). Later surveys showed that this response was seen primarily as a means of removing Jews from the country (the desire for migration must be viewed within the context of the problem of displaced persons in the postwar years, cf. Wetzel 1987; Königseder and Wetzel 1994) and not in terms of creating a nation-state for the Jews. In 1952, 37 percent declared that "It would be best for Germany if there were no Jews in the country," 44 percent were undecided or had no opinion (IfD vol. II, 1957, 126). In the course of time, interviewees lost "hope" that all Jews would leave Germany and go to Israel. Today, only 13 percent agree with the statement, and 65 percent view German Jews primarily as Germans (questions 10 and 2).

8. Only 5 percent rated Israel as very favorable, another 14 percent somewhat favorable, 38 percent neutral, 20 percent somewhat unfavorable, and 23 percent very unfavorable. As a comparison, here are the values from the same year for the United States: 12 percent rated Israel as very favorable, 21 percent as somewhat favorable, 53 percent neutral, 8 percent somewhat unfavorable, and 6 percent very unfavorable (EMNID-Informationen 15, 1957, 3).

9. Various Gallup Institutes determined the following public opinion in their respective countries:

Sympathies	Argentina %	Austria %	France %	Great Britain %	U.S. %	Netherlands %
Israel	31	54	56	56	55	67
Arabs	11	11	2	2	4	0
Indifferent	18	35	42	34	47	25
no opinion	40				7	7

Source: de Kadt 1967, 11.

10. The differences between the various age groups were relatively small. The twenty-one through thirty year-olds, followed by the thirty through fifty-year-olds, considered it right to give Israel moral support (55 percent and 53 percent, respectively) and blamed Egypt for the war (57 percent and 51 percent, respectively). Of the fifty through sixty-five-year-olds and those over sixty-five, 49 percent and 48 percent, respectively, supported Israel, but a lower percentage felt Egypt was responsible for starting the war: 47 percent and 43 percent, respectively (de Kadt 1967, 13). We feel that it is not possible, as de Kadt attempted (ibid.), to draw—on the basis of these relatively slight differences—

far-reaching conclusions as to the historical situations of the different generations, such as the identity crises of the twenty-one through thirty-year-olds in
view of the Nazi past, or efforts of the older generations to hold on to "the spirit
of the past."

11. The figures for France also show an influence of education. Of the most highly
    educated, 76 percent, as compared to 50 percent of the least educated, supported
    Israel, while in Argentina, the same effect was demonstrated by the distribution
    of social class. In the upper social classes, 60 percent were in favor of supporting
    Israel, 39 percent of the middle classes, and 17 percent of the lower classes (de
    Kadt 1967, 12, table 3).

12. The left-wing/right-wing distribution in Austria was even more clear, with the
    exception of the Austrian communist party (KPÖ), which supported the "anti-
    Zionist" line of the east bloc countries. Among SPÖ voters, 66 percent sup-
    ported Israel, as did 57 percent of ÖVP voters, 30 percent from the FPÖ and 11
    percent from the KPÖ. Four percent of SPÖ voters supported an Arab victory, as
    did 10 percent of ÖVP voters, 43 percent of FPÖ voters, and 57 percent of KPÖ
    voters (EMNID-Informationen 3, 1967, 6).

13. Wolffsohn did not consider the conspicuous difference between the findings of
    the Allensbach and EMNID surveys for October, 1973 to be significant. The
    difference in wording was negligible, so that it cannot be the only explanation
    for the large deviation. We assume that it was due to the fact that the IfD Allens-
    bach survey took place during the Yom Kippur War (6–23 October 1973), while
    the question used in the EMNID survey involved a retrospective look back after
    the war had ended: "For which side were your sympathies..." (EMNID-
    Informationen 11–12, 1973, 8). The great support for Israel during the war and
    the considerable decline (17 percent) after Israel's victory demonstrates the strong
    dependence of public opinion on specific events.

14. West German citizens were repeatedly very skeptical of peace efforts in the
    Middle East during the 1970s. In 1974, 68 percent expected renewed unrest and
    only 11 percent predicted a peaceful year (EMNID-Informationen 1/2/1974, 6).
    In 1978, only 33 percent of those questioned believed that the peace efforts of
    Egyptian President Sadat would lead to lasting peace (EMNID-Informationen 1/
    1978, 11). Cf. the similar answer distribution for this question for the years
    1977 and 1978 in IfD, vol. VIII, 1983, 649.

15. Cf. on developments from 1967 to 1983 in the United States, Great Britain,
    Denmark, the Netherlands, and West Germany, Connie de Boer 1983.

16. In 1988, 55 percent viewed Israel positively versus 67 percent in 1986. Still,
    Israel's image in the United States stayed more positive than the image of the
    Arab countries [with the exception of Egypt (Richman 1989, 417)].

17. In Austria, too, only 11 percent expressed approval of the Israeli side in 1991,
    but unlike the situation in Germany, sympathy for the Arab side was even lower
    [9 percent (Karmasin 1991, table 18). In Britain, 19 percent supported the Israe-
    lis, and only 13 percent the Arabs (Golub 1993, table 9), which may have al-
    ready reflected changed conditions in the Middle East, especially the policies of
    the new Israeli government. The Austrian and English studies distinguish be-
    tween approval of the Arab states and of the Palestinians. Here the Palestinians
    had a higher approval rating than the Israelis, because they are apparently per-
    ceived as a nation whose rights are being violated. In Austria, 13 percent sympa-
    thized with them, in Britain the figures were 14 percent for Israel and 20 percent
    for the Palestinians (Golub 1993, table 10).

18. In both Austria (Karmasin 1991, table 18) and Britain (Golub 1993, table 9), a majority supported neither side: 81 percent in Austria, 78 percent in Britain.
19. The German-Arab crisis as a result of the Ulbricht visit to Egypt (February, 1965) and German weapons deliveries to Israel did not lead to a projection of these complications onto Israel; instead, the West German federal government's behavior was considered the main cause (49 percent; 13 percent considered the Hallstein Doctrine to be the problem). Very few saw the weapons supplies and the efforts to establish diplomatic relations with Israel as causes of the crisis (6 percent each). Only a minority of 2 percent openly blamed Israel or the Jews (EMNID-Informationen 16, 1965, 4f.).
20. More favorable opinions on the immediate establishment of diplomatic relations with Israel were found by EMNID in March, 1965. According to that survey, 31 percent supported such relations, 30 percent supported relations at a later date, and 17 percent were fundamentally opposed. Among FDP voters, opposition was as high as 28 percent (EMNID-Informationen 17, 1965, 2ff.).
21. In the public consciousness, no distinction was made between various types of reparations payments. However, it was apparently the one-time, controversial reparations payment to Israel that formed opinions here. Our questions aimed both at this specific case and, more generally, at recompense of Jews in the form of return of confiscated property (restitution), pension payments, and the like.
22. Thus, Adenauer's expectation that reparations to Israel could function as an educational tool in response to public rejection in an insecure political situation were not entirely realized. There was no open resistance, but the payments to Israel have not been accepted to this day. Cf. the confirmation in Deligdisch 1974, 20f.
23. The number of those in all generations who considered the payments "too high" were as follows: 35 percent of the eighteen through twenty-nine-year-olds, 42 percent of the thirty through forty-four-year-olds, 49 percent of the forty-five through fifty-nine-year-olds, and 56 percent of those over sixty (EMNID 1989, tab. 81). The education factor apparently took effect only among those with higher education. While 54 percent of those with a basic education (*Volksschulabschluss*) considered reparations payments too high, 46 percent of those who had completed secondary school felt the same way. Among those with *Abitur* or a university degree, the figure fell drastically, to 22 percent (ibid.).
24. Cf., as virtual paradigms for the two positions, Jean Amery, who sees any criticism of Israel as an expression of anti-Semitism, and Erich Fried, who in the same volume of the magazine "Merkur" described Amery's position as an immunization strategy that attempted to avert any criticism of Israel by branding it anti-Semitism (1976).
25. Even operationalizations as undertaken by American surveys cannot be used here, because the domestic situation in the U.S., with its large, active Jewish minority, cannot be compared with the Jewish community in Germany (cf. Richman 1989). The "Index of Attitudes toward Israel" developed by Martire and Clark contains four items, of which two involved a continuation of U.S. assistance to Israel and a third concerned sympathy for Israel in the Mideast conflict, while only a negative response to the fourth question, whether the survival of Israel as a Jewish state is important, could be judged as anti-Zionism (1982, 82ff.). In other words, this index cannot be applied to the situation in West Germany. As far as the figures are concerned, 27 percent of Americans are critical of Israel according to this index, 41 percent are partially pro-Israel, and 32 percent are very pro-Israel (ibid.).

26. Michael May proposed a comparative procedure. He spoke of anti-Zionism when decisions and omissions by Israeli politicians were judged according to different criteria than those of Arab politicians (European Parliament 1985/86, Document A 2-160, L.20). This "relativist" defining process is not suited for operationalization in an empirical investigation.

27. The 1989 EMNID survey (table 83) contained some indications in this direction. Aside from those persons classed as very anti-Semitic, 47 percent of whom saw Israel's occupation policies as a possible cause of anti-Semitism, it was those classed as non-anti-Semitic who attached the greatest importance to this point (43 percent). Certainly one cannot infer people's own opinions from their views of the opinions of others; nevertheless, social psychology tells us that one's own views play an important role in such projective questions. That is, we can assume that for many non-anti-Semites, Israeli policies are one justification for a critical attitude toward Jews.

28. Of those questioned, 48 percent agreed with the statement that Israel is "a country whose behavior is influenced by a constant external threat." Among anti-Zionists, as index values rose, agreement fell from 41 percent to 28 percent.

29. The only exceptions were several anti-Zionists with a preference for the Green Party. While only 40 percent of non-anti-Zionist Green voters approved of these sales (as opposed to 56 percent of the population as a whole), 65 percent of this militant group approved of weapons sales to the Arabs. However, the correlation is not significant.

30. The largely anti-Semitic "Republikaner" voters also frequently (43 percent) assumed that Israeli occupation policies were the cause of critical views of Jews. Along with criticism of "enrichment of individual Jews through reparations payments" (67 percent), it was the most frequently mentioned point (EMNID 1989, table 83).

31. The influence of religion and church membership on anti-Zionism and opposition to reparations was not significant. Rejection of Israel was somewhat greater among Catholics than among Protestants. In addition to the fact that the Catholic Church's attitude toward Jews changed later than did Protestant views, the conflict between the Pope and the Jews over diplomatic recognition of Israel may have been responsible. However, the largest share of anti-Zionists was found among those not belonging to any religion (27 percent, as compared to 25 percent among Catholics and 18 percent among Protestants).

32. Our results were confirmed by the figures in the 1989 EMNID survey. While a linear educational effect was apparent in regard to feelings toward "German Jews," and a definite increase in positive views was found between persons with basic high school diplomas and those with Abitur and university degrees (from + 0.8 to + 1.3), this increase in positive views did not exist for "Israeli Jews" (each group received a value of + 0.7). In addition, the better-educated showed the greatest difference in positive views between "German Jews" and "Israeli Jews" [0.6 points, versus 0.1 or 0.2 points for other educational groups (table 61)].

33. For the well-educated (Abitur or university degree), Israel's occupation policies were by far the most frequently mentioned cause of possible critical views of Jews. One in two in this category felt this way (51 percent), while other points of criticism (economic or religious power, reparations) were accorded far lower importance (between 9 percent and 29 percent). People with lower levels of education, on the other hand, emphasized these points more strongly, while according Israeli policies less significance (EMNID 1989, table 83).

34. Willy Guggenheim, Secretary General of the Swiss Israelitischer Gemeindebund, proposed that the term anti-Zionism be used to refer to cases where criticism of Israel is characterized by historical blindness or one-sidedness. He said moral criticism applies a "double standard" when Israel is criticized for behavior that would be approved of or ignored for other countries—such as border changes after wars and the resulting refugee problems, Israel's religious or nationalist claims to territory, and so on. (1989, 171). Guggenheim would not subsume legitimate criticism of Israeli politics under the heading "anti-Zionism," but rather one-sided application and intensification of moral demands in the case of Israel.

8

Group Prejudice and Anti-Semitism

Since the famous "Studies in Prejudice" by Theodor W. Adorno et al. (1950), it has become an accepted fact in research on prejudice that rejection of an outgroup, such as Jews, always coincides with rejection of other groups not identified with one's own group because of skin color, language, culture, religion, or deviant social behavior. This antipathy and hostility toward alien groups goes hand in hand with a particularly high estimation, even overestimation, of the ingroup (ethnocentrism, nationalism). Thus we will examine anti-Semitism in the context of general xenophobia and negative attitudes toward groups stigmatized as socially deviant, in conjunction with strong nationalist views.

Because our investigation concentrated on the extent of existing prejudices, their demographic distribution, and their links with historical and political developments, we will not consider the psychological origins of prejudice, such as the thesis of the "authoritarian personality."

Xenophobia and Anti-Semitism

Rejection of the Jewish minority by Christian majority society underwent a historical transformation in which the forms of and motivations behind hostility toward Jews changed. Religious differences, economic competition, and biological and racial beliefs in a "racial struggle" succeeded one another and combined to justify hostility toward Jews. The Holocaust represented the end of one epoch and the beginning of another (cf. Strauss 1990). In Western countries, at least, and especially in Germany, this form of xenophobia was no longer acceptable in public political life (Bergmann and Erb 1986). But anti-Semitism did not disappear; Jews, like other minorities, continue to be rejected by a segment of the population. Because of its history, anti-Semitism is a singular phenomenon, but it is also part of a general xenophobic attitude, directed in today's Germany mainly against migrant workers and asylum seekers. Therefore, we would expect anti-Semitism to persist as a separate aggregate of attitudes with its own motivating structure, essentially determined by the consequences of Nazi crimes. But because it is politically combatted as a public taboo, it is likely to be less pronounced than rejection of groups newly immigrated to Germany. In addition to the aforementioned historical factors, social competition as a motivating force against Jews has lost its relevance in Germany. In countries such as the United States or France, with their larger Jewish minorities, anti-Jewish stereotypes and competitive motivations have persisted (cf. chapter 4; Weil 1990; Bergmann 1996). For these reasons, xenophobia is less apt to apply to Jews, especially among younger generations.

We did a factor analysis of the structures of xenophobia and rejection of socially stigmatized groups. It yielded six factors (see appendix 3).[1] Here we will limit our discussion to the factors onto which rejection of ethnic groups (described in colloquial terms) loaded. Factor 1, social distance from ethnic groups, included all the groups considered: blacks, Arabs, Israelis, Jews, Turks, asylum seekers (and, surprisingly, university students). Factor 2 included emotional xenophobia toward Turks, asylum seekers, guest workers, gypsies, Palestinians, and Jews. Anti-Semitism formed its own Factor (4), which included all anti-Jewish and anti-Israeli items.

The fact that "Jews" loaded onto the first two factors as well as onto a specific anti-Semitism factor confirmed the expectation expressed above that social and emotional rejection of Jews is part of a general complex of xenophobic attitudes, but that anti-Semitism also comprises a separate complex of attitudes (cf. our confirmational factor analysis in appendix 3).[2]

The correlations between rejection of individual outgroups, including Jews, was very high (see table 8.1). The correlation matrix (question 1: "Groups of people with which one would rather not have too much to do") showed the following relationship.

The strong correlation confirmed the assumption that xenophobia is a general complex of attitudes, in which the "objects" of rejection can change depending on current conflicts.[3]

Like/dislike values and the extent of social distance from ethnic groups themselves indicated that those groups most frequently rejected nowa-

TABLE 8.1
Correlation Matrix: Rejection of Ethnic Minorities

	Jews	Turks	Blacks	Israelis	Asylum seekers	Arabs
Jews	1.00	.74	.79	.83	.66	.73
Turks		1.00	.83	.73	.73	.77
Blacks			1.00	.75	.72	.78
Israelis				1.00	.67	.78
Asylum seekers					1.00	.70
Arabs						1.00

(Tetrachoric correlation, significant on the 1 percent level.)

days are those whose presence or immigration are perceived as an economic and social threat. In addition, rejection was quite pronounced for members of ethnic groups seen by the public to be politically and religiously radical, or in which respondents thought they recognized potential asylum seekers. In contrast, rejection of Jews and Israelis was significantly lower (see table 8.2).

TABLE 8.2
Sympathy and Social Distance toward Ethnic Groups (1987)[4]

	Like	Dislike	Not too much to do with	In circle of friends
	%	%	%	%
Jews	34	20	13	48
German Jews	—	—	8	49
Israel(is)	44	17	11	39
Guest workers	32	33	—	—
Turks	28	33	34	34
Gypsies	19	51	—	—
Asylum seekers	18	52	33	28
Palestinians	18	52	—	—
Arabs	—	—	30	30
Blacks	—	—	21	41

Columns 1 and 2: Word affinity test—question 5;
Column 3: People with which one would rather not have too much to do—question 1a;
Column 4: People you could have within your closest circle of friends—question 1b.

Of all the comparison groups we chose, Jews/Israelis achieved the highest affinity values, and were most frequently accepted as friends. Public opinion was far less distinct with regard to other groups. Like/dislike values and acceptance of Turks as friends more or less offset each other, while a majority disliked and rejected asylum seekers, gypsies, and Arabs. Aside from the high level of rejection of gypsies, which involves a traditional complex of prejudice not yet dealt with socially, the following overview indicates a particular pattern of rejection.

Of those who "do not want too much to do with Turks" (34 %, N = 721), the following percent also rejected contact:

with asylum seekers	66 %
with Arabs	64 %
with blacks	50 %
with Jews	25 %

Of those who "do not want too much to do with asylum seekers" (33 %, N = 700), the following percent also rejected contact:

with Arabs	67 %
with blacks	50 %
with Turks	32 %
with Jews	25 %

Of those who "do not want too much to do with Jews" (13 %, N = 273), the following percent also rejected contact:

with Turks	88 %
with Arabs	84 %
with blacks	80 %
with asylum seekers	80 %

Of those who "do not want too much to do with blacks" (21 %, N= 443), the following percent also rejected contact:

with Turks	85 %
with Arabs	76 %
with asylum seekers	75 %
with Jews	38 %

Rejection of a group based on actual or feared social conflicts also extended to a great degree to other supposedly competing groups, but

TABLE 8.3
Index: Xeno

Rejections	N	Share in %	Cumulative %
0	630	30.0	30.0
1	436	20.7	50.7
2	326	15.5	66.2
3	202	9.6	75.8
4	196	9.3	85.4
5	158	7.5	92.7
6	154	7.3	100.0
Total	**2102**	**100.0**	

Reliability coefficient alpha = .79.

not as heavily to "classic outgroups" such as Jews and blacks. Prejudice against these latter groups is based on cultural traditions and enjoys little environmental support today. But those who cling to such traditional prejudices, which may also have racist overtones, and thus reject Jews and blacks, also include other minorities and ethnic groups in their rejection.

The relatively low level of rejection of Jews can be explained, on the one hand, by the fact that no social conflicts exist at present with the small Jewish minority in Germany. However, a more important reason is the impact of decades of suppression of anti-Semitic prejudice, empathy with the fate of the persecuted Jews, and the success of education on the history of the persecution of the Jewish people. No similar efforts have been made for any other minority.[5] Thus, Jews have lost their traditional scapegoat role, while rejection of other groups does not violate norms of tolerance and freedom from prejudice, or at least not to the same degree.

We cannot necessarily infer anti-Semitism from xenophobia based on present social conflicts. But conversely, people with anti-Semitic opinions are almost always xenophobic.

The results of the correlation between the anti-Semitism index and a "xenophobia" index (xeno)—consisting of the items measuring rejection of Arabs, Turks, asylum seekers, gypsies, guest workers, and blacks (question 1a)—confirmed this connection ($r = 0.48$; see table 8.3).

The picture became even clearer when we related the different, sharply distinct groups of anti-Semites (measured by PAS and SAS) to the xeno index.[6] For pronounced anti-Semitism (SAS), we found a linear connection to rejection of outgroups (see figure 8.1).

Regarding the distribution of rejection by age group, two things become apparent: first, xenophobia is not an anthropological constant, but varies with social norms and their ability to resolve distribution conflicts in ways other than through ostracism and scapegoating; second, the objects of rejection change, and old prejudices can fade.

The proportion of people with xenophobic attitudes rose linearly with increasing age.[7] We used the xeno index to measure xenophobia. Those who rejected at least three ethnic groups were classed as xenophobic (the mean of all rejections was 2.0). The following graph (figure 8.2) shows the percentage of those with pronounced xenophobic views, and at the same time the rejection of closer contact with Jews by age group.

Among the very xenophobic in the younger age groups, Jews were included to only a very minor extent in the list of rejected groups. Only one-quarter to one-ninth did so. As age increased, Jews were increasingly included among the rejected groups. Among those over sixty-five, one in two xenophobes was also anti-Semitic. Political generations can be distinguished according to their rejection of Jews. That is, prejudices once inherited persisted even under completely altered circumstances. In younger age groups, rejection generally lacked any personal experiential context and was thus an "anti-Semitism without Jews," believed and held to despite public norms. The steady increase in xenophobia with increasing age was certainly, on the one hand, a result of the changing, more liberal political culture in West Germany; but it also demonstrates a life cycle effect, as indicated by the lack of generational gaps (cf. note 7).

The relationship between xenophobia and the demographic variables we investigated corresponded to the relationship we found for anti-Semitism. Gender and location and size of residential community showed no significant correlation to rejection of outgroups. Level of education and occupation had the same effects we had observed before: the higher the level of education and occupation, the lower the share among those we classified as xenophobic.[8]

The percentage of xenophobes among voters for parties in the Bundestag was distributed as follows (figure 8.3), with age and education again largely responsible for the differences.

This distribution corresponds to the statistical correlation between anti-Semitism and party preference, though on a quantitatively higher level;

FIGURE 8.1
Xenophobia and Anti-Semitism

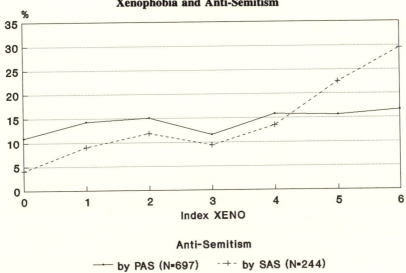

O "yes" responses = not xenophobic
6 "yes" responses = very xenophobic

FIGURE 8.2
Social Distance from Ethnic Groups by Age Group

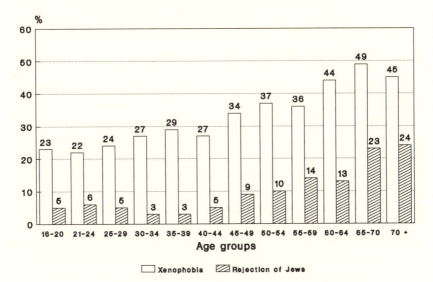

FIGURE 8.3
Xenophobia by Party Preference

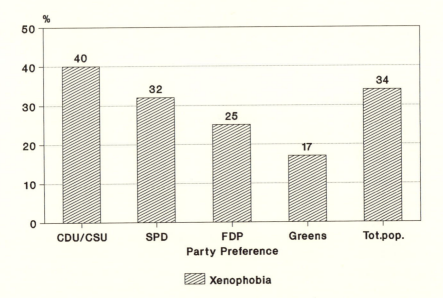

however, in this case the attitudes of FDP voters were considerably more negative than those of Green voters. The political trend of these findings accorded with those of Just and Mülhens (1982), though they found a higher level: in 1982, 54 percent of CDU/CSU voters were xenophobic, 47 percent of SPD voters, and 37 percent of FDP voters.

The findings of the 1989 EMNID study coincided with our findings on the relationship between party preference and rejection of outgroups. In that survey, for the first time, *Republikaner* voters provided a statistically significant group of people with radical right-wing convictions (N = 104). They expressed more xenophobic, anti-Semitic opinions than voters for other parties. Interestingly enough, these extremely nationalistic respondents rejected not only non-German foreigners; they also showed the greatest antipathy toward East German immigrants and ethnic Germans from Eastern Europe (cf. EMNID 1989, table 37). Given these facts, we considered it advisable to describe this complex of attitudes as

TABLE 8.4
Feelings toward Jews/Immigrant Groups

	Extremely	Very	Somewhat	Not
		anti-Semitic		
East German immigrants	-.1	.4	.5	1.2
Ethnic German immigrants	-.8	-.7	-.5	.4
Turks	-2.3	-1.8	-.7	.2
Asylum seekers from Eastern Europe	-3.5	-2.7	-1.5	-.2
Asylum seekers from Africa	-3.8	-3.1	-2.0	-.5
Asylum seekers from Asia	-3.9	-3.1	-2.1	-.5

N = 2272
Source: EMNID 1989, table 37.

xenophobia rather than racism. Republikaner voters reproduced a behavioral pattern familiar to scholars of migration: the most recent group
of immigrants encounters the greatest hostility, while earlier groups of
immigrants are more likely to be accepted. The rejection encountered by
the largest groups of immigrants indicates general xenophobia. This rejection is harsher, and can include racist convictions, when it involves
immigrants from African or Asian countries.

The correlation between anti-Semitism and strong xenophobia established above was confirmed by the EMNID study for groups that were
the focus of public discussion in March 1989. EMNID measured attitudes toward a number of groups on a like/dislike scale (from -5 to +5),
and then correlated them to attitudes toward Jews (see table 8.4).

The xenophobia we observed among hardcore anti-Semites was apparently so comprehensive that it even extended to members of their own
group. But because anti-Semitism, on the other hand, has a particularly
nationalistic, racist orientation (cf. EMNID 1989, table 75), the internal
contradictions of this ideology become apparent. In times of social and
economic conflict, people fall back on ethnocentrism, with particularly
restrictive definitions of their own group. Nevertheless, "national affinity" tempered rejection in the case of East German and ethnic German
immigrants, while immigrants or refugees who differed more perceptibly
from Germans in skin color, religion, or culture were rejected much more

vehemently. Here racist ideologies came to the fore, for example in opposition to "mixing the German people with other peoples."[9]

Rejection of Socially Deviant Groups and Anti-Semitism

In our question about groups with whom respondents would prefer not to have too much contact, we included groups that experience social discrimination because of socially deviant behavior, communicable diseases, social background, and the like. The factor analysis (see appendix 3: Antipathy and Social Distance) grouped the relevant variables around three factors. Factor 3 included groups bearing a relatively strong social stigma, such as convicted thieves, prostitutes, and people with AIDS, while factor 6 included categories such as divorced people, the unemployed, and university students—categories against which only older generations, if any, would have felt any hostility. Factor 5 included "dedicated communists and Nazis," categories of people experiencing very great rejection. We will leave the last two factors for our analysis of links between anti-Semitism and prejudice, and concentrate on the three categories surrounding the first three factors mentioned, which we combined in an index (deviance). We added to this the category "people collecting unemployment benefits, but not really looking for work," because they also violate an important social norm (at .31, this item loads relatively heavily onto Factor 3; see table 8.5).[10]

The correlations between the deviance index and the anti-Semitism index (.26) and between the deviance index and the xeno index (.49) showed that rejection of contact with socially deviant groups correlated considerably less closely with anti-Semitism than it did with xenophobia. Anti-Semites did reject socially deviant groups to a much greater degree than the population as a whole, but these groups encountered the greatest hostility from heavily xenophobic people. In other words, our findings tended to confirm the assumptions behind the "theory of the authoritarian personality" that intolerance felt by authoritarian persons extends to all outgroups, and that it is expressed in particular against socially weaker outsider groups.

An analysis of the relationship between prejudices against socially deviant groups and demographic characteristics provided some evidence—despite high correspondence with, for example, age patterns and party preference—that we might in fact be dealing with a complex of attitudes

TABLE 8.5
Index: Deviance

No. of groups rejected	N	share in %	cumulative %
0	348	16.6	16.6
1	462	22.0	38.5
2	495	23.5	62.1
3	496	23.6	87.5
4	301	14.3	100.0
Total	**2102**	**100.0**	

$\bar{x}$ = 2 rejected groups, reliability coefficient alpha = .59

only partially coincident with xenophobia and anti-Semitism. This was particularly true in regard to the influence of education and occupation. Higher educational level and better occupational standing did not lead—as with xenophobia and anti-Semitism—to a reduction in social rejection. People without high school degrees were just as likely to reject social deviants as those with *Abitur* (but without a college education; the only exception to this were college students). Higher-level civil servants and independent professionals did not differ from blue-collar and skilled workers; only farmers and farmworkers stood out, with a far above-average level of rejection. In contrast to anti-Semitism, expressed by more men than women, women were more likely to refuse social contacts in this category (57 percent, compared with 43 percent). Social distance from deviant groups seems to involve middle-class or petty bourgeois attitudes, in which deviance from social normalcy is stigmatized and contact avoided. Such class differences did not decrease with higher educational level and better occupational position, since social distance to these groups and the milieus associated with them tends rather to increase. This is also evidenced by the fact that FDP voters were no less likely to reject these groups than the population as a whole, whereas they, along with Green voters, expressed considerably fewer prejudices against Jews and other outgroups. Only Green voters—and here, the lower average age may have been significant—fell far below the average (38 percent), with a 17 percent level of rejection. They thus followed a party line that generally opposes discrimination against all (and not merely ethnic) minorities.

Thus, the choice of an object of prejudice was not uniform; groups were chosen or not chosen based on education, occupation, and political orientation. Though the small number of cases did not permit a statistically significant evaluation, only three of seven NPD voters opposed contact with socially deviant groups, while six of them were anti-Semitic and xenophobic.

Nationalism and Anti-Semitism

Surges of nationalism in Germany have generally gone hand in hand with a rise in discrimination against minorities. During such periods, the social and legal position of Jews, in particular, comes under increased attack. The historic finding that an increase in social cohesiveness of the ingroup is generally accompanied by ostracism of outgroups (defined as not belonging to the ingroup) is thought by social psychologists to be a general pattern of intergroup relations (Sherif et al. 1961).

In Germany, nationalism was for a long time deeply discredited by the crimes of the Third Reich and the defeat in the Second World War. International comparative studies showed that a basic, unreflected national consensus was taken far less for granted in Germany than in any other country (Noelle-Neumann and Köcher 1987). More than anything else, it has been "Auschwitz" that has stood in the way of an unbroken identification with German history and the German nation. Anyone trying today to identify completely and consistently with the German nation quickly comes up against this "obstacle;" the result is a tendency either to deny the facts and refuse to acknowledge guilt, or to respond with counter accusations and projections of guilt.[11] That is, we assume that nationalism and anti-Semitism are connected today in new ways. The issue is no longer primarily one of excluding an "un-German" minority from the national collective; instead, Jews are being held responsible for the precarious state of national consciousness, because of their demands that the Holocaust and its causes not be forgotten.[12]

In reaction to Germany's crimes, a segment of the population developed pronounced anti-nationalism, which also provides evidence of the difficulty of dealing with German history. We attempted to identify this group as well, to see whether we would also find the opposite position in attitudes to Jews.

To record nationalist attitudes, we created an ethnocentrism index containing the following variables: affinity for the terms "people" (*Volk*)

TABLE 8.6
Index: Ethnocentrism

Agreement	N	share in %	cumulative %
0	492	23.4	23.4
1	529	25.2	48.6
2	584	27.8	76.4
3	383	18.2	94.6
4	114	5.4	100.0
Total	**2102**	**100.0**	

Reliability coefficient alpha = 0.53.

(question 5/11), "race" (question 5/8), and "national" (question 5/10), and agreement with the statement "Germans are superior to other peoples" (question 6; see table 8.6).

Nationalism (ethnocentrism) correlated more closely with anti-Semitism (AS index $r = .33$) than with xenophobia (xeno $r = .22$, both significant at the 1 percent level). This suggests that nationalism today serves less as an integrative ideology to exclude newly immigrated minorities than as a factor connected with ways of dealing with the past.

This connection with the past is twofold: first of all, older generations cling to their German nationalist orientation, in which anti-Semitism was always a constitutive element; second of all, it is difficult for them, as contemporaries of the Third Reich, to reject Nazism and chauvinist attitudes. The fact that nationalism increased with age was evidence of this, as well as the fact that people over sixty rarely took anti-nationalist positions by responding negatively to concepts such as "Germany," "people (*Volk*)," or "national." The war generation's age-specific tendency to retain ultra-right, anti-Semitic views was revealed by the famous 1980 Sinus study. The most important reason for the survival of such views was explained in the survey as "positive experiences with an immediate environment that is nationalistically oriented (neighborhood, club, village)" (Sinus 1981, 102).

However, there was a significant correlation between nationalism and negative views of *Vergangenheitsbewältigung* (coming to terms with the past), such as opposition to reparations, the desire to stop talking about German history, ascribing to Jews a share of the blame for their own persecution, the accusation that many Jews profit from the Nazi period.

FIGURE 8.4
Anti-Semitism and Nationalism

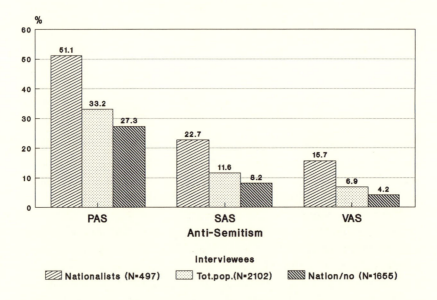

There was an equally significant correlation with anti-Semitism. Both correlations were apparent not only among older people raised during the Third Reich, but also as an independent factor among younger generations. Figure 8.4 shows that the proportion of anti-Semites among nationalists (defined by agreement with three and four statements on the ethnocentrism index) was significantly higher.

Anti-Semitism was reduced only slightly by a pronounced anti-nationalist position. The difference between this group and those classified on the ethnocentrism index as non-nationalist was minimal (the difference is 4 percent).

The relationship between anti-Semitism and nationalism was also explored by the 1989 EMNID survey. The results pointed in the same direction as ours (see table 8.7). The nationalist complex of attitudes was operationalized by EMNID through various questions. The relationship between agreement even with the more-or-less neutral statement, "I am

TABLE 8.7
Anti-Semitism and Nationalism

| National pride | Extremely | Very | Somewhat | Not Opposed to admitting foreigners |
| | anti-Semitic | | | |
%	%	%	%	%
Strong	82	76	61	43	61
Mid-range	16	18	34	40	33
Little	3	6	6	17	6
Total	**100**	**100**	**100**	**100**	**100**

Source: EMNID 1989, table 65.

proud to be German," and a negative view of Jews shows that strong identification with one's own collective leads to disproportionate rejection of Jews and other outgroups.

When nationalism was operationalized using the vocabulary of right-wing, populist hostility, the distinction between anti-Semites and non-anti-Semites became more defined.

These and a series of other questions asked by EMNID[13] suggested that the nationalism of many Germans has a precarious character. Nationalists saw themselves as the victims of external interference, foreign criticism, blame, and financial exploitation. For the politically disillusioned and socially deprived, nationalism also had a strongly compensatory function. Complaints of a lack of national self-confidence,

TABLE 8.8
Populist Resentment and Anti-Semitism

| "Politicians in Bonn are selling out German interests" | Extremely | Very | Somewhat | Not |
| | anti-Semitic | | | |
%	%	%	%
Complete agreement	77	46	34	15
Intermediate position	13	39	44	45
Disagreement	8	13	20	38

Source: EMNID 1989, table 75.

TABLE 8.9
Nationalism/Opinion Profile of *Republikaner* Voters

	Republikaner %	Total Pop. %
Proud to be German	80	55
National forces suppressed	63	19
Dislike Jews	37	8
Too much reparations	75	46
Germans are Europe's paymasters	92	55
N	104	2272

Source: EMNID 1989, table 65.

powerlessness, and common enemies are aspects of the complex of views forming a bridge to "Republikaner" voters, almost all of whom exhibit these characteristics (table 8.9).

In summary, the thesis that pronounced nationalism coexists with a tendency to reject and discriminate against outgroups can be confirmed. In regard to Jews, xenophobic rejection joins with the negative historical symbiosis of Germans and Jews. This gives current anti-Semitism a new dimension that distinguishes it from modern anti-Semitism before 1945, as well as from more general xenophobia.

Notes

1. The remaining three factors include the following groups: people facing heavy social discrimination, supporters of totalitarian ideologies, and people facing slight social discrimination. Cf. chap. 9.
2. In his 1960 study, Galtung came to the same conclusion: the attitudes of anti-Semites generally were part of an overall anti-minority position, that is, the anti-Semite rejects minorities in general, "but he specializes in Jews" (1960, 64).
3. The assumption that xenophobia is a learned behavior is evidenced by a finding of our pretest, in which 43 percent of those with anti-Semitic leanings said their parents had always been very cautious about people who were different (in comparison with 28 percent of the total population).
4. For more recent data see chap. 12.
5. The civil rights movement in the U.S. and the struggle against apartheid in South Africa were received positively by the public and political educators, leading at least in part to a decline in traditional negative attitudes toward blacks. In the sixties, in particular, an anti-racist learning effect was found among young people

as a result of their rejection of Nazi anti-Jewish racism (cf. DIVO Press Service, 1 March 1965).

6. If we compare the strongly xenophobic share of the respondents with non- or mildly xenophobic respondents with regard to anti-Semitic views, the close correlation between strong xenophobia and anti-Semitism becomes evident. Of the strongly xenophobic, 15.8 percent are "hardcore" anti-Semites (VAS); of the non- or mildly xenophobic, the share is 2.4 percent (total population, 6.9 percent).

7. All surveys on attitudes toward immigrant groups agree on this finding (cf. the overview in Geiger 1991, 31f.). Whether this is a case of generational or lifecycle effect remains open. The fact that, in recent decades, attitudes towards immigrants have not changed fundamentally suggests a lifecycle effect, according to Geiger. As people age, they tend to lose their earlier openness (ibid., 32). For the 1980 Allbus survey, Hoskin also interpreted the explanatory factor "age" in the sense of a lifecycle theory (1985, 21). In the case of anti-Semitism, in contrast, we believe our findings support the theory of political generations.

8. Here, too, our data confirmed the findings of all other surveys on these issues (cf. Geiger 1990, 32f.). This correlation between education and discriminatory attitudes was considered an artifact by van Dijk (1987, 350), who felt the better educated had learned to react with "socially desirable responses" in public situations like a survey (which we would consider a relatively anonymous situation, according to our results on the subject of latency). Wagner attempted to refute this assumption as early as 1982. Geiger suggests examining the artifact hypothesis in modified form; first of all, by assuming that only part of the difference can be explained this way; second of all, by modifying its content so that people with better education are seen to have learned to show an aversion to very undifferentiated, aggressively worded opinions (1990, 33f.).

9. In the 1989 EMNID survey (table 75), on a six-level response scale ranging from "agree completely" (6 points) to "disagree completely" (1 point), anti-Semites were much more likely to agree to the statement "We should be careful to keep the German people pure and prevent mixing of peoples" (4.9 points) than those free of anti-Semitism (2.4).

10. The overall mean was quite high, with an average in the total population of two groups with whom contact was not desired. Therefore, we drew the cutoff between two and three rejected groups, and treated all those with three or four rejections as people with strong hostilities toward socially deviant groups (rough estimate—38 percent of the respondents).

11. According to Herz, the particular fixation of German right-wing radicals and extreme nationalists on Nazism is reflected by the issues that were important to NPD voters in the 1960s: combatting "the war guilt lie," clandestine approval of anti-Semitism, and advocacy of "law and order." In Herz's opinion, this fixation on the past in the form of a "love-hate relationship"—love, because of positive identification with the goals of the Nazi regime; hate, because this identification is linked with negative sanctions—is typical of German right-wing extremists; in the United States, for example, there is no corresponding phenomenon (Herz 1975, 113).

12. Thus, those with anti-Semitic attitudes agreed to a very great extent with the statement, "National forces are suppressed today in Germany." On a six-point scale from "don't agree at all" (1) to "agree completely" (6), respondents classed as very anti-Semitic achieved the high agreement value of 5.0, while those classed as non-anti-Semitic rejected the statement, at 2.4 points. Seventy-seven percent

of hardcore anti-Semites chose answer categories 5 or 6, while only 5 percent of the non-anti-Semites did so (EMNID 1989, table 75).

13. Some examples: "When people in other countries always talk about German guilt from the past, they are often just jealous of German efficiency and wealth" (agreement among anti-Semites 98 percent, among non-anti-Semites 20 percent); "Germany is the scapegoat and paymaster for all of Europe" (agreement among anti-Semites 93 percent, among non-anti-Semites 35 percent, table 75).

9

Subjective Deprivation and Anti-Semitism

Historical research on anti-Semitism utilizes a crisis theory in analyzing the German Empire and Weimar Republic. According to this theory, groups threatened with social decline or loss of status were most susceptible to political anti-Semitism. This theory is applicable to periods of major societal change with a rapid social shift in which modern occupational structures, a social welfare system, and democratic political institutions are first formed. There was no economic and sociopolitical instrument of crisis management with which to confront dislocations in economic and occupational structures, so that political radicalization and regression to premodern, hierarchical models of society were regarded as plausible solutions to the crisis. Jews were seen as the cause of the crisis, the "winners" in the modernization process (Jochmann 1988, Stölzl 1975). Anti-Semitism took on the function of an integrative ideology, capable of combining totally contradictory ideas. As modern, internationalist forms of society, both capitalism and socialism were condemned as "Jewish inventions."

In view of this background, early empirical studies on anti-Semitism already examined the connection between loss of social status and mobility and the inclination to accept anti-Jewish prejudices (Massing 1949, Bettelheim and Janowitz 1950). Comprehensive research in the 1950s and 1960s based on these studies found extremely fine distinctions and came to somewhat contradictory conclusions. In societies characterized by a constant process of modernization and a high degree of social mobility, only extreme losses of status under specific conditions lead to assumption of ethnic prejudices (Bergmann 1988a, 155ff.). More recent theories of social mobility emphasize the addition of lower strata to the labor market through migrant laborers, which provides an opportunity for social advancement for the domestic laborers, thereby also decreasing competition (Bonacich 1972). In Hilde Weiss's mid-1970s Austrian study on anti-Semitism, she was unable to find any connection between social mobility and anti-Semitism (1984, 61f.).[1]

Empirical findings and theoretical considerations suggest that little is to be gained from further investigation of a connection between anti-Jewish prejudice and social mobility. In other words, an unreasonably elaborate empirical study would be required to ascertain causal connections between prejudice and objective positions of status. Furthermore, today few would consider it plausible to hold the small Jewish minority in the Federal Republic, whose occupational structure does not differ from that of society as a whole, responsible for the loss of status of either individuals or occupations as a whole. In contrast, in periods of economic recession, the demand to reduce the number of migrant laborers grows louder.

For this reason, we decided not to collect detailed data on objective social status, employment satisfaction, or social mobility in our survey, limiting our questions in this area to a subjective assessment of the individual's own present living situation. In evaluating the pretest, we noted that answers to less specific questions on general feelings about one's life were most likely to show some connection to rejection of Jews. In response to the question whether "all in all, we live in fortunate times," those with anti-Jewish attitudes more often said "no" (46 percent) than the population as a whole (29 percent), and they less often felt that "most people are trustworthy" (21 percent versus 33 percent in the population as a whole).[2] When respondents were asked if they felt they belonged to the disadvantaged (question 7/3) or the successful, upwardly mobile (question 7/7) in society, a self-assessment of their social position was sought; information on another aspect of dissatisfaction was explored by the question whether they see themselves among those disappointed by government and politics (question 7/5).

Subjective Deprivation

Aside from the connection between subjectively perceived disadvantage or individual success on the one hand, and anti-Semitism on the other, we also examined the impact of these feelings on xenophobia and a strong identification with the ingroup.

There was generally a significant correlation between subjective deprivation and anti-Semitism. This was true mainly if anti-Semitism was interpreted in a very broad sense (i.e., using the PAS index). Of those identifying themselves as "disadvantaged" (N = 257), 46 percent were considered anti-Semitic. Of the "non-disadvantaged" (N = 1845), only 31 percent were anti-Semitic. If anti-Semitism was defined more rigidly (SAS and VAS), the connection was less obvious. We explain this by assuming that hardcore anti-Semitism can be traced back primarily to motives other than social frustration.

Subjectively perceived deprivation was tied to an above-average level of rejection of the "other."[3] According to the xeno index, half of all those who saw themselves as "disadvantaged" had to be classified as xenophobic (population average: 34 percent). This rejection of outgroups did not correspond to a particular value judgment of the ingroup, as could be expected on the basis of group psychology theories. The "disadvantaged" did not demonstrate any significantly greater degree of nationalistic belief compared to the "non-disadvantaged." People who explicitly rated themselves as "successful and upwardly mobile," on the other hand, were somewhat more nationalistic.[4] The greater amount of satisfaction they gained from their success was "credited" to their own national collective. Their value judgment of the ingroup was not accompanied by a tendency to lower the status of the outgroups; neither, however, did it mean greater tolerance. Only when combined with a positive feeling toward life did judgments of Jews and other minorities tend to become more positive.

Deprivation and the resulting rejection of outgroups were not age-related phenomena; rather, they were tied to lower levels of education and the corresponding lower status, low income occupations. People who had not completed *Realschule* (basic high school equivalent) more often expressed a sense of disadvantage, and this feeling was particularly widespread among those not having completed *Hauptschule* (junior high school equivalent). There was a relatively stable, low level of subjective deprivation among those with high school and/or college diplomas. This finding was confirmed by statistics on occupation. A disproportionately high number of unskilled laborers and farmworkers felt disadvantaged. There was a linear correlation between income level and perceived deprivation; subjective deprivation decreased with increasing income.

This finding indicates that the connection between higher education and lower degree of outgroup rejection found by many studies, including ours, was not solely a result of knowledge gained in school and history lessons. More importantly, higher education opens the door to better jobs and higher income, thus increasing options for participation in cultural and political life. This leads to the development of a feeling of social success and trust in the ability to further one's own interests, thereby reducing the need to blame failure on social rivals or other external factors.[5] It was mostly less educated workers and recipients of welfare benefits who competed with less qualified migrant workers for jobs and resources. The higher degree of xenophobia demonstrated by the socially disadvantaged was a result of both real or imagined competition, as well as a projection of their own failures onto scapegoats.

The experience of losing social status leads to hostility toward those not belonging to one's own group.[6] This rejection of outgroups is related neither to increased nationalism nor to stronger prejudice against socially deviant groups.[7] This shows that we are not dealing with authoritarian personalities, where xenophobia is a component of a pronounced ethnocentric complex of prejudice in which not only outgroups, but also socially weak and deviant groups, are rejected.

The 1989 EMNID survey also measured the correlation between social deprivation and attitudes toward Jews, "guest workers," asylum seekers, and ethnic German immigrants from eastern Europe (*Aussiedler*). The following indicators were used to measure social deprivation: self-appraisal of one's economic status, hardship due to unemployment and the housing shortage, and self-assessment as belonging to the third of society that is not doing well, an allusion to the so-called "two-thirds society" that is supposedly thriving. All in all, the findings offered no obvious conclusions. Self-assessment as belonging to the deprived third in society did not correspond to any greater rejection of foreigners, and even the share among anti-Semites was only negligibly higher than in the population as a whole [25 percent of anti-Semites versus 20 percent non-anti-Semites; 22 percent of the total population (EMNID 1989, table 15)].

The "poor economic status" and "experiencing social hardship" indicators did not show any correlation to increased opposition with respect to the issue of immigration of families of guest workers, acceptance of asylum seekers, general appraisal of Nazism, or opinion on reparations paid to Jews. In measurements of sympathies held for certain social groups, such as Jews, Turks, *Aussiedler,* and asylum seekers, on the other hand, a correlation was found between dislike of these groups and assessment of one's own economic status as "poor" or experiencing social hardship. The deviation with respect to Jews and Turks was very small—0.5 points on a scale of 10—as compared to those well-situated socially. For *Aussiedler,* and especially asylum seekers, the difference was greater. Of those who appraised their own economic status as poor, 40 percent each rejected "asylum-seekers from Africa and Asia" totally. Of those who believed their economic status was good, only 26 percent and 28 percent did, respectively (EMNID 1989, table 37). Fifty-three percent of those affected by unemployment or the housing shortage responded with one of the two most negative categories, compared to 29 percent in the population as a whole. Even ethnic German immigrants from Poland and the Soviet Union were disliked by "those experiencing social hardship" to a much greater extent than by the population as a whole.

When asked if "guest workers" or asylum seekers cause social problems (unemployment, housing shortage, burdening the social security system), agreement was once again greater among the socially deprived. In this survey as well as our own, higher education and income were significant factors (EMNID 1989, table 46).[8]

In comparison with these EMNID findings, our measurement of subjective deprivation on the basis of self-assessment as "disadvantaged" proved to be relatively meaningful. This was most applicable to rejection of "foreigners," and less so—though still significantly—to a broadly defined anti-Semitism. The fact that the correlation is weaker for "hardcore" anti-Semites supports the thesis discussed above, that the Jewish minority has largely lost its status as a scapegoat for economic problems.

Hilde Weiss conducted a thorough examination of the impact on anti-Semitism of subjective deprivation as a function of occupation (job security, job prestige, competition, psychological and physical stress) and contentment in private life. She found no significant correlations. "The hypothesis that a greater perception of life goals that have not be achieved leads to greater prejudice (as suggested by theories of displacement of aggression and scapegoating) could not be confirmed by these data" (1984, 69ff.).

In view of the contradictory findings, it is necessary to carefully consider which indicators should be used in measuring subjective deprivation. As regards anti-Semitism, neither objective social situation (unemployment, housing shortage, stress, poor economic situation) nor subjective assessments of contentment at work and social status affect attitudes toward Jews. Our nonspecific indicator, which measures very general deprivation not related to specific life situations (self-appraisal as "disadvantaged"), appeared to better measure a dimension of subjective deprivation related to anti-Semitic prejudice. Self-appraisal as someone who "enjoys life" indicated the same trend, though in the opposite direction. Compared to those who said they enjoyed life, a significantly higher proportion of those who did not have such a positive attitude towards life were anti-Semitic or xenophobic.[9] Similarly, those with anti-Jewish attitudes who took part in the pretest less often felt they were living in fortunate times (see above).

Apparently, a diffuse feeling of discontentment and deprivation is responsible for more negative attitudes toward outgroups. An objectively poor social situation was not always translated into subjective deprivation and only indirectly influenced attitudes toward outgroups. The simple equation of unemployment and shortage of housing with xenophobia and anti-Semitism did not hold up to scrutiny.

Political Disillusionment and Anti-Semitism

An unexpectedly high percentage (22 percent) of people were found to be disappointed by government and politics. Two groups could be distinguished:

1. Supporters of opposition parties, that is, SPD and Green party voters. Their disappointment was directed at decisions made by the governing coalition and not at politics in general.

2. A smaller group of politically disillusioned people whose attitudes tended toward the right-wing of the political spectrum; this group was fundamentally opposed to the democratic system. Political apathy was also expressed in the form of political disenchantment ("don't know," "don't vote").[10]

There was a significant correlation between self-appraisal as "politically disillusioned" and anti-Semitism. The stricter the definition of anti-Semitism, the stronger this correlation became. However, there was no general pattern to the connection between political disillusionment and anti-Semitism. Thus, among younger people and Green party voters, political disillusionment was not expressed in the form of increased anti-Semitism. On the other hand, among older people, a higher proportion of anti-Semites were found among politically disenchanted people than among those expressing political contentment.

According to the data, it is apparent that a large proportion of strongly anti-Semitic people were politically disillusioned (35 percent). Since this group was comprised mostly of people over sixty years of age, we can assume that these political attitudes were acquired during the Nazi period and remained unchanged, as they could not be brought into line with a modern, democratic state and its principles.[11] Anti-Semitism was acquired together with the attitudes mentioned above, which now lead to disappointment; thus, anti-Semitism cannot be interpreted as a result of this disillusionment. Today, political disappointment stemming from current political conflicts is no longer connected to anti-Jewish projections. Even though half of all Green party voters identified themselves as politically disillusioned, there was no increased trend toward anti-Semitism among Green voters. The politically disillusioned among older voters for the two main parties, regardless of whether the party was in the opposition or in power, were more anti-Semitic than nondisillusioned voters. This indicated that the connection between anti-Semitism and political disappointment was not grounded in current politics, but in the common historical roots of antidemocratic and anti-Jewish thought. The fact that political disillusionment did not lead to significantly greater rejection of outgroups supports this historical congruence; in other words, political disillusionment did not have any additional impact on current cases of group conflict.

Political contentment was also examined in the EMNID survey. The findings largely coincided with ours with respect to age and education distributions, party preference, disapproval of admitting foreigners into the country, and attitudes toward Jews.[12] Among those who said they were somewhat dissatisfied with the political system, hardly any difference was found in attitudes toward Jews. No major deviation in the proportion of anti-Semites was ascertained until those who considered themselves "very disappointed." At 12 percent, the proportion of anti-Semites in this group was twice as high as among non-anti-Semites [5 percent (EMNID 1989, table 2)].

Political discontentment, which was particularly apparent on the left-wing and extreme right-wing fringes of the political spectrum, only showed a correlation with increased anti-Semitism among voters for the ultra-right parties. Although 51 percent of Green party voters were dissatisfied with the political system in West Germany (dissatisfied 7 percent, less satisfied 44 percent), this group had the lowest number of anti-Semites. Voters for the ultra-right *Republikaner* party, on the other hand, were both extremely critical of the political system (dissatisfied 30 percent, less satisfied 35 percent) and clearly anti-Semitic (cf. EMNID 1989, tables 2 and 61; Falter 1994).

In general, it was shown that valuable insights about respondents were gained when they identified with the descriptions "politically disillusioned," "disadvantaged," "successful," "enjoys life," and so on. These answers could not simply be traced back to objective social situations; rather, to some extent they seem to have developed from specific personal situations and personality traits. The connection between objective situations and subjective interpretations was difficult to measure quantitatively. Qualitative studies, on the other hand, can provide more detailed information on subjective construction of people's lives.

Notes

1. Silbermann did not examine the mobility hypothesis; cf. in contrast, Herz 1975, 134ff.
2. In the pretest, 51 percent of those with anti-Jewish attitudes agreed with the statement "Most people cannot be trusted." The average for the population as a whole was 43 percent. The difference from the pro-Jewish group was especially large. Only 28 percent of that group had no trust in people; in contrast, almost half felt that "most people can be trusted" (46 percent).
3. Empirical studies on xenophobia all emphasize that defensiveness against foreigners stems not from concrete experiences of competition, but from imagined competition, an inflexible need for security, and dissatisfaction with one's own life. These factors contribute to vague fears, which are then projected onto visible outgroups (Geiger 1991, 34ff.). The correlation we determined between a sense of deprivation and the rejection of Jews also confirms the theory that there is no direct correlation between the experience of competition and the rejection of outgroups, since Jews cannot be seen as competitors. Fears and fantasies are what lead outgroups to be seen as a threat and the cause of their own problems.
4. The EMNID survey of 1989 also found that those who classified their economic status as poor demonstrated less national pride than those who were economically content (EMNID 1989, table 65).
5. The 1989 EMNID survey (table 62) clearly illustrated this process of projecting one's own situation on the society at large. Only 16 percent of those who classified their own economic status as "poor" believed that "our society is by and large just" (54 percent of the total population), 30 percent believed that it is by and large unjust" (total population 10 percent).
6. In their theory on xenophobia, Hoffmann and Even (1983) stressed this aspect of shared knowledge within a society, which includes preliminary decisions about who clearly belongs to the national collective and who does not. In this sense, they see xenophobia as an integral component of the German view of society.
7. Both the "disadvantaged" and the "not disadvantaged" rejected socially deviant groups to an equally strong degree, as measured by the deviance index (cf. chap. 8).

8. The effect of education was especially great with respect to the question whether "there are too many foreigners in West Germany" (87 percent of those who completed *Volksschule* (elementary school equivalent) but not an apprenticeship or training program answered "yes," in comparison to 47 percent of those with a high school diploma and/or college education), though there was no correlation to either the assessment of one's economic status or the experience of social hardship.

9. Of those who said they "enjoy life," 30 percent had to be classified as potentially anti-Semitic in a broad sense. This corresponded approximately to the figure of 33 percent for the population as a whole. The figure was 41 percent for those respondents who did not feel they "enjoy life." Using a more strict definition of anti-Semitism, more than twice as many in each group said they "do not enjoy life" as those who did "enjoy life" (17.6 percent to 9.5 percent for SAS). The difference was even greater with regard to xenophobia: 46 percent versus 29 percent).

10. The relatively high correlation between the politically disappointed and the socially deprived (.26) might have been due to some overlap between the latter and the group of right-wing voters and those who were politically apathetic. The extreme discrepancy in levels of education also confirmed the fact that we were dealing with two very heterogenous groups of politically disappointed people. On the one hand, an above-average proportion of college students considered themselves politically disillusioned; on the other hand, this was also said by people who had at the most completed junior high school (*Hauptschule*). Whereas college students represented the group with the lowest proportion of anti-Semites, the latter group made up the largest proportion of anti-Semites.

11. This hypothesis was supported by a finding from the 1989 EMNID survey (table 2). The 17 percent of those interviewees who had moderately positive attitudes toward Nazism expressed dissatisfaction with the political system in West Germany. In comparison, of those who clearly rejected Nazism, only 4 percent were dissatisfied (6 percent in the population as a whole).

12. The figure of 33 percent who considered themselves politically dissatisfied in the 1989 EMNID survey was higher than the figure we measured (22 percent). The difference can be explained by the fact that EMNID used a milder wording of the question (EMNID asked about satisfaction/dissatisfaction, while we asked about disappointment). EMNID also provided more detailed response options, including the categories "less satisfied" and "dissatisfied." Many more chose the milder category [27 percent (cf. EMNID 1989, table 2)].

10

Anti-Semitism within the Context of "Coming to Terms with Nazism"

Since the end of World War II, anti-Semitism and Jewish history have become so closely tied to the Nazi persecution of the Jews that this subject dominates public consciousness, overshadowing any recollection whatsoever of German-Jewish history prior to 1933. Throughout the decades of political, legal, and scholarly discussion of the history and crimes of the "Third Reich," the murder of the Jews and anti-Semitism have taken on a central role. In the debate on the issue of guilt, in the question of national identity, and in public discussion on the German sense of history after 1945, Auschwitz has remained to this day an event that cannot be integrated into a positive national identity. This discussion has resurfaced whenever political decisions are imminent regarding issues such as reparations, prosecution of Nazi war criminals, and the lapse of the statute of limitations for Nazi crimes (cf. the public debates in 1965, 1969, and 1979). It has inevitably been accompanied by calls to end discussion of the Nazi past, by denial, rationalization, accusations, and counter charges. For this reason it is all the more surprising that no public opinion surveys had been conducted since the early 1960s on Jews and anti-Semitism within the context of coming to terms with German history (*Vergangenheitsbewältigung*).[1]

In surveys from the early postwar period, close links were drawn between anti-Semitism and Nazism. In research on the "authoritarian personality" and subsequent empirical studies at the Frankfurt Institute for Social Research (Pollock 1955, Schmidt and Becker 1967, von Freyhold 1971), anti-Semitic and Nazi attitudes were seen as an expression of a deeper-seated personality structure; early public opinion surveys by the Allied occupying powers and the IfD in Allensbach (1949) investigated the impact of Nazi politics and propaganda on attitudes toward Jews.

These studies still dealt with the experiences and influence of the Nazi period and their direct impact on contemporaries. In contrast to this, the passage of time has made it necessary to concentrate research on different questions. The main issue is no longer the direct impact, but the secondary effects that have emerged as a result of private and public discourse on the Nazi past. The focus is no longer actual experiences, but the discussion of the nature and consequences of those past experiences. This shift in perspective has made it impossible to continue using the concepts and questions of past studies.

Questions of German guilt and responsibility had not lost political relevance, but they were not taken into consideration as independent motives for anti-Semitism in the studies conducted in the 1960s and 1970s. This is true even though the 1954 EMNID study on anti-Semitism showed the great extent to which pro-Jewish attitudes were determined by feelings of guilt, and how strongly the word "Jew" was associated with the persecution of the Jews (cf. EMNID 1954, 56f.). Tumin's comparative study (1962) was conducted within the context of group relationships and racism, whereas Silbermann (1976, 1982; also Sallen 1977) avoided the context of Nazism entirely. Panahi (1980) investigated anti-Semitism within the framework of relationships among different nationalities. He focussed on the issues of racism, nationalism, and authoritarianism. In empirical studies on right-wing extremism, dealing largely with the persistent impact of Nazi ideology, anti-Semitism played only a secondary role (Herz 1975, Sinus 1981).

Public opinion research did not start dealing with this subject again until 1985 and 1986, when heated public debate was sparked by a series of anti-Jewish statements and events involving sensitive issues of German history (the Bitburg affair, the Fassbinder controversy, anti-Jewish comments by politicians). The 1986 IfD survey on "Germans and Jews forty years later" related attitudes toward Jews to feelings of German guilt and responsibility and to people's willingness to deal with the recent past. Our 1987 anti-Semitism study—in which the aspect of "coming to terms with the past" (*Vergangenheitsbewältigung*) was a major theme—and the EMNID surveys on this subject (1989, 1992), provide enough empirical data to verify our theory of "secondary anti-Semitism." We believe that, aside from persistent traditional prejudices, the relationship between Germans and Jews is influenced more and more by the way in which Germans deal with the Nazi past and the resulting responsibility toward Jews. In our opinion, the discrepancy between the desire to forget, that is, not to be reminded, on the one hand, and the continuing confrontation with German crimes, on the other, provides a new motive for prejudice, which to some extent is expressed in the revitalization of traditional accusations made against Jews (vindictiveness, greed, striving for power).[2]

We have concentrated on the following aspects of efforts to come to terms with the past, in order to verify our hypothesis:

1. The guilt issue and ending discussion of the past (*Schluβstrich*);

2. Attitudes toward the "Third Reich" and the truth of the Holocaust;

3. Reparations and responsibility toward the victims.

The Question of Guilt, Ending Discussion of the Past, and Attitudes toward Jews

In this study, the relationship between problems connected to coming to terms with the past (the guilt issue, trend toward ending discussion of the past, criticism of reparations) and anti-Semitism was systematically examined for the first time. Although early OMGUS surveys always included questions on German attitudes to the Nazi past, they were never viewed in their relationship to attitudes toward Jews. The questions mostly referred either to current domestic policy issues such as the reparations debate, the major concentration camp war trials, the debate on extending the statute of limitations for Nazi crimes, and the television mini-series "Holocaust," or were general questions about attitudes toward Hitler and Nazism. Often, any particular reference to Jews was omitted. The public was repeatedly asked its opinions of the following statement: "Aside from the war and the persecution of the Jews, the 'Third Reich' was not really all that bad" (IfD since 1975, cf. vol. VIII, 191). This statement already reflected a change in consciousness, as it recognized the Holocaust as *the* major Nazi crime. In preceding years, the question of Hitler's significance was posed with the war as the only reservation: "He would have become one of the greatest statesmen if it were not for the war" (IfD, vol. II, 277 and subsequent years).

In the period immediately following the war, when the impact of information about the extent of the crimes of the "Third Reich" against the Jews was still fresh, the notion of German collective guilt was largely opposed—particularly by anti-Semites—yet the majority of those questioned in the U.S. zone (63 percent) were willing to accept a certain amount of responsibility for the crimes of the Hitler regime and to supply aid for its victims. Fifty-nine percent acknowledged that Germany had tortured and murdered millions of innocent people in Europe (Merritt/ Merritt 1970, report no. 51, December 1946). Compared to these figures, the surveys conducted from 1949 to 1955 by the U.S. High Commission for Germany indicated a hardening of attitudes. Only 4 percent identified with the general charge of collective guilt; 21 percent acknowledged a certain responsibility to pay reparations; and 63 percent rejected both collective guilt and collective responsibility (Merritt 1977, 99). With respect to the Jews, collective guilt was also rejected (95 percent), though a somewhat higher proportion of 29 percent was prepared to accept some responsibility for paying reparations for past injustices. Of those questioned, 59 percent felt that only the perpetrators themselves bore any guilt or responsibility. The anti-Semitic counter-charge that Jews share the blame for their persecution served to qualify the sense of German responsibility (21 percent of the respondents; in 1991: 14 percent, EMNID 1992).[3]

Dishonest business practices, striving for power, and agitation against the "Third Reich" were mentioned as the main reasons for the persecution (ibid., 101f.). Regard for Nazism actually tended to rise until 1951 and 1952 [44 percent felt that there was more good than bad about the Nazi period (Merritt and Merritt 1980, report no. 167)], and the proportion of Germans who generally accepted no guilt for crimes against the Jews, and correspondingly rejected the payment of reparations, rose to 54 percent. According to the above-mentioned report, this position correlated significantly with pro-Nazi attitudes. It is difficult to determine whether this increased rejection of guilt and responsibility indicated an actual shift in opinion or whether it was the result of changing political circumstances. Earlier surveys had been commissioned by the Allied military administrations and had been met by a fearful, cautious population, so that it is possible that answers given at that time had been influenced in the direction of what was assumed a desirable political response.[4] On the other hand, historical research has determined that the practice of de-Nazification and the war crimes trials increasingly appeared in the eyes of the public, and especially among the German elite, as unsuitable and unjust. In the early 1950s, more and more doubt was expressed as to the fairness of the trials and the justness of the verdicts. In view of the fact that no punishment was forthcoming for Allied bombing of German cities, expulsion of the German population from the eastern territories, and so on, the judgments seemed an expression of arbitrary victors' justice (cf. Merritt 1977, 105ff.). Initial support for the Nuremberg trials and the principle of de-Nazification was replaced by increasing disillusionment and cynicism that ended in rationalization. In October, 1946, 78 percent of the population living in the U.S. zone felt the Nuremberg trials were fair and 6 percent felt they were unfair. Four years later these figures had changed to 38 percent and 30 percent, respectively (ibid., 105). Of those questioned in October, 1951, 11 percent felt the major mistake made by the occupying powers was "defamation of and unjust accusations against the Germans"; 8 percent named the war crimes trials and another 6 percent the de-Nazification process (IfD, vol.I, 1956, 140). Whereas the Nazi state and the war it waged were held responsible for the hardships experienced in the first few months after the war, by the autumn of 1945 the prevailing mood had deteriorated to such an extent that from that point on, the inability and/or political will of the occupying powers were increasingly blamed for critical shortages. This atmosphere continued until the monetary reform in 1948. These three years of deprivation were seen as sufficient atonement, and the tendency to "keep score" increased during this period (Holtmann 1989, 138ff.).

The intensive public opinion research on German attitudes toward punishment of the perpetrators and the question of guilt in general, as well as their willingness to deal with Nazism and its consequences, revealed the social and political virulence of these issues and the American and British occupying powers' intense need for information in the initial postwar years (cf. Allerbeck 1976, 7ff.).

The founding of the Federal Republic of Germany, economic reconstruction, and the cold war all served to decrease the importance of these issues in the 1950s. There was a broad political and social consensus to lay the issue of Nazi crimes to rest; this calm was disturbed only occasionally and public opinion research institutes collected hardly any relevant data during this time. Not until 1958, when a series of war crimes and concentration camp trials started (Ulm killing unit, Adolf Eichmann, and Auschwitz trials), did these events become topics of public opinion research. The debate over extending the statute of limitations for Nazi crimes was then followed by public opinion research in the 1960s and

1970s. In this context, questions were asked about acceptance of criminal prosecution and the desire to end discussion of the past (see table 10.1).

As time passed and more distance was gained to the "Third Reich," the population in the 1960s and 1970s increasingly expressed the desire to end discussion of Germany's criminal past. Since 1979, possibly in connection with the broadcast of the television mini-series "Holocaust," there appeared to be a shift in trends.[7]

One can certainly call this an evolution, even though it must be kept in mind that the surveys were all conducted against the background of different current political events. In those cases, for example, where a question on the continuation of criminal prosecution was asked in the context of a trial against a known war criminal, agreement was greater

TABLE 10.1

"I think they should stop taking people to court for things they did so many years ago. I think it would be good to finally end discussion of the past."

	Continue to prosecute Nazi crimes[5] %	End discussion of the past (Schlußstrich) %	Undecided %
1958	54	34	12
1963	34	54	12
1964*	53	39	8
1965	38	52	10
1966	—	46	—
1969	23	67	10
1974**	25	60	15
1978**	34	64	2
1979**	50	46	4
1979	40	47	13
1983	55	31	14
1988**	47	51	2
1990	48	43	10
1990+	74	20	6

Source: IfD Allensbach, Yearbooks III–VIII;
* DIVO Press Service July, 1964;
** EMNID-Informationen 1/2 1974; 2/1979; 4/1988.[6]
+ East Germans, Jodice 1991, table 8a

than when, during statute of limitations debates, the question involved legal and political decisions on all murder cases. In 1961, 67 percent were in favor of severe sentencing of Eichmann, and in 1983, in connection with the Klaus Barbie trial, 55 percent supported continued prosecution of Nazi criminals (IfD, vol. III, 225; and IfD, vol. VIII, 194). On the other hand, in 1979, in reference to the statute of limitations issue, only 40 percent supported continued prosecution. The general trend we identified was confirmed indirectly by EMNID and DIVO surveys, which found a noticeable decline in the interest shown in the Auschwitz trial in 1964 as compared to the close attention paid by the West German public to the Eichmann trial in 1961.[8] In 1964, only 60 percent of those questioned knew that the Auschwitz trial was going on, whereas in 1961, 95 percent knew about the Eichmann trial (DIVO press service, July 1961 and July 1964). Not only had the public begun to tire of the issue; opposition to such trials also increased. Whereas only 15 percent opposed the Eichmann trial and preferred not to rock the boat after so many years, during the Auschwitz trial, the figure rose to 39 percent (cf. Schmidt and Becker 1967, 114ff.). Schmidt and Becker even believe that demands to end discussion of the past increased in the course of the statute of limitations debate, as the population became aware of the large number of trials yet to be held (ibid., 117). When asked their reasons for these demands, the 52 percent who were in favor of discontinuing prosecution of Nazi criminals chose the following responses from a list they received (see table 10.2).

Aside from formal arguments involving lack of evidence and constitutional reservations, which served to exonerate the perpetrators and to some extent gave the impression that legal arguments were being used for political purposes, there was a prevailing trend toward rationalization and criticism of national critics. In other words, Nazi crimes were not denied, but an effort was made to neutralize the issue by resorting to counter attacks condemning those who sought to extend the statute of limitations for these crimes. Schmidt and Becker believed a weak sense of self-esteem was the reason for this inability to confront history directly, and why demands for prosecution of war criminals were perceived as an attack on the nation and, thus, on the people themselves. In extreme cases, the trials were seen as propaganda campaigns aimed against Germany [at the time of the Eichmann trial, 15 percent held this opinion (Schmidt and Becker 1967, 113, 118)].

TABLE 10.2
"Why are you in favor of ending discussion of the past?"

Because the other side also committed war crimes that are not being prosecuted for	66 %
Because as Germans we should finally stop denigrating our own country	57 %
Because so much time has passed that it is virtually impossible for the courts to prove guilt beyond the shadow of a doubt	54 %
Because the statute of limitations is 20 years and that should be adhered to	40 %
Because we should feel sorry for Nazi criminals	6 %
other or no response	2 %

base N = 196
(Multiple responses were allowed.)
Source: IfD 1965, cited in Schmidt and Becker 1967, 118.[9]

It can generally be said that until the late 1970s, only a minority felt that Nazi criminals should still be prosecuted.[10] The increase in support for continued prosecution of war criminals that became visible starting at the end of the 1970s was due to a generational effect. In 1979, almost half the youngest age group (sixteen through twenty-nine-year-olds) supported continued prosecution, while only about one-third of the older group (forty-five and older) held this opinion (IfD, vol. VIII, 194). In the 1960s, either no generational effect was noticeable at all—rejection of prosecution fluctuated only a maximum of 5 percent among all age groups in 1969 (IfD, vol. V, 232)—or there was a slight shift in attitudes only in the youngest cohort (DIVO press service, July 1964). We do not have the data necessary to carry out a sufficiently precise, secondary cohort analysis, since many of the available evaluations were not classified according to age. Although it cannot be absolutely verified based on the available data, it is likely that a parallel exists between the decline in anti-Semitism that we ascertained among younger generations and the greater degree of support they expressed for continued criminal prosecution.

The question of ending discussion of the past has been repeated in surveys in another form, namely, in the sense of generally laying to rest the Nazi past. This form of the question is more relevant for our pur-

TABLE 10.3

"Today, forty years after the end of the war, we shouldn't talk so much about the Nazi past and the persecution of the Jews anymore; instead, we should finally put an end to discussion of the past."

	1986	1987	1989*	1991		1994	
				West	East	West	East
	%	%	%	%	%	%	%
Right	66	67	68	68	48	56	39
Not right	24	21	32			37	58
Undecided	10	12	—			7	3

Source: IfD 1986, 1987; Emnid 1992; Forsa 1994;
* EMNID 1989, table 75, different wording of question and answers to choose from.[12]

poses, as it focuses more strongly on individual defense mechanisms used in coping with the past rather than on the prosecution of specific criminals, from whose crimes one can easily dissociate oneself. Any personal share of guilt for the persecution of the Jews during the "Third Reich" has been denied almost unanimously over decades. In 1951, the figure was 95 percent; in 1961, 88 percent; and in 1987, 83 percent (Merritt and Merritt, report no. 113; IfD, vol. III, 229; our question 12).[11] As temporal distance increases, the question as to prosecution of Nazi criminals is gradually losing its relevance, but Nazism as a sensitive epoch in German history is gaining significance and becoming a constant challenge to the political culture of the Federal Republic. It thus makes sense to use a different form of the question about ending discussion of the past than the one used in the 1960s (see table 10.3).

The figures show that a certain degree of willingness still exists to prosecute crimes, but there is widespread aversion to continued discussion of the Nazi past and the Holocaust.[13] This desire to close that chapter of history contrasts with the increasing scholarly and public attention being paid to Nazism, the persecution of the Jews, and attempts to cope with these issues in the history of the Federal Republic of Germany.

Our study was the first to reveal the correlation between rejection of guilt, the wish to end discussion of the past, and anti-Semitism.[14] Even though the accusation blaming all Germans personally has rarely been explicitly stated since the Nuremberg trials,[15] it has stubbornly remained in the public consciousness since the early debates on collective guilt and is rejected in that form by an overwhelming majority (see table 10.4).

TABLE 10.4
"I am not aware of any personal guilt toward the Jews."

	Total pop.	Age groups			
		16–29	30–44	45–59	60 and older
	%	%	%	%	%
Agreement	83.4	83.3	85.0	84.6	80.9

TABLE 10.5
"I am ashamed that Germans committed so many crimes against the Jews."

	Total pop.	Age groups			
		16–29	30–44	45–59	60 and older
	%	%	%	%	%
Agreement	61.2	59.1	63.7	62.0	59.4

In comparison with the findings of earlier surveys, it is amazing that today this statement is rejected less adamantly than in the period immediately after the war (1951: 95 percent; 1961: 88 percent; see table 10.5). It is also surprising that there are virtually no distinctions according to age. This widespread rejection of a very concrete assignment of guilt does not mean, however, that there is no collective sense of responsibility and regret with respect to the Holocaust.[16]

The concept of "collective shame" was introduced into public debate in 1949 by then West German President Theodor Heuss (Heuss 1964, 121ff.). It was intended to replace the concept of collective guilt—according to which merely belonging to the nation implied guilt—which was rejected by the public. Today it accurately describes a common reaction to reminders of the persecution of the Jews. The fact that the respondents' education and professional status influenced their answers to a certain extent indicates that the development of this feeling of shame and responsibility depends on knowledge of history and political judgment.[17] We cannot explain why there was no generational effect, since it could be expected that as contemporaries of the Nazi period, the older generation would express a greater degree of personal shame. On the other hand, the younger generations are better informed about the "Third Reich" and its "final solution" policies, or they are more willing to ac-

TABLE 10.6
"Do you think that most of what is reported about the concentration camps
and the persecution of the Jews is true, or is a lot of it exaggerated?"

	Total pop.	Age groups			
		16–29	30–44	45–59	60 and older
	%	%	%	%	%
Most is true	79.8	83.6	86.3	79.1	67.4
A lot is exaggerated	13.0	7.9	7.8	13.5	24.4
Undecided	7.2	8.5	5.9	7.4	8.1
Total	**100.0**	**100.0**	**100.0**	**100.0**	**100.0**

cept these as facts.[18] The truth of the Holocaust is acknowledged by a larger proportion of the younger generations without their necessarily translating this into a feeling of shame (see table 10.6).

The expected generational effect was well-defined here. The older generation obviously experienced a blocked learning process, that is, as contemporaries of the "Third Reich" they attempted to reduce their own responsibility by denying or minimizing the facts, or by blaming the victims.[19] Among younger generations, acknowledgment of the truth was clearly connected to level of education: 92 percent of the sixteen through twenty-nine-year-olds with higher education believed the reports to be true, while this was the case for only 74 percent of those in this age group with more than a *Hauptschule* education (junior high school equivalent). The significance of education was also evidenced by the fact that 13.3 percent of those having completed only junior high school were undecided, while only 4.4 percent of those with higher education gave this response. There was a significant correlation between acknowledging the truth of the concentration camps and feeling ashamed of the crimes. Two-thirds of those acknowledging the truth also said they were ashamed. Of those who saw the reports as exaggerated, only one-third felt shame. Acknowledging the extent of the Nazi crimes and feeling ashamed of them does not necessarily mean wanting to keep alive this subject and these feelings. By the same token, the wish to close this chapter of history does not mean *per se* a denial of this criminal period in German history. Nevertheless, there is a definite difference between those wish-

TABLE 10.7

"Recently someone said, 'Today, forty years after the end of the war, we shouldn't talk so much about the persecution of the Jews anymore; instead, we should finally put an end to discussion of the past.'"

	Total pop.	Age groups			Party preference			
		16–34	35–54	55+	CDU	SPD	FDP	Greens
	%	%	%	%	%	%	%	percent
For	66	58	66	76	78	61	60	41
Against	22	29	22	15	12	27	25	44
Undecided	12	13	12	9	10	12	15	15
Total	100	100	100	100	100	100	100	100

TABLE 10.8

Ending Discussion of the Past *(Schlußstrich)*/Level of Education

Level of education	1	2	3	4	5
	%	%	%	%	%
For	76	61	53	22	37
Against	14	26	36	59	51
Undecided	10	13	11	19	12
Total	100	100	100	100	100

(N = 2102)

Key: 1 = some secondary school, completed junior high school, some basic high school
2 = basic high school diploma, some higher education
3 = *Abitur* (university entrance qualification examination), no college
4 = students, some college
5 = college graduate

ing to end discussion of the past and the smaller group wanting to keep such discussion alive (see table 10.7). The responses of the latter group were coherent and can easily be described as follows: Those who consciously made a decision *against* ending discussion of the past did this in opposition to the majority opinion, retaining a firm, critical stance toward the Nazi past and the persecution of the Jews. Those in favor of ending discussion were not evenly distributed according to age, education, and voter preference groups.

Those who expressed opposition to ending discussion of the past were mostly younger people with higher education and politically left-wing,

FIGURE 10.1
Ending Discussion of the Past and Attitudes toward Nazi Past

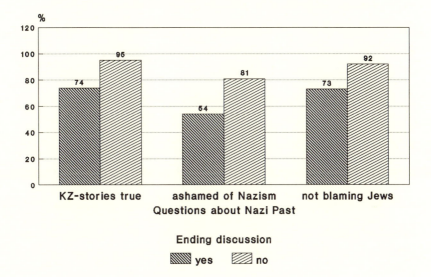

Questions about Nazi Past

Ending discussion

☒ yes   ☒ no

environmentally conscious attitudes.[20] The political orientation of the interviewees had an independent influence. In all age groups and most educational levels, the above-mentioned pattern remained basically intact. Political orientation had an even greater effect in the groups with the highest levels of education [college qualification exam (*Abitur*) and college]. Only 11 percent of college graduates who preferred the SPD were in favor of closing this chapter in history, while 73 percent of those college graduates preferring the CDU/CSU supported this. The ratio among college students was similarly extreme: 7 percent to 57 percent. The fact that differences along party lines were so pronounced among the highly educated, especially with respect to the issue of ending discussion of the past, while the differences were less extreme for those with less education, indicated that attitudes toward the Nazi past touched on a central factor in German identity and political culture.

The wish of the majority to close this chapter in history stemmed from a variety of motives, of which anti-Semitism represents only one. The contours of this group were thus less clearly defined. Since it involved

FIGURE 10.2
Ending Discussion of the Past and Anti-Semitism

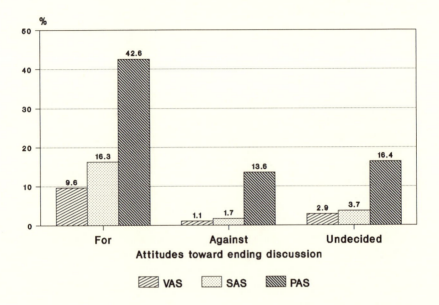

two-thirds of the total population, the proportion of anti-Semites in this group could be expected from a purely statistical standpoint to differ only slightly from the proportion in the population at large. However, there was a significant correlation between anti-Semitic attitudes and demands to end discussion of the Nazi past.

A comparison between those for and against ending discussion of the past clearly showed that a significant share of anti-Semites could only be found in the "against" group if a very broad definition of anti-Semitism (PAS) is used. If the perspective was shifted and questions dealing with anti-Semitism were posed, a virtually exact correlation could be seen between anti-Semitic attitudes and demands to end discussion of the Nazi past. Between 85 percent and 93 percent of all anti-Semites (depending on the strictness of the definition) supported this demand. Needless to say, a large majority of the anti-Semites felt no shame, and one out of two denied the truth of the concentration camps (47 percent using SAS figures).

Almost all anti-Semites refused to deal with the Nazi past any further. A large majority was also opposed to criminal prosecution of concentration camp guards (two-thirds to three-quarters). In this particular case, which involved a clearly defined, limited group of offenders, some anti-Semites felt it was indeed necessary to sentence the criminals. Even with respect to the truth of the concentration camps, denial by anti-Semites was not expressed to as great a degree as expected. Only among hardcore anti-Semites did 56 percent consider the reports to be exaggerated, while among those defined as potentially anti-Semitic in a broad sense (PAS), only 27 percent gave this response.

As already shown in the exploratory interviews (cf. chapter 2), many of those questioned could only explain the persecution of the Jews by attributing to them dishonest business practices and political power, which they said justified the persecution. In our survey, 21 percent were of the opinion that "Jews share the blame for hate and persecution." It was even widespread among people not classified as anti-Semitic according to the broadest definition of anti-Semitism. The correlation between anti-Semitism and projection of the blame was nevertheless significant. Among hardcore anti-Semites, 84 percent felt Jews shared the blame for the hate and persecution they experienced; in this way they attempted to exonerate Germans to some degree for the crimes (SAS: 71 percent; PAS: 50 percent).

Holding Jews responsible for their own persecution is a widespread explanation that is especially common among representatives of ultra-right revisionism. In the pretest, we asked who the guilty parties were (see table 10.9).

Those who had somewhat anti-Jewish attitudes were much less likely to blame Nazism in general than the control groups, though they were considerably more likely to project guilt onto the Jews or the enemy in World War I (Treaty of Versailles). A projection of guilt onto "World Jewry" by anti-Semites, along with the cliche of an international Jewish conspiracy, perpetuates the Nazi propaganda claim of a Jewish economic boycott of and declaration of war against Germany.[21] Primarily the older generations clung to this conviction (35 percent in the over-sixty category), while only 13 percent of the younger age groups were of this opinion.

The same proportation in all age groups admitted shame about the crimes committed against the Jews by Germans, though a certain impact of education could be identified. Political orientation also appeared to

TABLE 10.9

"What do you think was the major reason for the persecution of the Jews during the 'Third Reich'; that is, who was to blame?"

possible answers:	Total pop. %	Anti-Jewish leanings %	Pro-Jewish leanings %
Nazi leaders like Hitler, Himmler, and Goebbels	92	77	96
The Nazi party (NSDAP)	77	52	82
The entire Nazi ideology	72	53	82
Big business at the time, their attitudes toward Nazism	16	20	35
Most Germans who lived at the time	10	2	18
The Jews in Germany themselves	10	35	2
World Jewry, which was against Germany	10	59	5
The Treaty of Versailles	2	25	6
other	1	—	3
don't know	3	1	—

N = 344

have no influence on responses to this question. The long period that has since passed, and the knowledge of the extent of the crimes, led a majority to agree that the persecution of the Jews was a shameful fact. This agreement was limited to personal statements; while it might also have expressed humanitarian feelings,[22] it remained passive and unpolitical, and provided no motivation to continue remembering this event and its lasting consequences. On the other hand, demands to close this chapter in history, which is definitely more a subject of public debate, was influenced to a greater extent by political orientation, belonging to a particular political generation, and level of education achieved. The distribution of responses was similar to the pattern we often encountered in our anti-Semitism analysis. An above-average proportion of older, less educated, and more conservative interviewees agreed with this statement. There was a discrepancy in public opinion between personally expressed shame regarding the crimes committed by Germans, on the one hand, and the minimal tendency to deal with these issues in a responsible way publicly and politically (e.g., in reference to Israel), on the other. This tendency not to deal with the past combined a sense of failure when confronted with a past that one cannot truly "come to terms with," defense mechanisms, and rationalization strategies.

The 1989 EMNID survey confirmed our findings, both in terms of the amount of support for ending discussion of the past, and in the distribution of responses according to socio-demographic characteristics. Of those questioned, 32 percent did not agree with the statement "We should finally stop talking about the past; the other side did things that were just as terrible," thus rejecting the notion of "keeping score" by comparing crimes committed by the two sides. There was almost unanimous support for ending discussion of the past among voters for the ultra-right *Republikaner* party (92 percent); this was also true to a large extent for CDU/CSU voters (75 percent). The gap between CDU/CSU voters and SPD and FDP voters was minimal (two-thirds each of voters for SPD and FDP tended to support the statement). The response trend was reversed only for voters for the Green party; 61 percent of them rejected this demand. In addition to the special age and education patterns among Green party voters, their political and historical convictions played an important role here. The younger age groups and the more highly educated tended not to support demands to end discussion of the past, although the interface—deviating from the distribution we determined for education—was between the intermediate education levels and the "college qualification exam/college" level. Demands to end discussion of the past were seen as a way of removing the most terrible chapter in German history from public discussion. This was demonstrated by the fact that only people who had very negative attitudes toward Hitler and Nazism were opposed to the wishes of the majority to close this chapter in history. Full awareness of the criminal nature of Nazism is probably necessary in order to develop this attitude, as illustrated by the above-mentioned effect of education. As expected, people who expressed positive attitudes toward Hitler and Nazism or were undecided almost unanimously demanded an end to discussion of the Nazi past. However, even those who had "somewhat negative" feelings with respect to this issue deviated only slightly (approximately 80 percent agreement). The desire to end discussion did not necessarily imply a positive attitude toward Nazism. If the rejection was general and vague, it could express the sense that dealing with the consequences of Nazism was unpleasant. The need to continue to remember and deal with the past is only recognized once the full meaning of the Holocaust is comprehended. Such knowledge leads to problems in identifying with the national collective. Most of those opposed to closing this chapter in history expressed very little national pride (opposed to ending discussion: 66 percent). In contrast, a high level of national identification appeared possible only if German crimes were compared to the "terrible things that the other side did" and discussion was closed on this chapter in history (ending discussion: 81 percent—EMNID 1989, table 85). Our data show basically the same connection between a strong feeling of nationalism and the demand to end discussion of the past. Those who opposed closing the discussion or were undecided were seldom very nationalistic (one in eight), whereas the opposite was true for one in three of those supporting an end to discussion of the past.

Anticipation of Jewish Attitudes toward Germans

The analysis of German attitudes toward the Nazi past and persecution of the Jews has so far been one-sided; it has considered only what Germans think of Jews, but not German beliefs about Jewish attitudes toward Germans. Only by including these expectations in the analysis can we begin to trace the conflict between Germans' desire to put an end to discussion of the past, and their simultaneous "knowledge" that Jews harbor a critical, reserved attitude toward Germans.

Respondents were given a list of twelve statements projecting "what Jews think of us Germans" (question 9). We formulated these statements in two directions. In both cases, of course, these were perceptions in the minds of Germans.

1. What attitudes do Jews have toward Germans ("We Jews must...");

2. What feelings and intentions do Jews believe Germans have on issues involving the German-Jewish past and present ("The Germans...").

German expectations of Jewish expectations were marked by inhibition and skepticism, and there were differences between the attitudes expected of Jews and the expectations Jews are thought to have about Germans. Only about a third in each case assumed that Jews "wish to extend the hand of reconciliation to Germans," and that Jews believed the same of the Germans. The majority was convinced that "normalcy" between Germans and Jews was not yet attainable. On the contrary, the prevailing feeling was one of diffidence ["never again uninhibited," 34 percent; "Germans are ashamed," 48 percent; some believed Jews continue to distrust Germans ("You can never trust the Germans," 21 percent), and that they even suspect that hatred of Jews persists ("Many Germans still hate us Jews," 41 percent)]. Only 19 percent assumed Jews saw Germans as being like any other people and believed they "have nothing more and nothing less" against them. Many Germans assumed the Jews wanted to continue reminding them of their guilt ("We have to keep reminding Germans of their guilt," 47 percent), and would keep telling the Germans that "reparations alone are not enough" (40 percent). In contrast, only one in four Germans assumed that Jews today no longer reproach Germans. This conflicts with the expectation that Jews believe younger Germans, at least, "want nothing more to do with their past" (64 percent).

In contact with Jews, Germans expected a troubled relationship, laden with a heavy emotional burden. It was assumed that Jews do not leave the past alone, and thus do not want reconciliation; that they do not trust Germans and still feel Germans reject, even hate them. From the other perspective, it was expected that Jews believe Germans are ashamed of the persecution of Jews, but that they do not believe a majority of Germans feel guilty and are making efforts at reconciliation. That is, the respondents were skeptical, and suspected Jews of feeling just as skeptical and distrustful of Germans. Thus a contradiction exists between a desire for normalcy and wish to end discussion of the past, on the one hand, and the aforementioned expectations on the other—a contradiction that leads to oversensitivity, prejudice, and rejection.

In addition, the two stereotypes—that Jews are "unforgiving/unreconcilable" and "oversensitive" (26 percent and 32 percent agreement, respectively)—can be included in expectations of Jewish attitudes toward Germans. The stereotype of the "unforgiving Jew" may reflect traditional concepts of Jewish "vengefulness;" however, we assume this characterization had more to do with the current situation, in which many Germans felt they were constantly being reminded by the Jews of something they would prefer to forget.

The positive responses to the aforementioned "expectations of expectations" indicated the characteristic differences between respondents we classed as anti-Semitic (according to SAS) and all others. The following table (10.10) shows the distribution.

TABLE 10.10
Projective Statements on Jewish Attitudes toward Germans
(question 9)—Agreement

	Anti-Semites %	Non-anti-Semites %
unforgiving	66	20
not guilty	39	20
are ashamed	30	50
remind of guilt	70	44
reparations	56	37
distrust	41	18
hate Germans	59	38
reconciliation	15	34
N	244	1858

In all these questions, there was a significant correlation between anti-Semitic attitudes and projected expectations. Anti-Semites were especially likely to see Jews as a group that unforgivingly kept alive memories of the past in its own interests, with no desire for reconciliation. They suspected Jews of harboring a particularly negative view of Germany, characterized by distrust. This expectation was not based on their own negative image of Germany; rather, Jewish distrust of Germans was ascribed to "the bad character of Jews." For anti-Semites, a negative view of Germany among other peoples is explained not as a reflection of historical experience, but as a spiteful, distorted image.

However, the assumption that Jews harbor a negative view of Germany was not in every case an expression of anti-Semitism; Green voters, who evidenced levels of anti-Semitism far below the average, themselves had a self-critical view of Germany, and assumed Jews shared this skepticism. Here a negative self-image and the projected view of external perceptions coincided, so that the Jews' negative view of Germany was judged to conform with reality.

Certain characteristic differences appeared in the correlation between the projected image of Germany and party preference. FDP voters were distinguished by particularly positive expectations of the willingness for reconciliation on the part of both Germans and Jews. Their liberal view of

TABLE 10.11
Projective Statements:
"We have to keep reminding Germans of their guilt."
"We have to keep telling Germans that reparations alone are not enough."

Voters for	CDU/CSU	SPD	FDP	Greens
	%	%	%	%
Remind of guilt	52	49	47	32
Reparations not enough	44	42	34	34

Jews to a large extent excluded the possibility that the two peoples could continue to view each other with distrust or hate ("Many Germans still hate us Jews": FDP voters 28 percent, total population, 44 percent). In contrast, such a willingness for reconciliation was rarely assumed by Green voters ("The Germans are eager for reconciliation": Greens 25 percent; in comparison FDP 42 percent, total population, 36 percent). The two items that ascribed to Jews an interest in keeping alive German obligations based on guilt found the most support among voters for the two largest parties (CDU and SPD), while Green and FDP voters agreed less often.

While Green voters tended to make negative statements on Germany and were more reserved about negative judgments of Jews, the reverse was true of voters for the major parties. They had a high opinion of Germans, and were more likely to hold Jews responsible for the absence of the desired normalcy between the two peoples. FDP voters took an intermediate position; that is, they assumed greater willingness for reconciliation on both sides, and were less likely to hold Jews responsible.

The fact that neither education nor age had a measurable impact on these projective questions (with the exception of the two questions on reminding Germans of their guilt) suggests the significance of political attitudes that implicate specific views of the respondents' nation and its history. However, these political attitudes may be affected by age and education in ways that offset each other, making it impossible for them to be measured themselves.

Attitudes toward Nazism and the Truth of the Holocaust

Racial anti-Semitism that Nazism turned into state doctrine could still be found in the population in the 1947 OMGUS studies. This connection between pro-Nazi and anti-Semitic attitudes was confirmed again and again by studies on the "authoritarian personality" (Pollock 1955; Freyhold 1971, 96f.). Freyhold, whose study found a clear correlation between pro-Nazi and anti-Semitic responses, even went so far as to consider anti-Semitism in Germany a factor used to justify Nazism, rather than independent hostility (ibid., 97).

It is precisely this correlation that has been ignored so far in public opinion research; studies on attitudes toward Nazism or right-wing extremism have treated anti-Semitism only marginally (Herz 1975; Sinus 1981; Noelle-Neumann and Ring 1985; Forsa 1994), and studies on anti-Semitism have excluded right-wing extremist and pro-Nazi views (Tumin 1962; Silbermann 1982; Panahi 1980; Weiss 1984). Studies commissioned from commercial public opinion research institutes have merely compared Nazism, as a dictatorial regime, with democracy, and linked it with anti-Semitism in this operationalization. This ignores resistance to legal and material reparations and contexts of moral responsibility. These studies were correct to the extent that today's manifestations and effects of anti-Semitic prejudices differ from Nazi anti-Semitism; however, they throw out the baby with the bathwater by acting as though anti-Semitism today appeared in the same forms as in the nineteenth and early twentieth centuries, ignoring the fundamental effect of the Holocaust on the form, content, and motives of post-war anti-Semitism.

With West Germany's economic and political success, commitment to and positive assessments of an open, democratic, pluralistic society increased; at the same time, regard for dictatorship and Nazi ideology declined over the decades only slowly and discontinuously, and can still be found today among a minority of the population.[23] Both attitudes seem to have coexisted in the population for a long time. Empirical data on changes in anti-Semitic attitudes raise suspicions of certain parallels to this political transformation. To prove this process of transformation in attitudes toward Nazism, we chose four time frames, requesting for each of them a subjective assessment of the state of the nation, the idea and practice of Nazism, and Hitler's role in German history.

The tables clearly show, on the one hand, that with the collapse of the Hitler regime, it was politically discredited in the eyes of the majority of the public; that is, almost nobody would vote again for a man like Hitler.[25] On the other hand, however, National Socialism as an ideology continued to be approved of for a long time, despite its racist, anti-democratic,

TABLE 10.12
"When in this century do you feel Germany was doing best?"

	1951 %	1959 %	1963 %	1970 %
In the present, today	2	42	62	81
During World War II	—	—	1	—
Between 1933 and 1939	42	18	10	5
Between 1920 and 1933	7	4	5	2
Before 1914	45	28	16	5
Don't know	4	8	6	7

Source: IfD vol. V, 209.

TABLE 10.13
"Do you think National Socialism (Nazism) was a good idea that
was badly implemented?"

	1946 %	1947/48 %	1948 %	1969 %	1977 %	1979 %	1994 %
Yes	47	55	57	55	26	36	26
No	41	30	28	—	72	30	70
Undecided	12	15	15	—	2	37	4

Source: IfD vol. I, 134; Merritt/Merritt 1970, 32f.; Ernst 1979, 237—the deviating 1979 findings are probably based on the fact that the sample was not representative[24]; Forsa 1994, 15, the figures for the East Germans were: Yes—19 percent, No—70 percent, and 11 percent undecided.

aggressive nature (for the same observation, cf. Merritt 1977, 96). In 1947, it was mainly members of the younger generation (born between 1915 and 1930) who continued to support the ideology in 1947 (Holtmann 1989, 255). They failed either to completely comprehend the meaning of Nazism or to support democracy and the rule of law. The fact that people viewed the period from 1933 to 1939 in a positive light in the early postwar period shows that the aforementioned aspects of the Third Reich were rarely taken into account; only with respect to the war did people begin to withdraw the Nazis' legitimacy (cf. Niethammer and Plato 1985). There was little consciousness of the illegality of the political persecutions after 1933 and the emigration of Jews and opponents of the regime. The apolitical character of this view of Nazism, heavily oriented toward

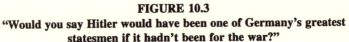

FIGURE 10.3
"Would you say Hitler would have been one of Germany's greatest statesmen if it hadn't been for the war?"

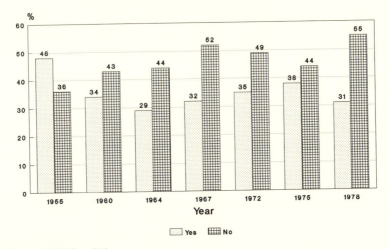

(Source: IfD Vol.V., p.204;
Vol.VIII, p.191)

FIGURE 10.4
"If there were a chance today, as in 1933, to vote in an election for or against a man like Hitler, how would you decide?"

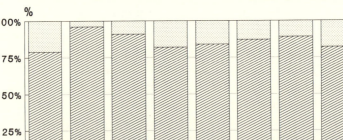

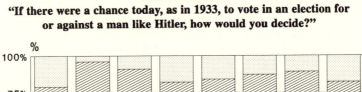

(Source: EMNID-Informationen 3/196
10/1983 cited in Stöss 1989, p.44)

personal experience, was demonstrated by the aspects that people classified as good or bad. In 1951, full employment, social welfare policies, security, and discipline were seen as good aspects of Nazism both by those who viewed it positively (41 percent of the respondents) and those who took a more critical position (36 percent). The ranking of negative aspects was also similar in the two groups, although critics placed more emphasis on the preparations for war and the war itself, as well as the limitations on freedom under the dictatorship, while those who saw Nazism more positively overall more frequently highlighted racial policies, persecution of Jews, and concentration camps as its negative aspects (Merritt 1977, 97ff.). Because of the lack of temporal distance, personal viewpoints prevailed, so that it was not yet possible for many to distinguish the important from the peripheral aspects of the Nazi dictatorship. Only when temporal distance and more extensive information facilitated a more objective overall assessment did a sharper polarization emerge between those who rejected Nazism in general and those who felt it had positive and negative sides. In the aforementioned survey, no one considered racial policies or persecution of Jews to be a positive aspect. But the fact that only 37 percent and 32 percent, respectively, mentioned the persecution of Jews as a negative aspect of Nazism shows how little the Holocaust was understood at the time to be the regime's central crime (ibid.).[26] The higher level of disapproval of the persecution of the Jews (37 percent) by those who saw more good than bad aspects of Nazism came as a surprise. It can be explained by an argumentation pattern used by those who attempt to rescue the reputation of the Nazi ideology by separating out the persecution of the Jews as a cardinal error, without which—aside from the war—they would have found it acceptable. War and persecution of the Jews are viewed not as original intentions of the regime and its ideology, but as the "bad practice" of a basically "good idea." This segment of the population was much less disturbed by the Nazi regime's domestic repression.[27]

For these reasons, the continuing decline in support for the Hitler regime found by G. R. Boynton and Gerhard Loewenberg on the basis of survey data collected between 1951 and 1967 must be viewed more critically—especially if we take into account that the political transformation of attitudes in the population had less to do with individual learning processes than with the emergence of untainted generations. Among the older generation, and on the extreme right, a point of view exists to this

TABLE 10.14
Affinity to the Third Reich and Anti-Semitism

Third Reich	N	Anti-Semitism according to		
		PAS %	SAS %	VAS %
positive	106	69.0	41.0	28.0
total population	2102	33.2	11.6	6.9

day that to some extent rejects the concrete political practice of Nazism, but refuses to abandon National Socialism and aspects of the Nazi ideology (on this, cf. Sinus 1981). Thus, it is not surprising that people continue to deny the immensity of Nazi crimes, emphasize Jewish responsibility for their own persecution, and compare Allied war policies with German crimes.[28]

The following evaluation involves the segment of the population that continued to view the Third Reich mainly positively in a "word affinity test." As studies on right-wing extremism overwhelmingly indicate, this assessment is linked with a particular view of history that includes denial or relativization of the Holocaust, as well as racism and anti-Semitism. In the word affinity test, 5 percent (N = 106) judged the concept "Third Reich" positively. Affinity for the concept "Third Reich" is strongly linked with anti-Semitism, but anti-Semitism does not necessarily go hand in hand with affinity for the Third Reich: even of the vehement anti-Semites only 21 percent show an affinity to the Third Reich.

Affinity for the Third Reich correlated disproportionately with anti-Semitism,[29] but this only partially explains the present-day distribution of anti-Semitic views. The theory that anti-Semitism is the position of a small group of die-hard Nazis is therefore incorrect.

However, the position of those for whom the concept "Third Reich" has a positive meaning was clear: only half of them acknowledged the truth of concentration camp reports (total population 80 percent), and about half of them said Jews shared the blame for their own persecution (total population 21 percent). This group's opposition to reparations was particularly strong; three-quarters were of the opinion that Jews profit from the Nazi past (total population 48 percent). The extent to which inconsistencies can coexist within this Nazi-like consciousness is shown

TABLE 10.15
**"When you think today about the Third Reich, what would you say:
did Nazism as a whole have..."**

	total pop.	Attitudes toward Jews			not
		extremely	very anti-Semitic	somewhat	
	%	%	%	%	%
Only bad sides	16	4	3	11	24
More bad sides	38	6	23	35	46
Good and bad sides	43	68	67	50	29
More good sides	3	22	7	3	—
Total	**100**	**100**	**100**	**100**	**100**
N	2272	94	205	960	1013

Source: EMNID 1989, table 78.[30]

by the fact that, despite their high regard for the Third Reich, 39 percent condemned the Israelis for carrying out policies toward the Palestinians that resembled the Nazi persecution of the Jews (total population 17 percent).

It is interesting that this estimation of the Third Reich was not based on positive experiences during this period, even among contemporaries, but was evidently purely ideological. Only 16 percent of those who said they "did well during the Third Reich," also expressed affinity for the Third Reich. This group, too, was disproportionately anti-Semitic, denied the truth of the concentration camps, and ascribed a share of the blame to the Jews. The group was comprised of older people who assumed the widespread anti-Semitism of their youth, without necessarily being closely involved with the Third Reich and its ideology. On the other hand, this ideology prevailed among Nazi sympathizers, approximately half of whom were contemporaries of National Socialism (over sixty years old) and half younger.

Our dichotomous question found only a core of 5 percent sympathizers with the Third Reich. However, this does not mean that 95 percent rejected it. The 1989 EMNID survey contained a similar question with more differentiated response choices, also permitting ambivalent judgments.

As in our sample, only a tiny minority clearly advocated Nazism; this minority was also anti-Semitic. However, with this more differentiated series of possible answers, it became clear that only half the respondents had an overwhelmingly negative view of Nazism. Among those who took an ambivalent position were also the majority of those classified as "extremely, very, and somewhat" anti-Semitic. However, here too the reverse was not true: those with ambivalent views of Nazism were not necessarily anti-Semitic.[31]

Aside from a relatively close correlation between positive attitudes toward Nazism and anti-Semitism, it could be expected that today, denial or relativization of the Holocaust would be a clear indicator of an anti-Jewish attitude. In comparison to the 1950s, today the truth of the Holocaust is generally accepted (in 1987: 79.2 percent; 13.3 percent consider much of it exaggerated; cf. above). In 1994, 60 percent of the German population said that they have heard of the "claim that the Nazi extermination of the Jews never happened," but for only 7 percent of former West Germans "it seemed possible that the Nazi extermination of the Jews never happened" [79 percent—impossible; 14 percent—No answer/Don't' know; the figures for former East Germans were 10 percent, 80 percent, and 8 percent, respectively (Golub 1994, table 12)].[32] In 1954, the distribution of opinions was practically the reverse. Only 29 percent considered the statement, "During the Hitler period more than five million Jews were killed" to be approximately correct or too low. Twenty-six percent believed it was somewhat exaggerated, and 37 percent thought it was very exaggerated (EMNID 1954, 40).

The consistency of rejection, and the lack of age differences and educational influences, suggest that opinions recorded then were not revisionist, anti-Semitic views that persisted despite knowledge to the contrary. Instead, it can be assumed that a whole series of influences formed these opinions, such as distrust of the "victor's" information, the incomprehensible large number of victims, and lack of knowledge about the genocide of the Jews, which was still less familiar than memories of "*Kristallnacht*" and observed mistreatment and boycotts of Jews in Germany.[33] Surveys today show that the facts uncovered through historical research and their presentation by the media and political educators have been widely accepted (see Forsa 1994, AJC 1994). The primary indicators of the success of such historical education are age and educational structures: of the respondents under forty-five years of age, 85 percent considered reports on the extermination of the Jews to be true, compared with only 67 percent of those over 60; among respondents with an elementary school education, the figure was 74 percent, while for those with higher education it was 87 percent. Those who continued to "believe a lot has been exaggerated" were also very likely to be anti-Semitic; 71 percent of them would have to be classed as such (according to PAS). Of the hardcore anti-Semites, 56 percent considered concentration camp reports to be exaggerated. People who doubted the truth of such reports were also to a large extent convinced that Jews shared the blame for their own persecution (57 percent), and that Jews attempt to take advantage of the Nazi past (79 percent). The attempt to relativize the Holocaust and ascribe shared blame to Jews is a central aim of Nazi revisionists and right-wing extremists, because the Holocaust is the event most responsible for delegitimizing their ideology (on the NPD, cf. Herz 1975, 113; Lipstadt 1993). Although only a small minority of Germans today denies the Holocaust, a much greater minority is of the opinion that the Holocaust is not relevant today, because it happened almost fifty years ago (37 percent) and disapproves of the idea to establish a national Holocaust memorial museum in Germany (37 percent—AJC 1994, tables 16 and 17).[34]

Reparations and Responsibility toward the Victims

With the end of the war and the release of prisoners from the camps, the problems of caring for them, compensation, and collective Jewish claims for reparations immediately emerged. Public opinion was split on these issues; on the one hand, most of the victims' claims were acknowledged, while on the other, efforts were made to keep the number of those entitled to make claims as small as possible. In autumn 1949, in response to the quite conservative question, "Do you believe Germany has an obligation to compensate German Jews who are still alive?", 54 percent answered "yes," 31 percent answered "no," and 15 percent were undecided (IfD 1949, 23). Many conflicts arose over restitution, return of Jewish property that had been confiscated or sold below value in response to political pressure (cf. Erb 1990, Goschler 1992). These claims were met with even less support. To the question, "If a non-Jew bought a Jewish business after 1933, and the previous owner demanded its return under the same conditions, would you say his claim is justified or unjustified?", only 39 percent acknowledged the justness of the claim "if the Nazi regime was clearly the reason for the sale." Twenty-eight percent considered the claim unjustified, and the remainder were undecided (IfD 1949, 21). In 1951, at a time when talks had begun with Israel on reparations, 68 percent believed that Jews who had suffered should be helped.[35] However, Jews were placed last on a list of victims of war and persecution—after war widows and orphans, bombing victims, refugees, and the families of the members of the Resistance Movement of the 20th of July 1944 killed for attempting to assassinate Hitler (Merritt/Merritt 1980, Report No. 113).

Faced with a lost war and postwar hardships, the German public saw itself as the victim, and had little understanding for the special situation of victims of persecution. In contrast to the view of the Western Allies and the West in general, who saw reparations as an issue of justice, moral obligation, and politics, the German population reduced the issue to its material, financial aspects. It was the democratic parties and the federal government, rather than the public, that accepted a broad political and moral responsibility (Vogel 1987, vol. 1; Herbst and Goschler 1989, Goschler 1992).[36]

In particular, public opinion was overwhelmingly opposed to collective reparations, as demanded of West Germany in the early 1950s by the state of Israel and the organizations joined in the Jewish Claims Conference. Compared with figures from 1949 and 1951, the public's willingness to help declined as the extent of reparations became more concrete. In December, 1952, 54 percent of Germans claimed they neither felt responsible for the persecution of the Jews nor had a duty to compensate this injustice (Merritt/Merritt 1980, Report No. 167). The result of reparations negotiations between Israel and the West German government, in which West Germany agreed to pay three billion marks to Israel and 450 million marks to the Claims Conference, met with even stronger disapproval. In August, 1952, 44 percent saw reparations as unnecessary, while 24 percent considered them basically correct, but the agreed upon amount too high; only 11 percent supported them, and 21 percent were undecided (IfD vol. I, 130).[37] Opposition to reparations was linked to a significant degree with pro-Nazi attitudes, which of course included anti-Semitism. Among respondents who saw more good than bad in Nazism, opposition was 20 percent higher than among those who saw more bad than good.

The issue disappeared from public opinion polls until 1966, but opposition apparently persisted. An indication of this is the fact that in 1966,

TABLE 10.16
"Is Germany morally obligated to pay reparations?"

	Before broadcast %	"Holocaust" viewers %	"Holocaust" non-viewers %
Yes, it is	45	54	40
Undecided	38	31	45
No, it isn't	17	15	15
Total	**100**	**100**	**100**

Source: Ernst 1979, 237.

this point was included on a long list of issues that made people at the time uncomfortable. Forty-six percent of the respondents agreed with the demand, "We should finally stop paying reparations to the Jews, they've already gotten too much" (IfD vol. IV, 204). In research done in connection with the television series "Holocaust" in 1979, respondents were asked, "Is Germany morally obligated to pay reparations?" (see table 10.16).

With 17 percent opposed, resistance to reparations seemed to have fallen sharply since 1966. However, if we take into account the high number of "undecideds," the majority of whom did not change their opinions even after viewing the emotionally charged film, it is apparent that opposition continued to be quite strong. Clearly, an emotional confrontation with the Holocaust, brought home through the individual life stories portrayed in the film, can sensitize and lead to greater acknowledgement of moral obligation. But the extent to which attitudes are changed by this learning effect is small, and most likely only short term, since our survey again indicated broad-based opposition.

We gave the issue of reparations a great deal of attention, because even the exploratory interviews showed that many people associated this issue, in particular, in negative fashion with Israel and the Jews (cf. chapter two and seven). In these interviews, it became clear that the willingness to pay additional reparations was slowly fading; in particular, reparations for new groups of victims "forty years after the end of the war" were seen as unacceptable. A significant number believed that accusations of guilt were being used for financial advantage, and linked this with traditional stereotypes such as "Jewish business sense," "Jewish

TABLE 10.17
"Many Jews try to profit today from the history of the Third Reich, and make the Germans pay."

	Total pop.	Age groups			
		16–29	30–44	45–59	60 and older
	%	%	%	%	%
Is absolutely true	11.4	6.5	7.0	12.9	19.7
There's some truth to it	37.0	32.0	33.0	41.6	42.2
Not true	29.0	36.0	36.4	25.0	17.7
Impossible to say	22.6	25.6	23.6	20.5	20.4
Total	100.0	100.0	100.0	100.0	100.0
N	2102	577	508	498	519

influence," and "Jewish vengefulness." A public statement, made by a CSU member of the *Bundestag* in connection with reparations demands from the Flick company's forced laborers, that he had the impression "Jews speak up quickly whenever money clinks in German coffers" was an expression of this widespread resentment.[38]

We asked a series of questions on the issue of reparations, ranging from the factual claim "Israel lives off our reparations payments" (question 14/13) to the conventional active protest "One should write letters to the editor strongly criticizing reparations payments to Israel" (question 16/16). Of course, the percentage of respondents who agreed with each depended on the sharpness of the wording of the question. The question that most clearly formulated resentment was agreed to by nearly half the population (see table 10.17).

This high level of agreement—among West Germans[39]—reflected a central cause of conflict in German-Jewish relations; that is, the Germans' distrustful assumption that they are being taken advantage of financially.[40] This is a general reservation aimed at any obligations arising from the Nazi period, irrespective of concrete demands. Thirty-nine percent of the respondents also expected Jews to think that "they have to keep telling the Germans that reparations alone are not enough."[41] Almost half of all Germans suspected Jews of intending "to keep reminding Germans of their guilt." This expectation expressed the fear that moral

TABLE 10.18
Index: Past (attitude toward the Nazi past)

"yes" responses	N	%	cumulative %
0	610	29.0	29.0
1	613	29.2	58.2
2	452	21.5	79.7
3	244	11.6	91.3
4	147	7.0	98.3
5	35	1.7	100.0
missing	1		
Total	**2102**	**100.0**	

(Reliability coefficient alpha = .59)

guilt persists, that it cannot be paid off, and that it has long been used for political purposes by Jews or Israel.[42] This attitude exhibited a lack of knowledge of the persecution and continuing suffering of the victims. There was often a lack of empathy and understanding of the complex and ongoing consequences of the destruction of Jewish life in Central Europe. Willingness to help Jews in Germany "because they suffered so much" was correspondingly low (26 percent).[43] The more solid their anti-Semitic world view, the more consistently help was opposed. Hardcore anti-Semites opposed such aid completely.[44]

Antipathy toward reparations did not necessarily lead to support for the demand that "no reparations be paid to Israel," advocated by 28 percent of the population. Active support for this demand, such as writing letters to the editor criticizing reparations, was limited to a small minority of 5 percent. Nevertheless, there was a correlation between antipathy toward reparations and the demand that they be discontinued. Approximately half were willing to translate their antipathy into demands.

We believe that present-day anti-Semitism is nourished not primarily by tradition, but by a past that has not yet been resolved in the present, with reparations and moral guilt playing a major role. To test this hypothesis, we created a past index[45] consisting of the following variables: "We should discontinue reparations payments to Israel," "Many Jews attempt to profit from the past," "Israel lives off our reparations payments," "We have to keep reminding the Germans of their guilt," and

FIGURE 10.5
Attitudes toward the Nazi Past and Social Distance from Jews

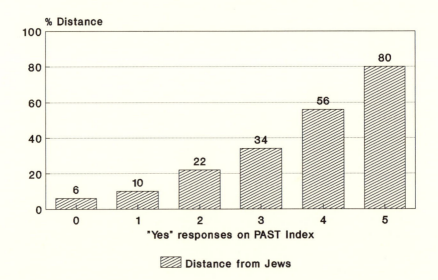

Distance from Jews

"One should write letters to the editor strongly criticizing reparations" (see table 10.18).

Rejection of the consequences of the Nazi past is connected with emotional rejection of the Jews.[46] The percentage of anti-Semites increased with an increasing number of "yes" responses on the past index.

Based on our data, we could not decide whether antipathy toward Jews led to opposition to reparations or if the reverse was true, that the reparations issue was a cause of the emergence or persistence of anti-Semitism (see figure 10.5). However, when seeking motives that could still exist today for anti-Jewish hostility, especially among younger people, there is much that suggests that rejection of the consequences of Germany's material and historical responsibility is a root cause of present-day anti-Semitism. Those who accept the moral and material responsibility seldom exhibit anti-Semitic attitudes (at 0 "yes" responses on the past index, 94 percent are free of emotional rejection of Jews). The respondents' own statements confirm that reparations payments are a focal point for

TABLE 10.19
"There are also people here with critical opinions about Jews.
What most likely upsets them?"

	total pop.	extremely	very	somewhat	not
			anti-Semitic		
	%	%	%	%	%
The Jewish faith	8	14	6	7	9
Social influence	14	23	16	11	14
Economic power	27	31	28	27	27
Reparations payments	29	45	53	32	19
Individual Jews making money off reparations payments	28	67	45	32	17
Israeli policies in the occupied territories	40	47	32	38	43
No response	1	1	1	1	1
Total in %	**147**	**228**	**181**	**148**	**132**
N	2272	94	205	960	1013

Source: EMNID 1989, table 83.

rejection of Jews. In 1989, EMNID used a list of possible choices to ask about causes of anti-Semitism.[47]

It is difficult to interpret this table, because the respondents were asked to give their opinions of the motives for other people's anti-Semitism. We assume that those identified as strongly anti-Semitic essentially mentioned what upset them personally, while the non-anti-Semites expressed assumptions on other people's possible motives. This was apparent from the fact that they considered traditional criticisms to be important, such as the Jewish faith and Jewish economic power, while not ascribing the same importance as anti-Semites to the reparations complex. In their assessment of causes, people without an anti-Jewish attitude clung to traditional criticisms that have no basis in today's relationship between Jewish and non-Jewish Germans in the Federal Republic.[48] Anti-Semites were upset by all the listed responses, as well as, with disproportionate frequency, by traditional cliches. But they were clearly most upset by the

TABLE 10.20
Attitude toward Nazi Past and Anti-Jewish Stereotypes

Index	Anti-Jewish Stereotypes				
Past	Unforgiving	Over-sensitive	Greedy	Crafty	Power hungry
	%	%	%	%	%
0	5	19	9	22	4
1	16	30	18	35	12
2	29	34	33	50	21
3	53	43	53	68	36
4	75	57	73	76	49
5	89	63	86	86	69
Total population	**25**	**31**	**27**	**42**	**18**

N = 2102

historical complex; that is, they confirmed and strengthened their prejudices on the basis of current conflicts and scandals. The fact that anti-Semites see reparations as the main point of criticism does not clarify whether they do so because their judgments stem from an already anti-Semitic perspective, or whether their anti-Semitism first emerged from this issue. This fact at least suggests that this complex of problems has an important function in reinforcing their prejudices.

In chapter 4 we left open the question of the extent to which ascribing certain stereotypical characteristics correlates with the view that Jews take advantage of the Nazi past. We assumed that traditional accusations that Jews are "unforgiving, oversensitive, greedy, crafty, and power-hungry" were constantly "confirmed" by Jewish reminders and political and material demands. Here, too, we can draw no conclusions about the existence of such causality; we can only determine the extent of the correlation, which was very strong for the stereotypes mentioned (see table 10.20).

Those who rejected Jewish demands and the need to keep memories alive largely tended to believe these demands had their roots in negative Jewish character traits. Older people with anti-Jewish attitudes saw a confirmation of their traditional prejudices, while younger people explained the demands by way of such negative characterizations. It is not

TABLE 10.21
"What do you think of the reparations payments that we pay to
Jews living here?"

| | Total population | National pride | | |
| | | strong | medium | little |
	%	%	%	%
Too high	46	56	38	19
Appropriate	47	40	54	66
Too low	5	3	6	13
No response	2	2	3	3
Total	**100**	**100**	**100**	**100**
N	2272	1249	782	233

Source: EMNID 1989, table 81.

the rejection itself, which can sometimes be explained with rational arguments, that is problematic here; it is the great inclination to project and
interpret these demands as an expression of malicious intent and negative Jewish characteristics.[49]

When rejection of efforts to come to terms with the past (*Vergangenheitsbewältigung*) were differentiated according to socio-demographic
characteristics, the pattern revealed was already familiar from the analysis of anti-Semitism. Unwillingness to deal critically with the past increased with increasing age. There were two "generational leaps": the
inclination increased only slightly up to the forty-year-olds, continued to
rise at a slightly higher rate among the forty- to sixty-four-year-olds, and
peaked among those over sixty-five. If we break down the data by educational level, rejection of *Vergangenheitsbewältigung* was relatively equal
in intensity among those with lower and intermediate level diplomas; it
became weaker among those with the *Abitur* or college educations.

As far as party preference is concerned, the expected left-right pattern
emerged. While only 20 percent of CDU/CSU voters never answered
"yes" on the past index, the figure was 30 percent for the SPD and FDP,
and nearly half of Green voters.[50] Independent of the influence of the
various age and educational structures of these parties' voters, there was
also a separate political and ideological element. Nationalist orientation,
emphasized by the CDU/CSU, is especially useful in explaining the rela-

TABLE 10.22
"What do you think of the reparations payments that we
pay to Jews living here?"

	Attitude toward Nazism			
	Very negative	Moderately negative	Fifty-fifty	Moderately positive
	%	%	%	%
Too high	25	38	59	80
Appropriate	61	55	38	15
Too low	12	4	3	4
No response	2	3	—	1
Total	100	100	100	100
N	368	855	973	69

Source: EMNID 1989, table 81.

tively strong rejection of *Vergangenheitsbewältigung* among their voters. There was a significant correlation between nationalism and rejection.

The 1989 EMNID survey also found a high correlation between strong national pride and the view that reparations to the Jews were too high (see table 10.21).

Because the large majority agreed with the statement, "I am proud to be German" (on a six-point scale from 1: "completely" to 6: "not at all," 79 percent were in categories 1 to 3), the deviance of strong nationalists from the popular average is not very significant from a statistical viewpoint. But when measured according to the difference between them and those with weak national attitudes, the great influence of national orientation on reparations became clear. Apparently, an ability and willingness to achieve critical distance from one's ingroup is necessary in order to fully accept claims on one's nation arising from the past.

Only those who viewed history very critically and assessed Nazism as thoroughly negative were also prepared to a great extent to see reparations payments as appropriate or too low. Among those with a *moderately critical* view of Nazism, this willingness already began to drop. Those who considered Nazism *moderately positive* were hardly ever willing to consider reparations appropriate.

The EMNID survey's analysis of party preference found a pattern similar to the one we established. Once again, it was CDU/CSU voters who opposed reparations more strongly than SPD (51 percent versus 42 percent), FDP (44 percent), and Green voters [25 percent (EMNID ibid.)]. For the first time, *"Republikaner"* voters made a statistically significant appearance; they confirmed their extremist position, with 74 percent opposition.

Only a quarter of the population accepted reparations and was willing to accept a special obligation toward survivors of Nazi persecution. The demand that discussion of the past be put to an end, accompanied by rejection of special responsibility for the victims and the state of Israel, is more popular. In 1994, only 12 percent of all Germans accepted that the younger generations would be answerable for the nazi crimes (Forsa 1994, 16), but nevertheless, 28 percent of the West and 39 percent of the East Germans agreed to the statement "Because of the events of the Third Reich, we have a special obligation toward Jews and also toward Israel." We cannot treat Israel like any other country on earth (Jodice 1991, table 2a). While the desire to no longer be confronted with the Nazi past is less widespread among those born between 1935 and 1964, there are no generation gaps on the issue of aid to the Jews. The impression predominates that forty years after the end of the war, that chapter of history is closed. Because this debt has not been paid off, because new, untreated historical fields are constantly being discovered and problems dealing with the Nazi period are already being criticized [the phrase "renewed guilt" (*die zweite Schuld*) recently formulated this concept (Giordano 1987)], this wish to "close that chapter" collides with the persistence of conflict-laden contradictions. The inclination of many Germans to "make peace" with the past leads them to view reminders of that past as disturbances originating from outside. They are seen as serving the interests of troublemakers attempting to exploit memories for material profit. This projection confuses cause and effect, often substituting secondary hostilities for a rational analysis of emerging problems.

Notes

1. Empirical research done in 1979 in connection with the television series, "Holocaust," represented an exception to a certain extent. It examined the persecution of the Jews entirely within the context of attitudes toward Nazism and treatment of Nazi crimes (Magnus 1980, Ernst 1979). This evaluation serves the interests of anti-Semitism research only minimally, however, since it did not determine whether those with and without anti-Semitic attitudes differed in their sentiments toward Nazism and ways of coping with its consequences. The question

as to how confrontation with the consequences of Nazism negatively influenced attitudes toward Jews, a question central to anti-Semitism research, was not investigated.

2. The concept of secondary anti-Semitism is traditionally employed in "Critical Theory" in a way differing from our definition. Claussen regards anti-Semitism in the post-fascist era as secondary, insofar as it is no longer Jews who are denounced as representatives of wealth and learning, but anyone who can be connected to wealth and learning (1987, 48). We do not feel it makes sense to use the term anti-Semitism to mean anti-intellectualism and irrational chauvinism. Schönbach (1961, 80) comes closer to our use of the term, characterizing secondary anti-Semitism as an act of defiance, maintaining anti-Semitic ideas after the war in order to justify one's own attitudes or those of one's parents. Anti-Semitic convictions are thus retained or even strengthened in order to preserve one's own and one's parents' identities, which are threatened by criticism of Nazism. Similar to our views, Schönbach sees secondary anti-Semitism as a reaction to problems arising in attempts to deal with the Nazi past.

3. In the 1994 survey by the American Jewish Committee, 8 percent gave a positive answer to a similar question: "Do the Jews behave in a manner which provokes hostility toward them in your country?"; 69 percent of the West Germans disagreed, 22 percent said "Don't know.

4. Surveys conducted in Austria by the U.S. military administration also showed this negative trend toward anti-Semitic and anti-democratic responses. Hiller interpreted this finding, as well as the high number of those who expressed no opinion, to mean that respondents were initially cautious, not expressing their opinions openly. In the course of time, fear of sanctions faded and "real" opinions were then expressed in a more open manner (Hiller 1974, 152). Sodhi and Bergius also observed a pronounced suspicion of surveys in their 1951 studies on national prejudices. Germans suspected that such questions were a political trap and preferred not to make any admissions that could later be used against them (1953, 29f.).

5. When interpreting this data, it must be taken into account that the wording of the question varied. In 1958, 1963, and 1965, the IfD used the same wording, while in 1969/79 a shorter version was used, though the meaning was basically the same. EMNID used identical wording three times in their question: "Recently, public discussion has once again increased regarding continued prosecution of crimes that were committed during the Nazi period. What is your personal opinion? Should crimes committed during the Nazi period still be prosecuted—or should we close that chapter in history?" They referred more strongly to the context of the statute of limitations debate, though their wording was very similar to that used by the IfD. The 1964 DIVO survey on the Auschwitz trial included a comparable choice of possible responses: "I think it is right that this mass murder trial for crimes committed during the Nazi period is still being conducted today, in order to show the German people the horror and suffering that were caused by Germans;" "I think it is right that these trials are being held, so that those guilty of mass murder in Auschwitz are convicted and punished;" "It would be better not to conduct such trials; after so many years, these things shouldn't be constantly stirred up." The question on the Eichmann trial in 1961, on the other hand, was posed in a very different way and, thus, not included in our table.

6. According to EMNID, the large increase between 1978 and 1979 in support for continued prosecution of Nazi criminals was caused solely by the reception of the TV series "Holocaust." Among "Holocaust" viewers, 60 percent were in favor of continued prosecution, while only 39 percent of nonviewers were. See also the figures for viewers and nonviewers in the study conducted in connection with the TV series: 39 percent of viewers and 25 percent of nonviewers supported continued prosecution (Ernst 1979, 236). On the question of the stability of the change in attitude, see note 7.

7. It cannot be definitively determined whether this change was indeed a shift in trends or a short-lived effect of the TV miniseries "Holocaust." The Sample Institute survey data suggest a temporary effect, based on responses in November 1978, February 1979, and January 1980 to a question on extending the statute of limitations for Nazi crimes (using the identical wording each time); the figures were 53 percent, 45 percent, and 57 percent, respectively, in favor of letting the statute of limitations lapse, and 31 percent, 51 percent, and 34 percent, respectively, against a lapse (Sample Telegram, January 1980). Though this might not suggest a shift in trends, the above-mentioned data from 1983 and the age distribution ascertained by IfD, according to which the younger generations less often rejected continued prosecution, would support such a shift (IfD, vol. VIII, 194).

8. Despite this attention, the Eichmann trial did not change the distribution of attitudes in the population. Surveys conducted before (1961) and after (1962) the trial had almost identical results (Schmidt and Becker 1967, 133).

9. These are the findings of a nonrepresentative spot survey conducted by IfD in Allensbach in January 1965. Nevertheless, the prevailing arguments for ending discussion of the past seem to have been adequately recorded.

10. There was also always a foreign policy justification for rejection of further criminal prosecution of Nazi criminals. It was felt that the world should not be reminded of the horrors of the Nazi concentration camps, since there were fears of a negative impact on the international opinion of Germans and Germany. Such a reminder was supported by a majority outside of Germany (70 percent in Switzerland, 62 percent in the U.S., and 56 percent in Great Britain), but by only 35 percent in Germany. Forty-five percent considered a reminder harmful (EMNID-Informationen 24, 1961). On the actual, low impact on opinions in the countries mentioned, see EMNID-Informationen 30, 1961: Only 16 percent to 18 percent each of Americans and British liked Germans less as a result of the Eichmann trial.

11. There was, however, a greater tendency to ascribe collective guilt to contemporaries of Nazism. In the research done in connection with the TV series "Holocaust," only 53 percent disagreed with the following statement: "All Germans who were adults during the Nazi period share the guilt for what happened then." Sixteen percent agreed and the remainder were undecided (Ernst 1979, 238). It is probably above all younger generations, not themselves affected, who see contemporaries of Nazism as bearing a share of guilt.

12. In the 1986 EMNID survey on anti-Semitism, a similar proportion, namely 60 percent, supported putting an end to discussion of the past, and 40 percent were in favor of constant reminders of the Nazi past, so that nothing like it could ever happen again (EMNID 1986, table 3). This greater opposition to ending discussion as compared to the 1986 IfD findings can be explained by the lack of a neutral response category in the EMNID survey.

13. This aversion appears to have increased over time. On the occasion of the Eichmann trial in 1961, 53 percent wanted to deal only with the present and the future, and wanted to hear nothing more about the Nazi past (IfD vol. III, 227).
14. In our study we use the term "guilt" in a diffuse sense, in accordance with what we consider the common usage of the word. Especially in the guilt debates in the early postwar period, philosophers, clergy and even politicians used a more differentiated and precise concept of guilt [i.e., Karl Jaspers's (1946) distinction between criminal, political, moral, and metaphysical guilt); in everyday communication even today, however, one can observe an application of the term in which aspects of political responsibility in the sense of obligatory reparations, on the one hand, and personal, moral guilt or shame, on the other, are not clearly distinguished. For an interesting new attempt at defining political criteria for guilt in regard to the Nazi regime and its crimes, see Buchheim, 1988.
15. The German philosopher, Günther Anders, correctly indicates that the accusation of collective guilt was initially raised by the Allied powers; however, they dropped it quickly, as did well-known German journalists. It is more the "guilty ones" who keep it alive, in their attempts to refute any form of guilt and responsibility. "No newspaper mentions it [the term collective guilt] with such tenacity, not to say devotion, as the 'Deutsche National- und Soldatenzeitung'" (Anders 1985, 195ff.).
16. For the question of personal guilt, the only category listed in the survey was rejection, so that nonrejection cannot be interpreted as a recognition of guilt. The large degree of rejection of personal guilt covers such a broad range of attitudes that no significant correlations to anti-Semitism, to the concentration camp crimes, or to acknowledgment of the concentration camps could be determined in the evaluation.
17. The extent to which a verbal expression of shame denotes a corresponding feeling of shame, especially among the well educated, is fundamentally disputed by researchers. The well-educated were particularly likely to express agreement, because they learned to publicly comply with the norm of expressing shame and sympathy in view of Nazi crimes (van Dijk 1987). An analysis of the experience of guilt and shame, and the resulting behavioral directives and self-images, indicates that both these emotions were very rare in Germany, that is, an expression of shame could have been purely verbal, with no equivalent in experience (cf. Lindsay-Hartz 1984).
18. The success of political education and public instruction can be clearly discerned if we look back over the past decades. In the 1954 EMNID anti-Semitism study, 37 percent still considered the figure of 5 million murdered Jews to be "greatly exaggerated," and another one in four for "somewhat exaggerated." That means that only one-third accepted the truth of reports on the extent of the Holocaust (EMNID 1954, 40). In contrast to today, no effect of age or education level could be observed in 1954.
19. Of those sixty years of age and older, 35 percent felt that Jews "share the blame if they are hated and persecuted." Only 13 percent of the sixteen through twenty-nine-year-olds felt this way. There was a significant correlation between qualifying the concentration camp reports as exaggerated and a projecting blame onto the Jews for their own persecution. Of those who felt reports of the camps were exaggerated, 57 percent blamed the Jews to some extent; of those who believed the truth of the reports, the figure was only 15 percent.

20. Even in the 1979 IfD survey, it was in the under-forty-four age group that a majority felt it was good "that films about the Nazi period are shown." In the forty-five through fifty-nine age group, the figure was 32 percent, and 28 percent of the over sixty age group (cited in Zinnecker 1985, 341). In 1984, 74 percent of the sixteen through twenty-four-year-olds thought it was "important" or "very important" "that we deal with the Nazi period and Hitler" today. Among the forty-five through fifty-four-year-olds, only 54 percent gave this response. According to Zinnecker, it could be shown "that the interface between the age groups is located at those who, as contemporaries, consciously perceived Nazi fascism and were actively involved in it" (ibid.). The evaluation of spontaneous reactions to letters to the editor about the TV mini-series "Holocaust" yielded the same results. It was the older age groups that exhibited the least amount of willingness to deal with the subject (Gast 1982, 360).

21. In a DIVO survey conducted in 1965 within the context of racial unrest in the United States, the following question was asked: "What was the reason for anti-Jewish incidents during the 'Third Reich?'" Only 9 percent attributed any guilt to the Jews ("best positions," "work-shy," "cut-throat"), although multiple responses were possible. A majority held the Nazi regime responsible (DIVO press service, March 1965). The difference between this and our findings can be explained by two factors: First of all, DIVO did not take the international dimension of guilt projection (the conspiracy theory) into account in their list of possible choices; secondly, feelings that Jews shared in the blame is more widespread than seeing them as bearing all the blame. In the pretest, even anti-Semites did not question the fact that the main share of guilt was born by the Nazi leadership.

22. The fact that women more often felt "ashamed" (65 percent) than men (56 percent) can also be interpreted in this way. Women always responded with greater agreement to all statements in our questionnaire involving humanitarian aid and personal sympathy.

23. In contrast to the Nazi ideology itself, whose central tenets were quickly "renounced," the corresponding mentality persisted for a long time. An example was the discussion on integration of foreign nationals, in which social change was hindered and delayed by conservative views of what was normal and right.

24. The growing proportion of respondents between 1946 and 1947–48 that approved of the idea of Nazism can also be found in survey data for Austria. Between August 1947 and December 1947, the percentage rose from 39 percent to 51 percent. A large number of those with no opinion changed their views during the difficult winter months (Hiller 1974, 155). Contemporary sources found two reasons for this increase: first of all, with greater distance from the end of the war, people were less afraid to express their views openly in surveys; second of all, the American occupiers were blamed for economic difficulties. This observation was true for the occupied zones of both Austria and Germany.

25. After the end of the war, public trust in and sympathy for Hitler and his closest associates was low. Only 12 percent recalled having trusted Hitler as their leader until the very end; 35 percent claimed they had never trusted him or had lost their trust at the outbreak of war in 1939 (16 percent). A large majority also found the indictments at the Nuremberg trials to be justified (cf. Merritt 1977, 96). Nevertheless, Nazism had not completely lost support; based on survey data from summer-fall 1947, British military authorities estimated the "hard core" of

Nazi supporters in the British zone at around 10 percent of the population over seventeen years of age (PORO, Rep. 111 A, cited in Holtmann 1989, 373).

26. A confirmation of the change is found in the evaluation of youth studies by Zinnecker (1985, table 5). While in 1955, only 9 percent of young people (fifteen through twenty-four years old) considered persecution of the Jews a negative characteristic of Nazism; in 1984 the figure was 74 percent of the same age group. Racial hatred and persecution of the Jews had become the most frequently mentioned negative characteristics, while dictatorship and lack of freedom, which topped the list in 1955 with 39 percent, fell to second place (64 percent). The 1955 age cohorts were also questioned in 1984 (forty-five through fifty-four-year-olds). At 41 percent, they ascribed greater significance to racial hatred and persecution of the Jews than in 1955, but dictatorship and lack of freedom retained first place among the negative characteristics, with 48 percent. Zinnecker ascribed this shift of accent in the image of Nazism first of all to "impressive thematization by the media," and second of all to the long-term change of opinion regarding condemnation of discrimination against and persecution of minorities (ibid., 346f.). Heitmeyer reached a similar conclusion (1988, 149ff.).

27. Young people, in particular, remained fixated on authority until the late 1950s, and must be categorized as right-wing conservative. Hitler's reputation, in particular, remained intact for quite some time, beginning to fade only in the late 1950s. In 1951, 30 percent of all young people judged him positively, 17 percent in 1953, 10 percent in 1955, and 3 percent in 1961 (Zinnecker 1985, 331). In research on youth, the period around 1960–61 is generally seen as a turning point toward a more critical view of Nazism.

28. According to Heitmeyer (1988, 151), for young people with an undecided attitude toward Nazism, persecution of Jews represented the limit of relativization, while other fascist elements—excepting war—went unrecognized, concealed beneath positive legends.

29. For many of those who continued to express affinity for the Third Reich, racist convictions might also have had an effect: 57 percent of them assessed the word "race" positively (total population 20 percent).

30. In May, 1961, in the context of the Eichmann trial in Jerusalem, an almost identical question was asked: "When you think back today to the period of the 'Third Reich,' what would you say; did Nazism as a whole have…"

only bad sides	7 percent
more bad sides	41 percent
as many good as bad sides	28 percent
more good sides	5 percent
only good sides	— percent
no response	19 percent

(*Source:* Freyhold 1971, 94).

If we compare the results from 1961 and 1989, the picture is largely the same. Clear rejection hardly increased (from 48 percent to 54 percent), while the ambivalent position, surprisingly, is more widespread today than it was in 1961. However, we can assume that many people who refused to respond in 1961 did so more out of fear of admitting positive views of Nazism. The answers to a similar question posed by the IfD in September, 1991 show a much greater rejection of the Third Reich: 65 percent of the West Germans are of the opinion that it was "a bad thing without any doubt" (East Germans: 64 percent), 23 percent agreed that "the Third Reich was not as bad" (12 percent of the East Germans), and 12 percent were undecided (IfD, Jahrbuch IX, 1993, 382).

31. Von Freyhold found the same basic pattern on the basis of data from the 1961 Eichmann survey. A slight pro-Nazi attitude correlated weakly with anti-Semitism; on the other hand, approximately half of those who expressed mild anti-Semitism were susceptible to pro-Nazi arguments. The correlation with anti-Semitism rose with increased support for Nazism (v. Freyhold 1971, 97).

32. The Forsa-Institut posed the question of "Holocaust denial" in another way: "Do you believe that it is only allied propaganda, that millions of people were killed by the Nazis?" (1994, 14) only 3 percent agreed, but 91 percent disagreed.

33. In the 1954 EMNID survey (27ff.), anti-Jewish measures observed in Germany itself ("boycotts, *Kristallnacht,* plundering, arrests," etc.) had been the experience that remained most strongly in the memories of some 40 percent of the respondents. Only 10 percent primarily recalled operations connected with the Holocaust ("deportation, shootings, concentration camps, mass murders"). In general, it can be said that the Holocaust as the central crime of Nazism entered the German consciousness relatively late; at the outset, responsibility for the war and dictatorship were the most important reasons for condemning Nazism.

34. The rejection to remember the Holocaust today is much more widespread among West Germans than among East Germans: while only 22 percent of the latter denies the relevance of the Holocaust, 40 percent of the West Germans do. The idea of a national Holocaust museum was disapproved by 42 percent of the West and only by 20 percent of the East Germans (AJC 1994, tables 16 and 17).

35. Decades later, the question of limiting responsibility was once again posed. In 1986, 23 percent acknowledged a general responsibility and obligation to help all Jews, 57 percent would have limited this to those directly persecuted and their families, and 20 percent were undecided (IfD 1986, 71). This statement cannot be compared with that of 1951 in either the wording of the question or the contemporary historical context. Here there was no alternative choice opting to reject responsibility, and the refusal to extend responsibility to all Jews need not be seen as a criticism of reparations.

36. It was the intention of Chancellor Konrad Adenauer and his deputy in charge of reparations, Franz Böhm, that reparations have an educational function, given the uncertain political situation and the strong presence of radical right-wing views in many parties (Deligdisch 1974, 20). Adenauer's strategy failed. In the 1953 election campaign, the subject of reparations was so unpopular that it was agreed to not even mention it. It cannot be ruled out that IfD's 1952 findings on the strong opposition to reparations influenced this decision.

37. The aforementioned Report No.167 of December, 1952 found a similarly high level of opposition; 49 percent opposed Bundestag ratification of the agreement, while only 26 percent supported it (25 percent undecided). The arguments used by opponents of reparations involved the magnitude of the payments (24 percent), the fact that Israel had not suffered in World War II (11 percent), and rejection of collective guilt represented by state assumption of the payments (only the perpetrators should pay: 7 percent).

38. Attempts by the West German media to treat the "Nachmann case" (Werner Nachmann was the former head of the Central Council for Jews in Germany) involving embezzlement of interest on reparations payments, with discretion

and reserve shows *ex negativo* that there was fear of arousing public hostility toward continued reparations payments, and ultimately also toward Jews.

39. The AJC survey of 1990 shows that the West German population differs on that issue from the Eastern Germans: as in 1987, 45 percent of the former agreed to the statement "Jews are exploiting the National Socialist Holocaust for their own purposes," while only 20 percent of the latter did (Jodice 1991, table 3a). Another AJC survey in 1994 yielded the same results: 44 percent and 19 percent (AJC 1994, table 19).

40. Thus, consistently, 36 percent also disliked the concept of "reparations" and 42 percent disliked the concept of "coming to terms with the past." Approximately the same proportion viewed these concepts positively (38 percent and 28 percent).

41. This general expectation was overwhelmingly a negative assumption, but it was also expressed affirmatively by about 40 percent of the respondents, who did not share the opinion that Jews profit from the Nazi period. Here the expected Jewish demands were not rejected as unjustified.

42. The first German ambassador to Israel, Dr. Rolf Pauls, expressed a similar fear in his first speech: "It is with great concern that we observe how the suffering of the past is terribly agitated again and again for political purposes and selfish motives, in order to disturb the present and keep it from serving the future. Such forces, hostile to today's Germany for political reasons, are not helping their own country with their agitation" (cited in Vogel, 1967, 203ff.). This statement triggered a strong public reaction in Israel. In a radio interview, SPD Bundestag member Jahn said that this insensitive speech and the Israeli reaction to it had revealed the central difference of perspective on this point. The Germans hoped for a limitation of and end to claims and to discussion of the Nazi past, while the Israeli public was unable to perceive Germany independently of its past. From the German point of view, this is all too easily seen as political or economic manipulation.

43. Data from a more recent survey indicate that especially among those born after 1940 attitudes seem to have changed: 40 percent of them hold that the indemnities paid to the victims of Nazism were not sufficient [sufficient: 24 percent, too much: 7 percent, don't know: 29 percent (Forsa 1994, 18)].

44. Only 13 percent of anti-Semites, measured according to PAS, agreed that "Jews in our country should be helped in every way, because they have suffered a lot."

45. Question 11 (concentration camp stories true), question 12 (end to discussion), and question 15 (Nazi comparison) were not considered because the correlation was too low.

46. Measured by the AS-Social Distance index; correlation Past/AS-Social Distance 0.43. We used this partial index of emotional anti-Semitism because the overall Anti-Semitism index contained variables that we also used for the PAST index. Double use of the variables "reparations too high" as a separate question and as part of the anti-Semitism index in the EMNID survey (1989, table 81) invalidated the high correlation found there between strong anti-Semitism and negative assessments of reparations payments.

47. As early as 1954, EMNID (31ff.) had asked a question about the causes: "To what main causes would you attribute the emergence of anti-Semitism, that is, hostility toward Jews?" The wording of the question was aimed more at a historical than a contemporary explanation, and thus cannot be compared exactly with the 1989 EMNID survey. Economic reasons were the most common re-

sponse (approximately 25 percent), ahead of the Third Reich's anti-Semitic propaganda (12 percent). These were followed by racial (8 percent), political, and religious reasons and social behavior (between 4 percent and 7 percent). In this historical context, reparations were not yet mentioned in 1954.

48. This historically based description of suspected causes of contemporary anti-Semitism by non-anti-Semites poses the question whether the struggle against anti-Semitism really attacks its most virulent present-day causes. Thus, only traces of anti-Judaism can be found, while the refusal to draw appropriate conclusions from the Holocaust can be seen today as a significant area of conflict in German-Jewish relations and a motivating force behind anti-Semitism as well as anti-Zionism.

49. In dealing with the Holocaust, the individual often had to acknowledge his or her superficial knowledge of the context, lack of reflection, and incapability, in comparison with the broad knowledge and self-reflective memory of the Jews. This awareness, which people were unable to cope with, put them on the communicative defensive and encouraged a stereotyping of behaviors. Once again, as in the Christian-Jewish debate, Jews were seen as hairsplitting, unrepentant, crafty, opinionated, and ineducable.

50. Conversely, the proportion of those who rejected reparations with particular vehemence (three or more "yes" responses on the Past index) was highest among CDU/CSU voters, at 27 percent, followed by 18 percent for SPD voters, 15 percent for the FDP, and 7 percent for Green voters.

11

Latent Anti-Semitism

No term has been more frequently used, yet less frequently explained, in descriptions of German anti-Semitism since the 1950s than the term *latent anti-Semitism*. It was coined in the mid-1950s (Pross 1956), and reflects a new manifestation of anti-Semitism differing from the open, politically instrumentalized forms of preceding decades. Harry Pross and others have observed the disappearance of public anti-Semitism, but have determined that it persists in private opinion. Here the concept of latency is applied at the level of the social system, and means the exclusion of certain issues and views from public communication. But the term *latency* is used much more frequently in the sense of unknown, unconscious, or repressed. This is meant to indicate that many people do not even realize they have anti-Jewish attitudes, and that the relative calm on the surface of society conceals the true extent of anti-Semitism. In this view, making anti-Semitism a public taboo has not led to a decrease in anti-Jewish views among the public; these continue in the form of latent dispositions. If we follow this hypothesis, it is virtually impossible to form a realistic estimate of the extent of anti-Semitism in the population, as it is difficult for empirical research to determine latent psychological information of which the respondents themselves are unaware—except through population-wide psychoanalysis. From this point of view, which is immune to empirical refutation (cf. on this strategy Luhmann and Fuchs 1989, 178ff.), public opinion surveys are an entirely unsatisfactory instrument for measuring the true extent of latent anti-Semitism.

We have countered this psychologization and personalization of latency with the sociological concept of *communicative latency,* which is more closely linked with the above observation on the banishment of anti-Semitism from public discourse (Bergmann and Erb 1986). System theory distinguishes between psychological and social systems. Depend-

ing on which of these is the point of reference, we can distinguish between consciousness latency (lack of knowledge, lack of awareness) and
communicative latency [lack of certain issues to facilitate and direct communication (Luhmann 1984, 458)]. Of course, there are relationships
between the two system levels, to the extent that communication presup-
poses awareness and people want to speak their minds. We assume that
anti-Semitic views exist and that their supporters are aware of them, and
express them in certain social situations in which the public moral taboo
regarding anti-Semitism does not apply. In our view, the relatively anonymous interview situation of a public opinion survey is one of the social
situations in which personal attitudes toward Jews are openly expressed.
We tested this hypothesis in the exploratory interviews, the pretest, and
the main survey.

Theoretically, we must also distinguish between actual and functional
latency. Capacity limitations require that consciousness and communication always operate selectively, leaving a multitude of possibilities
unexplored, while keeping them open as options. Thus, there is always
an actual latency in the form of nonexploration of issues, ignorance, and
the impossibility of knowledge. We should therefore not leave unexplored
the cases in which people have no explicit opinion on, or know very little
about, issues such as Jews, *Vergangenheitsbewältigung* (coming to terms
with the past), and anti-Semitism. This should not be prematurely interpreted as the consequence of taboo or repression. The pretest indicated
the minor significance of these issues in many people's lives.[1] In the
methodological discussion of public opinion surveys, this phenomenon
is treated under the heading of "non-attitude;" it is assumed that a
prestructured questionnaire artificially constructs opinions by allowing
the respondent only a few possible responses to choose from (see for
discussion Bogart 1967; Converse 1970; Schuman and Presser 1983;
Reuband 1990). In our survey, too, it is possible that the spectrum of
opinions established on attitudes toward Jews was more contoured than
what actually existed in the minds of the respondents. As the evaluation
of the anti-Jewish stereotypes showed, an incoherent image of Jews is
quite widespread (cf. chapter 4). To test whether those with "no opinion"
and the "undecideds" were cases of actual latency or a form of repression or avoidance, we evaluated the categories "don't know" and "undecided" separately (for criticism of the widespread survey practice of not
taking those with no opinion into account, Reuband 1990).

But latency also has the function of maintaining structures in the system; that is, it blocks awareness or communication when these would lead to destruction or restructuring of the system. Certain "dangerous" themes or opinions are excluded from the public arena because they violate important norms or systemic interests. That which is latent does not simply disappear, and it never vanishes entirely; instead, the system creates structures to regulate what must be said or left unsaid, seen or ignored in what situations (Luhmann 1980, 68). In Germany various norms and rules were developed to force anti-Semitism into latency and keep it there. The rules ranged from moral discrediting and communication strategies to criminal prosecution.[2] This structural protection through latency can be interpreted as a reaction to the persecution and murder of European Jewry. Public anti-Semitism was unacceptable for the process of establishing a democratic system in post-war Germany; right from the start, the allies saw combatting it as a prerequisite for Germany's acceptance into the community of nations (Stern 1992).[3] The wish for German integration and international recognition forced myriads of politicians and writers to keep to themselves, for political reasons, their deviating opinions on reparations, the "Jewish question" before 1933, and the like.[4]

In addition to these external political requirements for integration, domestic problems of integration and continuity also required that Nazi convictions, the core of which included anti-Semitism, no longer be permitted. The political elimination of Nazism took place through firings, reeducation, de-Nazification, and war crimes trials. To facilitate the rebuilding of state and society, which had to be carried out by the same "personnel," a fiction of discontinuity was necessary, best illustrated by the concept of "Zero Hour" (*Stunde Null*). Since it was impossible to change in one fell swoop the anti-Jewish attitudes that continued to be widespread after the war, anti-Semitism was turned into a social taboo that could no longer be expressed publicly. Legal regulations against racial hatred were passed, for example, in 1946 in Bavaria, and similar bills introduced by the SPD and CDU was discussed in the Federal Parliament in 1950 (cf. Cobler 1985, 161). The platforms of the reestablished democratic parties, as well as the declarations of principle of the churches and trade unions, expressed opposition to any form of "racial arrogance" and discrimination. The extreme right-wing parties that had emerged with the founding of the Federal Republic of Germany were hindered in their political development by both administrative and more concrete measures. The SRP was ultimately outlawed by the Constitutional Court in 1952. In the GDR right-wing organizations were totally banned. Anti-Semitism was thus no longer socially acceptable, and could only be insinuated, indirectly and weakly (on the SRP, cf. Furth 1957, 156ff. and 226).

Prohibiting communication of anti-Semitism is closely interconnected with the broad-based latency of the concrete Nazi past in general. In reaction to this normative pressure, many former Nazi supporters had decided to keep quiet. Sociological studies of young people in the early 1950s provide evidence of young people's great caution with regard to politically sensitive issues (Zinnecker 1985, 344), and Schönbach's study found that people from the generation most linked to the Nazis—those born between 1910 and 1920—were most likely to try to reduce their discomfort through silence and denial of the past (1961, 61). To this extent, the latency of anti-Semitism forms one aspect of the overall problematic of *Vergangenheitsbewältigung* (cf. in detail on this complex Bergmann and Erb 1986, 227ff.).

Advocates of this way of dealing with the past see in this strategy the only realistic way to integrate former Nazis and parts of the population that succumbed to that ideology into the democratic state.[5] But its opponents criticize this strategy as denial and restoration. This denial thesis, based on a psychoanalytical model,[6] emphasizes the pathological consequences of denial, which fails to dissolve identification with the "Führer" and does not lead to a healthy society—there are consequences of this latency.[7] To this day, the two camps continue to disagree: the first pleads for an end to the discussion of the past (*Schlussstrich*) and sees the democratic reconstruction of Germany as a successful means of overcoming the past. These people now point to the negative effects this insistence on remembrance and guilt has had on Germans' collective sensibilities (the phrase used is "the wounded nation," see the book of the same name by Noelle-Neumann and Köcher 1987). The second group emphasizes the deficiencies in this area, and points to the necessity of continuing to face up to the Nazi past. These two viewpoints also differ in their evaluation of the current extent and virulence of anti-Semitism (Bergmann 1988b). For the former, anti-Semitism has receded to such an extent that it is no longer a political problem, making continuing structural protection of the social system through norms of anti-anti-Semitism no longer necessary. Communicative prohibitions appear to them to be dysfunctional, and they blame the persistence of such prohibitions in part on the interests of those benefitting from them.[8] The latter, meanwhile, see a major, merely repressed potential that could reappear whenever the norms are relaxed.

These different evaluations are themselves based on the communicative latency of anti-Semitism, and always appear when anti-Semitic incidents are being discussed. The first group sees such incidents as merely "unfortunate faux pas" by individuals, which however do not permit drawing the conclusion that anti-Semitic views are widespread. The second group sees these incidents as symptoms that old hostilities persist to a great degree under an apparently calm surface.[9] For them, it is not visible, but invisible anti-Semitism that is most significant (the "iceberg" metaphor). The political reaction to anti-Semitic incidents is correspondingly different. The first group suggests "drying them out" by disregarding them, while the second group would place them on the agenda and publicly attack them. Both groups typically criticize the results of social science research on the extent of anti-Semitism. The first group finds the results vastly exaggerated, while the second believes questioning techniques are not equipped to determine latent anti-Semitism.

Thus, taking a cue from the sociological concept of "pluralistic ignorance" and the "spiral of silence," we must investigate the extent to which *projected* anti-Semitism correlates with personal attitudes towards Jews and overall political beliefs.

Communicative Latency and Response Patterns

A general criticism of public opinion research on the sensitive subject of anti-Semitism holds that respondents give socially desirable answers, attempting to conceal anti-Jewish attitudes. Therefore, survey results are systematically falsified.[10] We paid particular attention to this problem by offering several statements (all question 19) in which respondents were asked about their discomfort with the subject and their willingness to express themselves openly.

"I'm always careful when talking about Jews, because you can easily end up getting in trouble that way" (20 percent agreement).

"Somehow I don't like the whole subject of Jews" (23 percent agreement).

"I don't share my true feelings about Jews with just anyone" (15 percent agreement).

TABLE 11.1
Index: Latency

"yes" responses	n	%	cumulative %
0	1310	62.3	62.3
1	474	22.5	84.9
2	211	10.0	94.9
3	107	5.1	100.0
Total	**2102**	**100.0**	

(Reliability: alpha = .57)

These three questions measured personal reactions to a subject per-ceived as sensitive. Approximately one-fifth of the respondents reacted cautiously to the pressure of latency, avoiding the issue in certain situations.[11]

We summarized these three statements in a latency index (table 11.1).

About two-thirds of the population believed themselves personally free of latency pressures. The remaining third felt the taboo and the moral weight of the subject and admitted to being cautious with their state-ments. These statements imply a negative attitude toward Jews, which could come into conflict with the norm of anti-anti-Semitism if expressed publicly. Thus we can assume that fear of communication is linked with an anti-Jewish point of view.

In the opinion of survey critics, those people who claim they wouldn't tell just anyone their opinion of Jews are the ones who would not reveal themselves as anti-Semites in an interview. But this was not the case for the great majority. The latency index has a correlation of r = .47 with the anti-Semitism index. This showed that anti-Semites were perfectly aware of the latency pressure and knew their views were not tolerated in public. The fact that they could be recognized in our survey despite the latency pressure they perceived shows they apparently defined the survey situa-tion as *anonymous* and thus answered the questions in a way compatible with their true attitudes. Nevertheless, it cannot be entirely ruled out that under conditions of public repression of prejudices, respondents hide their true feelings and supply socially desirable responses. In various steps of our evaluation, we attempted to narrow down this percentage. The fol-lowing table, which shows the correlations between latency pressure and

FIGURE 11.1
Communicative Latency and Anti-Semitism

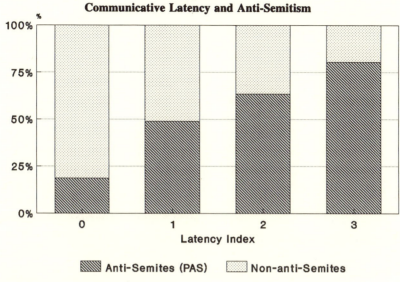

0 agreement - no latency pressure
3 agreements - high latency pressure

FIGURE 11.2
Distribution of Anti-Semites and Non-anti-Semites using the Latency Index

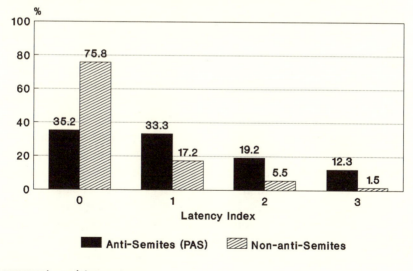

0 agreement - no latency pressure
3 agreements- high latency pressure

a relatively broadly defined anti-Semitism (using PAS), provides some indications of this.

As communicative inhibitions increased, the percentage of anti-Semites also increased. While 19.5 percent of those without communicative reservations were anti-Semites, 80.5 percent were non-anti-Semites. When latency was particularly pronounced, the relationship was reversed. Communicative inhibitions increased further when anti-Semitic views were particularly pronounced.[12]

Communicative inhibitions and anti-Semitism are thus closely linked, but do not coincide entirely. There were people who admitted to great communicative inhibitions (agreement with two to three statements on the latency index), but whom we did not classify as anti-Semitic (using PAS). Among these ninety-eight respondents (4.6 percent of the sample), there may have been many anti-Semites who had adjusted their entire response behavior to public norms. Since this behavior could not be the case for all of the ninety-eight people, we estimated the maximum amount of concealed anti-Semitism which was also not revealed in the survey situation at less than 4 percent.[13] This view was supported by the fact that, from a psychological point of view, it would be difficult to sustain total mimicry throughout the length of a survey questionnaire; response behavior that consistently deviates from one's actual opinions requires a high degree of concentration and knowledge of the desired responses.[14] Therefore, we assume that the distribution of anti-Semitic views we determined corresponded to the actual distribution of opinions in the population, with a small margin of error of 2 percent to 4 percent.

Evaluation of "No Opinions" and "Undecideds"

Our assumption that people with anti-Semitic views express their actual opinions in survey situations was also supported by findings we arrived at by evaluating the "undecided/impossible to say" responses. We would have assumed that people with anti-Jewish views who wished to conceal their true opinions would be very likely to take the opportunity of choosing these neutral response categories. But this was patently not the case. For those questions in our survey that contained a neutral response choice, we measured the mean value using the anti-Semitism and latency indexes. A comparison of the mean values for the "Agreed/Disagreed/Undecided" response categories revealed the following: The

TABLE 11.2
Mean of the Anti-Semitism Index, "Some people believe the Jews think they
are special and look down on others because it says in the Old Testament that
God declared the Jews to be his Chosen People."

Mean/AS Index	
Agreement	1.74
Disagreement	.94
Undecided	.31
Total Population	**.03**

TABLE 11.3
Mean of the Latency Index (question 17)

Mean/Latency Index	
Agreement	.90
Disagreement	.40
Undecided	.58
Total population	**.58**

mean values of the "undecided" category in all the questions examined
were always closer to the non-anti-Semitic and non-communicatively
latent response choices. Two examples follow (see tables 11.2 and 11.3).

An evaluation of the other questions with the response choice "undecided" revealed the same pattern. The difference between the mean values
of the "undecided" and "agreement" response categories was particularly
great for crassly-worded anti-Jewish statements. Here the "undecideds"
closely resembled those who disagreed with such statements.

All this suggests that an undecided response pattern is more likely to
result from uncertainty and lack of knowledge of the subject than from a
desire to conceal one's own anti-Semitism. The fact that the undecideds
were hardly more likely to express communicative inhibitions than the
non-anti-Semites additionally suggests that their choice of neutral response categories did not at all mean avoidance of negatively judged
responses. It cannot be ruled out that anti-Semites sought "refuge" in
these neutral responses; however, given the below-average mean values
on the anti-Semitism index, this can only be a rare occurrence.

The more broadly anti-Semitism was defined (using PAS), that is, the larger the group of those classified as anti-Semites, the larger the proportion of "undecideds" who must be assigned to this group (an average of 16 percent of the "undecideds"). When anti-Semitism was more narrowly defined, isolating the group of vehement anti-Semites, the proportion of "undecideds" who sympathized with these views tended to drop (an average of 11 percent of "undecideds"). The more strongly pronounced the anti-Semitic views, the greater the need to express them and have one's own opinion confirmed, and the stronger the perception of latency pressure (see Bergmann and Erb 1991). Thus, anti-Semitic potential becomes largely estimable.

The choice of the responses "don't know/undecided/no opinion" also points to an *actual* latency. Many people are not interested in the subject, pay no attention to it, and know little or nothing about it.[15] In the pretest, we asked how important the respondents found the subject and whether they spoke about it with family or friends. On a list of fourteen possible topics of conversation, such as nuclear energy, the arms race, terrorism, the death penalty, and the like, 27 percent felt the subject "Jews" was of little interest anymore; thus it fell somewhere in the middle. Half of the respondents said they had almost never spoken in private conversation over the past three or four years about the persecution of Jews in the Third Reich; only 4 percent said they had done so often, and 41 percent occasionally. The exploratory interviews confirmed this low level of interest and widespread lack of knowledge.[16] Of course, disinterest and ignorance also reflect avoidance of a subject considered unpleasant, sensitive, and difficult.

Distribution of Communicative Latency

Evaluation of communicative latency by age group showed increasing inhibitions about expressing opinions on "Jews and anti-Semitism" as age increased (see figure 11.3).

Up until the mid-thirties, communicative inhibitions remained at a plateau; they began to rise with increasing age. Of the older generation, from which most anti-Semites are recruited, half were afraid to express their opinions openly.[17]

Latency pressure and party preference of the respondents revealed an interpretable relationship for the four parties represented in the *Bundestag*

FIGURE 11.3
Communicative Latency by Age Group

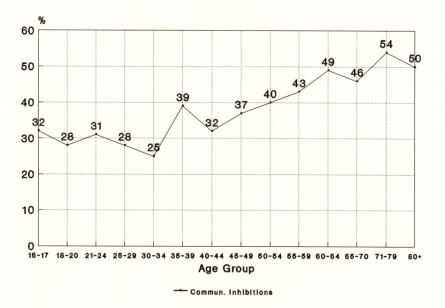

— Commun. Inhibitions

(1986–1990). CDU/CSU voters indicated above-average inhibitions in communication, SPD voters coincided with the average, and FDP and Green voters were disproportionately free of latency pressure. A left-right pattern could be determined in the difference between the major parties, that is, the CDU/CSU and the SPD, but it was eclipsed by the distinction between the major parties and the smaller ones with specific constituencies. Here the "more right-wing" FDP did slightly better than the "more left-wing" SPD. After controlling for age and education, an independent influence of political orientation could be pinpointed. In the respective age and educational groups, CDU/CSU voters exhibited greater latency than SPD voters; theirs was in turn greater than that of FDP voters. Overall, the latency level was lowest for Green voters, but it varied between the different age and educational groups.

The congruence in distribution of age, education, and political preference between anti-Semitism and communicative latency once again indi-

FIGURE 11.4
Communicative Latency and Party Preference

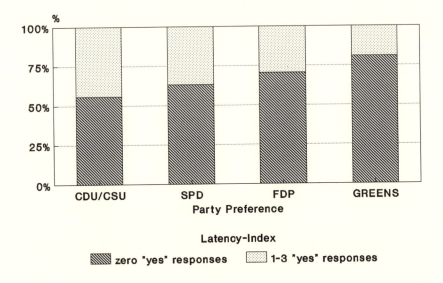

cated that anti-Semites knew their views were socially undesirable and could not be expressed in any and every social situation. The communicative strategies chosen by social elites, the media, and the press to make anti-Semitism taboo have been successful to the extent that they have restricted anti-Semitic statements to a narrow sphere of communication, making it more difficult to pass them along (cf. Bellers 1990). However, this strategy could only change existing anti-Semitic convictions to a very limited degree. Public treatment of anti-Semitic incidents by politicians, the media, and educational institutions throughout the history of the Federal Republic condemned them thoroughly, thus constantly reinforcing the prevailing norm of anti-anti-Semitism. This norm also had to take into account extreme right-wing parties, such as the *"Republikaner,"* that deny being anti-Semitic,[18] although a majority of their members and voters in fact hold anti-Semitic views (Noelle-Neumann 1993). The anti-anti-Semitic consensus has clear taboos; thus vandalism is always rejected. But there are also marginal areas, such as verbal slips of the tongue, where public condemnation is less universal. Such "slips" and

TABLE 11.4
"Do you believe there are a lot of people today who do not like Jews?"

	N	%
A lot	420	20
Not that many	778	37
Very few	610	29
Impossible to say	294	14
Total	**2102**	**100**

insinuations are the forms in which anti-Judaism is expressed today, and which are capable of igniting public, political conflicts.

Public condemnation of anti-Jewish vandalism is increasingly accepted and encouraged by the population.[19] Because of these negative experiences, anti-Semites prefer to avoid public discussion of such incidents; in addition, they consider them very rare,[20] and would rather see anti-Jewish incidents ignored. If this is not possible, they use a strategy of trivialization in order to avoid prosecution or political and educational measures.[21] For anti-Semites, negative discussion of anti-Semitic views led to cognitive dissonance between the opinions established as morally correct by society, and their own stigmatized views.[22] As long as they did not consider their views to be the prevailing views, they preferred noncommunication to a discussion that would discredit them.

Analysis of the State of Public Opinion

Anti-Semites perceive the public resistance to their views, and prefer to remain silent.[23] According to the theory of the "spiral of silence" developed in recent years by Elisabeth Noelle-Neumann (1977, 1978; for criticism of the concept, cf. Noetzel 1978; Glynn 1989; Fuchs et al. 1992), they could be expected to view themselves as a minority, isolated in their inopportune opinions. To test the relationship between public discrediting and estimation of the number of those sharing their opinions, our survey included the following question (see table 11.4).

The majority of the public believed there was indeed some degree of hostility to Jews; a fifth even thought it was widespread. It would be interesting to know whether there is a systematic difference of perception

TABLE 11.5
"Do you believe there are a lot of people today who do not like Jews?"
by Anti-Semitism

	PAS		SAS		VAS	
	no	yes	no	yes	no	yes
	%	%	%	%	%	%
A lot	15	28	17	41	18	45
Not that many	37	37	37	35	37	35
Very few	34	20	32	9	31	9
Impossible to say	14	15	14	15	14	12
Total population	**67**	**33**	**88**	**12**	**93**	**7**

(p < .001)

of public opinion between anti-Semitic and non-anti-Semitic people. There are in fact significant differences between these two groups of people that contradict the theory of the spiral of silence (cf. for a more extensive discussion Bergmann and Erb 1991). In this case, it was people with anti-Semitic views who assumed their views were shared by many in the population, and that very few were not anti-Jewish. The following table (11.5) illustrates the relationship.

Very few anti-Semites saw themselves as the small minority they actually are. Many of them believed their opinion was "really" widespread.[24] Their view clearly distinguished them from the average, as well as from people not classified as anti-Semites. The more stringent the criteria used in defining anti-Semitism, the more frequently the anti-Semites overestimated the number of those sharing their views. Here we found a pronounced tendency to project, which has been observed within the scope of authoritarianism theory to be a central character trait of xenophobic and anti-Semitic people.[25]

In 1989, the EMNID Institute survey on "contemporary history" also asked about the presumed extent of anti-Semitism in West Germany. The evaluation suggested a close relationship between anti-Semitic views and systematic overestimation of the extent of these views.

The classifications made by EMNID according to degree of anti-Semitic attitude corresponded very closely with assessments of the extent of anti-Semitism (see table 11.6). While two-thirds of the extreme anti-Semites assumed it was widespread, the number was half that among

TABLE 11.6
"How would you assess the general attitude of West Germans to Jews?"

	Total pop.	Attitudes toward Jews			
		extremely	very	somewhat	not
			anti-Semitic		
	%	%	%	%	%
Most against Jews	4	23	12	3	2
A large number	22	43	35	25	14
A small number	52	21	42	51	59
Hardly any	21	13	12	20	24
No response	1	—	—	1	1
Total in %	100	100	100	100	100
N =	2272	94	205	960	1013

Source: EMNID 1989, table 82.

those with very anti-Semitic attitudes, a quarter among the somewhat anti-Semitic, and a sixth among non-anti-Semites.

These results seem to limit the validity of the spiral of silence theory. Apparently there are groups sharing certain opinions, such as devout anti-Semites, who are so convinced of the truth of their worldview that they take it for granted that many others must share it. Paradoxically, they do not perceive communicative pressure and the infrequency of anti-Semitic incidents as an indication that they represent a minority opinion; on the contrary, latency pressure, which anti-Semites perceive particularly strongly, is interpreted as a repressive measure against a point of view that is widespread, but politically undesirable.[26]

Thus, they disproportionately support the view that "Many people are afraid to give their true opinions of Jews."[27] This leads them to have optimistic expectations regarding the development of their group. In the pretest, we asked the following question on this (see table 11.7).

This inclination to presume widespread anti-Semitism stemmed, first of all, from wishful thinking on the part of anti-Semites; however, for another segment of the population, it arose both from fear of anti-Semitism and a need to preserve the concept of an identifiable enemy. Sixteen percent of the non-anti-Semitic respondents presumed that "most" or a "very large number" of West Germans did not like Jews (EMNID 1989, table 82).[28]

TABLE 11.7
"What do you think is going to happen? In ten years, will more people
or fewer people in West Germany not like Jews?"

	Total population %	anti-Jewish %	pro-Jewish leanings %
More people	4	30	8
Fewer people	42	17	42
Nothing will change	30	32	26
Undecided/D.K.	24	21	24
Total	**100**	**100**	**100**
N	121	95	128

The phenomenon that liberal, progressive people overestimate the extent of prejudice against minorities in society is discussed in the English-speaking world as part of the concept of "pluralistic ignorance." This includes two mechanisms that systematically influence perceptions of opinion distribution in the population:

1. The mirror effect of perception—people with conservative views of minorities and those who reject them project their own views and values on everyone else.

2. Underestimation of changes in opinion—it is more liberal people who tend to believe that other peoples' conservative and rejecting attitudes towards minorities have changed less for the better than have theirs (Fields and Schuman 1976, 437; Banton 1988).

We have already determined a mirror effect of perception among anti-Semites (see table 11.8). Our research also provided evidence of the second mechanism included in the concept of "pluralistic ignorance." It was voters for the Green party, a party that fights for the rights of minorities, criticizes what it sees as insufficient treatment of the Nazi past, and makes combatting prejudice and discrimination a central element of its platform, who judged the decline in anti-Semitism most pessimistically. Liberal voters, on the other hand, were particularly optimistic, while the two major parties fell within the national average.

Depending on party preference, agreement with various response choices meant different things. The view that many people do not like

TABLE 11.8
"Do you believe there are a lot of people today who do not like Jews?"

	Total pop. %	Voters for			
		CDU/CSU %	SPD %	FDP %	Greens %
A lot	20	20	20	11	22
Not that many	37	38	39	38	35
Very few	29	30	30	35	24
Impossible to say	14	12	11	16	19
Total	100	100	100	100	100

(chi^2 64.6 df .30, p < .05)

Jews was, for the 20 percent of voters for the major parties, to some extent a projection of their own anti-Jewish views.[29] The fact that 22 percent of Green voters shared this view, although the proportion of anti-Semites among them is very small, can be seen in connection with their socially critical attitude, which makes them skeptical that a great change of attitude could have taken place among the West German population. The significantly lower assessment of 11 percent of FDP voters can be explained, on the one hand, by the small share of anti-Semites among them, and on the other, by their affirmative attitude towards West Germany's political achievements.[30]

The effect of socially critical or affirmative positions among the respondents was underlined by the lack of expected age and educational effects. People with higher levels of education feared anti-Semitism was widespread, though they themselves had disproportionately low levels of anti-Semitic prejudice. The age-related increase in anti-Semitism was not reflected in answers to the statement on the estimated extent of anti-Semitism. The estimates were more or less equally high in all age groups. Thus we may assume that the perceptions of older generations were structured by the above-mentioned mirror effect, while those of younger generations were affected by skepticism regarding a change of attitude in the population.

Other surveys contain additional indications that estimations of the extent of anti-Semitism vary greatly depending upon people's own attitudes toward Jews, assessments of Nazism, and political positions

(Schönbach 1961, 31 and 40; Galtung 1960, 74 and 86; and EMNID 1986, table 4).

It is important to know how Jews directly threatened by anti-Semitic statements and attacks estimate the extent of anti-Semitism. In 1979, Alphons Silbermann asked a representative sample of Jews in West Germany about their estimation of the extent of manifest anti-Semitism (1982, 123ff.). They held 80 percent of non-Jewish Germans to be moderately to heavily anti-Semitic. This skeptical view is undoubtedly based on the experience of the terrible past, which is projected on the present and future in what Michael Banton called "playing it safe" or "risk avoidance" (Banton 1986; 1988).[31] Historical experience leads to selective perceptions, in which anti-Jewish incidents or those seen as such are ascribed increased significance. This perception by Jews must be taken seriously, as they are the targets of the attacks, the ones receiving threatening letters and telephone calls, and the like. However heavily or weakly distributed anti-Semitism may be, it is a threat from the Jewish point of view. However, this pessimistic view cannot substitute for empirical studies of the actual, quantitative extent of anti-Jewish attitudes.

The data from the Silbermann survey found a difference between the suspected great degree of anti-Semitism and everyday personal relationships between Jews and non-Jews. The study on the Jewish community in Germany conducted by Silbermann and Sallen in 1990 reveals the same pattern (1992; see table 11.9).

The very negative assessment of the extent of anti-Semitism in West Germany was more an expression of learning from the past than the result of present-day experience. The tendency of Jews and their representatives to overestimate the extent of anti-Semitism, compared with survey results, is a general phenomenon also reported in other Western democracies (see for the United States Curtis 1990; Chanes speaks of a perception gap between beliefs and survey data, 1994, 98ff.).[32] The extent to which selective concentration on anti-Semitism leads to overdramatization of its appearance, resulting from understandable concern as well as occupational blindness, was shown by Gary A. Tobin's study of perceptions of anti-Semitism by officials of Jewish organizations in the United States (1988).

People with close personal contacts to Jews or those who see themselves as "pro-Jewish" seemed to share this perspective. Their response behavior in the pretest of our study showed that those with pro-Jewish

TABLE 11.9
"'In general,' how would you describe the relationship between German Jews and German non-Jews?"
"And how would you describe your 'personal' relationship to German non-Jews?"

	personal %	general %
Very good	28.9	3.6
Good	69.6	56.4
Moderate	10.2	37.0
Bad to very bad	1.4	2.9
Total	**100.0**	**100.0**

Source: Silbermann 1982, 110.

leanings more frequently assumed that "a lot of people don't like Jews" than the national average (22 percent versus 14 percent).[33]

The empirical findings of a 1986 EMNID study on anti-Semitism show the extent to which estimates of the distribution of anti-Semitism and assessments of certain incidents such as statements by public figures or anti-Jewish jokes depend on historical and political convictions. Opinions on the issues mentioned were affected by positions toward the Nazi past, even more so than by personal attitudes toward Jews. Those respondents who demanded an end to discussion of the past were more likely to assume that there was no anti-Semitism in Germany or that it was minimal, that anti-Jewish jokes and political statements were "not to be taken seriously." Conversely, a majority of those who wanted the Nazi period to be remembered so that nothing like it could ever happen again tended to judge these incidents as "very bad" and assume that anti-Semitism was widespread (EMNID 1986, table 3). The desire to downplay such incidents is related to the close linkage between anti-Semitism and Nazism in the public consciousness.[34] At the same time, a reemergence of anti-Semitism recalls the issue of the "unresolved past" onto the agenda. Those who would prefer to close that chapter of history and avoid reigniting such controversies in the domestic press and abroad have an interest in "overlooking" or denying the existence of anti-Semitism or downplaying its significance. Those holding the opposite view, on the other hand, see the persistence of anti-Semitism as reason enough to keep alive the memory of the Nazi period. Thus they are critical of anti-Jewish jokes and statements, and consider concern over the extent of anti-Semitism to be "very justified" (EMNID 1986, table 4). It is communicative latency itself that permits such opposing interpretations. The mere existence of a taboo creates the incentive to break it, as we have seen in the provocative use of Nazi symbols by young people. A debate has been sparked about whether breaking the taboo represents the exception that proves the rule of the insignificance of anti-Semitism, or whether it is a sign that latent anti-Semitism persists.

In estimates of the extent of anti-Semitism and assessments of it, we find a majority of opinion categories that can be traced to the involvement, interests, political and historical beliefs, and attitudes toward the German state and society of those holding the opinion. Diametrically opposed groups ascribe great significance to present-day anti-Semitism. Anti-Semites hope their view is the majority view, overestimating the potential of those sharing their opinions. A socially critical, more "left-wing" position,[35] which sees anti-Semitism as a sign of an "unresolved past" also tends to overestimate the potential in order to guard against unpleasant surprises, as expressed in the slogan *"Wehret den Anfängen"* (Nip the danger in the bud). The latter motive is certainly also the basis for the Jewish perception that anti-Semitism continues to be widespread. Anti-Semitism is ascribed minimal significance or none at all by those who believe the past has been "resolved" or would like to believe this. Those sharing this view would like to avoid discussion of the Nazi past, and are thus forced wherever possible to avoid acknowledging anti-Semitic incidents for what they are.

This points to a more general problem, namely, how anti-Semitism is defined from different points of view. There is no consensus, whether scholarly or social, on what should be categorized as anti-Semitism in individual cases (cf. on this problems recently Chanes 1994, 88ff.). This disagreement came to light clearly in the so-called Fassbinder controversy, in which views of the anti-Semitic character of the play "Garbage, the City, and Death" and the dangers that could arise from its performance varied considerably, even among liberals (Lichtenstein 1986; cf. Zollinger 1986). The limits to tolerance of critical statements about Jews are judged very differently. For some, against the backdrop of the Holocaust any criticism of Jews or Israeli politics is an expression of an anti-Semitic attitude; others see such criticism as part of freedom of expression in a pluralistic society, and accept a certain amount of polemics. Where this limit is drawn will remain controversial, and conflicts will flare up again and again, with no ultimate resolution. The incongruence of perspectives and interests we found, which cannot be circumvented, make appeals for "objectivity, lack of inhibition, and normalcy" in German-Jewish relations do not seem sufficiently thought through. Demands for normalcy ignore the fact that the communicative latency of anti-Semitism was the result of a political decision to control communication in a society hostile to Jews. Making anti-Semitism a taboo has undoubtedly led to a reduction of the problem; whether the problem has already disappeared, making further "tabooization" unnecessary, remains doubtful, given the figure of 12 percent dedicated anti-Semites.

Notes

1. In 1954, there was not only disinterest, but a pronounced reluctance to deal with the issue of anti-Semitism. Of all the respondents, 88 percent showed no interest at all, 6 percent showed minimal interest, and only 5 percent showed a pronounced interest. A special survey of grade school and college students and teachers recorded somewhat higher figures: 70 percent showed no interest, 21 percent minimal interest, and 9 percent pronounced interest. Only college students showed any great degree of interest: 34 percent said they had a pronounced, or at least minimal, interest in the issue (EMNID 1954, 42 and 69).
2. This tabooization was assisted by the fact that anti-Semitism was offered a substitute during the Cold War in the form of anti-communism. Little is known as yet on the function of anti-communism in the context of the changeover from Nazism and anti-Semitism. See the remarks on this in Mitscherlich and Mitscherlich 1976.
3. In 1950, Franz Böhm, later head of the German delegation to the reparations talks with Israel, clearly described the precarious situation of West German politics: on the one hand, it had to assume that a "considerable stratum of anti-Semitism remained" and that at the time no climate of public opinion had developed which "anti-Semites had to fear." On the other hand, the belief existed among politicians that they could under no circumstances admit this "if we do not want to cause Germany incalculable harm abroad" (Böhm 1950, 10f.). Böhm opposed this "bad diplomacy" of begging for a clean bill of health at home and abroad, calling instead for decisive opposition of, in particular, moderate anti-Semitism, in order to gain public power and authority (ibid. 13).
4. For example, at the third reading of the reparations agreement with Israel in the *Bundestag,* this was how FDP deputy Dr. Hasemann explained why his party did not want to publicly "bargain" over the agreement. It was feared this would "dissipate" the moral effect (Negotiations of the German Bundestag, first legislative period, 254th sitting, 3 March 1953, 12, 278f.).
5. This latency of Nazism and anti-Semitism, whether created through prohibition, moral discrediting, or voluntary reserve, was described by Hermann Lübbe as a

"certain silence," which in his opinion was the socio-psychological and political medium with which to transform the post-war population into citizens of West Germany (Lübbe 1983, 334).

6. For a critical view of the denial theory, see Luhmann and Fuchs (1989, 195ff.), who revealed the paradox that the observed system is ascribed experiences and psychological treatment that it does not itself experience or remember. Resistance to the observers' interpretations "confirms" their view that that which is experienced is denied and repressed. The denial thesis is incontrovertible, because it uses circular argumentation.

7. Thus, the psychologist Birgit Rommelspacher saw bad relations with other ethnic groups in Germany as a result of its "culture of denial," because the anti-Semitic past has never been resolved (taz, 7 May 1990, 11).

8. The negative consequences of the anti-Semitic taboo were the subject of the controversial play "Garbage, the City, and Death," by Rainer Werner Fassbinder, who hoped to use his character, "the rich Jew," to illustrate the business machinations of a Jewish real estate speculator, protected by the "false philo-Semitism" of local West German politicians. His criticism was aimed not at the Jew, but at those who helped him for historical reasons (cf. interview with Fassbinder 1976).

9. The collection of materials published by Heiner Lichtenstein in 1986 on the Fassbinder controversy is a treasure trove of this type of assessment.

10. Such objections are supported in part by "unobtrusive studies" on racial prejudice. Similar studies in the U.S. show that survey data do not fully record prejudice and discrimination (Crosby et al. 1980).

11. The correlations between the three statements dealing with the personal experience of latency pressure are relatively high, ranging from .39 to .42.

12. Of the 146 (6.9 percent) vehement anti-Semites, only 18.5 percent were free of any feeling of latency pressure, while 55 percent of them felt it very strongly.

13. On the basis of the same survey, Renate Köcher also examined whether the number of those with anti-Jewish views, as distilled from survey data, did not underestimate their actual potential in society. She estimated that only 3 percent of those classified as free of prejudice had great communicative inhibitions—approximately one percent of the population (IfD 1987, 66ff.).

14. Schönbach (1961, 23f.) discussed the psychological problem of anti-Semites in postwar Germany. He found that this consisted of a precarious juxtaposition of rationalizations and denial reactions, which forced anti-Semites partly to search for confirmation of their views, and partly to trivialize and conceal them. In an anonymous survey situation in which no sanctions need be feared, honest expression of opinion could therefore be anticipated. The two contradictory tendencies made it unlikely that one complete response pattern would prevail.

15. Cf. the minimal interest, 11 percent, in the subject of anti-Semitism in the 1954 EMNID survey (42). On interest in the Holocaust, see *Media Perspektiven 4*, 1979, 230.

16. Despite decades of political education and the visibility of the subject in the media, after broadcast of the television series "Holocaust," 51 percent of the respondents said the film had taught them "things about the Nazi period that they hadn't known." Even 48 percent of those who did not define themselves as strongly interested in politics said their knowledge had increased (Ernst 1979, 234).

17. In the Schönbach study (1961, 64ff.), these age groups had already indicated a particularly pronounced tendency to "cover up and deny" the past, while younger generations (born between 1930 and 1942) expressed their opinions "with fewer

inhibitions and worries." They tended toward honesty and were more likely than older people to admit their own anti-Semitic feelings. Schönbach interpreted this behavior as indicating that older people concealed their anti-Semitism due to inhibitions stemming from their memories as contemporaries of Nazism, while younger people, lacking the burden of direct experience, believed they could be less inhibited in expressing their opinions. In our study, this age group revealed a higher latency that the next generation (born in 1943 or later). Communicative inhibitions have remained a generational problem to this day. This is not insignificant in the dialogue between the generations. The tendency of younger people today to express themselves freely and radically leads to exaggerated fears among older people, who sense and respect the communicative prohibitions more strongly, that anti-Semitism could reemerge among young people. In 1991, only 12 percent of those aged sixteen through twenty-nine were of the opinion that "one cannot speak about some aspects of the Third Reich in public" (thirty thorough fifty-nine age group: 17 percent, sixty years and older: 21 percent). The great majority of Germans agreed that "one can talk about everything" (IfD, Jahrbuch IX, 1993, 382).

18. Cf. Lepszy 1989, 8. In Germany, extreme right-wing parties could express themselves only in a veiled, indirect fashion. They were frequently forced to distance themselves from their members' statements and actions. Thus, the DRP immediately expelled two party members who were responsible for desecrating the Cologne synagogue, and sent an apology to the Cologne Jewish Community (cf. Bergmann 1990, 259ff.). This strategic party maneuver, which was intended to prove the party's democratic legitimacy and constitutionality, served indirectly to confirm the validity of the norm.

19. In 1990, 79 percent of the Germans thought the government should ban anti-Semitic groups (Jodice 1991, table 6a). Today 90 percent demand punishment of anti-Semitic perpetrators [6 percent reject it (Emnid 1992, table 23)]. In comparison, in 1949 this demand was only supported by 41 percent, while 15 percent refused.

20. *"One occasionally hears and reads about attacks by Germans on Jewish sites such as cemeteries, synagogues, and the like. What do you think: does this happen often or only rarely?"*

	Total Pop.	anti-Jewish leanings	pro-Jewish leanings
	%	%	%
Happens often	9	3	17
Rarely happens	83	85	70
Don't know	8	12	13

Source: Pretest 1987.

21. Some survey results underscore these statements. In response to the wave of anti-Semitic graffiti in the winter of 1959–60, only 37 percent of the population supported condemnation of the incidents, while 35 percent favored ignoring them (IfD vol. III, 320). In our 1987 pretest, 69 percent of the respondents believed in publicizing all anti-Jewish incidents such as cemetery and synagogue desecrations, while only 9 percent preferred to ignore them. Characteristically, of those with anti-Jewish leanings, only 39 percent would have publicized such incidents, but 85 percent of those with pro-Jewish views would have done so. Of those with anti-Jewish views, 16 percent preferred to hush them up, while another 44 percent of them favored publication, depending on the circumstances.

22. In a study on the wave of graffiti, Schönbach found a precarious juxtaposition of satisfaction/rationalization and denial/trivialization among anti-Semites. On the one hand, they saw public confirmation of their private opinions; on the other hand, the wave of graffiti renewed the discussion—fateful for anti-Semites—on Nazism, persecution of the Jews, and guilt (1961, 24). These contradictory tendencies among anti-Semites probably still exist today. Consequently, in 1986 the majority of them did not consider concern over reignited hostility towards Jews in West Germany to be justified (cf. EMNID 1986, table 4).

23. In the pretest, 40 percent of anti-Semites defined the subject "Jews" as one about which one should say nothing because one could easily end up getting into trouble; 33 percent said this about the subject "concentration camps," and 27 percent about Nazism (at 13 percent through 17 percent, the average of communicative inhibitions in the population as a whole was considerably lower). None of the otherwise mentioned political issues revealed such high latency pressure among anti-Semites).

24. The 1991 Emnid study reaffirmed these findings for East Germans as well: while half of the anti-Semites supposed that most or a large number of their fellow Germans are in fact anti-Semitic, only 18 percent of the non-anti-Semites did [West Germans: even more (57 percent) anti-Semites believed that the other Germans are anti-Semitic (19 percent of the non-anti-Semities—EMNID 1992)].

25. When asked about the motives of adult perpetrators in the wave of graffiti, those classified as anti-Semitic were significantly more likely to assume anti-Semitic views than other respondents: "racial hatred," "bad experiences with Jews," and above all, "protest against the recent Jewish political upswing" (Schönbach 1961, 39).

26. In the pretest, 91 percent of those with anti-Semitic views agreed with the statement: "Many of our politicians can't give their true opinions on Israeli politics, because there would immediately be trouble" (the popular average was 65 percent; for those with pro-Jewish views, 44 percent). Anti-Semites thus assumed that even politicians were subject to strong communicative pressure, and that their "true opinions" would be very critical of Israel.

27. The backdrop here is formed by conspiracy theories that claim public opinion is purposely manipulated, and that those who make public opinion are victims of "reeducation policies." With this construction, one can "discover" the "true, anti-Semitic public opinion" behind distorted media images. This is another indication that anti-Semitism today is mainly a phenomenon of the political right-wing (see for an analysis of right-wing-publications Erb 1994).

28. In surveys on xenophobia, this difference between expressed personal opinions and those ascribed to fellow citizens was especially crass; while 45 percent of the respondents were against the presence of foreigners in Germany in a 1985 IfD survey, 72 percent believed most Germans were opposed to foreigners. This discrepancy can be interpreted in two ways: on the one hand, that personal hostilities that respondents did not want to admit openly were concealed in this projection (this was the interpretation in Geiger 1990, 21f.); on the other, that it was an underestimation of the positive change in public opinion on minorities on the part of liberal citizens who tended toward a pessimistic, socially critical attitude (cf. below, the concept of "pluralistic ignorance").

29. The March 1989 EMNID survey, which included *Republikaner* voters in a representative survey for the first time, showed that personal views were very heavily projected by the extreme right. Forty percent of them believed that most, or a

large number, of Germans were anti-Semitic (EMNID 1989, table 82). The findings of the 1991 EMNID study corroborates this projective attitude: two thirds of the East and half of the West German voters of the Republikaner believed most or a lot of the Germans are anti-Semitic, only a minority of voters of the CDU/CSU or SPD shared this view [17 percent in East Germany and 25 percent resp. 23 percent in West Germany (EMNID 1992).)]

30. In applying the concept of "pluralistic ignorance," we must keep in mind that in the English-speaking world, "liberal" generally means a left-oriented intellectual, and is not identical to West Germany's political liberalism. To this extent, the concept is most applicable to Green party voters.

31. At a hearing before a committee of the European Parliament on "Revival of Fascism and Racism in Europe," Michael May of the Institute of Jewish Affairs in London stated, "Because of the trauma of the Hitler period, we (the Jews) can never feel entirely secure in free and apparently enlightened societies. The history of Western culture is burdened by the tragic legacy of anti-Semitic prejudice. We feel that, though it may be concealed from one period to the next, this prejudice lurks beneath the surface of our civilization" (European Parliament, Meeting Documents 1985/86, Document A 2-160/85/Appendix 4, S.L.1).

32. According to Martire and Clark (1982, 108), Jewish perceptions of anti-Jewish attitudes are consistently more strongly negative than opinions expressed by non-Jews (on a restrictive critique of the interpretation by Martire and Clark, cf. Tobin 1988, 218f.; Chanes 1994). In 1960, Galtung determined that a higher proportion of Jewish schoolchildren assumed a very high number of incidents of anti-Semitic graffiti than did the non-Jewish comparison group; in the latter, a larger proportion of those with anti-Jewish views than of those with positive views assumed there had been a large number of such incidents. Jewish schoolchildren were also more likely to assume that such activities could recur (Galtung 1960, 110).

33. This tendency was confirmed by Galtung's survey. The closer the contact to Jews, the more frequently non-Jews report anti-Jewish statements (Galtung 1960, 69).

34. This evaluation pattern was also found in reactions to the wave of anti-Semitic graffiti in 1960. Those who clearly opposed the vandalism considered it a warning of impending danger ("it's come to this again"—37 percent; only 5 percent of anti-Semites shared this opinion), and only 19 percent saw it as "childish pranks" (41 percent of the anti-Semites). Opinions also differed significantly on the perpetrators themselves; opponents of the vandalism more often saw it as the work of Nazis and right-wing extremists (26 percent) than did the anti-Semites (8 percent), and less often as "kids looking for attention" [16 percent versus 30 percent of the anti-Semites (Schönbach 1961, 31)]. Views about those sympathizing with synagogue desecrators conflicted. Of non-anti-Semites, 30 percent believed many people sympathized with the perpetrators, while 14 percent of anti-Semites shared that view (ibid. 40). In contrast to the tendency toward projection that we had found, in this concrete, scandalous case, anti-Semites wanted to keep the number of supporters small in order to interpret the incident as the act of a few individuals and thus reduce its significance.

35. Green Party and SPD voters were much more frequently critical of anti-Jewish statements by politicians (80 percent of the Greens and 63 percent of SPD voters found them "very bad") than were CDU/CSU and FDP voters [45 percent and 43 percent (EMNID 1986, table 4)].

12

Anti-Semitism in United Germany
(1990–1995)

The collapse of the GDR and the opening of the Berlin Wall were welcomed around the world. It did not take long, however, before talk was heard, both inside and outside Germany, of a feared slackening of Western ties, the rise of a new sense of nationalism in a united Germany, and the possibility that, with unification, Germans would lose their sense of responsibility for the consequences of World War II and the Holocaust (Huelshoff 1993; Moyle 1994; Heydemann 1994). Such anxiety was directed in particular toward East Germans, since very little was known of their political attitudes; therefore, anti-democratic, authoritarian, and nationalistic views were anticipated. There were also expectations that the political system of the former West Germany would shift to the right after full sovereignty was attained, with the change manifesting itself in revanchism, efforts to become a superpower among neighboring countries to the east, and Germany once again "going its own way" ["*deutscher Sonderweg*" (Le Rider 1994)].[1]

The GDR *Volkskammer* that convened in April, 1990 after the first free elections issued a declaration asking Jews throughout the world and the Israeli people for forgiveness for the hypocrisy and hostility of East Germany's anti-Israel policy and for the continued persecution and degradation of Jewish citizens after 1945. Nevertheless, many Jews feared that the "prescribed antifascism" in East Germany had not led to any fundamental change in attitudes toward Jews and Judaism, and in fact that there was strong opposition to the state of Israel and Jews in general as a result of GDR anti-Zionist policies. Numerous political decisions served to fuel these fears. For example, a proposal by the Central Council of Jews in Germany to include a passage in the preamble of the German Unification Treaty between the governments of the GDR and the

Federal Republic was turned down. The passage would have included a clear acknowledgement of responsibility for the consequences of the dictatorship from 1933 to 1945.[2] Skepticism was reinforced by the secondary importance given the restitution of Jewish property in the former East Germany and the hardship clause for Jewish victims of persecution.

In addition, since the opinion was widespread that the Federal Republic had fulfilled its reparations obligations solely because of external political pressure and not out of any sense of moral conviction, it was feared both that continued reparations payments might be threatened once Germany acquired full sovereignty,[3] and that the anti-Semitism taboo might also be eliminated.

Germany's image was also harmed when the public learned that German companies had supplied technology for the production of poison gas in Libya and missiles in Iraq. Historic parallels were drawn in light of Germany's support of Israel's adversaries by supplying them with "gas." The wave of violence against asylum seekers that started in Germany in 1991 also recalled the state's weak response to severe political unrest toward the end of the Weimar Republic. Parallels were also drawn between the persecution of Jews and attacks on immigrant ethnic minorities, as these were interpreted as an expression of a German need to seek scapegoats in times of social and economic crisis. Asylum seekers were initially the primary targets of such violent crimes, but as the influence of right-wing extremist ideology increased within these violent groups, attacks on Jewish targets also became more frequent.

The sensational pogromlike riots in Hoyerswerda (September, 1991) and Rostock-Lichtenhagen (August, 1992) not only triggered a wave of crimes throughout Germany (see figure 12.1), but were met with public approval locally. This gave the impression that a broad-based xenophobic movement was developing in Germany. Because of these fears, the tools of social science were employed to observe the process of German unification. Thus, numerous studies are available on this period, making it possible to provide answers to the above questions on the basis of empirical data.

Sociological analyses of offender profiles and public opinion did not confirm participation by a broad base of the population. A 1991 evaluation of 1379 police investigations revealed that most of the apprehended suspects were young, male, blue-collar workers with little education. Approximately 90 percent were under twenty-five years of age, and one-

FIGURE 12.1
Right-Wing Extremist Crimes 1990–1995[4]

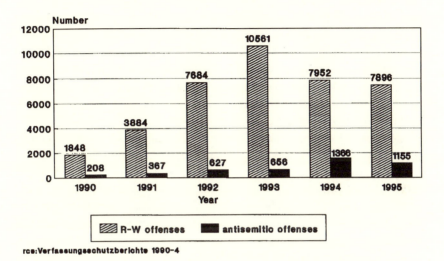

rce:Verfassungsschutzberichte 1990-4

third were even under seventeen (Willems 1993, 110f.). Only 4 percent of the suspects were girls and young women.[5]

In light of the great influx of asylum seekers and the heated debate on changes in the right to asylum, right-wing extremists enjoyed a certain degree of public approval in 1991 (27 percent of western and 13 percent of eastern Germans expressed understanding for right-wing extremist activities). This figure dropped considerably at the end of 1992 in response to the riots in Rostock and the resulting broad-based movement protesting violence and racism [16 percent of western and eastern Germans (EMNID 1992, table 23)]; right-wing extremists became the group with the most negative rating [in December, 1992, 77 percent of western Germans and 79 percent of eastern Germans expressed firm rejection of right-wing extremists (Noelle-Neumann, 1993, table A1)]. Public disapproval of anti-Semitic attacks and groups was even greater.[6]

The analysis of public attitudes does not suggest growing xenophobia. On the contrary, data collected for the EMNID survey conducted at the end of 1991—at the height of the so-called asylum debate—show that compared to 1989, the antipathy expressed toward asylum seekers and Turks actually decreased.[7] With respect to West Germans—a comparison is only possible for them—EMNID had used the same like-dislike scale in March, 1989 as it had in 1991 (EMNID 1989, 1992). The proportion of those who expressed clear dislike for Turks (1989: 30 percent; 1991: 19 percent), asylum seekers from eastern Europe (40 percent to 31 percent) and Africa (49 percent to 38 percent), and ethnic Germans from eastern Europe (27 percent to 20 percent), decreased between 7 percent and 11 percent from 1989 to 1991. Since it is unlikely that attitudes would shift so drastically within three years, we assume that in the context of the existing violent, xenophobic atmosphere, the positive attitudes of the respondents were an expression of their desire for a political solution to the problem. They undoubtedly continued to harbor negative attitudes toward these subpopulations in their everyday lives, but the respondents clearly opposed "vigilante justice."

The rise in xenophobic and anti-Semitic attacks alone cannot be taken as evidence of a corresponding change in public opinion. Waves of violence emerge as a result of a favorable "opportunity structure" and certain contagion and bandwagon effects, particularly when a subculture inclined to violent behavior (xenophobic skinheads and racist neo-Nazis) exists and learns by example, adding such activities to their own repertoire.

Times of dramatic social change and crisis that are perceived by many as a threat, and for which a political solution appears impossible, encourage the development of ultraright-wing parties and unconventional protest. We have discussed the recent success of these parties at the polls and outbreaks of violence elsewhere (Bergmann and Erb 1994a; 1994b). In order to ascertain the extent and significance of anti-Semitism in society, we can analyze various phenomena, such as anti-Jewish offenses and actions; public opinion; attitudes of the intellectual elite; treatment by the media; government treatment of Jews and anti-Semites in politics, the courts, and education; and the ideology and activities of right-wing organizations. The results vary depending on the subject of analysis. This analysis is concerned with anti-Semitic attitudes of the public as a whole that change only in the long term and apparently do not react immediately to conflict-laden incidents.

TABLE 12.1
Dislike of Jews

	yes	no
Eastern Germans	10.8%	89.2%
Western Germans	14.4%	85.6%

Source: EMNID 1992.

The Frequency of Anti-Semitic Attitudes in Eastern and Western Germany

The following analysis rests upon a broad-based survey on anti-Semitism conducted from 3 to 17 December 1991 throughout all of Germany by the EMNID Institute for the Hamburg news magazine *Der Spiegel*.[8] The 1990 and 1994 anti-Semitism surveys conducted by the American Jewish Committee, both of which used a shorter list of questions, were also taken into consideration (Jodice 1991; Golub 1994), which made it possible to compare attitudes over four years. To supplement the data, all studies on subjects relating to anti-Semitism were included, above all studies on adolescents and right-wing extremism, and a series of voter profiles prepared in the "super election year 1994" (see chapter 1).

The anti-Semitic potential of respondents' attitudes could be determined in two ways. The first was based on subjective self-evaluation. In our case, respondents were asked to rate their emotional attitudes toward Jews living in Germany on an eleven-point like-dislike scale (from -5 to +5). Those expressing a mild or strong dislike of Jews (from -2 to -5) were regarded as anti-Jewish. The resulting distribution for eastern and western Germans was as follows (see table 12.1).

Since self-evaluation can deviate from scientific measurements, especially with respect to a strongly stigmatized prejudice, it is important to measure anti-Semitic potential over a series of indicators expressing objective anti-Jewish statements. Therefore, the second method we used to measure anti-Semitic potential (see table 12.2) was to create an additive index summarizing agreement with eight anti-Jewish statements.[9]

Both the subjective emotional assessment of Jews and the measurement using the index revealed a significantly lower percentage of anti-Semites among eastern Germans. The difference between East and West

TABLE 12.2
INDEX: Anti-Semitism 1991

yes responses	East Germans			West Germans		
	N	%	cum. %	N	%	cum. %
0	424	50.8	50.8	607	35.1	35.1
1	219	26.3	77.1	437	25.3	60.4
2	109	13.1	90.2	266	15.4	75.7
3	47	5.6	95.8	137	7.9	83.6
4	22	2.6	98.4	114	6.6	90.2
5	9	1.1	99.5	70	4.0	94.3
6	2	0.2	99.8	52	3.0	97.3
7	2	0.2	100.0	35	2.0	99.3
8	—	—	100.0	12	0.7	100.0
Total	**834**	**100.0**		**1730**	**100.0**	

was smaller for emotional attitudes (dislike) than using the index, which consisted almost exclusively of items from the cognitive dimension of prejudice. We will base our further evaluation on the index, since western Germans tend to view themselves as not anti-Jewish even when they objectively express anti-Semitic opinions, as was already found in our 1987 survey (cf. chapter 2). We attribute this difference to the specifically West German climate of public opinion, in which the subject of "Jews" is treated in an extremely moralist manner characterized by stigmatization of deviating opinions. There was no corresponding climate in East Germany, as the official antifascist consensus there left no room for conflicting interpretations to develop as in the Federal Republic. We thus assume that respondents from the East openly admit their emotional antipathy toward Jews; on the other hand, western Germans sometimes avoid expressing such feelings (that is, they respond with categories -1 and 0), while still agreeing with objectively discriminatory statements. In this respect there is a greater discrepancy between subjective assessment and objective characterization by western Germans. The response distribution for two questions, which were also used in our 1987 survey to measure the level of communicative latency (cf. chapter 11), clearly show that western more often that eastern Germans wish to avoid the morally burdened subject "Jews." In response to the statement "I think that many people are hesitant to express their true opinion of Jews," 32 percent of eastern Germans and 43 percent of western Germans agreed entirely; 30 percent and 17 percent, respectively, completely disagreed with the statement. A similar distribution was found for the following statement: "Somehow I don't like the whole subject of 'Jews'" (total agreement: 19 percent of those from the East, 26 percent of those from the West; total disagreement: 47 percent to 39 percent, respectively).

A preliminary finding in the East-West comparison showed that far fewer eastern Germans agreed with the anti-Semitic items included in the index than western Germans.[10] The eastern Germans rated more favorably in all dimensions of prejudice: they agreed less often with anti-Jewish stereotypes, they exhibited less emotional rejection, and very few denied the truth of, and German responsibility for, the persecution of the Jews and the consequences of that persecution (cf. note 9, this chapter).[11]

This finding, of course, raises the question why anti-Semitic attitudes declined more sharply in the GDR than in West Germany where, after all, the goal of postwar re-education has been actively pursued. There are three possible explanations for this: First, the presence of a dogmatic ideology centered around anti-fascism is able to eradicate dissenting prejudices and world views more thoroughly than the open, wide range of ideologies that coexist in a pluralistic society, even if that society generally rejects and opposes extreme right-wing ideas. In the former GDR, fundamental reference points were antifascism, resistance, and the idea of socialism. Nazism and the Holocaust do not—and never did—play anything like the role they did in the West. At least the generation that built up East Germany in the 1950s and 1960s could be expected to faithfully support a humanist-oriented form of antifascism, therefore rejecting anti-Semitism.

Secondly, East German state doctrine treated anti-Semitism and neofascism as problems of capitalist countries, exonerating its population of any historical responsibility for Nazi fascism. The East German population itself thought this, living in the belief, in the words of writer Stephan Hermlin, "that half the German population were antifascists during the Nazi period." This freedom from guilt appears to explain why East Germans are less anti-Semitic and show less rejection of memories of the Holocaust. They feel free of the need to deal with their share of guilt and responsibility, issues that we believe represent an essential motive for post-Holocaust anti-Semitism among West Germans today. Attitudes toward Jews and Nazism may have been preserved unchanged, whereas in the West, ongoing discussion of guilt and responsibility and debates on reparations have pressured people to change their views.

Third, it is possible that the psychoanalytic model, which theorizes that something can be overcome by being worked through, does not apply to societies as a whole. Anti-fascism as proclaimed by the East German state made it impossible to constantly reiterate anti-Semitic ideas. Consequently, the handing down of anti-Jewish stereotypes was effectively blocked. In West Germany, on the other hand, the very intense preoccupation with Nazism in schools and public life meant that, like it or not, prejudices toward Jews were also communicated. This is particularly apparent with regard to religious anti-Judaism, which virtually disappeared in the secularized GDR.

Other surveys on subjects of contemporary history, such as Nazism or World War II, also reveal the impact of the specifically "antifascist political culture" in East Germany. Thus a slight decrease in anti-Semitic and historically revisionistic opinions can be confirmed for the population of the united Germany. Debate on the end of the postwar period and the position of the new "Berlin Republic" in world affairs, as well as discussion on the German nation initiated by right-wing intellectuals, represent issues of political and intellectual interest rather than matters of concern to the public.

Subgroup Differences

Age Groups

A difference between political generations in West Germany has been discernible since the 1960s. Younger generations socialized after 1945 have less often taken on anti-Semitic opinions. These different generational categories could still be clearly recognized in our 1987 survey, though at that time it was already apparent that anti-Semitism in the youngest age cohorts no longer continued to decline. This trend, as well as the fact that the oldest group, which had been most strongly influenced by nationalistic and Nazi anti-Semitism, is gradually dying off, have caused the differences among age groups to become less distinct. In terms of anti-Semitism, only two age categories can be distinguished: the

FIGURE 12.2
Antisemitism by Age Group: East and West Germans 1991

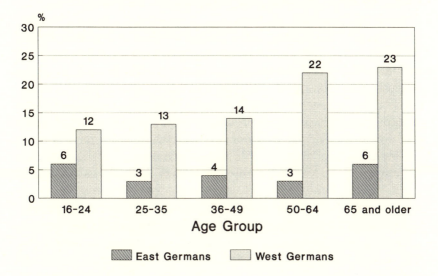

younger cohorts up to forty-nine years old, and the fifty and older age group. Generational differences within the sixteen through forty-nine age group are insignificantly small, and the difference between this group and the over-fifty-year-olds is also less clear-cut than previously.

The distribution of anti-Semitic attitudes in the western German age groups reflects a delayed and tenacious process in the early 1960s involving an active campaign against anti-Semitic prejudices. In the East, on the other hand, political generations can barely be distinguished at all. We believe that this is because the GDR's definition of itself as an anti-fascist state included banning anti-Semitism and Nazism from the public arena and declaring them successfully eliminated. In contrast to the Federal Republic, where education focussed on democracy and self-determination rather than anti-Nazism specifically, education in the GDR concentrated on socialism and included an active campaign against fascism. The over-sixty-five generation, already adults when the GDR was established, exhibited an above-average proportion of anti-Semitic attitudes. The diagram shows a second peak for the youngest cohort (sixteen through twenty-four years old).[12] This is the generation that started protesting against socialism in East Germany even before 1989, and was later responsible for most of the racist violence against asylum seekers and other foreigners.[13]

Youth studies of age groups fourteen and older show strong political polarization into right- and left-wing camps in the former East Germany, while political ties to the democratic center parties are weak (Förster et al. 1993, 114–16). Youth researchers in Leipzig, who had conducted a study on young people in 1990, repeated their study in 1992 and determined that right-wing extremist orientations, including xenophobia and anti-Semitism, had increased among German adolescents in the East during those two years. In 1992, anti-Semitic statements met with less approval (12 percent in Saxony and Saxony-Anhalt), and were more often disapproved of (71 percent) than xenophobic items (29 percent approval; 45 percent disapproval). A negative trend is evident between different age groups, however, with fourteen through eighteen-year-olds harboring the most anti-Semitic attitudes; 14 percent agreed with the old anti-Jewish slogan "The Jews are Germany's misfortune" (*"Die Juden sind Deutschlands Unglück"*), a far larger proportion than among those in the twenty through twenty-five age group.[14] Gender and education shape this anti-Jewish potential. Of male apprentices, 33 percent dislike Jews (female apprentices: 10 percent), compared to 16 percent of male high school students in eleventh and twelfth grades (4 percent of the girls). The dislike of foreigners by German youth in the East also increased sharply (by about 10 percent) between 1990 and 1992.

Since the attention of the public and of research has been directed in the past few years entirely toward eastern Germany, no corresponding youth studies exist for western Germany. We have access to only one study conducted in one of the former West German states. In a representative telephone survey conducted in December, 1992, the Infas Institute asked young people in Schleswig-Holstein to respond to a similar statement: "The Jews are a people who bring nothing but disaster" (*"Die Juden sind ein Volk, von dem nur Unheil ausgeht"*). Compared to eastern German youth, fourteen- to eighteen-year-olds in the West agreed less often with this statement—5.1 percent; nineteen to twenty-four-year-olds: 4.2 percent [Institut für angewandte Sozialforschung (Infas) 1992, table 28]. Nevertheless, this cohort proved to be more anti-Semitic than the middle generations.[15]

In the past, successive political generations were characterized by the fact that each was more liberal and tolerant than the next older one. This trend appears no longer to apply in western Germany. With respect to anti-Jewish attitudes, the age groups under fifty are no longer as distinct from each other as they once were, though as a whole they differ significantly from older age groups. While the continued, progressive decline in anti-Semitism no longer applies to the younger age groups, it would be wrong to say that the trend has reversed for western German adolescents. The image is more that of a plateau that has ceased its downward trend in the 1990s.

There is little difference with respect to anti-Semitism among the different generations in eastern Germany. As in western Germany, the generation in the East that experienced Nazism (those now over sixty-five years of age) seems to have retained remnants of anti-Jewish attitudes to a greater degree than younger generations; but unlike the situation in western Germany, members of the younger age groups, to some extent not included in representative surveys because of their age, have assumed anti-Semitic prejudices in addition to xenophobic attitudes. It cannot yet be definitively determined, on the basis of presently available material, whether this represents long-term, stable attitudinal patterns or temporary reactions to the crisis-laden transformation period in the new former East Germany. West German sociologists have conducted a broadly based analysis of the structure of political generations [from the Hitler Youth generation to the "skeptical" generation (Schelsky) and the 1960s "student protest" generation to the post-materialists], but there are no corresponding analyses of the succession of political generations and the political experiences that influenced them in East Germany.[16] These gaps in the research make it difficult to interpret the age-specific distribution of anti-Semitic attitudes among East German generations.

Education and Career

Because of the very different educational systems and occupational structures in West and East Germany, it is difficult to compare the effects of education and career on adoption of anti-Semitic attitudes. In the Federal Republic, level of education essentially determined one's career options, whereas it was more common in the GDR for further qualifications to be acquired through night school and vocational training programs. For example, in the Federal Republic a college degree is a prerequisite to becoming a teacher; in the GDR, on the other hand, there were some fifteen different ways of attaining teaching certification. Accordingly, career groups in the GDR were not as clearly separated by education, income, and status differences as was the case in the Federal Republic. Another problem regarding the EMNID survey is that career groups were distributed according to West German career categories, which did not reflect the real employment situation in the East. It can generally be expected that attitude differences among eastern Germans will be less clearly related to level of education or employment positions. Empirical findings confirm this assumption. As in western Germany, formal schooling in the East has a positive effect; that is, those with college educations very rarely express negative attitudes toward Jews, whereas the corresponding figures for those having completed only the regular ten years of schooling (polytechnic high school) are above the population average. Attitudinal differences between individual educational or career groups are less distinct in the East than in the West. Blue-collar and skilled workers are more anti-Semitic than white-collar employees, civil servants, and professionals. For western Germans, the correlations determined in the 1987 and 1989 studies continued to apply in the early 1990s.

Aside from the effects of acquired or practiced occupation, significant factors can also be loss of a job, on the one hand, and subjective assessment of contentment with one's economic situation, on the other. As we know from both sociological theories and political experience, periods of social change, especially when connected with severe economic crises, lead to dissatisfaction, which is often directed at scapegoated ethnic minorities. In eastern Germany the unemployed are somewhat more often anti-Semitic than those with work; unemployed people in the West are not conspicuous in this regard. Unemployed eastern Germans are generally not more xenophobic, however, since they do not dislike Turkish "guest workers" and asylum seekers any more than those who have jobs. Even appraisal of one's own economic status did not reveal a connection between social dissatisfaction and anti-Jewish attitudes.[17] The effects are different among western Germans, for whom unemployment does not have any direct impact on relationship to Jews. Western Germans have perhaps learned to consider unemployment a "normal," usually temporary situation for which the capitalist economic system is responsible, rather than a particular group of people. In cases where an individual economic situation was appraised as threatened or unsatisfactory, dis-

like of Jews was much greater (30 percent) than among those who expressed satisfaction with their situation (14 percent). Asylum seekers
from eastern Europe and Turks living in Germany were also disliked
more often by those who are "dissatisfied." This higher proportion of
anti-Semites and xenophobes among the "economically dissatisfied" can
partly be explained by the particular composition of this group with regard to education and occupation, that is, lower educational and occupational levels predominate. In western Germany, in comparison, this group
is comprised of an above-average number of young people who are just
beginning their careers and thus still evaluate their economic situation as
poor. This high proportion of younger people leads us to expect less anti-
Semitism among the dissatisfied. As this is not the case, it must be assumed that the factor "appraisal of one's own economic situation" has
an individual effect on attitudes toward Jews.

Political Orientation

Political orientation was measured in two ways in the 1992 EMNID
study: first, according to plans to vote for a particular party, and second,
in a self-evaluation on a ten-point scale ranging from extreme left wing
to extreme right wing. Responses to both questions showed a significant
correlation between extreme political orientation and negative attitudes
toward Jews.[18] As expected, anti-Semitism is widespread among those
with extreme right-wing views, as it has remained a central aspect of
chauvinistic, ultraright wing, and nationalistic attitudes. Left-wing extremists, in keeping with their anti-pluralistic, anti-Zionist views and
critical view of religion, also rejected Jews whenever these assert group
claims. The correlation between political orientation and anti-Semitism
reveals the same pattern for both eastern and western Germany, albeit to
different degrees.

An evaluation of voter intention also reflects this right-left pattern in
both eastern and western Germany. It shows that right-wing extremists
feel "at home" with the "Republikaner;" two-fifths of "Republikaner"
voters in both East and West are anti-Semitic. The distribution according to age reveals a characteristic difference, however. More than half of
"Republikaner" voters in the East are under thirty-five years of age,
whereas three-quarters of western "Republikaner" voters are over thirty-
five. This variance in voter potential creates a dilemma for the "Repub-

FIGURE 12.3
Anti-Semitism by Political Orientation 1991

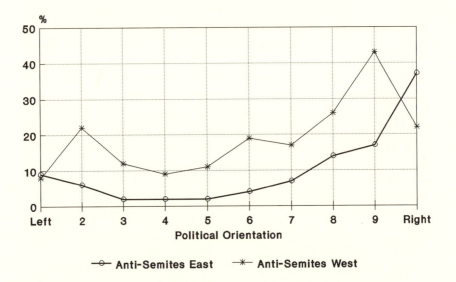

likaner." In the West, their supporters are mostly older, passive, and authoritarian, while in the East, they are young and favor spontaneous action. The party leadership has responded to this situation by becoming more politically radical and expressing anti-Semitism more openly.[19]

Most extreme left-wing anti-Semites do not vote for the PDS, since they probably consider this party more of a left-wing social democratic party than a revolutionary force. Extreme left-wing voters are thus spread out over various parties (PDS, SPD, Greens, non-voters).

The distribution of anti-Semitism among voters for all other parties corresponds to the expected right-left pattern in both East and West. The findings of political party research can be used in interpreting this pattern. An above-average proportion of anti-Semites are CDU/CSU voters. This is due in part to their conservative, nationalist platform, but also in part to the fact that they have a very large proportion of older voters. Since the founding of the Federal Republic, the FDP has had two wings: a nationalist, liberal economic wing and a "social liberal" wing primarily committed to protecting civil rights and liberties. In recent years,

FIGURE 12.4
Anti-Semitism by Party Preference, East and West 1991

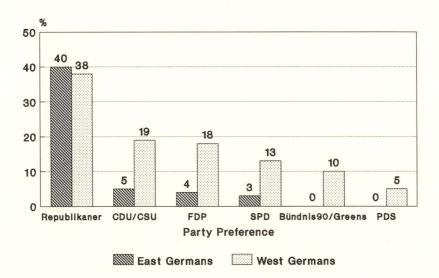

voters and members have tended to move away from this liberal wing, allowing the nationalist wing to dominate. As a result, anti-Semitism among FDP voters is currently more widespread than in the 1980s. Using our index, we could not find any anti-Semitism in eastern Germany among Bündnis 90 (Alliance 90) or PDS voters. For the civic movement Bündnis 90, this can be explained by its special social structure and ideological status; it was comprised of a young, educated avantgarde that came together to fight for political rights and civil liberties in the GDR. The PDS boasts a disproportionately high number of college graduates and members of the intelligentsia, as well as members of the generation that built up the GDR who are still committed to their socialist self-image as antifascists.

Summary

The variables age, education, and political orientation are the three major factors influencing the extent of anti-Semitic prejudice in both eastern and western Germany. Gender is a major factor with respect to membership in ultraright-wing parties and organizations and participation in criminal acts motivated by xenophobia and anti-Semitism (90 percent to 95 percent of all offenders are male). In terms of anti-Semitic attitudes, however, gender plays a much smaller role (56 percent of anti-Semites in the West and 63 percent of those in the East are male). These demographic variables can be used to explain the distribution of anti-Semitism. Neither age, educational level, or gender forms per se a social group or collective. When social groups that have historically propagated anti-Semitic ideology are analyzed, however, it can be shown that neither membership in a particular occupational group nor religious denomination or social milieu indicate any special affinity for anti-Semitism. Ultraright-wing organizations provide the only backdrop that incorporates and actively spreads hatred of Jews as a central issue. Anti-Semitism exists in Germany today only in ideological fragments and as personal prejudice. Assumption of anti-Semitic prejudice can be attributed only to an individual's active receptivity; outside of a right-wing extremist context, it is no longer accepted as an integral component of other political or ideological orientations. Acquisition of anti-Jewish attitudes is therefore highly individualized, which distinguishes the present situation in the Federal Republic from anti-Semitism in Germany prior to 1933. At that time, anti-Semitism was a central part of the world view of almost all leading social groups and institutions (i.e., student fraternities; officer corps; churches; nationalist, conservative parties, etc.). Also, anti-Semitism today does not appear as a form of intergroup conflict. For one thing, the small Jewish minority is socially integrated, thus providing very few occasions for conflict; secondly, those opposed to Jews have been able to establish themselves collectively only as a marginalized subculture. Since anti-Semitism is discredited at a moral level and is criminally prosecuted, any expression of anti-Jewish attitudes must be avoided, at the risk of social and political isolation.

A complex set of motifs does exist in Germany that anti-Semites share with larger segments of the population, namely, feelings of guilt, shame, and awkwardness. These are a result of inadequate attempts to deal with a criminal national past. When Jews are spoken of in Germany or when German-Jewish-Israeli conflicts surface, this almost always occurs in conjunction with efforts to deal with the Nazi past, the Holocaust and its consequences.

Anti-Semitism and the Nazi Past

All surveys conducted in unified Germany that have included questions on opinions toward World War II, Nazism, and the Holocaust have indicated that eastern Germans more often have more specific knowledge about National Socialism and more often acknowledge the extent of Nazi crimes and responsibility for World War II, as well as the resulting responsibility for the victims (cf. EMNID 1992; Forsa 1994, 1996; Jodice 1991; Golub 1994). Contemporary research offers two basic explanations for this difference between Germans from the East and those from the West.

1. The transition to socialism and its close ties to the Soviet Union caused the GDR to consider the events and consequences of Nazism as not part of its own history; rather, they were universalized under the category of fascism. This allowed a distinction to be made between "Hitler fascists" and the German people. By linking fascism with capitalism, the socialist GDR rid itself of any relationship to Nazism. This could then be used in criticizing the Federal Republic, which remained capitalist. This was not an option for the Federal Republic, since it was the legal successor to the German Reich. West Germany attempted to deal with Nazism through reform of state institutions, establishment of a democratic value system, and ties to Western democracies.[20]

This fundamental decision by the East German state and the associated view of history enabled East German citizens to see themselves as part of the tradition of communist resistance to Nazism. As "victims of Nazism" they could renounce any responsibility for the crimes, on the one hand, and ground themselves ideologically in antifascism, on the other.

2. An additional factor was East Germany's membership in the opposing political bloc in the cold war. The major crimes East Germans dealt with involved the Nazi war of extermination in eastern Europe; East Germans felt the most empathy with the Soviet victims of that campaign. For West Germans, the Soviet Union remained a threatening hegemonical power; they preferred not to acknowledge Soviet suffering during World War II. In the Federal Republic, the Holocaust was emphasized as the major crime of the "Third Reich" (cf. on German recollection of Jews and Russians, Niethammer 1990). State reparations corresponded to the respective perceptions of who the victims had been: in the GDR they were limited to the countries of the Eastern bloc, while

in the Federal Republic, reparations went primarily to Jews and the state of Israel.

We believe this constellation in the East-West conflict had a considerable impact on attitudes of the respective populations, though this effect is difficult to quantify. While East Germans were told the Red Army had "liberated" them from the "yoke of fascism," many West Germans saw the establishment of communist rule behind the Iron Curtain as a justification for the war against the Soviet Union in retrospect.

These differences in political culture are reflected in the survey findings. The eastern German population is much more often willing to accept the burden of historical facts, while less often attempting to excuse the past. Two-thirds of eastern Germans blame Germany for starting World War II [only half of western Germans agree (FORSA 1994, 2)], while 87 percent say reports of concentration camp crimes are true (western Germans: 71 percent). Very few from the East (5 percent) reject these reports as exaggerated (West: 17 percent). Agreement with the facts is not only an expression of more accurate knowledge; it is also connected to a widespread feeling of shame for the crimes committed against the Jews (East: 73 percent agreement, 9 percent disagreement; West: 55 percent agreement, 15 percent disagreement). Despite knowledge of and personal feelings about the past, considerably fewer people in both East and West accept any special collective responsibility toward the Jews (eastern Germany: 43 percent; western Germany: 30 percent). When the abstract term "responsibility" was made more concrete in the form of questions on making up reparations payments that the former GDR had never paid, only a small minority still expressed agreement (eastern Germans: agreement 11 percent, disagreement 61 percent; western Germans: agreement 8 percent, disagreement 76 percent).[21] The fact that a majority of the population is opposed to perpetuation of a special responsibility corresponds to the desire to end public discussion of this chapter in German history. Although eastern Germans support this demand less often (48 percent) than those from the West (68 percent), a majority in unified Germany still supports closing that chapter in German history. These demands are based, first of all, on the fact that so much time has passed since then, and secondly, on the belief that the other side did "things that were just as terrible." There was a high level of agreement for this "keeping score" type of logic (55 percent, in the West: 60 percent). This shows that below the ideological level, defense mechanisms that frequently resort to comparison by way of "keeping score" and stylization of one-self as a victim were and are at work in everyday discussions in unified Germany.

The public is not sure what is to be gained by further discussion of Nazism. They see the issue as being imposed from outside, and thus attribute to "other countries" in general, and Jews in particular, special selfish, anti-German interests. Other countries are presumed to continually remind Germans of their guilt because they actually envy German efficiency (eastern Germans 36 percent, western Germans 45 percent).[22] And Jews are accused of profiting from the past (eastern Germans 44 percent, western Germans 60 percent). Based on the stereotype of a Jewish conspiracy and world power, it is assumed that international Jewish organizations use their influence toward this end.[23] This anti-Semitic cliche still exists among the older generation, while the younger and better educated prefer rational explanations.

The necessity of continuing to deal with the Nazi past and accepting special responsibility depends on who is regarded as belonging to the group of those responsible. Opinions in East and West coincide insofar as not all Germans living at the time—or even all Germans—are held responsible for crimes against the Jews. Rather, the category of guilty persons is more often limited to those actively involved in the persecution of the Jews (45 percent) and those who knew what was happening (32 percent). The number of those who knew about the Holocaust is estimated by both eastern and western Germans to be relatively small.[24] A majority of Germans thus limit the number of those actively responsible for the persecution of the Jews to a very small figure. Combined with the fact that some of the perpetrators have been convicted and that the vast majority of them have already died, it is apparent that for many Germans, the chapter is closed.

In spite of the antifascist socialization in the GDR, the eastern German population was not willing to condemn all aspects of Nazism. Although only 2 percent in both the East and the West rated the Nazi period positively, two-fifths of the respondents attributed to it both good and bad aspects.[25] This indicates that neither the pluralist Federal Republic nor the East German "opinion dictatorship" succeeded in controlling everyday discussion among family and friends. Thus personal experiences and myths that offered a contrast to a totally negative stigmatization of this period could be passed on.

Anti-Semitism and Xenophobia

Anti-Semitism and xenophobia are often mentioned in the same breath and treated as problems cast from the same mold. There are indeed great similarities between the two phenomena, but particularly in Germany there are differences in dislike of Jews and of "foreigners", both in extent and in motive. Responses to questions on sympathy and antipathy and social distance toward these groups indicate a hierarchy in which "gypsies" are most disliked, followed by asylum seekers from Africa, Asia, and eastern Europe, and finally Turks and ethnic Germans from the former Soviet Union. Jews are disliked the least in this hierarchy (see table 12.3 below). There is also a qualitative difference between hatred of Jews and xenophobia. The latter is motivated by allocation conflicts as a result of large waves of immigration, especially in times of economic depression, and fear of cultural "infiltration" by too many foreigners. Throughout Europe, laws regulating asylum and immigration are becoming more restrictive in response to growing immigration and shortages on the labor and housing markets. Right-wing parties have also been able to gain a foothold all over Europe as "anti-immigration parties." "Foreigners" have thus become the subject of heated domestic policy debates. Neither politically nor in the public consciousness are Jews in Germany part of this discourse. Dislike of Jews is primarily motivated by their image as admonishing representatives of the burden of the past. This difference in motives for hostility corresponds to a difference in the stereotyping of the two groups. While Jews are seen as internationally influential, powerful, unforgiving, and successful in business, immigrants are generally stereotyped as lower class. They are regarded as "uncivilized," loud, dirty, poor, and having many children, and are assumed to have come to Germany in search of easy money.

Part of the motivation behind anti-Semitism is the opinion that Germans are special and superior to other peoples, so that immigration is feared as a cultural threat and a source of undesirable interbreeding. In rejecting immigrants, a "cultural, racist hierarchy" (Geiger 1991) can be observed, directed at the cultural, economic, and physical manifestations of "otherness." Anti-Semites are frequently also xenophobic; one half to three-quarters of them dislike asylum seekers from eastern Europe and Africa, as well as "gypsies." Eastern and western Germans differ only slightly in this respect. The only significant exception to this involves attitudes toward Turks living in Germany. While eastern German anti-Semites dislike Turks to the same degree as asylum seekers (66 percent), only 42 percent of western German anti-Semites express antipathy toward Turks. This is apparently because western Germans have grown accustomed to Turks to some extent after decades of living together, leading to a weakening of the antipathy typically expressed by anti-Semites toward all outgroups. The harsh rejection of Turks by eastern German anti-Semites (66 percent) and eastern Germans in general can be partly explained by the fact that East Germans did not have this experience of coexistence (up to 1990, almost no Turks lived in East Germany, compared to 1.6 million in West Germany), but instead are left with the fear that this large immigrant minority represents competition for blue-collar jobs and scarce resources. In their hostility toward all "foreigners", anti-Semites make up an extremist subpopulation.[26] On the other hand, xenophobic people are less often anti-Semitic. From a purely statistical perspective, this can be inferred from the different numbers of anti-Semites and xenophobes in the population. Nevertheless, xenophobic people are more often anti-Semitic (East: 12 percent to 15 percent; West: 21 percent to 35 percent) than the popular average (4.3 percent in the East; 16.4 percent in the West).

The differing causes of xenophobia and anti-Semitism are also indicated by the two groups' differing demographic structures. However, differences are also found with regard to different "foreigner" and immigrant groups; thus, hostility toward Turks has a different demographic structure than hostility toward asylum seekers, gypsies (Romany and Sinti), and ethnic German immigrants, mainly from the former Soviet Union.

A large majority of western and eastern Germans sees foreign nationals living in Germany and immigrants, including ethnic Germans, as undesirable competition for jobs, housing, and government benefits. It is not surprising that almost everyone with a xenophobic attitude holds this view, but a majority of non-xenophobic people shares these views as well. This indicates that most Germans do not view their society as immigrant. Minorities already living in the country, such as Turks, are tolerated, but all further immigration is opposed. Only a small minority sees immigration as culturally and economically enriching.

Western Germans have become accustomed in the last few decades to living with a large Turkish minority. This group is the focus of much less hostility than asylum seekers and Gypsies. Age and occupation have hardly

TABLE 12.3
Anti-Semitism and Dislike of Foreigner Groups in Eastern
and Western Germany in 1991

Antipathy toward:	Anti-Semites		Non-anti-Semites	
	East %	West %	East %	West %
Turks	66	42	25	16
Asylum seekers from eastern Europe	51	55	29	27
Asylum seekers from Africa	69	64	33	34
Gypsies	74	72	45	41
Eastern European immigrants of German heritage	26	31	18	19

Interpretation guide: Of anti-Semites, 66 percent in eastern Germany and 42 percent in western Germany expressed strong feelings of antipathy toward Turks; of non-anti-Semites, 25 percent and 16 percent in the East and West, respectively, expressed such feelings.

TABLE 12.4
Xenophobia and Rejection of Jews

Antipathy toward:	Anti-Semites	
	East %	West %
Turks	12	35
Asylum seekers from eastern Europe	15	28
Asylum seekers from Africa	12	27
Gypsies (Romany and Sinti)	15	24
Eastern European immigrants of German heritage	15	21

Interpretation guide: Of those people who expressed strong feelings of antipathy toward Turks, 12 percent in the East and 35 percent in the West are also anti-Semitic.

any influence whatsoever on attitudes toward Turks, though the familiar connection between education and reduction in prejudices can be observed. The dividing line lies between *Volksschulabschluß* (elementary school completed) with an apprenticeship, and higher education levels. The eastern

TABLE 12.5
Antipathy toward Ethnic Minorities (1991)

Minority	Antipathy	
	Eastern Germans %	Western Germans %
Eastern European immigrants of German heritage	18	20
Turks in Germany	26	19
Asylum seekers from eastern Europe	30	31
Asylum seekers from Africa	34	38
Gypsies (Romany and Sinti)	47	45

Germans more often see Turks—the only group disliked more in the East than in the West—as competitors who, depending on the economic situation, should either stay in the country or return to Turkey, on the "hire and fire" principle (72 percent of eastern Germans would prefer such a rotation of "guest workers;" in the West, the figure is 67 percent). Turks, and not the dominant western Germans, are seen as a symbol of competition for jobs and government benefits. Thus it is primarily less educated, younger eastern Germans, above all apprentices and skilled and unskilled laborers, who have negative feelings toward Turks.

There is hardly any difference in the frequency with which eastern and western Germans express dislike of asylum seekers, but the distribution is not the same. In the former East Germany, where social distinctions were less pronounced, opinions do not vary significantly on the basis of age, level of education, and occupation, whereas age and education have a greater impact in western Germany. To the same degree in both East and West, people with secure career positions (civil servants and salaried employees) are more tolerant of refugees, but the converse is not true, namely, that the unemployed show less tolerance. The deciding factor is a feeling of subjective deprivation, that is, those who are very dissatisfied with their living situation with respect to income, housing, and benefits tend to dislike immigrants with above-average frequency (not including those from Turkey!). At the end of 1991, when the EMNID Institute conducted the survey, two other groups were in the public eye: Romany (Gypsy) refugees, mostly from Romania, and ethnic Germans from eastern Europe (*Aussiedl*). The latter enjoy a "national" advantage in comparison to all other immigrant groups and are less often viewed negatively. Unlike other groups, they have a political and media lobby in the government and among conservatives. The Romanian Gypsies, on the other hand, meet with rejection across the board, even among an unusually large number of left-wing, liberal Green party voters. This is because of a combination of objections to immigration. Europe has a long, unbroken tradition of anti-Gypsy sentiment, as a result of which they lack a lobby in both Romania and potential host countries. Further, the difference between their lifestyle and prevalent lifestyles in the host countries make it unlikely that Gypsy refugees would be able to integrate successfully.

Aside from the demographic factors described above, such as age, education, and subjective assessment of contentment with one's own situation, political and ideological orientation exercises an independent influence on attitudes toward foreigners. Those who have a strong right-wing orientation or vote for right-wing radical or established conservative parties more often dislike non-German immigrants than those on the left or left-wing liberal end of the political spectrum. Those who believe their country is locked in a social Darwinist struggle with other peoples ("Germans are superior to other peoples") and races ("It is important to keep Germans pure and prevent interbreeding") often oppose immigration, feeling it is a threat that weakens the substance of their nation.

From this analysis we conclude that xenophobia can most aptly be described as a form of defensive nationalism, in which the be-all and end-all is preservation of own's own affluence. In contrast, an aggressive, nationalistic sense of mission with respect to other peoples is far less common. Many Germans believe their country is being overwhelmed by large numbers of refugees and other countries' demands for financial aid from Germany. Opposition to these demands, including reparations for victims of Nazi persecution, does not mean that a majority of Germans holds extreme right-wing political views, although ultraright-wing parties have focussed on these issues.

Notes

1. Some weeks after the downfall of the Berlin wall, the news magazine *Der Spiegel* published an article on the anxiety and rejection of Jews concerning the rapprochement of the two German states: *"Ein Volk, ein Reich, ein Führer"* (No. 50,

1989, 150ff.) quoting newspapers from Israel like *Jediot Achanot, Haaretz,* and the *Jerusalem Post,* as well as Elie Wiesel. On the attitude of the American Jewish community toward the unification of Germany see Shafir 1993, 42ff. ("An Ambiguity that Will Not Disappear").

2. The Central Council of Jews in Germany was disappointed by the wording suggested by Minister of the Interior Wolfgang Schäuble, which acknowledged the continuity of German history and the resulting responsibility for peace, human rights, and democracy, but did not explicitly mention the Nazi period (*Der Tagesspiegel,* 22 August 1990). On the difficulties of German Jews in accepting unification. See Gisela Dachs: *"Der nationale Traum als Trauma"* (*Die Zeit,* 4 May 1990).

3. In conversations with German Jews in Israel, Rafael Seligmann, a German-Jewish writer (*"Durch Hitler geboren."* *Die deutschen Juden in Israel, Der Spiegel,* no. 44, 1994, 188) was often confronted with the belief "that a strong Germany would no longer need to fear anyone, and so the first thing it would do would be to stop paying reparations pensions to Jews."

4. The Office for the Defense of the Constitution (*Verfassungsschutz*) includes the following in the category "Violations of the law with proven or assumed right-wing extremist motivation": Violent crimes (killings, bodily injury, arson, etc.), propaganda offenses (graffiti, leafletting campaigns, the Nazi salute), and other violations (libel, slander, incitement to hatred). There has been a rise in anti-Semitic crimes in all three offense types, whereby the increase in crimes of libel has been disproportionately high (libelous and provocative letters to Jewish communities and representatives, etc.).

5. A follow-up study for the period from May, 1992 to December, 1993 reveals almost the same picture (cf. Willems, Würtz, and Eckert 1994).

6. Today, 90 percent of the population demand punishment of anti-Semitic offenders (6 percent opposed punishment). In comparison, this demand was supported in 1949 by only 41 percent of the population, while 15 percent were opposed to such punishment (IfD 1992). In 1990, a majority (80 percent) of Germans advocated a ban on anti-Semitic organizations (cf. Jodice 1991, table 6a).

7. An evaluation of the EUROBAROMETER data and the ALLBUS study (the latter is conducted in Germany every two years) found no increase in xenophobia. They confirmed a positive development in attitudes for the 1980s in West Germany; starting in 1990, they found a stagnation and polarization of the different positions (cf. Hill in Willems 1993, 33ff; Wiegand 1992).

8. EMNID-Institut, Antisemitismus in Deutschland, Bielefeld 1992. A preliminary evaluation was published in *Der Spiegel,* nos. 3 and 4, 1992, and in *Spiegel-Spezial,* Juden und Deutsche, Hamburg 1992. We would like to thank Mr. Werner Harenberg of *Der Spiegel* for allowing us access to the survey data for our evaluation.

9. The following questions were included in the index: (1) "If someone were to tell you that many Jews try to profit from the history of the 'Third Reich' at German expense, would you say that is true or false" [response: "That is true" (East: 8.5 percent; West: 20 percent)]; (2) "Jews share the blame if they are hated and persecuted" ["That is totally true" (8 percent; 17 percent); (3–5) "Are Jews modest or arrogant?" [clearly "arrogant" (10 percent; 17 percent); clearly "ruthless" (7 percent; 16 percent); clearly "suspicious" (14 percent; 19 percent)]; (6) "Do you think that most of what is reported about the concentration camps and the persecution of the Jews is true, or is a lot of it exaggerated?" ["exaggerated" (5 percent; 16 percent)]; (7) "Jews have too much influence in the world" [response:

"That is true" (20 percent; 40 percent)]; (8) "How do you feel about Jews living in Germany?" [-5 to -2: strong to mild dislike (10.8 percent; 14.4 percent)]. *Spiegel-Spezial: Juden und Deutsche, 2*, 1992, 70. Two of the questions used seem to us to be problematic, as they do not actually measure anti-Semitic attitudes. EMNID classed as having anti-Semitic leanings those who answered the question "How many Germans knew about the extermination of Jews in the Third Reich" with "very few." Contemporary research has been unable to determine or even to quantify with certainty how well the Holocaust was concealed from the public. Thus, those who gave this answer might have been expressing the state of research; they need not necessarily have been following a rationalization strategy. Agreement with the second indicator, "Somehow I don't like the whole subject of 'Jews,'" taken from our 1987 survey—with which we measured communicative latency (cf. Bergmann and Erb 1991)—may also result from various motives: diffidence, ignorance, feelings of shame and guilt, as well as rejection of Jews.

10. The decision on where to draw a dividing line in the additive index between persons considered anti-Semitic and those regarded as not anti-Semitic is an arbitrary one. We utilized the coherence criterion, as we had done in constructing the index in our 1987 survey (chap. 2); that is, we did not categorize respondents as clearly anti-Semitic unless they agreed with more than three statements. The resulting proportion of anti-Semites among western Germans was 16.4 percent; among eastern Germans, the figure was 4.2 percent.

11. This difference in attitudes between Germans from the East and from the West has also been found by other studies on anti-Semitism conducted since 1990 (Wittenberg et al. 1991, 1995; Jodice 1991, Golub 1994).

12. The study conducted in late 1990 by Wittenberg et al. (1991) already showed that the eighteen through thirty generation displayed slightly greater agreement than thirty-one through forty-three-year-olds. A survey in December, 1991 of ninth- to twelfth-grade high school students in Jena found that young people were more likely than the population as a whole to say they "would not like to have too much to do with Jews" (13 percent versus 8 percent total population) and "with Israelis" [26 percent versus 16 percent total population (Wittenberg et al. 1995)]. This clearly shows that a potential for xenophobia and anti-Semitism existed among young people even before the collapse of the East German state, and that this potential had the opportunity to become more brutal and radical afterwards. Anti-Semitism in the youngest age group was considerably below the level for forty-four through fifty-nine-year-olds, and was especially under that for the over-sixty age group (Wittenberg et al. 1991), whereby the generational difference in general was markedly smaller than among western Germans.

13. On young peoples' opposition to the East German communist state in the 1980s, cf. GDR youth research by Friedrich and Griese 1991; on an analysis of the wave of violence in 1991–92, cf. Willems 1993, which found that 90 percent of all offenders were under twenty-five years of age.

14. In a youth survey conducted in Brandenburg in 1993, even 25 percent of all students in comprehensive high schools agreed strongly or mildly with this anti-Jewish statement (cf. the high school student survey by the Institut für angewandte Familien-, Kindheits- und Jugendforschung, Potsdam). This Brandenburg youth study used the item "Jews share the blame if they are hated and persecuted" from the 1991 EMNID survey. In the seventeen through eighteen age group, 25 percent agreed with the statement (32 percent of the fifteen

through sixteen-year-olds), whereas 19 percent of the eighteen through twenty-four age group in the 1991 EMNID study expressed agreement.

15. Only 3.2 percent of those aged twenty-five through thirty-four agreed with the statement, and the figure was even lower for thirty-five through forty-four-year-olds (2 percent). Anti-Semitism is more prevalent among the older age groups. Among forty-five through fifty-nine-year-olds, 5.3 percent must be classified as anti-Semites, and for respondents over sixty the figure is even higher (9.4 percent). The distribution of responses to xenophobic and right-wing statements in the same questionnaire does not reveal a negative deviation from the attitudes of the intermediate generations. With respect to xenophobia and right-wing orientation, forty-five years of age was the interface between the two generations, with the older group expressing considerably stronger xenophobia and right-wing orientation.

16. Cf., for preliminary research conducted before the fall of East Germany on the generation responsible for establishing socialism, Niethammer, von Plato, and Wierling 1991.

17. On the contrary, it is precisely those who consider their economic situation to be good who are more often anti-Semitic in eastern Germany. We can offer no explanation for this phenomenon, which also holds true for western Germans. This correlation is found in all age groups, so it cannot be explained by the higher proportion of anti-Semites among the older generations. The much higher proportion of people with higher education who considered themselves "very satisfied" could actually be expected to ensure a very small proportion of anti-Semites. The only possible explanation is the specific political orientation of this small subpopulation (4.2 percent of the western German population). This group is almost exclusively right-of-center politically, and a majority supports either the "*Republikaner,*" the CDU/CSU, or the FDP.

18. The flattening of the curves (see diagram) in the extreme ranges (1 or 10) represents a change in trends which was also found in other surveys on the attitudes of Germans towards foreigners; it cannot be traced to the small number of cases in these ranges in the sample or to the sociodemographic structure of the extremists (Kühnel and Terwey 1994, 82). Up to now, we are unable to explain this deviation.

19. At a press conference, former "*Republikaner*" party chair Franz Schönhuber referred to Ignatz Bubis, president of the Central Council of Jews in Germany, as an "incitor," after Bubis had spoken of the political Right as "intellectual arsonists" following the arson attack on the synagogue in Lübeck. Political observers interpreted Schönhuber's intentionally slanderous remark as an attempt to make anti-Semitism an issue in the 1994 election year and to motivate his supporters.

20. The way West Germany dealt with the Nazi system and anti-Semitism led many western Germans to view the subject "Jews" as a difficult and unpleasant one, and to feel that "many people are hesitant to express their true opinion of Jews" (45 percent). In particular, it is the anti-Semites (73 percent) who suspect this is the case and avoid the subject because they find it unpleasant (44 percent, total population: 22 percent). Ostracization of people making anti-Semitic statements has been successful, insofar as anti-Semites are the main ones to feel this public pressure. In eastern Germany there was no public, conflict-laden debate on the subject, so the population had fewer inhibitions about expressing their opinions openly. In eastern Germany, 56 percent do not consider the subject unpleasant (western Germany: 38 percent). In eastern Germany, the anti-Semites also feel

less public pressure and are thus less likely to see any reason to avoid the subject (51 percent).

21. The opposition to anti-Semitism and racism by East German citizens is credible. When asked about material compensation, however, a different motive takes over: the opinion prevails that reparations have been made politically ("tearing anti-Semitism out by the roots"), and it is therefore considered unnecessary to pay financial reparations, especially since material motives are generally viewed with skepticism.

22. It is above all the older generation that uses this reasoning (55 percent of those over sixty-five; 37 percent of the youngest age group), thus perpetuating the so-called Siegfied Complex, which holds that Germany is surrounded by envious enemies. This justification had been used once before in response to the defeat in World War I and the Versailles Treaty.

23. Twenty percent of respondents in eastern Germany and 40 percent in western Germany agreed with the statement "Jews have too much influence in the world" (EMNID 1992). The 1994 AJC study included the question "Do you feel the Jews have too much influence in our society?" Twenty-four percent of western Germans and 8 percent of eastern Germans answered affirmatively (Golub, 1994, table 4b). Compared to other groups (big business, media, Americans, Japanese, churches), Jews were least often attributed too much influence.

24. There was a typical East-West distinction in responses to the question "Between 1933 and 1945, how much did Germans know about the persecution of the Jews?" Eastern Germans consider the number of those who know what was going on to be smaller than western Germans. We believe this is due to the different discourses in East and West on the persecution of the Jews. In the West, the involvement of large segments of the state, bureaucracy, and Wehrmacht was emphasized. It was also stressed that anti-Jewish policies, from the 1933 boycott to the pogroms in November, 1938, took place before the eyes of the public.

25. The 1994 Forsa survey also found that 19 percent of eastern Germans and 26 percent of western Germans judge the ideas of Nazism to be "not all that bad" (15).

26. Western German anti-Semites dislike even ethnic Germans from Russia, though these enjoy a slight "national" advantage over asylum seekers from eastern Europe and Africa. This is not the case for eastern German anti-Semites. This might be due to the different age structures of anti-Semites in East and West. Most of the anti-Semites in western Germany are old or very old, and they consider Russian Germans displaced members of the German people who should come "heim ins Reich" (back to the Reich). This nationalist ideology does not play a role for the relatively large proportion of younger people among anti-Semites in eastern Germany; they dislike all immigrants.

Appendix 1:
Problems in the Development of Anti-Semitism Scales

The first, most influential anti-Semitism scale was developed after 1944 as part of the famous "Studies in Prejudice" project. The scale, which in an earlier form included fifty-two disparaging comments on Jews, was intended to provide as complete a picture as possible of the elements that could trigger rejection of Jews. The weighting of responses (from +3, meaning strong agreement, to -3, meaning strong disagreement with an item) was intended to make it easier to quantify the degree of anti-Semitism. This AS scale was divided into subscales to measure specific attitude patterns, while different, shorter versions were also developed. Unlike the famous F (fascism) scale, the AS scale was not used later as an index in actual anti-Semitism studies; instead it served, in shortened form, in psychological studies as an instrument to segregate populations into anti-Semitic and non-anti-Semitic test samples (cf. Berkowitz 1959; Weatherley 1963). This AS scale was no longer utilized in later studies because of its close link to a particular theory of anti-Semitism. It was created in the context of studies on fascism and on the authoritarian personality as an instrument to measure personality structures; it ultimately formed a partial scale within the framework of efforts to devise a comprehensive scale to measure personality structures predisposed to fascism.[1] Of the partial scales, only the authoritarianism scale is still part of the scientific debate, in studies on right-wing extremism.

The change in the hypotheses posed by international anti-Semitism researchers since the 1960s made it necessary to develop new scales. Research no longer focussed on recording complex personality structures or on empirical examination of theories; rather, on a theoretically less ambitious level, it aimed at a representative investigation of anti-Semitic attitudes and the changes they underwent. Almost every anti-Semitism study developed its own scale, resulting in what Lucy Dawidowicz called a "patchwork of scales" (1970, 39). Each study hoped to provide a "standard" for future research; as far as we know, however, repeated use occurred only in one case. In the 1960s, Selznick and Steinberg developed an index as part of a large-scale, five-year study on anti-Semitism in the United States, conducted by Charles Y. Glock at the University of California, Berkeley. It consisted of eleven statements in which negative judgments were made about Jews.[2] These statements were obtained through a factor analysis of twenty-four questions. Each affirmative response to a statement received one point, resulting in an additive average index with which the interviewees could be classified according to degree of anti-Semitism. The authors established three groups: not or only slightly anti-Semitic (31 percent), intermediate (32 percent) and strongly anti-Semitic (37 percent). They considered the precise dividing line between anti-Semites and non-anti-Semites to be "arbitrary" (1969, 26).

   In fact, there is no general solution to the problem of drawing such a line. Selznick and Steinberg justified their boundary line with two arguments. One criterion was the average of the index values of all those questioned. Those scoring above the average were classified as pronounced anti-Semites. Using this criterion, in 1964, 47 percent of all Americans would have had to be so classified. However, the average value seemed to Selznick and Steinberg to be an external, purely statistical instrument. Instead, they proposed drawing the line at the point where the cumulative rate of agreement with all items on the index was higher than the percentage that each of these items achieved in the questionnaire. This interface was drawn between index values 4 and 5. The anti-Semitic group was reduced accordingly, redefined as five to eleven affirmative responses, or 37 percent (24ff.)[3] Ultimately, the decision was made primarily on the basis of quantitative considerations.

   Such a procedure becomes problematic when the index combines "soft" and "hard" questions. For soft questions, the ratio of agreement of the total sample is reached very quickly; harder questions take longer. Thus, the hardest indicator in Selznik and Steinberg ("Too much power in the U.S.") does not fit within the boundary they established between extreme and intermediate anti-Semites. Using the condition that agreement to all items on the index must exceed average agreement, the line would have to be drawn at a much higher level (in this case, between 6 and 7). The conditions chosen for the category interface assume that all questions discriminate to the same extent. The criteria chosen by Selznik and

Steinberg show that the rules for deciding where to draw the line cannot be set in advance; instead, they must conform to the existing distribution of responses. In our opinion, the interface between anti-Semites and non-anti-Semites cannot be determined with clarity *a priori,* but only by weighing statistical and content criteria.[4]

The Validity of the Anti-Semitism Construct

The indices from the United States discussed so far measured anti-Semitism solely according to the strength of anti-Jewish convictions. They thus limited themselves in the operationalization of anti-Semitism to the cognitive dimension of the prejudice. First of all, it is doubtful that agreement with some of the chosen stereotypes actually allows us to conclude the existence of a clearly hostile attitude toward Jews; secondly, limiting indices to the cognitive dimension neglects the complexity of the prejudice. They must be supplemented by measurements of emotional rejection and social distance, as well as inclination to discriminate actively or passively, in order to evaluate the extent to which the negative stereotypes are more than merely "opinions" with little emotional depth (cf. chapter 4). At the same time, this must be qualified by pointing out that the method of questioning can determine emotional attitudes and behavioral orientations only indirectly, through verbal statements about emotions and intended behavior.

While the U.S.-American studies introduced so far formed the AS index via negative stereotypes, Melvin Tumin, in his comparative study of "Intergroup Attitudes of Youth and Adults in England, France and Germany" of 1961–62 (Princeton University, 1962), constructed an index of social distance from Jews. He used various contexts in which contacts to Jews could be disapproved of—a Jew as son-in-law, employer, friend, co-worker, fellow student, and neighbor—to form a five-tiered scale of rejection. Those who did not reject contact with Jews in any of these contexts received a 1; those who would only reject a Jew as son-in-law, a 2; those who would also avoid them as employers got a 3; those fulfilling both of these conditions and also rejecting friendship with Jews received a 4; and those who rejected at least two of the following three relationships—co-worker, fellow student, or neighbor—received the highest index score, a 5. There is certainly something to be said for creating an anti-Semitism index using criteria other than stereotypical judgments of Jews, including rejection of Jews in everyday life.

It is surprising that this hierarchy of social distance is not formed according to the distance levels of the Bogardus scale. Tumin assigned his social distance levels according to decreasing rates of rejection. Forty-eight percent of those questioned would reject a Jew only as son-in-law (the least amount of social distance); 30 percent would refuse a Jew as son-in-law and as employer; 25 percent as son-in-law, employer, and friend; and 11 percent or 13 percent in all the named categories plus co-worker, fellow student, or neighbor [greatest social distance; Tumin 1962, Part I, 12; cf. also the basic count of interviewees in International Prejudice Study, DIVO Frankfurt/M. (n.d.), Question 40]. In this type of scale, it is not clear how to classify those who agree with a weaker distance level and not with a stronger one for example, those who reject Jews as employers without rejecting them as sons-in-law.

Tumin formed his anti-Semitism index using only this distance scale, but to validate it, he correlated it, for example, with questions on emotional and cognitive attitudes toward Jews. The validity test of emotional attitudes, for which he used the question "How do you personally feel about Jews?" showed a comparatively high and significant correlation in the expected direction. People with positive feelings indicated little social distance on the AS index, while people with negative feelings showed the greatest distance (Tumin 1962, Part I, 14). The same pattern emerged for the extreme groups in a test using a list of ten anti-Jewish stereotypes; they either strongly (six to ten "yes" responses) or mildly (zero to one) agreed with the stereotypes. Only the intermediate group (two to five "yes" responses) showed no clear correlation with the AS index. From these results, Tumin drew the conclusion that a linear correlation exists between anti-Semitism (measured by social distance) and anti-Jewish stereotyping, but that this is true only for the extremes and not for the intermediate range of stereotyping (ibid., 32). He concluded that this intermediate group had an ambivalent, mixed image of Jews, indicating a degree of social distance without complete rejection. That is, in constructing an anti-Semitism scale that incorporates a list of stereotypes, it must be taken into account that selective agreement with a small number of stereotypes includes non-agreement with those not chosen, and thus indicates an inconsistent attitude that is difficult to interpret (see chapter 4).

Because he measured anti-Semitism only through social distance, Tumin was unable to classify this intermediate group, and therefore concentrated on the extremes—anti-Semites and philo-Semites. Only those who indicated no social distance toward Jews whatsoever were not counted as anti-Semites. In this way, Tumin obtained the high figure of 55 percent to 61 percent of English, German, and French people who exhibited a certain degree of anti-Semitism. By using this method, he avoided the problem of defining the interface between strong and weak anti-Semitism.

Galtung took a different approach. Like Tumin, he created an anti-Semitism index on the basis of social distance. However, he considered it unrealistic to separate the sample dichotomously into anti-Semites and philo-Semites, as many gradations of negative feeling are possible. It made more sense to him to interpret the extremes in light of the intermediate group (Galtung 1960, 14ff.). He gave points for each of the five social distance indicators (rejection, two points; undecided, one point; agreement, zero points), thus obtaining a scale of ten index values. In accordance with the aforementioned theoretical decision, he distinguished three groups. His explanation of the interfaces between the groups was relatively lacking in insight—he wanted to have approximately three groups of equal size. In this way, he obtained 29 percent anti-Semites (six to ten points), 41 percent philo-Semites (zero to three points), and an intermediate group of 30 percent (four to five points). Aside from the questionable nature of this decision, in which the percentage of anti-Semites can hardly fall below a third of the population, it seems problematic to us that the five social distance indicators are treated as having equal weight, although each one expresses a different degree of social distance. Disapproval of marriage to a Jew may be much less an expression of anti-Jewish sentiment than refusal to work with a Jew.[5]

Silbermann and Sallen attempted to take account of the three-dimensionality of prejudice (cognitive, affective, and conative dimensions) by developing an AS index for the Federal Republic of Germany that consisted of a combination of three partial scales: one AS scale in the narrower sense, a social distance parameter, and a measurement of behavioral orientation.

The AS scale consisted of twenty anti-Semitic statements with which, as in the U.S.-American study, only stereotypical attitudes were measured (Silbermann 1982, 33ff. and Sallen 1977, 228ff.). As a method of scaling, the authors used a Likert scale with four possible responses (strong/mild agreement; strong/mild disagreement) and the category "don't know." In the distribution of responses, using criteria that were not made clear, five groups were distinguished based on their degree of agreement with the anti-Semitic statements. It is not clear how the total score was obtained; nor were the criteria for defining interfaces provided. There was no discussion of the typical problem with the Likert scale, which provides no information on how the intermediate scores were calculated, whether through consistent intermediate attitudes or by having extreme answers in both directions cancel each other out (cf., in contrast, Weiss, see below).

In addition, the distance parameter used in the Silbermann and Sallen study did not measure what sociologists refer to as social distance, which is generally measured with distance scales (such as those of Bogardus 1925 and 1933; Triandis and Triandis 1960; and others). Instead, they used the difference between the German self-image and the image of the Jew as alien, which they measured using a list of twelve positive and negative characteristics ["greedy, insolent, intelligent," etc. (Sallen 1977, 232f.)]. Here, too, five groups were distinguished according to intensity of prejudice, determined through the degree of deviation from the mean. This procedure reflects alienness, but measures it once again through cognitive schemes, and thus ultimately through the same dimension of prejudice as their AS scale. The distance parameter did not include the emotional significance of the negative judgment or the intensity of approval or disapproval of social contacts with Jews.

As a measure of behavioral orientation, Silbermann and Sallen utilized a single question, in which the interviewee was asked to indicate how he or she would advise a friend wishing to become involved in an advantageous business deal with a Jewish businessman. Those questioned had the choice of five possible responses, ranging from avoidance of the deal to a particularly positive assessment of Jewish businesspeople.[6] We leave open the question whether behavioral intention can be sufficiently operationalized by means of a single question.

The three individual measurements were not truly combined into a new AS scale, and the considerable deviations were not discussed; instead, the results were presented as "consistent with respect to trends and magnitude" (Sallen 1977, 236, and Silbermann 1982, 63).[7] But consistency and similar magnitude are precisely what should not be expected in measuring various dimensions of prejudice, since agreement with stereotypes, as our survey showed, is usually greater than emotional and social distance, which in turn is greater than an anti-Jewish behavioral intention. We are faced with the fundamental problem of how to combine and weight separate scales in creating a comprehensive AS scale. The problem of weighting is of course also posed in forming an integrated scale from the items in the various dimensions of prejudice and content-related expressions of anti-Semitism.

To evaluate her 1976 anti-Semitism survey in Vienna, Hilde Weiss formed an AS scale comprised of twenty-one items that included stereotypes as well as emotionality, social distance, and inclination to discriminate (1984, 52f.). Each question was allowed four possible responses, ranging from strong agreement to strong disagreement; for each person, a point value was set up from all the responses. The problem with this form of scaling is that, aside from extreme forms of agreement or disagreement, intermediate positions may result arising from the addition of extremely positive and extremely negative responses, or from a consistent choice of neutral positions. Here, too, defining interfaces between strong, medium and weak forms of anti-Semitism poses a serious problem. Weiss's dividing lines cannot be reconstructed with clarity on the basis of her explanation. Apparently she did not create partial groups on the basis of each overall score, but instead formulated a series of response combinations that were necessary in order to classify an interviewee. All those who tended completely or partially toward anti-Semitism in all the questions were classed as very strongly anti-Semitic; those who disagreed completely or partially with half the items in each case were classed as free of prejudice. The range of intermediate attitudes was never explained sufficiently. Only one group with strong prejudices was more closely defined; it was made up of those who partially agreed with approximately half of the items and partially disagreed with approximately half, while the groups "medium prejudice" and "slight prejudice" remained undefined altogether.

To avoid the problem of the response set, which had also led Silbermann and Sallen to combine the responses of extreme rejection with those of partial rejection, we largely dichotomized the responses, or in any case included the category "undecided/don't know." Therefore, Hilde Weiss's criteria for delimitation did not apply in our study.

A study that utilized wordings of questions and possible responses comparable with those in our study was carried out in 1986 by the Institute for Public Opinion Research in Allensbach (IfD) for *Stern* magazine. Renate Köcher rightly pointed out that an analysis of negative attitudes demands an aggregation of various indicators. Therefore, to identify clearly anti-Semitic persons, she used a scale which—after a preliminary factor analysis of the various dimensions of anti-Jewish attitudes—included not only stereotypes, but also emotional rejection, tolerance of anti-Jewish views and actions, social distance, and willingness to deal with Germany's past. The scale consisted of nineteen items, in which positive attitudes were given two points, indifferent attitudes one point, and negative attitudes zero points. A maximum of thirty-eight points could be achieved if all nineteen questions received positive responses; this was given the index value of 100 percent.[8] Through a cluster analysis, eight clusters were established; a strongly anti-Semitic cluster (lower third of the scale) stood out, achieving an index value of twenty-nine (15.3 percent of the sample). Three other clusters could be combined into three additional groups of attitudes: mildly negative views (index values fifty-six to fifty-eight, or 29.5 percent of the sample), mildly positive views (seventy-one, or 13.1 percent of the sample), and pronounced positive views (seventy-seven to eighty-five, or 42.1 percent of the sample). The interface between the last two groups was arbitrary, as no clear discontinuity could be determined here (IfD 1986, appendix). In a second step, a hardcore group within the 15.3 percent anti-Semites was identified. For this purpose, agreement with seven statements was taken out of the overall scale and counted separately. Those who answered "yes" to four of the statements were considered part of the hardcore group (6 percent). The content of the questions chosen to determine the hardcore group was surprising; by concentrating on stereotypes (such as greedy, stingy, arrogant), rather than including strongly discriminatory questions, they took into account only the dimension of prejudice. In our opinion, it makes more sense to determine hardcore anti-Semites by looking at their agreement with anti-Semitic statements that (1) find little agreement, and (2) reveal a high degree of emotional involvement and inclination to discriminate (such as "all Jews should emigrate to Israel," or "desecration of Jewish cemeteries shouldn't be taken so seriously").

In her evaluation of our 1987 survey, Köcher took a somewhat different tack in devising an anti-Semitism index. She first conducted a factor analysis of thirty-seven questions that she believed reflected anti-Semitic attitudes, obtaining seven dimensions of anti-Jewish bias: (1) emotional rejection and exclusion; (2) aggressive rejection; (3) anti-Israeli stereotypes; (4) and (5) anti-Jewish stereotypes: the dangerous Jew and the greedy Jew; (6) religious bias; and (7) resentment of Jewish influence and elitist self-assurance. Here, Köcher combined the three components of prejudice with the most important forms of present-day anti-Semitism. For each dimension, the degree of agreement was assigned a point value: zero points is equal to zero or one "yes" response per dimension; one point is equal to agreement with more than one and up to half the statements; two points is equal to agreement with the majority of statements per dimension. This yields an overall scale covering all seven dimensions, ranging from zero to a maximum of fourteen points. Those satisfying a majority of the conditions, that is, receiving eight or more points, were classified as clearly anti-Jewish (15 percent of those questioned). The choice of this particular cut-off point was not elaborated upon; it seems to have been more or less "arbitrary." This procedure is questionable in that a different number of partial questions (between three and seven questions) was used to form each of the individual dimensions. To achieve the highest point value of two, the interviewee would have to voice agreement four times in one dimension, but only twice in another. Through this procedure, the responses in the various dimensions receive varied weights, without this being justified by content (cf. the critique by Jesse, 1989).

The EMNID study of 1989 measured attitudes toward Jews by assigning points to responses to seven questions, some of which allowed a range of responses. In our opinion, however, this "super code" combined very heterogeneous elements, some of which have only limited value in measuring anti-Jewish attitudes. It is true that anti-Semites are more likely than the average to agree with the statement "Many people are afraid to give their true opinions of Jews," and are more likely to deny that "the majority of Germans knew about the extermination of the Jews," but agreement with these statements need not imply rejection of Jews. With the exception of the two like-dislike scales on attitudes towards German and Israeli Jews, all the other statements ("Brandt's genuflection at the Warsaw Ghetto was going too far," reparations are excessive, the estimated number of murdered Jews is too high) are more a measure of attitudes toward Nazism and reparations for its crimes, which correlate to only a limited degree with anti-Semitic attitudes (cf. the question of ending discussion of the issue in our study). The possible number of points is between zero and twenty-seven. Neither a criterion nor a norm orientation is discernible in the interfaces between categories (twenty through twenty-seven being extremely anti-Semitic; fourteen to nineteen, quite anti-Semitic; six to thirteen, somewhat anti-Semitic; zero to five, not anti-Semitic).

Notes

1. The work of von Freyhold belongs in this tradition of the analysis of "authority-related behavior." In addition to indices of Nazism and fascism, she also created an anti-Semitism index (1971, 269). This consisted of a cross-tabulation of two questions on attitudes toward Jews. The nine possible responses (yes/no/no opinion) were combined in a five-level index: two yes responses (AH), two yes/no responses, two yes/undecided responses (TH), two undecided responses (U) forming the neutral intermediate group, two no/undecided responses (TN), and two no responses (AN). The following distribution was established for the representative data, gathered in 1961 in light of the trial of Adolf Eichmann:

	%	(N)
pronounced authoritarian (AH)	6	(118)
authoritarian leanings (TH)	15	(302)
undecided (U)	22	(439)
non-authoritarian leanings (TN)	22	(433)
pronounced non-authoritarian (TA)	35	(697)
	100	**(1989)**

2. Martire and Clark used these eleven statements from the 1964 survey in their Yankelovich survey of 1981. They correctly pointed out that repeated use of an index is only acceptable if the structure of anti-Semitic attitudes has remained the same. Therefore, they combined the eleven questions from the index with a range of new questions and subjected them to a factor analysis. The analysis resulted in the same four anti-Semitism dimensions, and the factor load of the items also remained remarkably stable, justifying use of the 1964 AS index in 1981. In 1992, Martilla and Kiley conducted a survey of American attitudes toward Jews for the ADL using once again the criteria (index) first developed by the Berkeley Group and used by Yankelovich in 1981. They found that 20 percent of Americans answered "yes" to six or more questions on the index and are therefore "most antisemitic," 41 percent were rated in the "middle" category, and 39 percent "not antisemitic" (cf. Chanes 1994, 92).

3. In their survey, Martire and Clark used the same index, also drawing the interface between anti-Semites and "neutrals" between the scores of 4 and 5. In this way, in 1981 they found a 23 percent share of anti-Semites. However, they went about separating the "neutrals" from the "non-prejudiced" in a different way, by combining agreement with four or fewer statements with the number of abstentions (1982, 32ff.). This points to the basic problem of how to count undecided answers and abstentions. Selznick and Steinberg counted only "yes" answers, while counting abstentions as rejection of anti-Semitic items. For a different procedure, see Martire and Clark, xenophobia and Israel scales (1982, 124 ff.). See for a criticism of the variations in these two studies and in the Martilla and Kiley study of 1992 Tom W. Smith (1993).

4. In his 1978 study on anti-Semitism among blacks in Los Angeles, Tsukashima only partially utilized Selznick and Steinberg's index (four questions were borrowed), and developed his own six-point index. In contrast to his preliminary theoretical remarks, in which he described anti-Semitism as a complex phenomenon consisting of stereotypes, emotions, and behavioral orientations, Tsukashima expressly limited his index to measuring stereotypical anti-Semitic views (1978, 18). Similarly to Selznick and Steinberg, he ranked agreement on a scale of zero to six points, and divided the sample into two groups using the mean value. Tsukashima provided no discussion or justification of this choice of criteria.

5. The extreme differences in rejection of the various distance indicators by the interviewees (53 percent rejected marriage, but only 10 percent would not accept a Jew as co-worker) should have made Galtung aware of the qualitative difference.

6. Incomprehensibly, in the final grouping of these five response indicators to create an index, not only was the category "no response" omitted, but Sallen excluded the positive assessment of Jewish businesspeople from further consideration, calling it a "positive prejudice" (235). In this way, the pool from which percentages were established was reduced, and skewed toward an increase in the number of anti-Semites. While Sallen indicates this questionable methodological operation, the diverging figures appear without any commentary in Silbermann's book (55 and 63; cf. table 15 and table 21).

7. An overview of the three anti-Semitism measurements:

Anti-Semitic Attitudes (%)

Instrument	none	mild	strong
AS scale	29.8	43.0	27.2
Distance parameter	26.2	37.8	36.0
Behavioral orientation	40.4	43.5	16.1
(Basis of all interviewees = 100%)	42.3	38.7	14.3 (4.7 no resp.)

(*Source:* Sallen 1977, 236; Silbermann 1982, 63).

8. "Calculated as the relation of the average number of times mentioned in a cluster to the maximum possible number of 38" (IfD 1986).

Appendix 2:
Questionnaire with Basic Count Questionnaire for the Main Survey conducted by IfD Allensbach— September 1987

2102 people interviewed, minimum age: 16 years
Subgroup A: 1016
Subgroup B: 1086

1. a) Interviewer gives interviewee List 1.
   "This list includes a range of very different groups of people. Could you please select all those with whom you would not like to have too much to do?"

	% agreement
Divorced people	3.7
People infected with the AIDS virus	58.8
Turks	33.6
People with a record of conviction for theft	48.7
Blacks	21.3
Jews (subgroup A)	13.0
German Jews (subgroup B)	8.2
dedicated Nazis	66.4
People who have spent a few months in a psychiatric clinic	24.1
People who receive unemployment benefits, but aren't really looking for work	30.3
Prostitutes	59.7
Israelis	10.7
College students	3.3
Asylum-seekers	32.7
Children of criminals	15.3

People with a lot of children	3.5
Arabs	29.7

b) "And which groups could easily be part of your closest circle of friends? Which groups would you have no objections to?"

	% agreement
Divorced people	84.5
People infected with the AIDS virus	21.1
Turks	33.8
People with a record of conviction for theft	19.9
Blacks	40.6
Jews (subgroup A)	48.4
German Jews (subgroup B)	48.9
dedicated Communists	19.5
dedicated Nazis	9.8
People who have spent a few months in a psychiatric clinic	34.0
People who receive unemployment benefits, but aren't really looking for work	29.2
Prostitutes	14.3
Israelis	39.3
College students	71.6
Asylum-seekers	27.8
Children of criminals	33.9
People with a lot of children	78.4
Arabs	29.8

2. "What do you think about the following: Would you consider a Jew who was born and raised in Germany more a German or more a Jew?"

	% agreement
More a German	64.7
More a Jew	20.4
Undecided	14.9

3. "Do you think there are a lot of people today who don't like Jews, or not that many, or very few?"

	% agreement
A lot	20.0
Not that many	36.8

Very few	29.0
Can't say	14.3

4. "If Jews and other people have problems living together, do you think the problem often lies in the Jewish religion, or are there other reasons?"

Other answer:

	% agreement
In the Jewish religion	23.0
Other reasons	55.2
Undecided	21.3
Other answer	0.8

5. Interviewer gives interviewee a set of cards and List 2. "There are various words printed on these cards. You can react in various ways to these words; you can like them or dislike them. Could you please sort out these cards on the paper, according to how you feel? If you really cannot decided about a certain word, then lay that card aside."

	% like	% dislike
Peace movement	71.9	14.6
Jew	37.6	20.0
Anti-Semite	5.4	60.2
Palestinian	15.9	51.7
Communism	6.1	75.7
Germany	83.9	3.9
Asylum-seekers	18.2	52.0
Race	20.1	47.4
Third Reich	5.3	78.6
National	45.4	27.1
The people (Volk)	63.5	11.4
Gypsy	18.9	51.3
Talmud	13.0	22.5
Reparations	38.4	35.7
Tolerance	86.6	4.1
Fanatic	4.4	84.0
Pacifist	30.9	34.7
Zionist	8.9	41.0
Coming to terms with the past	27.5	41.8
Guest worker	31.9	32.6
Israel	44.1	16.9

Capitalism	27.3	41.0
Turk	28.8	32.9

6. "If someone says that we Germans are superior to other people, in your opinion is there some truth to this, or would you not say that?"

	% agreement
Some truth to it	29.3
Wouldn't say that	59.3
Undecided	11.5

7. Interviewer gives interviewee List 3. "For which of these groups of people could you always say, 'That could mean me'—that is, to which of these groups would you say you belong?"

	% agreement
Religious, devout people	34.6
Liberals	32.2
Disadvantaged	12.2
People who like to live, who enjoy life	74.0
People who consider justice more important than anything else	50.3
Successful, upwardly mobile people	11.2
People who don't like Jews	5.8
Tolerant people	67.2
People who can adapt	61.5
Progressives	22.6
Conservatives	18.7
People who suffered a lot in the last war	20.9
Artistic people, artists	15.3
People who distinguished themselves in World War II	3.6
People who support law and order	64.6
People who did well during the Third Reich	3.7
none of the above	1.3

8. "Are there any Jews in your circle of acquaintances?"

Yes, many	4.0%
Yes, one or two	7.9%
No	66.6%*
Don't know	21.6%*

* And do you now of any people who live around here, or who are on television, who are Jews?"

Yes, many	18.3%
Yes, one or two	20.0%
No	49.9%
Not questioned	11.9%

9. Interviewer gives interviewee List 4. "We all have some idea of what other people think of us Germans. What do you think: What do Jews think of us Germans? Please tell me on the basis of this list.

	% agreement
Many *Jews* surely think that...	
Younger Germans don't want to have any more to do with their past	63.7
Germans don't feel any sense of guilt	22.3
Many Germans are ashamed of the persecution of the Jews	47.5
After everything that the Germans did to us Jews, we will never again be able to deal with them normally	33.7
We have to keep reminding the Germans of their guilt	46.9
We have to keep telling the Germans that reparations alone are not enough	39.8
You can never trust the Germans	20.8
Many Germans still hate us Jews	41.0
Germans are genuinely interested in reconciliation with the Jews	32.0
We shouldn't always reproach the Germans; they don't deserve that	24.5
Germans have nothing more and nothing less against us than other people do	19.4
We should reach out our hands to the Germans in reconciliation	30.1
Others—please indicate	1.2

10. "If someone says, 'It would be best for us Germans if all the Jews would go to Israel,' would you agree or disagree?"

Agree	13.1%
Disagree	66.8%
Undecided	20.1%

11. "Do you think that most of what is reported about the concentration camps and the persecution of the Jews is true, or is a lot of it exaggerated?"

Most is true	79.2%
A lot is exaggerated	13.3%
Undecided	7.5%

12. "Recently someone said, 'Today, forty years after the end of the war, we shouldn't talk so much about the persecution of the Jews anymore; instead, we should finally put an end to discussion of the past.' Would you say that's true or not true?"

True	66.9%
Not true	21.5%
Undecided	11.6%

13. "Should people who are involved in anti-Jewish activities in Germany today be prosecuted or not?"

Yes, definitely	38.5%
Yes, in serious cases	43.0%
No, not as a rule	5.1%
No, it would be undemocratic	5.0%
Undecided	8.5%

14. Interviewer gives interviewee List 5. "Here is a list of things that you might hear about the State of Israel. To which of the points would you say, 'That's true; that's how I see it, too'?"

	% agreement
They sometimes act like they are the center of the world	21.5
There is a curse on that people	20.8
The State of Israel deserves our special support	22.7
They are dependent on the Americans	35.2
Israel can truly be proud of itself	21.0
That country has a lot of covert influence in the world	38.9
There is a lot we can learn from the Israelis	7.7
A state that stops at nothing	18.0
They have a good army and a good secret service	45.5
Israeli politics are ruthless and narrow-minded	18.5
They are like us. The Germans of the Middle East	9.9

An industrious people	36.9
Israel lives off our reparations payments	16.8
Religious fanatics are pulling the strings there	20.0
Israel has exemplary agriculture	27.2
They take land away from their neighbors illegally	21.3
A country whose behavior is influenced by a constant external threat	48.1
A country that simply does not want peace	11.6
They start wars and blame others	14.9
A country like any other	20.7

15. "If someone says, 'The way the State of Israel treats the Palestinians is in principle no different from how the Nazis treated the Jews in the 'Third Reich,' would you agree or disagree?"

Agree	16.9%
Disagree	50.1%
Undecided	33.0%

16. Interviewer gives interviewee List 6. "Here is a list of things we have heard in the course of our surveys. Which of these demands would you agree with?"

	% agreement
Jews should be helped in every way possible, since they have suffered a lot.	26.0
Jews should not become government ministers or high level civil servants here.	16.1
The Federal Republic of Germany should support Israeli policy more.	8.7
Former concentration camp guards should still be sought out and punished.	49.5
The struggle of the Palestinians for their homeland should be supported.	16.0
Jewish children should go to the same schools as other children.	68.7
The Federal Republic of Germany should definitely not sell weapons to the Arabs.	44.1
We should discontinue reparations payments to Israel.	27.9
There should be more schools and streets named after German Jews.	7.8
People shouldn't go to Jewish doctors.	2.1

Travel to Israel should be publicly supported.	26.1
There should be more partnerships between Israeli and German cities.	37.4
Jews should no longer be permitted to immigrate or return to Germany.	6.4
People should support people who say things against Jews in conversation.	6.9
Jews and non-Jews should be treated the same, legally and generally.	70.1
People should write letters to the editor strongly criticizing reparations payments to Israel	5.1

17. "Some people think that Jews believe they are special and look down on others, since it says in the Old Testament that God declared the Jews to be his Chosen People. Do you think it's true that Jews believe they are special, or don't you think that?"

I think they do believe that	30.8%
I don't think they do	52.5%
Undecided	16.7%

18. "Jews have too much influence in the world. Would you say that's true or not true?"

It is true	33.0%
It is not true	42.6%
Undecided	24.4%

19. Interviewer gives interviewee a set of cards. "Could you please look through these cards and tell me which points apply to you?"

	% agreement
I am not aware of any personal guilt towards the Jews.	83.4
In my family, we used to have very anti-Jewish attitudes.	10.0
My family had Jewish friends and acquaintances before the war.	18.7
I am always careful when talking about Jews, because you can easily end up getting in trouble.	20.4
I am ashamed that Germans committed so many crimes against the Jews.	60.9
I don't make any distinction between Jews and other people.	74.7

I believe you always have to be somewhat careful with Jews.	19.4
I find it incomprehensible that there are people who have something against Jews.	49.3
I think Jews share the blame if they are hated and persecuted.	21.6
In order to form my own picture, I would like to get to know some Jews more closely.	33.7
I don't share my true feelings about Jews with just anyone.	15.3
I think that many people are hesitant to express their true opinion of Jews.	39.8
Somehow I don't like the whole subject of "Jews."	22.7

20. Interviewer gives interviewee a set of cards. "Here is a list of things that other people have told us about Jews. In your opinion, which of these characteristics can often be found in Jews?"

	% agreement
Radical politics	21.6
Intelligent, smart	49.4
Successful in business	74.6
Artistically talented	38.5
Unforgiving, unreconcilable	25.5
Brave	33.5
Arrogant	14.7
Ambitious	48.7
Loyal	10.8
Honest	10.5
Orderly, clean	20.3
Conspiratorial	11.3
Religious	75.0
Stick together	69.9
Cowardly	3.5
Industrious	46.0
Stingy	20.1
Sense of duty	28.7
Modest, unpretentious	11.4
Ugly	3.6
Sense of tradition	64.6
Ruthless	15.3
Oversensitive	31.6

Weak	4.1
Destructive, subversive	4.4
False, conniving	8.7
Avaricious, greedy	27.8
Crafty, shrewd	42.4
Power-hungry	18.5
Unpredictable	15.2
Sinister	7.4
None of these	7.7

21. Interviewer gives interviewee illustration 7, a cartoon with a person talking. "This is something we were told recently. Would you say there is some truth to it, or do you disagree?"

    Balloon text: "Many Jews try to profit from the history of the 'Third Reich' at Germans' expense."

It is the exact truth	11.4%
Some truth to it	37.1%
Not true	29.0%
Can't say	22.6%

22. "What would you estimate—how many Jews are now living in the Federal Republic of Germany and West Berlin?"

Up to 10,000	3.3%
From 11,000–20,000	1.8%
21,000–30,000	1.6%
31,000–50,000	2.7%
51,000–90,000	1.6%
91,000–100,000	4.1%
101,000–200,000	2.1%
201,000–300,000	1.4%
301,000–500,000	4.1%
More than 500,000	7.3%
Can't say	70.0%

23. "Sometimes you hear that the Jews have so much trouble because God is punishing them for crucifying Jesus Christ. Would you agree or disagree?"

Agree	8.0%
Disagree	75.7%
Undecided	16.4%

24.a) "Austrian President Kurt Waldheim is accused by Jewish organizations of having been involved in the persecution of Jews during World War II. Have you heard anything about this issue?"

Yes	83.0%
No	17.0%

b) "Some say the World Jewish congress interfered too much, and others say it was necessary to look into Waldheim's role in World War II. What is your opinion?"

Interfered too much	30.0%
Necessary to look into Waldheim's role	47.0%
Undecided	23.0%

(only asked of those who answered 'yes' to Question 24 a)

c) "Heads of state are normally invited to visit the Federal Republic of Germany from time to time. Because of the charges against Waldheim, some now say that the Federal Republic should not invited Waldheim. Others are in favor of inviting him, since they do not feel the charges have been proven. How do you feel, like the former or the latter?"

Like the former (Waldheim should not be invited)	23.0%
Like the latter (Waldheim should be invited)	52.0%
Undecided	25.0%

(only asked of those who answered 'yes' to Question 24 a)

Appendix 3:
Factor Analyses

Factor Analysis: Stereotypes about Jews

31 variables / varimax rotation
>1.0

Factor	Eigenvalue Value	Explained variance %	Cumulative variance
1	5.89859	18.4	18.4
2	4.29342	13.4	31.9
3	1.95124	6.1	38.0
4	1.30238	4.1	42.1
5	1.21392	3.8	45.9
6	1.00495	3.1	49.0

% Variable	Factors (Load >.40)						
	F1	F2	F3	F4	F5	F6	Common.
15 Ruthless	.72	.06	-.05	.11	-.02	.09	.55
15 Unpredictable	.71	.01	-.03	.09	.09	.08	.52
19 Power-hungry	.66	.02	-.01	.24	-.01	.13	.51
4 Destructive	.60	-.02	.01	-.09	.29	-.12	.47
15 Arrogant	.57	.05	-.03	.18	-.04	.35	.49
9 False, conniving	.57	-.07	-.05	.14	.33	.00	.46
7 Sinister	.55	.02	.00	.06	.21	-.18	.38
22 Radical politics	.55	.27	-.05	-.14	-.11	.21	.45
11 Conspiratorial	.53	.07	.05	.03	.23	.10	.34
26 Unforgiving	.52	.13	-.03	.16	.06	.46	.53
28 Greedy	.45	.01	-.13	.60	.14	.12	.62
75 Religious	.03	.74	.09	.03	.04	.11	.57
65 Sense of tradition	.06	.68	.17	-.03	-.07	.05	.50
70 Stick together	.10	.68	.16	.10	.02	.05	.51

75 Successful							
in business	-.04	.61	.06	.46	-.01	-.04	.59
49 Ambitious	.22	.42	.30	.32	-.11	-.26	.49
11 Honest	-.08	-.02	.73	-.02	.07	.06	.54
11 Loyal	-.01	.00	.67	.08	.05	.07	.46
20 Orderly, clean	-.04	.13	.66	.03	-.03	.10	.47
29 Sense of duty	.01	.22	.65	.09	-.04	.01	.48
12 Modest	-.03	.06	.54	-.06	.16	-.09	.33
20 Industrious	-.02	.37	.50	.22	-.14	-.13	.47
34 Brave	.14	.36	.45	-.03	-.16	-.30	.46
42 Crafty, shrewd	.33	.21	.00	.62	.03	-.06	.55
28 Greedy	.45	.01	-.13	.60	.14	.12	.62
20 Stingy	.31	-.01	.03	.53	.29	.08	.47
49 Intelligent, smart	-.02	.35	.30	.51	-.09	-.08	.49
75 Successful							
in business	-.05	.61	.06	.46	-.01	-.04	.59
4 Cowardly	.24	-.01	.03	.02	.69	.09	.54
4 Weak	.11	-.02	.10	.02	.69	.18	.54
4 Ugly	.20	.06	-.02	.08	.60	-.20	.44
32 Oversensitive	.21	.23	.26	.07	.04	.59	.52
26 Unforgiving,							
unreconcilable	.52	.13	-.03	.16	.06	.46	.53

Of those stereotypes that were not categorized, "artistically talented" loaded relatively high (.38) for factor 4.

Factor Analysis: Image of Israel

32 variables / varimax rotation
Intrinsic value > 1.0

Factor	Eigenvalue Value	Explained variance %	Cumulative variance
1	4.70513	14.3	14.3
2	3.46414	10.5	24.8
3	1.65231	5.0	29.8
4	1.38993	4.2	34.0
5	1.14299	3.5	37.4
6	1.08837	3.3	40.7
7	1.07940	3.3	44.0
8	1.03462	3.1	47.1

% Variable	Factors (Load >.40)								
	F1	F2	F3	F4	F5	F6	F7	F8	C.
15 Start wars	.68	-.06	.19	.01	-.12	.08	.05	.02	.54
19 Ruthless politics	.65	.14	-.00	-.12	.00	.10	.15	.05	.49
12 Country that doesn't want peace	.62	-.21	.16	.07	-.09	.08	-.06	-.09	.48
18 State that stops at nothing	.58	.11	.13	-.14	.01	.16	.12	-.01	.42
20 Religious fanatics pull strings	.56	-.02	.21	-.03	-.04	-.05	-.08	-.06	.37
21 Take land away from neighbors	.42	.22	.21	-.08	-.16	.01	.45	.05	.51
46 Good army	.03	.68	.17	.03	.09	.04	.13	-.06	.52
35 Dependent on the Americans	.10	.61	.08	-.06	.08	-.04	.22	-.03	.45
27 Exemplary agriculture	-.06	.58	-.01	.32	-.05	-.07	-.04	.10	.46
48 Constant external threat	.00	.57	-.09	.13	.29	-.04	-.03	-.24	.49
37 Industrious people	-.08	.53	-.09	.34	.03	-.02	-.12	.16	.46
21 Israel can be proud of itself	-.06	.46	-.01	.49	-.00	-.08	-.10	.11	.48
39 A lot of covert influence	.08	.41	.35	-.10	.21	.13	.06	-.03	.38
28 No reparations to Israel	.11	.08	.67	-.15	-.12	.11	.05	.02	.53
48 Profits from the past	-.19	-.07	-.65	.03	.06	-.06	.06	-.05	.48
17 Israel lives off reparations	.27	-.04	.60	.10	-.16	-.04	-.01	-.03	.47
5 Letters opposing reparations	.18	-.18	.46	.10	-.06	.21	.24	-.10	.41
9 More support of Israeli politics	-.04	.02	.01	.63	.09	.03	-.01	-.02	.41
8 A lot to learn from Israel	-.02	.12	-.02	.60	-.02	.07	-.04	.18	.41
23 Israel; deserves support	-.09	.11	-.16	.59	.22	-.05	.09	-.04	.46

21 Israel can be proud of itself	-.06	.46	-.01	.49	-.00	-.08	-.10	.11	.48
26 Support travel to Israel	.03	-.01	-.02	.43	.55	-.13	.04	-.01	.51
39 No Israelis in circle of friends	.06	-.17	.15	-.02	-.64	-.02	.00	-.09	.48
37 City partnerships/ sister cities	-.09	.11	-.09	.38	.56	-.06	.10	-.10	.51
26 Support travel to Israel	.03	-.01	-.02	.43	.55	-.13	.04	-.01	.51
11 Don't want to have anything to do with Israelis	.23	-.11	.18	.15	-.45	.21	.12	-.28	.46
22 Dislike Talmud	.08	.03	.04	.07	-.05	.75	-.02	.12	.60
17 Dislike Israel	.34	-.12	.09	.01	-.18	.63	.09	-.09	.58
36 Dislike reparations	-.04	.15	.43	-.23	.08	.50	-.07	-.04	.52
16 Support Palestinian struggle	.19	.11	.06	.02	.16	.04	.70	.10	.58
21 There is a curse on this people	.40	.01	.13	.02	.17	.08	-.46	.16	.44
21 Take land away from neighbors	.42	.22	.21	-.08	-.16	.01	.45	.05	.51
21 A country like any other	-.21	-.15	.09	.15	.20	-.02	.11	.64	.57
10 The Germany of the Middle East	.06	.22	-.03	.24	.00	.09	-.13	.48	.40

Of those statements that were not categorized for Israel, the following loaded relatively high: "the way the State of Israel treats the Palestinians is in principle no different from how the Nazis treated the Jews in the Third Reich", with -.37 for factor 8; "They sometimes act like they are the center of the world", with .31 for factor 1 and .39 for factor 3.

Factor Analysis: Antipathy and Social Distance

26 variables / varimax rotation
Intrinsic value > 1.0

Factor	Eigenvalue Value	Explained variance %	Cumulative variance
1	6.35845	24.5	24.5

2	1.94109	7.5	31.9
3	1.71553	6.6	38.5
4	1.25753	4.8	43.4
5	1.13937	4.4	47.7
6	1.02135	3.9	51.7

%	Variable	Factors (Load >.40)						
		F1	F2	F3	F4	F5	F6	Common.
21	Blacks	.68	.13	.35	.08	.05	.08	.62
30	Arabs	.54	.27	.24	.05	.11	.12	.57
11	Israelis	.64	.06	.04	.35	.14	.15	.58
11	Jews/German Jews	.60	.09	.06	.46	.17	.14	.63
34	Turks	.59	.33	.39	.03	.00	.00	.61
33	Asylum-seekers	.54	.29	.34	.02	-.00	.10	.50
3	College students	.46	.07	-.23	-.04	.01	.50	.52
33	Dislike Turks	.24	.72	.09	.13	-.06	-.02	.61
52	Dislike asylum-seekers	.19	.69	.19	-.01	-.03	.03	.56
33	Dislike guest workers	.17	.69	.10	.16	-.07	.01	.54
51	Dislike Gypsies	.12	.65	.17	.06	.03	.02	.46
52	Dislike Palestinians	.01	.63	-.05	-.01	.20	.12	.42
20	Dislike Jews	.20	.52	-.06	.48	.00	.07	.55
49	People with conviction record for theft	.11	.06	.67	.07	.11	.13	.51
60	Prostitutes	.06	.08	.66	.00	.13	.10	.47
59	People with AIDS	.25	.17	.61	.02	-.01	-.06	.54
6	People who don't like Jews	.23	.14	.01	.71	.06	.00	.59
6	Jews shouldn't be allowed to immigrate	.17	.07	.10	.68	-.10	-.07	.52
13	All Jews to Israel, disagree	.20	-.03	-.04	-.65	.04	-.17	.50
20	Dislike Jews	.19	.52	-.06	.48	.00	.07	.55
11	Jews/German Jews	.60	.09	.06	.46	.17	.14	.63
66	Dedicated Nazis	-.01	-.10	.01	-.09	.84	.02	.73
50	Dedicated Communists	.16	.20	.29	.06	.66	.02	.59
4	Divorced people	.15	-.02	.11	.09	-.05	.63	.44
30	Unemployed	-.07	.14	.31	.04	.15	.63	.54

3 College students   .46   .07   -.23   -.04   .01   .50   .52

Of those groups that were not categorized, the following loaded relatively high: "Psychiatric patients" with .39 for factor 1 and .38 for factor 3; "Children of criminals" with .34 for factor 1 and .37 for factor 3; "A Jew born and raised in Germany is more a Jew than a German" with .39 for factor 1 and .39 for factor 3.

Appendix 4:
AS-STEREOTYPE Index

List of the 17 indicators

Question 17: "Some people think that Jews believe they are special and look down on others, since it says in the Old Testament that God declared the Jews to be his Chosen People." (Response: I think they do believe that)

Question 18: "Jews have too much influence in the world." (Response: It is true)

from

Question 19: "I think Jews share the blame if they are hated and persecuted."

from

Question 20: "In your opinion, which of these characteristics can often be found in Jews?"

The characteristics: Unforgiving, unreconcilable
Arrogant
Conspiratorial
Ugly
Ruthless
Destructive, subversive
False, conniving
Greedy, avaricious
Crafty, shrewd
Power-hungry
Unpredictable
Sinister

Question 21:   "Many Jews try to profit from the history of the 'Third Reich' at Germans' expense." (Response: it is the exact truth / Some truth to it.)

Question 23:   "Sometimes you hear that the Jews have so much trouble because God is punishing them for crucifying Jesus Christ." (Agreement)

Bibliography

Sources and Survey-Analyses

Adorno, Theodor W., Else Frenkel-Brunswik, Daniel J. Levinson, and R. Nevitt Sanford. *The Authoritarian Personality*. New York, 1950.

Ahren, Yizhak, Christoph Melchers, Werner Seifert, and Werner Wagner. *Das Lehrstück "Holocaust." Wirkungen und Nachwirkungen eines Medienereignisses*. Opladen, 1982.

Allerbeck, Klaus R. *Demokratisierung und sozialer Wandel in der Bundesrepublik Deutschland. Sekundäranalyse von Umfragedaten 1953–1974*. Opladen, 1976.

Antisemitismus in Österreich. Ergebnisse einer Untersuchung der Demoskopischen Institute Österreichs. Leitung: H. Kienzl, and E. Gehmacher. Wien, 1987 (MS).

Bensimon, Doris, and Jeannine Verdes-Leroux. Les Français et le probleme juif. Analyse secondaire d'un sondage de l'I.F.O.P. In *Archives de sociologie des religions 29*, 1970: 53–91.

Bergmann, Werner. Public Beliefs about Anti-Jewish Attitudes in West Germany: A Case of "Pluralistic Ignorance." In *Patterns of Prejudice 22*, 1988: 15–21.

———. Antisemitism in (East and West) German Public Opinion, 1987–1992. In *Patterns of Prejudice 27, 2*, 1993: 21–28.

———. Anti-Semitism and Xenophobia in the East German Länder. In *German Politics 3, 2*, 1994a: 265–76.

———. Xenophobia and Antisemitism after the Unification of Germany. In *Patterns of Prejudice 28, 1*, 1994b: 67–80.

Bergmann, Werner, and Rainer Erb. Extreme Antisemiten in der Bundesrepublik Deutschland. In *Jahrbuch Extremismus und Demokratie 3*, 1991: 70–93.

———. Wie antisemitisch sind die Deutschen? Meinungsumfragen 1945–1994. In W. Benz (ed.), *Antisemitismus in Deutschland*, 47–63. München, 1995.

———. Antisemitismus—Umfragen nach 1945 im internationalen Vergleich. In *Jahrbuch für Antisemitismusforschung 5*, 1996: 72–195.

Berkowitz, Leonhard. Anti-Semitism and the Displacement of Aggression. In *Journal of Abnormal and Social Psychology 59*, 1959: 181–87.

Bettelheim, Bruno, and Morris Janowitz. *Dynamics of Prejudice*. New York, 1950.

Brusten, Manfred. Wie sympathisch sind uns die Juden? Empirische Anmerkungen zum Antisemitismus. Aus einem Forschungsprojekt über Einstellungen deutscher Studenten in Ost und West. In *Jahrbuch für Antisemitismusforschung 4*, 1995: 107–29.

Chanes, Jerome A. Interpreting the Data: Antisemitism and Jewish Security in the United States. In *Patterns of Prejudice 28*, 3/4, 1994: 87–101.

Cohen, Renae, and Jennifer L. Golub. Attitudes Toward Jews in Poland, Hungary and Czechoslovakia. A Comparative Study. Working Papers on Contemporary Anti-Semitism, American Jewish Committee 1991.

de Boer, Connie. The Polls: Attitudes Toward the Arab-Israeli Conflict. In *Public Opinion Quarterly 47*, 1983: S.121–31.

de Kadt, Emanuel. What People Thought of the Middle East War. In *Patterns of Prejudice 1*, 1967: 10–13.

DIVO-Pressedienst. Zu den Spannungen im Mittleren Osten, 2 July 1958.

———. Bekanntheit und Beurteilung des Eichmann-Prozesses/ Frage der Mitarbeit von Angehörigen der jüdischen Bevölkerungsgruppe und des Emigrantenkreises in der Bundesregierung, July II 1961.

———. Bekanntheitsgrad des Auschwitz-Prozesses und die Einstellung der Bundesbürger zu seiner Durchführung "zwanzig Jahre danach," July I/ July II 1964.

———. Einstellungen zu den Bürgerrechtsgesetzen und zu den Rassenunruhen in Amerika, 1 March 1965.

Emnid-Institut. Zum Problem des Antisemitismus im Bundesgebiet. Eine Spezial-Erhebung im Auftrage der Bundeszentrale für Heimatdienst, Bonn, Bielefeld 1954.

———. Emnid-Informationen 45/1956-Völkermeinungen zum Nahost-Konflikt.

———. Emnid-Informationen 15/1957-Sympathien und Antipathien gegenüber anderen Ländern.

———. Emnid-Informationen 41/1959-Gruppeneinflüsse in der Öffentlichkeit des Bundesrepublik.

———. Emnid-Informationen 9/1960-Antisemitische Äußerungen im Urteil der westdeutschen Bevölkerung.

———. Emnid-Informationen 17/1961-Meinungen über Gruppeneinflüsse in der Bundesrepublik.

———. Emnid-Informationen 24/1961-Weltmeinungen zum Eichmann-Prozeß.

―――. Emnid-Informationen 30/1961-Wirkungen des Eichmann-Prozesses auf die Einstellungen gegenüber Deutschland.

―――. Emnid-Informationen 32/1961-Wie die Deutschen sich sehen.

―――. Emnid-Informationen 7/1962-Gruppeneinflüsse in der Bundesrepublik.

―――. Emnid-Informationen 37/1963-Zu den Gruppeneinflüssen in der Bundesrepublik.

―――. Emnid-Informationen 7/1965-Religiöse Gruppeneinflüsse in der Bundesrepublik von 1959 bis 1964.

―――. Emnid-Informationen 35/1965-Internationales Meinungsbild: USA. Vorurteile in der Politik.

―――. Emnid-Informationen 3/1967-Was NPD-Anhänger von einem "Mann wie Hitler" halten. Der Einfluß der Interessenverbände.

―――. Emnid-Informationen 7/1967-Einstellung zum Nahost-Konflikt.

―――. Emnid-Informationen 8/1967-Einstellung zum Nahost-Konflikt in der Weltmeinung.

―――. Emnid-Informationen 6/1968 und 11-12/1968-Heirat.

―――. Emnid-Informationen 2/1969-Völkerstereotypen im Wandel eines Jahrzehnts.

―――. Emnid-Informationen 11-12/1970-Gruppeneinflüsse.

―――. Emnid-Informationen 11-12/1971-Gruppeneinflüsse.

―――. Emnid-Informationen 11-12/1973-Wenig Sympathien für die Araber während des Nahost-Konflikts.

―――. Emnid-Informationen 1-2/1974-Eine Untersuchung über Nahost-Sympathien und unsere jüdischen Mitbürger.

―――. Emnid-Informationen 7/1975-Gruppeneinflüsse in der Bundesrepublik Deutschland.

―――. Emnid-Informationen 12/1975-Einstellungen zu Problemen der Außen- und Deutschlandpolitik.

―――. Emnid-Informationen 1/1977-Gehört Israel zu Europa?

―――. Emnid-Informationen 1/1978-Friedensbemühungen Präsident Sadats.

―――. Emnid-Informationen 6/1978-Israels Politik wird ausgleichend gesehen.

―――. Emnid-Informationen 11-12/1978-Verjährungsfrist für NS-Verbrechen.

―――. Emnid-Informationen 1/1979-Gruppeneinflüsse in der Bundesrepublik Deutschland.

―――. Emnid-Informationen 2/1979-Verjährungsfrist für NS-Verbrechen-Umdenken durch "Holocaust"?

―――. Emnid-Informationen 11/1981-Zur Akzeptanz pogromistischer Judenwitze.

―――. Emnid-Informationen 12/1981-Untersuchungsergebnisse aus dem Ausland: Israel-U.S. Politik im Nahen Osten.

————. Emnid-Informationen 5-6/1982-Zum aktuellen Image von Reagan, Thatcher, und Begin.

————. Emnid-Informationen 3-4/1984-Zum Image von Reagan, Kohl, Honecker, und Shamir.

————. Emnid-Informationen 11-12/1984-Gruppeneinflüsse.

————. Emnid-Informationen 8-9/1986-Verschiedene Länder und ihre Produkte (question of boycott).

————. Antisemitismus. Repräsentativbefragung im Auftrag des WDR, 1986.

————. Zeitgeschichte, Repräsentativbefragung im Auftrag des "Spiegel." Bielefeld, 1989.

————. Antisemitismus in Deutschland. Repräsentativumfrage im Auftrag des "Spiegel," December 1991. Bielefeld, 1992.

Erlebach, R., T. Kissenkötter, R. Krieger, and D. Wacker. Nationalsozialismus. Kenntnisse und Meinungen von Abiturienten 1961 und 1979. In *Politische Psychologie,* hrsg.v. Hans Dieter Klingemann/Max Kaase, Sonderheft der Politischen Vierteljahresschrift 12. Opladen, 1981: 337–43.

Ernst, Tilman. "Holocaust" und politische Bildung. In *Media Perspektiven,* 1979: 230–40.

————. "Holocaust" in der Bundesrepublik. In *Rundfunk und Fernsehen 28,* 1980: 509–33.

Falter, Jürgen W. *Wer wählt rechts? Die Wähler und Anhänger rechtsextremistischer Parteien im vereinigten Deutschland.* München, 1994.

Fields, James M., and Howard Schuman. Public Beliefs About the Beliefs of the Public. In *Public Opinion Quarterly 40,* 1976: 427–48.

FORSA. Die Deutschen und der Nationalsozialismus: Kenntnisse, Einschätzungen, Urteile, Repräsentative Umfrage im Auftrag "Die Woche" (published 1 June 1994), 1994.

————. Deutsche und Juden Anfang 1996. Repräsentative Umfrage im Auftrag "Die Woche" (26 January) 1996.

Förster, Peter, Walter Friedrich, Harry Müller, and Wilfried Schubarth. *Jugend Ost: Zwischen Hoffnung und Gewalt.* Opladen, 1993.

Freyhold, Michaela von. Autoritarismus und politische Apathie. Analyse einer Skala zur Ermittlung autoritätsgebundener Verhaltensweisen, Frankfurt a.M. 1971 (Frankfurter Beiträge zur Soziologie Bd. 22).

Galtung, Johan. *Anti-Semitism in the Making. A Study of American High School Students.* Oslo, 1960.

Gast, Wolfgang. "Holocaust" und die Presse. In *Rundfunk und Fernsehen 30,* 1982: 355–62.

Gehmacher, Ernst. Vorurteil und Politik. Ein sozialwissenschaftliches Modell. In *SWS-Rundschau 27,* 1987: 69–74.

Geiger, Klaus F. Einstellungen zur multikulturellen Gesellschaft—Ergebnisse von Repräsentativbefragungen in der Bundesrepublik. In *Migration 9*, 1991: 11–48.

Glock, Charles Y., and Rodney Stark. *Christian Beliefs and Anti-Semitism.* New York, 1966.

Golub, Jennifer. British Attitudes Toward Jews and Other Minorities. Working Papers on Contemporary Anti-Semitism, American Jewish Committee. New York, 1993.

————. *Current German Attitudes toward Jews and Other Minorities.* New York, 1994.

Gudkov, Lev, and Alex Levinson. Attitudes Toward Jews in the Soviet Union. Public Opinion in Ten Republics. Working Papers on Contemporary Anti-Semitism, American Jewish Committee. New York, 1992.

Haerpfer, Christian. Antisemitische Einstellungen in der österreichischen Gesellschaft in der Periode 1973–1989. In NS-Ideologie und Antisemitismus in Österreich, in *Schriftenreihe der Liga der Freunde des Judentums, 1*. Wien 1989: 35–45.

Herz, Thomas A. *Soziale Bedingungen für Rechtsextremismus in der Bundesrepublik Deutschland und in den Vereinigten Staaten.* Meisenheim a.G., 1975.

Hoskin, Marilyn. Die öffentliche Meinung in der Bundesrepublik Deutschland und die ausländischen Arbeitnehmer. In M. Rosch (ed.), *Ausländische Arbeitnehmer und Immigranten. Sozialwissenschaftliche Beiträge zur Diskussion eines aktuellen Problems.* Weinheim, Basel, 1985: 2–30.

Institut für angewandte Sozialforschung (infas) Bad Godesberg, Jugend und Rechtsextremismus in Schleswig-Holstein, on behalf of the NDR. Hamburg 1992.

Institut für Demoskopie Allensbach. Ist Deutschland antisemitisch? Ein diagnostischer Beitrag zur Innenpolitik Herbst 1949. Allensbach, 1949.

————. *Jahrbuch der öffentlichen Meinung 1947–1955.* E. Noelle and E. P. Neumann (eds.). Allensbach, 1956.

————. *Jahrbuch der öffentlichen Meinung,* vol II. Allensbach, 1957.

————. *Jahrbuch der öffentlichen Meinung,* vol. III, 1958–1964. Allensbach, 1965.

————. *Jahrbuch der Öffentlichen Meinung,* vol. IV, 1965–1967. Allensbach, 1968.

————. *Jahrbuch der öffentlichen Meinung,* vol. V, 1968–1973. Allensbach, 1974.

————. *Allensbacher Jahrbuch für Demoskopie,* vol. VI, 1974–1976. Allensbach, 1977.

————. *Allensbacher Jahrbuch für Demoskopie,* vol. VIII, 1978–1983. Allensbach, 1984.

————. *Allensbacher Jahrbuch für Demoskopie*, vol. IX, 1984–1992. Elisabeth Noelle-Neumann and Renate Köcher (eds.). Munich, Allensbach, 1993.

————. *Zwischen Toleranz und Besorgtheit. Einstellungen der deutschen Bevölkerung zu aktuellen Problemen der Ausländerpolitik.* Allensbach, 1985.

————. Deutsche und Juden vier Jahrzehnte danach. Eine Repräsentativbefragung im Auftrag des "Stern," Renate Köcher. Allensbach, 1986.

————. Ausmaß und Formen des heutigen Antisemitismus in der Bundesrepublik Deutschland, Renate Köcher. Allensbach, 1987.

ISIS-Meinungsprofile. Antisemitismus in Österreich und Westdeutschland 1987 (red. Bernd Marin). *Journal für Sozialforschung 28*, 1988: 77–104.

Jaide, Walter, and Hans-Joachim Veen. *Bilanz der Jugendforschung. Ergebnisse empirischer Analysen in der Bundesrepublik Deutschland von 1975–1987.* Paderborn, Munich, 1989.

Jodice, David A. United Germany and Jewish Concerns. Attitudes Toward Jews, Israel, and the Holocaust, American Jewish Committee. New York, 1991.

Just, Dieter, and Peter Caspar Mülhens. Ausländerzunahme: objektives Problem oder Einstellungsfrage? Aktuelle Einstellungen der Deutschen gegenüber ausländischen Mitbürgern. In *Aus Politik und Zeitgeschichte B 25*, 26 June 1982: 35–38.

Karmasin, Fritz. Austrian Attitudes Toward Jews, Israel, and the Holocaust. Working Papers on Contemporary Anti-Semitism, American Jewish Committee. New York, 1992.

Katz, Daniel, and Kenneth W. Braly. Racial Stereotypes of 100 College Students. In *Journal of Abnormal and Social Psychology 30*, 1933: 280–90.

————. Racial Prejudice and Racial Stereotypes. In *Journal of Social Psychology 30*, 1935: 175–93.

Költringer, Richard, and Ernst Gehmacher. Antisemitismus und die "Waldheimdiskussion" während des österreichischen Bundespräsidentschaftswahlkampfes 1986. In *Kölner Zeitschrift für Soziologie und Sozialpsychologie 41*, 1989: 555–62.

Krauth, Cornelia, and Rolf Porst. Sozioökonomische Determinanten von Einstellungen zu Gastarbeitern. In K. U. Mayer, and P. Schmidt (eds.), *Allgemeine Bevölkerungsumfrage der Sozialwissenschaften. Beiträge zu methodischen Problemen des ALLBUS 1980.* Frankfurt, New York, 1980: 233–66.

Kühnel, Steffen, and Michael Terwey. Die Einstellung der Deutschen zu Ausländern in der Bundesrepublik. In Michael Braun and Peter Ph.Mohler (eds.), *Blickpunkt Gesellschaft 3. Einstellungen und Verhalten der Bundesbürger.* Opladen, 1994: 71–105.

Lang, Kurt, Gladys Engel Lang, Hans-Mathias Kepplinger, and Simone Ehmig. Collective Memory and Political Generations. A Survey of German Journalists. In *Political Communication 10*, 1993: 211–29.

Lederer, Gerda, Joachim Nerger, Susanne Rippl, Peter Schmidt, and Christian Seipel. Autoritarismus unter Jugendlichen der ehemaligen DDR. In *Deutschland-Archiv 6*, 1991: 587–96.

Lukawetz, Gerd. Antisemitismus—Versuch einer Klärung. Theorieorientierte Analyse der großen Antisemitismusumfrage 1986. In *SWS-Rundschau 27*, 1987: 75–81.

Magnus, Uwe. "Holocaust" in der Bundesrepublik: Zentrale Ergebnisse aus der sicht der Rundfunkanstalten. In *Rundfunk und Fernsehen* 28, 1980: 534–542.

Martire, Gregory, and Ruth Clark. *Anti-Semitism in the United States. A Study of Prejudice in the 1980s*. New York, 1982.

Marwell, Gerald, Michael T. Aiken, and N. J. Demerath, III. The Persistence of Political Attitudes among 1960s Civil Rights Activists. In *Public Opinion Quarterly 51*, 1987: 359–75.

Melzer, Wolfgang. *Jugend und Politik in Deutschland. Gesellschaftliche Einstellungen, Zukunftsorientierungen und Rechtsextremismus-Potential Jugendlicher in Ost- und Westdeutschland*. Opladen, 1992.

Merritt, Anna J., and Richard L. Merritt (Eds.). *Public Opinion in Occupied Germany. The OMGUS Surveys, 1945–1948*. Urbana, 1970.

Merritt, Richard L. Digesting the Past: Views of National Socialism in Semi-Sovereign Germany. In *Societas 7*, 1977: 93–119.

Middleton, Russell. Do Christian Beliefs Cause Anti-Semitism? In *American Sociological Review 38*, 1973: 33–52.

Noelle-Neumann, Elisabeth. Rechtsextremismus in Deutschland. *Eine Dokumentation des Beitrags in der Frankfurter Allgemeinen Zeitung vom 18 March 1993*. Allensbach, 1993.

Noelle-Neumann, Elisabeth, and Erp Ring. *Das Extremismus-Potential unter jungen Leuten in der Bundesrepublik Deutschland 1984*. Bonn, 1985.

Noelle-Neumann, Elisabeth, and Renate Köcher. *Die verletzte Nation*. Stuttgart, 1987.

Oesterreich, Detlef. *Autoritäre Persönlichkeit und Gesellschaftordnung. Der Stellenwert psychischer Faktoren für politische Einstellungen-eine empirische Untersuchung von Jugendlichen in Ost und West*. Weinheim und München, 1993.

Panahi, Badi. *Rassismus, Antisemitismus, Nationalismus...in der Bundesrepublik Deutschland heute. Eine empirische Untersuchung*. Frankfurt a.M., 1980.

Peres, Yochanan. Antisemitismus in Österreich. Bemerkungen und Eindrücke. In *SWS-Rundschau 27*, 1987: 83–86.

Pollock, Friedrich. *Das Gruppenexperiment*. Frankfurt a.M., 1955 (Frankfurter Beiträge zur Soziologie Vol. 2).

Radio Free Europe, and Radio Liberty. Stereotypes Projected to Jews, Blacks, and Gypsies by East Europeans and Austrians. Typoskript, 1980.

Richman, Alvin. The Polls—A Report. American Attitudes toward Israeli-Palestinian Relations in the Wake of the Uprising. In *Public Opinion Quarterly 53*, 1989: 415–30.

Robb, James H. *Working Class Anti-Semite. A Psychological Study in a London Borough.* London, 1954.

Robinson Duane, and Sylvia Rohde. Two Experiments with an Anti-Semitism Poll. In *Journal of Abnormal and Social Psychology 41*, 1946: 136–44.

Roof, Wade Clark. Religious Orthodoxy and Minority Prejudice: Causal Relationship or Reflection of Localistic World View? In *American Journal of Sociology 80*, 1974: 643–64.

Rosenfield, Geraldine. The Polls: Attitudes Toward American Jews. In *Public Opinion Quarterly 46*, 1982: 431–43.

Roth, Dieter. Sind die Republikaner die fünfte Partei? Sozial- und Meinungsstruktur der Wähler der Republikaner. In *Aus Politik und Zeitgeschichte B 41-42/89*, 6 October 1989: 10–20.

Roth, Rainer A. 40 Jahre nach dem Holocaust. Umfrage über antisemitische Einstellungen bei deutschen Schülern. In *Tribüne*, No. 100, 1986: 59–72.

Sallen, Herbert A. *Zum Antisemitismus in der Bundesrepublik Deutschland. Konzepte, Methoden und Ergebnisse der empirischen Antisemitismusforschung.* Frankfurt a.M., 1977.

Sample-Institut, Sollten NS-Verbrechen verjähren? Repräsentativerhebung. Hamburg, 1978.

———. Verjährung von NS-Verbrechen: nach "Holocaust" ist jeder Zweite dagegen. Repräsentativumfrage. Hamburg, 1979.

———. Umfrage zum Thema NS-Verbrechen: Kurzlebiger "Holocaust-Effekt." Repräsentativerhebung. Hamburg, 1980.

Schmidt, Regina, and Egon Becker. *Reaktionen auf politische Vorgänge. Drei Meinungsstudien aus der Bundesrepublik.* Frankfurt a.M., 1967.

Schönbach, Peter. *Reaktionen auf die antisemitische Welle im Winter 1959/1960.* Frankfurt a.M., 1961.

Selznick, Gertrude, and Stephen Steinberg. *The Tenacity of Prejudice. Anti-Semitism in Contemporary America.* New York, 1969.

Silbermann, Alphons. *Sind wir Antisemiten? Ausmaß und Wirkung eines sozialen Vorurteils in der Bundesrepublik Deutschland.* Köln, 1982.

Silberman, Alphons, and Herbert A. Sallen. Latenter Antisemitismus in der Bundesrepublik Deutschland. In *Kölner Zeitschrift für Soziologie und Sozialpsychologie 28*, 1976: 706–23.

———. *Juden in Westdeutschland. Selbstbild und Fremdbild einer Minorität.* Köln, 1992.

Sinus-Institut, 5 Millionen Deutsche: *"Wir sollten wieder einen Führer haben." Die Sinus-Studie über rechtsextremistische Einstellungen bei den Deutschen.* Reinbek, 1981.

Smith, Tom W. What Do Americans Think About Jews? Working Papers on Contemporary Anti-Semitism, American Jewish Committee. New York, 1991.

————. The Polls—A Review. Actual Trends or Measurement Artifacts? A Review of Three Studies of Anti-Semitism. In *Public Opinion Quarterly* 57, 1993: 380–93.

Sodhi, Kripal Singh, and Rudolf Bergius. *Nationale Vorurteile*. Berlin, 1953.

Sodhi, Kripal Singh, Rudolf Bergius, and Klaus Holzkamp. Geschlechtsspezifische Unterschiede nationaler Stereotypen. In *Jahrbuch für Psychologie und Psychotherapie 4*, 1956: 263–96.

Sturzbecher, Dietmar, Peter Dietrich, and Michael Kohlstruck. *Jugend in Brandenburg 93, Brandenburger Landeszentrale für politische Bildung*. Potsdam, 1994.

SWS-Meinungsprofile: Antisemitismus in Österreich. In *SWS-Rundschau 27*, 1987: 90–96.

SWS. Was blieb von der NS-Ideologie in Österreich? In NS-Ideologie und Antisemitismus in Österreich, in *Schriftenreihe der Liga der Freunde des Judentums, no. 1*. Wien, 1989: 9–34.

Tobin, Gary A. Jewish Perceptions of Antisemitism and Antisemitic Perceptions About Jews. In *Studies in Contemporary Jewry, An Annual, IV,* J. Frankel (ed.). New York, Oxford, 1988: 210–31.

Triandis, Harry C., and Leigh M. Triandis. Race, Social Class, Religion, and Nationality as Determinants of Social Distance. In *Journal of Abnormal and Social Psychology 61*, 1960: 110–18.

Tsukashima, Ronald T. *The Social and Psychological Correlates of Black-Antisemitism*. San Francisco, Calif.: 1978.

Tumin, Melvin. Intergroup Attitudes of Youth and Adults in England, France, and Germany. Unpublished Typoscript. Princeton University, N.J.: 1962.

Weatherley, Donald. Maternal Response to Childhood Aggression and Subsequent Anti-Semitism. In *Journal of Abnormal and Social Psychology 66*, 2, 1963: 183–85.

Weil, Frederick D. The Extent and Structure of Anti-Semitism in Western Populations since the Holocaust. In Helen Fein (ed.), *The Persisting Question. Scoiological Perspectives and Social Contexts of Modern Antisemitism*. Current Research on Antisemitism, vol. 1. Berlin, New York, 1987: 164–89.

————. The Imperfectly Mastered Past: Anti-Semitism in West Germany since the Holocaust. In *New German Critique 29*, 1980: 135–53.

————. Umfragen zum Antisemitismus. Ein Vergleich zwischen vier Nationen. In W. Bergmann, and R. Erb (eds.), *Antisemitismus in der politischen Kultur nach 1945*. Opladen, 1990: 131–78.

Weiss, Hilde. Antisemitismus: Inhalte und Ausmaß antijüdischer Einstellungen in der Wiener Bevölkerung, Part I–III. In *Journal für angewandte Sozialforschung 17/3*, 1977: 13–26; *17/4*, 1977: 12–22; and *18/1*, 1978: 9–16.

———. *Antisemitische Vorurteile in Österrreich.* Wien, 1984.

Wickert-Institut. Adolf im Kopf. In *Wiener,* May 1988: 3–6.

Wiegand, Erich. Zunahme der Ausländerfeindlichkeit? In *ZUMA-Nachrichten 16*, 31, 1992: 7–28.

Willems, Helmut. *Fremdenfeindliche Gewalt. Einstellungen, Täter, Konflikteskalation.* Opladen, 1993.

Willems, Helmut, Stefanie Würtz, and Roland Eckert. *Analyse fremdenfeindlicher Straftäter. Texte zur inneren Sicherheit.* Edited by the Bundesminister des Innern. Bonn, 1994.

Wittenberg, Reinhard, Bernhard Prosch, and Martin Abraham. Antisemitismus in der ehemaligen DDR. In *Tribüne 30,* Nr.118, 1991: 102–20.

———. Struktur und Ausmaß des Antisemitismus in der ehemaligen DDR. Ergebnis seeiner repräsentativen Umfrage unter Erwachsenen und einer regional begrenzten schriftlichen Befragung unter Jugendlichen. In *Jahrbuch für Antisemitismusforschung,* vol. 4, 1995: 88–106.

Wolffsohn, Michael. Deutsch-israelische Beziehungen im Spiegel der öffentlichen Meinung. In *Aus Politik und Zeitgeschichte B 46-47,* 1984: 19–30.

———. German Opinion on Israel, 1949–1986. In *Jerusalem Journal of International Relations 10,* 1988: 79–105.

Zinnecker, Jürgen. Politik, Parteien, Nationalsozialismus. In A. Fischer (ed.), *Jugendliche und Erwachsene '85. Generationen im Vergleich,* vol. 3. Leverkusen, 1985: S.321–408.

Zollinger, Peter. Der Normalbürger spricht. Eine Schnellumfrage zum Theaterstreit. In *Pflasterstrand-Flugschrift 1,* 1986: 52–65.

Works on History and Theory

Ajzen, I., and M. Fishbein. *Understanding Attitudes and Predicting Social Behavior.* Englewood Cliffs, N.J. 1980.

Allport, Gordon W. *Treibjagd auf Sündeböcke, Berlin, Bad Nauheim.* 1951. (*ABC's of Scapegoating.* Chicago, 1948).

Amery, Jean. Der ehrbare Antisemit. Eine Rede. In *Merkur 30,* 1976: 532–46.

Anders, Günther. Kollektivschuld? In ibidem, *Besuch im Hades*, second ed. Munich, 1985.

Baker, Kendall L., Russel J. Dalton, and Kai Hildebrandt. *Germany Transformed. Political Culture and the New Politics.* Cambridge, 1981.

Banton, Michael. Pluralistic Ignorance as a Factor in Racial Attitudes. In *New Community 13*, 1986: 18–26.

———. Optimism and Pessimism about Racial Relations. In *Patterns of Prejudice 22*, 1988.

Bauer, Yehuda. Abwehr aus zionistischer und israelischer Sicht. In *Lerntag über den Antisemitismus und dessen Abwehr. Lerntage des Zentrums für Antisemitismusforschung 1*. Berlin, 1984: 52–60.

Bellers, Jürgen. Moralkommunikation und Kommunikationsmoral. Über Kommunikationslatenzen, Antisemitismus und politisches System. In W. Bergmann, and R. Erb (eds.), *Antisemitismus in der politischen Kultur nach 1945*. Opladen, 1990: 278–91.

Benninghaus, Hans. *Ergebnisse und Perspektiven der Einstellungs— Verhaltensforschung*. Meisenheim a.G., 1976.

Benz, Wolfgang (ed.). *Antisemitismus in Deutschland. Zur Aktualität eines Vorurteils*. München, 1995.

Berg-Schlosser, Dirk, and Jakob Schissler (eds.). Politische Kultur in Deutschland. Bilanz und Perspektiven. In *Politische Vierteljahresschrift, Special Issue 18*. Opladen, 1987.

Bergmann, Werner (ed.). *Error Without Trial. Psychological Research on Antisemitism* (Current Research on Antisemitism, Vol. 2). Berlin, New York, 1988a.

———. Politische Psychologie des Antisemitismus. Kritischer Literaturbericht. In *Politische Psychologie heute, Sonderheft Leviathan* 1988b: 217–34.

———. Antisemitismus als politisches Ereignis. Die antisemitische Schmierwelle im Winter 1959/60. In W. Bergmann and R. Erb (eds.), *Antisemitismus in der politischen Kultur nach 1945*. Opladen, 1990: 253–76.

———. Prejudice and Stereotypes. In *Encyclopedia of Human Behavior, 3*. San Diego, Calif. 1994: 575–86.

———. Effekte öffentlicher Meinung auf die Bevölkerungsmeinung. Der Rückgang antisemitischer Einstellungen als kollektiver Lernprozeß. In *Öffentlichkeit, öffentliche Meinung, soziale Bewegungen*, edited by Friedhelm Neidhardt, Kölner Zeitschrift für Soziologie und Sozialpsychologie, Special Issue 34, 1994: 296–319.

———. Antisemitismus in öffentlichen Konflikten 1949–1994. In W. Benz (ed.), *Antisemitismus in Deutschland*. München, 1995: 64–88.

Bergmann, Werner, and Rainer Erb. Kommunikationslatenz, Moral und öffentliche Meinung. Theoretische Überlegungen zum Antisemitismus in der Bundesrepublik Deutschland. In *Kölner Zeitschrift für Soziologie und Sozialpsychologie, 38*, 1986: 223–46.

———. "Mir ist das Thema Juden irgendwie unangenehm." Kommunikationslatenz und die Wahrnehmung des Meinungsklimas im Fall des Antisemitismus. In *Kölner Zeitschrift für Soziologie und Sozialpsychologie 43*, 1991: 502–19.

———. (eds.), *Antisemitismus in der politischen Kultur nach 1945*. Opladen, 1990.

———. (eds.), *Neonazismus und rechte Subkultur*. Berlin, 1994a.

———. Eine soziale Bewegung von rechts? Entwicklung und Vernetzung einer rechten Szene in den neuen Bundesländern. In *Forschungsjournal Neue Soziale Bewegungen, 2*, 1994b: S.80–98.

Bergmann, Werner, Rainer Erb, and Albert Lichtblau (eds.). *Schwieriges Erbe. Der Umgang mit Nationalsozialismus und Antisemitismus in Österreich, der DDR und der Bundesrepublik Deutschland*. Frankfurt, New York, 1995.

Billerbeck, Rudolf. *Die Abgeordneten der ersten Landtage (1946–1949) und der Nationalsozialismus*. Düsseldorf, 1971.

Böhm, Franz. Der Antisemitismus und die Deutschen. In *Die Gegenwart 5*, Nr. 18, Sept. 1950: 110–13.

Bogardus, Emory S. Measuring Social Distances. In *Journal of Applied Sociology 9*, 1925: 299–308.

———. A Social Distance Scale. In *Sociology and Social Research 17*, 1933: 265–71.

Bogart, L. No Opinions, Don't Know, and May Be No Answer. In *Public Opinion Quarterly 31, 1967*: 311–45.

Bonacich, Edna. A Theory of Ethnic Antagonism: the Split Labor Market. In *American Sociological Review 37*, 1972: 547–59.

Boyens, Armin. Das Stuttgarter Schuldbekenntnis vom 19. Oktober 1945. Entstehung und Bedeutung. In *Vierteljahrshefte für Zeitgeschichte 19*, 1971: 374–97.

Brigham, John C. Racial Stereotypes: Measurement Variables and the Stereotype-Attitude Relationship. In *Journal of Applied Social Psychology 2*, 1972: 63–76.

Broder, Henryk M. Antizionismus-Antisemitismus von links? In *Aus Politik und Zeitgeschichte, B 24/76*, 12 June 1976: 31–45.

———. *Der ewige Antisemit. Über Sinn und Funktion eines beständigen Gefühls*. Frankfurt a.M., 1986.

Broszat, Martin. Hitler und die Genesis der "Endlösung." Aus Anlaß der Thesen von David Irving. In *Vierteljahrshefte für Zeitgeschichte 25*, 1977: 739–75.

Brumlik, Micha. Die Angst vor dem Vater. Judenfeindliche Tendenzen im Umkreis neuer sozialer Bewegungen. In A. Silbermann and J. H. Schoeps (eds.), *Antisemitismus nach dem Holocaust*. Köln, 1986: 133–63.

Buchheim, Hans. Politische Kriterien der Schuld an der NS-Herrschaft und deren Verbrechen. In *Politik, Philosophie, Praxis*. Festschrift für Wilhelm

Hennis zum 65. Geburtstag, edited by Hans Maier et al., Stuttgart 1988: 513–25.

Bundesministerium der Finanzen, Dokumentation 7/94: Härteregelungen des Bundes zur Entschädigung von NS-Unrecht, Bonn, 1994.

Bungenstab, Karl Ernst. *Umerziehung zur Demokratie? Re-education—Politik im Bildungswesen der US-Zone 1945-1949.* Düsseldorf, 1970.

Bunzl, John, and Bernd Marin. *Antisemitismus in Österreich. Sozialhistorische und soziologische Studien.* Innsbruck, 1983.

Chamberlin, Brewster S. "Todesmühlen." Ein früher Versuch zur Massen-"Umerziehung" im besetzten Deutschland 1945–1946. *Vierteljahrshefte für Zeitgeschichte 29,* 1981: 420–36.

Claussen, Detlev. *Grenzen der Aufklärung. Zur gesellschaftlichen Funktion des modernen Antisemitismus.* Frankfurt a.M., 1987.

Cobler, Sebastian. Das Gesetz gegen die "Auschwitz-Lüge." Anmerkungen zu einem rechtspolitischen Ablaßhandel. In *Kritische Justiz 18,* 1985: 159–70.

Conradt, David P. Changing German Political Culture. In Gabriel Almond, and Sidney Verba (eds.), *The Civic Culture Revisited.* Boston, 1980: 212–72.

Converse, P. E. Attitudes and Non-Attitudes. Continuation of a Dialogue. In E. R. Tufte (ed.), *The Quantitative Analysis of Social Problems.* Reading, Mass., 1970: 168–89.

Crosby, Faye, Stephanie Bromley, and Leonard Saxe. Recent Unobtrusive Studies of Black and White Discrimination and Prejudice. A Literature Review. In *Psychological Bulletin 87,* 1980: 546–63.

Curtis, Michael. Antisemitismus in den Vereinigten Staaten. In H. A. Strauss, W. Bergmann, and C. Hoffmann (eds.), *Der Antisemitismus der Gegenwart.* Frankfurt, a.M., New York, 1990: 226–59.

Dawidowicz, Lucy S. Can Anti-Semitism Be Measured? In *Commentary 50,* 1970.

Deligdisch, Jekutiel. *Die Einstellung der Bundesrepublik Deutschland zum Staate Israel. Eine Zusammenfassung der Entwicklung seit 1949.* Bonn-Bad Godesberg, 1974.

van Dijk, Teun A. *Prejudice in Discourse.* Amsterdam, Philadelphia 1984.

———. *Communicating Racism. Ethnic Prejudice in Thought and Talk.* Newbury Park, 1987.

Diner, Dan. Negative Symbiose—Deutsche und Juden nach Auschwitz. In Micha Brumlik, et al. (eds.), *Jüdisches Leben in Deutschland seit 1945.* Frankfurt a.M., 1986: 243–57.

Dudek, Peter. *Kleine Geschichte der antifaschistischen Jugendarbeit in der Schule.* In P. Dudek and H. -G. Jaschke. Jugend rechtsaussen. Analysen, Essays. Bensheim, 1982: 109–31.

Dudek, Peter, and Hans-Gerd Jaschke. *Entstehung und Entwicklung des Rechtsextremismus in der Bundesrepublik* (2 Vols.). Opladen, 1984.

Erb, Rainer. Die Rückerstattung: ein Kristallisationspunkt für Antisemitismus. In W. Bergmann and R. Erb (eds.), *Antisemitismus in der politischen Kultur nach 1945*. Opladen, 1990: 238–52.

———. Antisemitismus in der rechten Jugendszene. In W. Bergmann and R. Erb (eds.), *Neonazismus und rechte Subkultur*. Berlin, 1994: 31–76.

———. Gesellschaftliche Reaktionen auf Antisemitismus. In W. Benz (ed.), *Antisemitismus in Deutschland*. München, 1995: 217–30.

Erb, Rainer, and Werner Bergmann. *Die Nachtseite der Judenemanzipation. Der Widerstand gegen die Integration der Juden in Deutschland 1780–1860*. Berlin, 1989.

Erler, Wolfgang, and Ursula Schlude. Zertrümmerte Stühle und abgesägter Baum. Zur Sprache der Dinge im Rückblick auf die NS-Zeit. Zwei Fallbeispiele aus einem fränkischen Dorf. In Lutz Niethammer and Alexander von Plato (eds.), *"Wir kriegen jetzt andere Zeiten." Auf der Suche nach der Erfahrung des Volkes in nachfaschistischen Ländern. Lebensgeschichte und Sozialkultur im Ruhrgebiet 1930 bis 1960*, vol. 3. Berlin, Bonn 1985:152–71.

Estel, Bernd. *Soziale Vorurteile und soziale Urteile. Kritik und wissenssoziologische Grundlegung der Vorurteilsforschung*. Opladen, 1983.

Europäisches Parlament. Bericht im Namen des Untersuchungsausschusses "Wiederaufleben des Faschismus und Rassismus in Europa." Berichterstatter: Dimitrios Evrigenis, Sitzungsdokumente, 23 January 1985, Series A.

Faßbinder, Rainer Werner. Philosemiten sind Antisemiten, Interview, in *Die Zeit*, 9 April 1976. In Heiner Lichtenstein (ed.), *Die Fassbinder-Kontroverse oder Das Ende der Schonzeit*. Königstein, 1986: 43–45.

Fiedler, Peter. *Das Judentum im katholischen Religionsunterricht. Analysen, Bewertungen, Perspektiven* (Lernprozeß Juden-Christen, Vol. 1). Düsseldorf, 1980.

Fogt, Helmut. *Politische Generationen. Empirische Bedeutung und theoretisches Modell*. Opladen, 1982.

Fried, Erich. Ist Antizionismus Antisemitismus? Eine Widerrede. In *Merkur 30*, 1976: 547–52.

Friedrich, Walter, and H. Griese (eds.). *Jugend und Jugendforschung in der DDR*. Opladen, 1991.

Frey, Hans-Peter. Die Brauchbarkeit von Einstellungen als Prädikator für Verhalten. In *Soziale Welt 23*, 1972: 257–68.

Fritzsche, K. Peter. Hat der Antisemitismus eine Chance? Thesen zur Gefahr und zu den Grenzen der politischen Eskalation des Antisemitismus in der Bundesrepublik. In *Gegenwartskunde 3*, 1987, 311–20.

Fromm, Erich. *Arbeiter und Angestellte am Vorabend des Dritten Reiches.* Stuttgart, 1980.

Fuchs, Peter, Jürgen Gerhards, and Friedhelm Neidhardt. Öffentliche Kommunikationsbereitschaft. Ein Test zentraler Bestandteile der Theorie der Schweigespirale. In *Zeitschrift für Soziologie 21,* 1992: 284–95.

Funke, Hajo. Bitburg und die "Macht der Judem." Zu einem Lehrstück anti-jüdischem Ressentiments in Deutschland. In A. Silbermann, and J. H. Schoeps (eds.), Antisemitismus nach dem Holocaust. Köln 1986: 41–52.

Furth, Peter. Ideologie und Propaganda der SRP. In *Rechtsradikalismus im Nachkriegsdeutschland. Studien über die "Sozialistische Reichspartei"* (SRP). Berlin, Frankfurt a.M., 1957.

Geiger, Heinz. *Widerstand und Mitschuld. Zum deutschen Drama von Brecht bis Weiss.* Düsseldorf, 1973.

Giordano, Ralph. *Die zweite Schuld oder Von der Last Deutscher zu sein.* Hamburg, 1987.

Glynn, Caroll J. Perceptions of Others' Opinions as a Component of Public Opinion. In *Social Science Research* 18, 1989: 53–69.

Goschler, Constantin. Wiedergutmachung. Westdeutschland und die Verbrechen des Nationalsozialismus (1945–1951). München, 1992.

Gottschlich, Maximilian, and Karl Obermair. Antisemitismus in Österreich und die Rolle der Medien. Drei Studien zum Thema, Typoscript. Institut für Publizistik- und Kommunikationswissenschaft der Universität Wien. Wien, 1988.

Grimm, Reinhold, et al. (eds.). Der Streit um Hochhuths "Stellvertreter." *Theater unserer Zeit 5.* Basel and Stuttgart, 1963.

Guggenheim, Willy. Antisemitismus und die Einstellung zu Israel seit dem Zweiten Weltkrieg in der Schweiz. In *Judenfeindschaft,* edited by Erhard R. Wiehn. Konstanz, 1989: 163–86.

Hamel, Iris. *Völkischer Verband und nationale Gewerkschaft. Der Deutsch-nationale Handlungsgehilfen-Verband 1893–1933.* Frankfurt a.M., 1967.

Hansen, Niels. Verbindungen in die Zukunft. 25 Jahre diplomatische Beziehungen zwischen Deutschland und Israel. In *Aus Politik und Zeitgeschichte B 15/90,* 6 April 1990: 8–18.

Harding, John, Harold Prohansky, Bernard Kutner, and Isidor Chein. Prejudice and Ethnic Relations. In *Handbook of Social Psychology, V,* second edition, edited by G. Lindzey and E. Aronson. Reading, Mass., 1969.

Hartman, Geoffrey H. (ed.). *Bitburg in Moral and Political Perspective.* Bloomington, 1986.

Heinsohn, Gunnar. *Was ist Antisemitismus? Der Ursprung von Monotheismus und Judenhaß-Warum Antizionismus?* Frankfurt a.M., 1988.

Wilhelm Heitmeyer. *Rechtsextremistische Orientierungen bei Jugendlichen.* Weinheim/München, 1988.

Herbst, Ludolf, and Constantin Goschler (eds.). *Wiedergutmachung in der Bundesrepublik Deutschland.* München 1989.

Hermle, Siegfried. Die Evangelische Kirche und das Judentum nach 1945. Eine Verhältnisbestimmung anhand von drei Beispielen: Hilfe für Judenchristen, theologische Aufarbeitung, offizielle Verlautbarungen. In W. Bergmann and R. Erb (eds.), *Antisemitismus in der politischen Kultur nach 1945.* Opladen, 1990: 198–217.

Heßdörfer, Karl. Die finanzielle Dimension. In L. Herbst and C. Goschler (eds.), *Wiedergutmachung in der Bundesrepublik Deutschland.* München, 1989: 55–59.

Heuss, Theodor. Mut zur Liebe. In ibidem., *Schriften und Reden 1906–1963,* collected and edited by Hans Lamm. Düsseldorf, Wien 1964: 121–27.

Heydemann, Günther. Partner or Rival? The British Perception of Germany during the Process of Unification 1989–1991. In Harald Husemann (ed.), *As Others See Us. Anglo-German Perceptions.* Frankfurt a.M, Berlin, 1994: 123–48.

Hiller, Alfred. Amerikanische Medien- und Schulpolitik in Österreich (1945-1950). *Phil. Diss.* Wien, 1974.

Historikerstreit. *Die Dokumentation der Kontroverse um die Einzigartigkeit der nationalsozialistischen Judenvernichtung.* Munich, 1987.

Hochheimer, Wolfgang. Vorurteilsminderung in der Erziehung und die Prophylaxe des Antisemitismus. In *Psyche 16,* 1962: 285–94.

Hoffmann, Lutz, and Herbert Even. *"Die Belastungsgrenze ist überschritten."* *Entwurf einer Theorie der Ausländerfeindlichkeit.* Bielefeld, 1983. Zentrum für Wissenschaft und Praxis, Materialien Heft 18.

Holtmann, Everhard. *Politik und Nichtpolitik. Lokale Erscheinungsformen politischer Kultur im frühen Nachkriegsdeutschland.* Opladen, 1989.

Hortzitz, Nicoline. >Früh-Antisemitismus< in Deutschland (1789–1871/72). Tübingen, 1988.

Hübner-Funk, Sibylle. Jugend als Symbol des politischen Neubeginns. Strategien zur Bannung der rassistischen Vergangenheit. In W. Bergmann and R. Erb (eds.), *Antisemitismus in der politischen Kultur nach 1945.* Opladen, 1990: 218–35.

Huelshoff, Michael G., Andrei Markovits, and Simon Reich (eds.). *From Bundesrepublik to Deutschland.* Ann Arbor, 1993.

Husemann, Harald (ed.). *As Others See Us, Anglo-German Perceptions.* Frankfurt a.M, Berlin, 1994.

Jeggle, Utz (ed.). *Nationalsozialismus im Landkreis Tübingen. Eine Heimatkunde.* Tübingen, 1988.

Jesse, Eckhard. Antisemitismus in der Bundesrepublik? In *Jahrbuch Extremismus & Demokratie 1*, 1989: 285–88.

Jochmann, Werner. *Gesellschaftskrise und Judenfeindschaft in Deutschland 1870–1945*. Hamburg, 1988.

Kampe, Norbert. *Studenten und "Judenfrage" im Deutschen Kaiserreich. Die Entstehung einer akademischen Trägerschicht des Antisemitismus.* Göttingen, 1988.

Kastning-Olmesdahl, Ruth. *Die Juden und der Tod Jesu. Antijüdische Motive in evangelischen Religionsbüchern für die Grundschule.* Neunkirchen, 1981.

Katz, Jacob. A State within a State. The History of an Anti-Semitic Slogan. In ibidem., Zur Assimilation und Emanzipation der Juden. Darmstadt, 1982: 124–53.

Kellermann, Henry. Von Re-education zu Re-orientation. Das amerikanische Reorientierungsprogramm im Nachkriegsdeutschland. In Manfred Heinemann (ed.), *Umerziehung und Wiederaufbau*. Stuttgart, 1981

Kiderlen, Elisabeth (ed.). Deutsch-jüdische Normalität...Faßbinders Sprengsätze. In *Pflasterstrand, Flugschrift 1*. Frankfurt a.M., 1986.

Kloke, Martin W. *Israel und die deutsche Linke. Zur Geschichte eines schwierigen Verhältnisses* (Schriftenreihe des Deutsch—Israelischen Arbeitskreises für Frieden im Nahen Osten, Vol. 20). Frankfurt a.M., 1990*a*.

———. Kathartische Zerreißproben: Zur Israel-Diskussion in der Partei Die Grünen. In H. A. Strauss, W. Bergmann, and C.Hoffmann (eds.), *Der Antisemitismus der Gegenwart*. Frankfurt a. M., 1990*b*: 124–48.

Königseder, Angelika, and Juliane Wetzel. *Lebensmut im Wartesaal. Die jüdischen DPs (Displaced Persons) im Nachkriegsdeutschland.* Frankfurt a.M., 1994.

Knütter, Hans-Joachim. Die Linksparteien. In Werner E. Mosse and Arnold Paucker (eds.), *Entscheidungsjahr 1932. Zur Judenfrage in der Endphase der Weimarer Republik.* Tübingen, 1965: 323–45.

Lämmermann, Godwin. Christliche Motivierung des modernen Antisemitismus? In *Zeitschrift für evangelische Ethik 28*, 1984: 58–84.

Lang, Jürgen, and Patrick Moreau. PDS. Das Erbe der Diktatur. In *Politische Studien, Sonderheft 1*, 1994.

Lange, Thomas. *Judentum und jüdische Geschichte im Schulunterricht nach 1945*. Bestandsaufnahmen, Erfahrungen und Analysen aus Deutschland, Österreich, Frankreich und Israel, *Aschkenas, Beiheft 1*. Wien, 1994.

Laschet, Armin, and Heinz Malangré. *Philipp Jenninger. Rede und Reaktion.* Aachen, 1989.

Le Rider, Jacques. *Mitteleuropa. Auf den Spuren eines Begriffes.* Wien, 1994.

Lepszy, Norbert. Die Republikaner. Ideologie-Programm-Organisation. In *Aus Politik und Zeitgeschichte, B 41-42/89*, 6 October 1989: 3–9.

Leiris, Michel. Rasse und Zivilisation. In ibidem., *Die eigene und die fremde Kultur.* Frankfurt a.M., 1977: 72–118.

Levkov, Ilya (ed.). *Bitburg and Beyond. Encounters in American, German and Jewish History.* New York, 1987.

Lewis, I. A. American Jews and Israel. In *Public Opinion,* July/August 1988, 53–55.

Lichtblau, Albert. *Antisemitismus und soziale Spannung in Berlin und Wien 1867–1914.* Berlin, 1994.

Lichtenstein, Heiner (ed.). *Die Faßbinder-Kontroverse oder Das Ende der Schonzeit.* Königstein, 1986.

Lindsay-Hartz, Janice. Contrasting Experiences of Shame and Guilt. In *American Behavioral Scientist 27,* 1984, 689–704.

Lipstadt, Deborah E. *Denying the Holocaust. The Growing Assault on Truth and Memory.* New York, 1993.

Ludwig, Andrea. *Neue oder Deutsche Linke? Nation und Nationalismus im Denken von Linken und Grünen.* Opladen, 1995.

Lübbe, Hermann. Der Nationalsozialismus im politischen Bewußtsein der Gegenwart. In *Deutschlands Weg in die Diktatur. Internationale Konferenz zur nationalsozialistischen Machtübernahme,* edited by Martin Broszat, et al. Berlin, 1983, 329–49.

Luhmann, Niklas. Soziologie der Moral. In ibidem/Stephan H. Pfürtner (eds.), *Theorietechnik und Moral.* Frankfurt a.M., 1978, 8–116.

———. Gesellschaftsstruktur und Semantik. *Studien zur Wissenssoziologie der modernen Gesellschaft, 1.* Frankfurt a.M., 1980.

———. *Soziale Systeme. Grundriß einer allgemeinen Theorie.* Frankfurt a.M., 1984.

Luhmann, Niklas, and Peter Fuchs. *Reden und Schweigen.* Frankfurt a.M., 1989.

Marin, Bernd. Ein historisch neuartiger "Antisemitismus ohne Antisemiten." In *Geschichte und Gesellschaft 5,* 1979, 545–69.

Massing, Paul W. *Rehearsal for Destruction.* New York, 1949.

Mayhew, Leon H. *Law and Equal Opportunity. A Study of the Massachusetts Commission against Discrimination.* Cambridge, Mass., 1968.

McGuire, William. Attitudes and Attitude Change. In Gardner Lindzey and E. Aronson (eds.), *Handbook of Social Psychology.* New York, 1985 (3rd edition).

Mertens, Lothar. "Westdeutscher" Antisemitismus? MfS-Dokumente über eine Geheimaktion in der Bundesrepublik Deutschland. In *Deutschland Archiv 12,* 1994: 1271–73.

Mitscherlich, Alexander. Die Vorurteilskraukheit. In *Psyche 16,* 1962: 241–45.

Mitscherlich, Alexander and Margarete. *The Inability to Mourn.* New York, 1976 (German edition: 1967).

Mitten, Richard. *The Politics of Prejudice. The Waldheim Phenomenon in Austria.* Boulder, Colo., 1992.

Moyle, Lachlan R. The Ridley-Chequers Affair and German Character. A Journalistic Main Event. In Harald Husemann (ed.), *As Others See Us.* Frankfurt a.M., Berlin, 1994: 107–22.

Niethammer, Lutz. Juden und Russen im Gedächtnis der Deutschen. In Walter H. Pehle (ed.), *Der historische Ort des Nationalsozialismus.* Frankfurt a.M., 1990: 114–34.

Niethammer, Lutz, and Alexander von Plato. *Lebensgeschichte und Sozialstruktur im Ruhrgebiet 1930–1960.* Berlin, Bonn, 1985.

Niethammer, Lutz, Alexander von Plato, and Dorothee Wierling. *Die volks-eigene Erfahrung. Eine Archäologie des Lebens in der Industrieprovinz der DDR.* Berlin, 1991.

Noelle-Neumann, Elisabeth. *Öffentlichkeit als Bedrohung. Beiträge zur empirischen Kommunikationsforschung,* edited by J. Wilke. Freiburg, München, 1977.

———. Unruhe im Meinungsklima. Methodologische Anwendungen der Theorie der Schweigespirale. In *Publizistik 23,* 1978: 19–31.

———. *Die Schweigespirale. Öffentliche Meinung-Unsere soziale Haut.* München, Zürich, 1980.

Neustadt, Ammon. *Die deutsch-israelischen Beziehungen im Schatten der EG-Nahostpolitik.* Frankfurt/Main, 1983.

Noetzel, Dieter. Über einige Bedingungen des Erwerbs politisch-ideologischer Deutungsmuster. Kritische Anmerkungen zur Theorie der Schweigespirale. In Dieter Oberndörfer (ed.), *Wählerverhalten in der Bundesrepublik Deutschland. Studien zu ausgewählten Problemen der Wahlforschung aus Anlaß der Bundestagswahl 1976,* Berlin 1978: 215–63.

Paucker, Arnold. *Der jüdische Abwehrkampf gegen Antisemitismus und Nationalsozialismus in den letzten Jahren der Weimarer Republik.* Hamburg, 1969.

Pelinka, Anton, and Erika Weinzierl (eds.), *Das große Tabu. Österreichs Umgang mit seiner Vergangenheit.* Wien, 1987.

Porst, Rolf. *Praxis der Umfrageforschung. Erhebung und Auswertung sozialwissenschaftlicher Umfragedaten.* Stuttgart, 1985.

Postone, Moishe. Antisemitismus und Nationalsozialismus. In *Alternative 140/41,* 1981: 241–58.

Prokop, Dieter. *Medien-Wirkungen.* Frankfurt a.M., 1981.

Pross, Harry. Antisemitismus in der Bundesrepublik. In *Deutsche Rundschau 82,* 1956: 1069–76.

Puhle, Hans Jügen. *Agrarische Interessenpolitik und preußischer Konservatismus im Wilhelminischen Reich, 1893–1914*. Bonn, 1975.

Rendtorff, Rolf, and Hans Hermann Henrix. *Die Kirchen und das Judentum. Dokumente von 1945 bis 1985.* München, 1988.

Reck-Hog, Ursula. *Das Judentum im katholischen Religionsunterricht. Wandel und Neuentwicklung.* Freiburg, 1990.

———. Unterrichtserfahrungen zum Thema Judentum und zur jüdischen Geschichte im katholischen Religionsunterricht. In Thomas Lange (ed.), *Judentum und jüdische Geschichte im Schulunterricht nach 1945.* Ashkenas, Beiheft 1, 1994: 313–20.

Reuband, Karl-Heinz. Meinungslosigkeit im Interview. In Zeitschrift für Soziologie 19, 1990: 428–443.

Ruhrmann, Georg. *Rezipient und Nachricht. Struktur und Prozeß der Nachrichtenrekonstruktion.* Opladen, 1989.

Sagi, Nana. Die Rolle der jüdischen Organisationen in den USA und die Claims Conference. In L. Herbst, and C. Goschler (eds.), *Wiedergutmachung in der Bundesrepublik Deutschland.* München, 1989: 99–118.

Sherif, Muzafer, et al. *Intergroup Conflict and Cooperation. The Robbers Cave Experiment.* Norman, Ok., 1961.

Scheuch, Erwin K., and Hans D. Klingemann. Theorie des Rechtsradikalismus in westlichen Industriegesellschaften. In *Hamburger Jahrbuch für Wirtschafts- und Gesellschaftspolitik 12,* 1967: 11–29.

Schörken, Rolf. *Jugend 1945. Politisches Denken und Lebensgeschichte.* Opladen, 1990.

Schuman, Howard, and Jaqueline Scott. Generations and Collective Memories. In *American Sociological Review 54,* 1989: 513–36.

———, and S. Presser. *Questions and Answers in Attitude Surveys. Experiments in Question Form, Wording and Content.* New York, 1983.

Shafir, Shlomo. Die SPD und die Wiedergutmachung gegenüber Israel. In L. Herbst, and C. Goschler (eds.), *Wiedergutmachung in der Bundesrepublik Deutschland.* München, 1989: 191–204.

———. American Jews and Germany After 1945. Points of Connection and Points of Departure. American Jewish Archives, 1993.

Stern, Frank. Entstehung, Bedeutung und Funktion des Philosemitismus in Westdeutschland nach 1945. In W. Bergmann, and R. Erb (eds.), *Antisemitismus in der politischen Kultur nach 1945.* Opladen, 1990: 180–96.

———. *The Whitewashing of the Yellow Badge. Antisemitism and Philosemitism in Postwar Germany.* Oxford, 1992.

Stölzl, Christoph. *Kafkas böses Böhmen.* München, 1975.

Stöss, Richard. *Die extreme Rechte in der Bundesrepublik.* Opladen, 1989.

Strauss, Herbert A. Einleitung—Vom modernen zum neuen Antisemitismus. In H. A. Strauss, W. Bergmann, and C. Hoffmann (eds.), *Der Antisemitismus der Gegenwart.* Frankfurt a.M., 1990: 7–25.

———. Der Holocaust als Epochenscheide der Antisemitismusgeschichte: historische Diskontinuitäten. In W. Bergmann, and R. Erb (eds.), *Antisemitismus in der politischen Kultur nach 1945.* Opladen, 1990: 38–56.

Vetter, Dieter. Hebräische Bibel-antisemitischer Mißbrauch. In Günter Brakelmann, and Martin Rosowski (eds.), *Antisemitismus. Von religiöser Judenfeindschaft zur Rassenideologie.* Göttingen 1989: 9–26.

Vogel Rolf (ed.). *Deutschlands Weg nach Israel. Eine Dokumentation.* Stuttgart, 1967.

——— (ed.). *Der deutsch-israelische Dialog. Dokumentation eines erregenden Kapitels deutscher Außenpolitik,* 8 Bände, München, New York, 1987.

Volkov, Shulamit. *The Rise of Popular Antimodernism in Germany. The Urban Master Artisans 1837–1896.* Princeton, 1978.

———. Antisemitismus und Anti-Zionismus: Unterschiede und Parallelen. In ibid., *Jüdisches Leben und Antisemitismus im 19. und 20. Jahrhundert,* München, 1990: 76–87.

von Jena, Kai. Versöhnung mit Israel? Die deutsch-israelischen Beziehungen bis zum Wiedergutmachungsabkommen von 1952. In *Vierteljahrshefte für Zeitgeschichte 34,* 1986: 457–80.

Wagner, Ulrich. *Soziale Schichtzugehörigkeit, formales Bildungsniveau und ethnische Vorurteile: Unterschiede in kognitiven Fähigkeiten und der sozialen Identität als Ursachen für Differenzen im Urteil über Türken.* Berlin, 1982.

Wetzel, Dietrich (ed.). *Die Verlängerung der Geschichte. Deutsche, Juden und der Palästinakonflikt.* Frankfurt a.M., 1983.

Wetzel, Juliane. *Jüdisches Leben in München 1945–1951. Durchgangsstation oder Wiederaufbau?* (Miscellanea Bavarica Monacensia, vol. 135). München, 1987.

Wodak, Ruth, et al. *"Wir sind alle unschuldige Täter." Diskurstheoretische Studien zum Nachkriegsantisemitismus.* Frankfurt a.M., 1990.

Wolffsohn, Michael. *Ewige Schuld? 40 Jahre deutsch-jüdisch-israelische Beziehungen.* München, 1988.

———. *Die Deutschland Akte. Juden und Deutsche in Ost und West.* München, 1995.

Zielinski, Siegfried. *Veit Harlan. Analysen und Materialien zur Auseinandersetzung mit einem Filmregisseur des deutschen Faschismus.* Frankfurt a.M., 1981.

Index